Consequences of Contact

Consequences of Contact

Language Ideologies and Sociocultural
Transformations in Pacific Societies

Edited by
Miki Makihara
Bambi B. Schieffelin

OXFORD
UNIVERSITY PRESS

2007

OXFORD
UNIVERSITY PRESS

Oxford University Press, Inc., publishes works that further
Oxford University's objective of excellence
in research, scholarship, and education.

Oxford   New York
Auckland   Cape Town   Dar es Salaam   Hong Kong   Karachi
Kuala Lumpur   Madrid   Melbourne   Mexico City   Nairobi
New Delhi   Shanghai   Taipei   Toronto

With offices in
Argentina   Austria   Brazil   Chile   Czech Republic   France   Greece
Guatemala   Hungary   Italy   Japan   Poland   Portugal   Singapore
South Korea   Switzerland   Thailand   Turkey   Ukraine   Vietnam

Copyright © 2007 by Oxford University Press, Inc.

Published by Oxford University Press, Inc.
198 Madison Avenue, New York, New York 10016

www.oup.com

Oxford is a registered trademark of Oxford University Press

Library of Congress Cataloging-in-Publication Data
Consequences of contact : language ideologies
and sociocultural transformations in Pacific societies /
edited by Miki Makihara and Bambi B. Schieffelin.
    p. cm.
Includes bibliographical references and index.
ISBN 978-0-19-532497-6;   978-0-19-532498-3 (pbk.)
1. Languages in contact—Pacific Area.
2. Sociolinguistics—Pacific Area.
I. Makihara, Miki. II. Schieffelin, Bambi B.

P40.5.L382P163 2007
306.44091823—dc22   2006053269

9 8 7 6 5 4 3 2 1

Printed in the United States of America
on acid-free paper

CONTENTS

CONTRIBUTORS

J. Joseph Errington is professor of anthropology and chair of the Council on Southeast Asian Studies at Yale University.

Courtney Handman is a Ph.D. candidate in anthropology and linguistics, University of Chicago.

Christine Jourdan is professor of anthropology in the Department of Sociology and Anthropology at Concordia University.

Miki Makihara is assistant professor of anthropology at Queens College and The Graduate Center at the City University of New York.

Susan U. Philips is professor emerita of anthropology at the University of Arizona.

Kathleen C. Riley is a part-time faculty member in linguistics and anthropology at Concordia University.

Joel Robbins is professor of anthropology at the University of California, San Diego.

Bambi B. Schieffelin is professor of anthropology at New York University.

Rupert Stasch is associate professor of anthropology at Reed College.

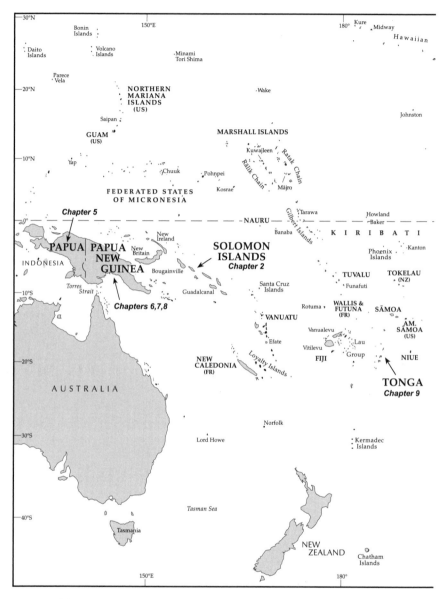

Map of the Pacific Islands. © 2006. Center for Pacific Islands Studies, University of
Hawai'i at Mānoa. All Rights Reserved. Cartography by Manoa Mapworks, Inc.
Modified and reproduced with permission.

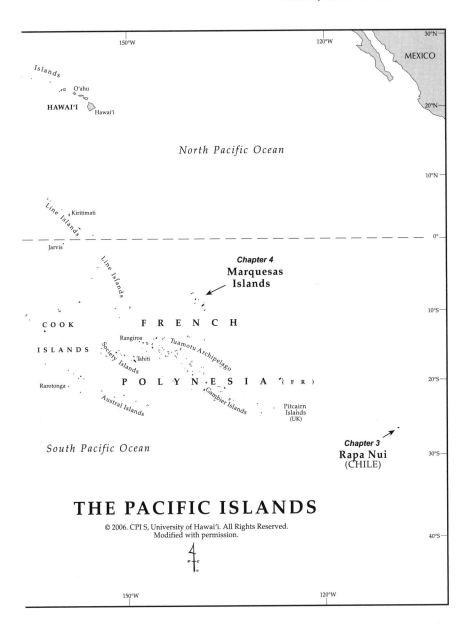

Islands

O'ahu

HAWAI'I   Hawai'i

MEXICO

30°N

20°N

North Pacific Ocean

10°N

Line Islands   Kiritimati

0°

Jarvis

Chapter 4
Marquesas Islands

Line Islands

10°S

C O O K   **F R E N C H**

Rangiroa

Tuamotu Archipelago

I S L A N D S

Society Islands   Tahiti

P O L Y N E S I A (F R)

20°S

Rarotonga

Austral Islands

Gambier Islands

Pitcairn Islands (UK)

South Pacific Ocean

Chapter 3
Rapa Nui
(CHILE)

30°S

THE PACIFIC ISLANDS

40°S

150°W   120°W

Consequences of Contact

MIKI MAKIHARA AND BAMBI B. SCHIEFFELIN

Cultural Processes and Linguistic Mediations

Pacific Explorations

The contemporary Pacific is culturally and linguistically diverse, a complex, interrelated socioecological zone composed of islands with a variety of polities, including nation states (Papua New Guinea, Solomon Islands, Tonga), and overseas collectivities (French Polynesia) and provinces (Rapa Nui or Easter Island, Papua) of nations.[1] These political designations have shifted over at least three centuries as these islands were taken, traded, and governed by various colonial and then postcolonial states. Though some achieved independence, issues of self-governance continue to be raised by others, as is the case of the West Papua independence movement.

No one can ignore the profound historical changes that contact with colonial and postcolonial governments and religious institutions have spurred throughout indigenous language communities of the Pacific. In recent years, large-scale socioeconomic transformations linked to globalization, urbanization, militarization, and environmental changes have reshaped communities through the movement of people, ideas, and commodities. However, the effects of contact on languages and their speakers, though no less pervasive, have proved easier to overlook—especially given characterizations of language still prevalent in the West as a transparent, culturally indifferent referential medium. Contemporary cross-cultural contact brought about by activities ranging from missionization, education, and tourism to conservation efforts, sustainable agriculture, the extraction of resources (timber, minerals, petroleum and fish), and nuclear testing continue to influence local language communities in both predictable and unpredictable ways.

The essays collected in this volume examine situations of intertwined linguistic and cultural change unfolding in specific Pacific locations in the late twentieth and early twenty-first centuries. They have in common a basic concern with the multiple ways that processes of historical change have shaped and been shaped by linguistic ideologies: reflexive sensibilities about languages and language use, held by Pacific peoples themselves. In this introduction, we outline some relevant broader contexts within which these chapters can be read. These contexts include: the complex history of cultural crossings and recrossings characteristic of Pacific societies; the varied history and political conditions of linguistic research in Pacific settings across different colonial and postcolonial phases of interaction between Europeans and Pacific Islanders; and the linguistic diversity of Pacific Island societies, and the social centrality of talk in them. We particularly seek to outline some of the main ways in which situations of linguistic and cultural change in the Pacific *vary*, and we suggest some strategies for understanding the dynamics of linguistic change by identifying its key agents, institutional sites, and linguistic forms within a wider historical conjuncture.

The Pacific has always been a place of intercultural contact, and these recent patterns must be understood in terms of the long and pervasive history of contact into which they figure. Melanesia had already been inhabited for at least forty thousand years by ancestors of Papuan- (non-Austronesian-) speaking peoples who had built extensive trading networks and complex interisland and broad interregional interactions extending possibly to Southeast Asia (Summerhayes 2007). Austronesian-speaking people migrated from Taiwan or sites nearby and started moving through Island Southeast Asia into Melanesia about four thousand years ago. Over the next three thousand years, they and their descendants, using sophisticated navigational skills, traveled vast distances from their origins. They settled as far east as Rapa Nui, as far west as Madagascar, to the north in Hawai'i and to the south in New Zealand. They had substantial cultural and ecological influence, including long-term fusions of traditions with Papuan peoples and among one another.[2] In the sixteenth century, European explorers began to chart the waters and bring news of exotic places and people (and sometimes the people themselves) back to Europe. During this time, Europeans conceptualized the Pacific region as "empty." They were ignorant about this area, vast expanses of ocean separated its small islands, and they believed that many of these islands (and those islands' resources) had no legitimate owners (Ward 1989). Later, this final sense of "emptiness" would enable various colonial powers to legitimize their own claims over Pacific territories, frequently accomplished through the use of written deeds transferring indigenous sovereignty to their own colonial nations. At the beginning of the nineteenth century, European Catholic and Protestant missionaries of various denominations, backed by their colonial governments, intensified contact first with Polynesia and then with other parts of the Pacific. Newly missionized Pacific Islanders often served as pastors and teachers alongside or independent of their European counterparts. Simultaneously, merchants, planters, and "blackbirders" (slavers) voyaged to these islands, initiating large-scale social, demographic, and ecological changes that would reverberate throughout the region.

This contact history remains relevant today, as evidenced in postcolonial debates about modernity, tradition, indigeneity, sovereignty, indigenous agency, and other political and social topics. Competing local, national, and transnational interests and perspectives have given rise to cultural activism concerned with indigenous rights, customs and cultural revival, political autonomy, and local resource management. These concerns have been articulated by elites and other members of local communities, and in political, religious, and academic contexts as well.[3] Whereas some have argued that changes initiated by earlier contact have been desirable and beneficial, leading to economic development and social improvement, others have seen them as essentially negative, causing people to lose their land, cultural and linguistic practices, and identity. Others view change as simply an inevitable consequence of globalization and other world-reshaping processes. Emerging from the arena of local politics, these divergent perspectives have informed scholarly attempts to theorize, model, or describe the dynamics of change in terms of continuity/discontinuity, assimilation, adaptation, and hybridity.[4]

Even the terms usually used to label the major Pacific Island regions—Melanesia, Micronesia, and Polynesia—show the instability that comes with being forged in the heat of historical processes of contact and colonialism. Though these three divisions have some correspondence to language groups, they were Western categories that originated in the 1830s and did not initially correspond to local perceptions or categories of identity and place. These three labels circulate in a variety of ways, both complicating and complementing indigenous perspectives, which emphasize a holistic view of the Pacific as "a sea of islands" (Hau'ofa 1993; Levinson, Ward, and Webb 1973) and of peoples as connected, rather than isolated, by the ocean. At the same time, localist discourses give importance to specific places, ethnicities, customs, languages, and histories. Most important, there are no singular or simple views of the Pacific to speak of.[5] Thousands of indigenous communities with diverse histories have had greater or lesser contact. Many are linked locally, and also have extensive and extending ties to diasporic communities both in and outside of the Pacific. Hence indigenous views are multiple and always changing.

Describing language(s) in culture

In the Pacific, language is intricately linked to the sociocultural and political transformations that we have briefly outlined above. As we will see, language is transformed by and transforms changing social realities. The multilingualism in vernaculars, lingua francas, and colonial and national languages that characterize many Pacific communities is a clear product of contact. What happens to linguistic structures, practices, and values mirrors, reinforces, and sometimes changes presuppositions about social relations and social relations themselves (Silverstein 1998). The role of language and the forms it takes, though central to cross-cultural contact situations, is rarely written about and remains undertheorized. Historical accounts, for example, often are vague about verbal interactions, failing to indicate languages used in contact moments, much less what might have been said or heard when partially shared languages were used to establish rudimentary forms of communication. For example, passionate debates within Pacific historiography about Captain Cook's 1779 death in Hawai'i have long engaged native and nonnative anthropologists, historians, linguists, and others.[6] There are multiple speculations regarding how Hawaiians addressed and referred to Cook at the time of his death and afterward. If we had more or less reliable, ethnographically annotated transcripts of what participants were saying, we would be able to begin to understand the multiple interpretations and viewpoints based on different interests regarding Cook's identity. Without such clues, we are faced with trying to make sense against the grain of multiplying uncertainties as to what has been said, done, or meant, which is often misremembered or revised.[7]

The inherent complexity of communication in cross-cultural encounters must be kept in mind as we investigate the different interpretive strategies, translation conventions, and encoding procedures, as well as the broader language ideologies, which may converge in moments of contact. All of these have long-term consequences for indigenous people regarding resources and power. One clear example is the case of Maori and the British signing of the 1840 Treaty of Waitangi, which transferred sovereignty from the Maori to the British Crown. Translating culture-bound concepts such as *mana* and sovereignty has proved to be quite difficult and complicated (Biggs 1989). In addition, the parties involved had different understandings of the acts of signing and textual authority (McKenzie 1987). Both issues continue to be in play to this day, as evidenced by debates and legal contestations which now include discussions about contemporary multiethnic civil society in Aotearoa/New Zealand (Kawharu 1989).

Though Captain Cook and his crew collected word lists in the 1770s, noting similarities and possible historical connections among Polynesian languages, there was little systematic linguistic research on Pacific languages until the later part of the nineteenth century. Vernaculars were unwritten, structurally different from European languages, and there were an overwhelming number of them, often with dialectal differences. Though speakers were often multilingual, there were few trade languages or lingua francas as bridges. For those wanting to missionize, colonize, or carry out anthropological research in the Pacific, language learning and analysis presented a number of challenges, many of which remain today.

The first systematic and sustained linguistic work in the Pacific was carried out by missionary linguists, who focused on language analysis for translating the Bible.[8] Many faced the task of devising orthographies to write down previously unwritten languages, often producing the first word lists, dictionaries, and grammatical sketches. In many communities, these texts still influence local perceptions, use of the vernacular, and the shape of the language itself. It is ironic that through a process often referred to as phonological "reduction" (Pike 1947), these words on paper came to exert such power. Languages were often simplified through selective processes, and decisions about orthography and other issues of graphic representation and grammatical analysis were often based on ideological and ethnocentric grounds rather than sociolinguistic research.

R. H. Codrington was among the first and best known missionary linguists. At the British Melanesian Mission on Norfolk Island, he trained Pacific Islanders coming from a range of islands in the region. He also interviewed these teachers-in-training about their vernacular languages and native cultures, and over twenty-four years produced grammatical descriptions of more than two dozen languages of (present-day) Vanuatu and the Solomon Islands (Codrington 1885). Later work (Codrington 1891) focused on indigenous religious beliefs, and it introduced to Europe the concept of *mana*, which became influential in early debates about the nature of religion in native societies. His writing showed an appreciation of the complexity and systematicity of these languages, and of the importance of native knowledge, albeit from interview data, for understanding local concepts. Although Codrington's writing is recognized as one of the earliest to contextualize language in cultural concepts, it was Bronislaw Malinowski's work that established the importance of systematic ethnographic fieldwork and redefined the place of language within it.

In *Coral Gardens and Their Magic* ([1935] 1978), Malinowski's focus on Trobriand Island agricultural practices enmeshed him in the study of magic and religious beliefs. One clear message from this work was that knowledge and use of the local language is essential for ethnographic understanding. Though Malinowski's emphasis was on the role of language for the ethnographer in generating a "native outlook," we can reframe this idea and see language as articulating natives' points of view, thus acknowledging that perspectives are multiple, knowledge is socially distributed, and language expresses social variation.

Conceptualizing language "as a mode of action," Malinowski propounded an ethnographic theory of language in Trobriand society that suggests his attempts to define context and pragmatics. His emphasis on utterances as effective achievements and speech as a component of concerted activity foregrounds a pragmatic and action-focused view of speech. Linking descriptions of Trobriand language practices to cultural activities, he argues that "the speech of a pre-literate community brings home to us in an unavoidably cogent manner that language exists only in actual use within the context of real utterance" ([1935] 1978, 2:v). His work demonstrates the importance to ethnographers of thinking about translation, inference, and cultural meaning, and his focus on chants and spells displays sensitivity to the interpenetration of linguistic and cultural processes. Though Malinowski paid close attention to language as a cultural practice, he also struggled to achieve a synthetic analysis of cultural and linguistic processes. In the end, he settled on two separate volumes, published under a single title. Today, many linguistic anthropologists realize the challenge of integrating the narrative of ethnographic description and the details of linguistic and sociolinguistic transcripts, which are themselves theoretically constructed.

Language(s) in the Pacific

From our perspective, two things stand out about language and speech practices in Pacific societies: their centrality in the construction of self and sociality, and social life more broadly, and their extraordinary diversity. In communities that are overwhelmingly organized through face-to-face encounters, language is an expressive resource that individuals must manage carefully and artfully. A variety of verbal resources and performative genres—oratory, narrative, song, lament, conversation, arguments, gossip, teasing in activities from the everyday to the ritual—have been linked not only to a rich tradition of expressive culture, but also to politics and memory. Social relationships are established and maintained through talk and acts of reciprocity and exchange, which are accomplished through talk. Signaled throughout the lexicon, morphology, syntax, and pragmatics are ideas about social relationships and personhood, identity, and affect, for example, in naming practices, honorifics, and pronoun systems. Language is key to socialization and in establishing and understanding ethnopsychological dimensions. These and other features central to language and speech communities have been documented in the last fifty or so years by strong lineages of linguistic and cultural anthropologists in the Pacific.[9]

Anthropologists have theorized talk as a form of action in Pacific politics and political discourse, connecting it to different social systems. We do not wish to reify cultural models that oppose Melanesian, Big Man egalitarian societies in which power is achieved with Polynesian hierarchical chiefdoms in which power is ascribed. We recognize that there is variation across different regions and societies and the arenas within them, and that although talk and code selection often reflect different types of social organization and status relations, these are not static features. To the extent that communities or interactional contexts might be shown to be organized on more or less egalitarian grounds, talk is still crucial in creating and re-creating egalitarian relations. Open disagreement, which may be expected in more egalitarian communities, is often expressed indirectly in public and private domains, as settling conflict is carefully managed. In more hierarchical language communities, where power is more likely to be ascribed on the basis of kinship and other preexisting arrangements, those with power are often at risk and must verbally justify their positions and persuade others to maintain hierarchies in political arenas. Thus, general cultural preferences toward ascription and achievement must still be constituted verbally. For both kinds of polities, talk is also what challenges and sometimes transforms the status quo, and those who are eloquent with words are highly regarded (Duranti 1994; Myers and Brenneis 1984).

Talk is central not only in acting politically but in managing interpersonal conflict, where it plays an informative and persuasive role in Pacific communities. Taking as a starting point the embeddedness of personhood in complex matrices of social relations, it is clear that talk functions to negotiate and reestablish moral, social, and emotional boundaries, especially when they have become strained (White and Watson-Gegeo 1990). It is in these affectively charged contexts that new ideas and feelings about identity are articulated and tried out, thus providing opportunities for change or revision.

The impression of the centrality of language in Pacific communities might be an academic artifact, the result of intense attention that anthropologists (mostly American) have paid to language, starting with early work in folk classification, ethnoscience, and ethnography of speaking. However, a variety of co-occurring factors suggest that many Pacific societies do indeed place a high value on talk, regardless of scale or social organization. Language and speech practices are tied to issues of truthfulness, practices of revealing and concealing specific forms of knowledge, and the efficacy of many forms of social or ritual action. Not only are speech genres varied and elaborated, but metalinguistic vocabulary is often extensive. People talk about, and think about, talk a lot. They judge and circulate talk, and they remember certain forms of talk—in verbal activities ranging from stories to land claims—for generations.

Further evidence of the centrality of talk to Pacific societies comes from the way indigenous scholars and local activists have always recognized its importance in native communities, especially its rootedness in their histories and places. The centrality of native language and indigenous discourse has been described in several ways: "as markers of deep difference" (Diaz and Kauanui 2001b: 320), as resources for decolonization projects, and as ways to reclaim cultural knowledge and political autonomy. This has become even more salient with the implicit and explicit language policies of missionization and colonization, which have changed patterns of language transmission, disrupting local speech ecologies.[10] These disruptions have led to language shift and loss in many communities, often increasing consciousness about language itself. In particular, Maori and Hawaiian language activists have been leaders in language revitalization efforts, which include establishing language immersion schools (language nests),[11] promoting the connectedness of linguistic and cultural practices in pursuing broader social and political projects.[12]

The centrality of a shared vernacular in identity-making is also linguistically marked and made salient in other kinds of contact situations. In Papua New Guinea and the Solomon Islands, the importance of a shared local language is expressed in the creole languages (Tok Pisin and Pijin) spoken there. The word <u>wantok</u>, which derives from English 'one talk,' originated on plantation settings in the early part of the twentieth century, which brought together laborers from diverse parts of Melanesia. This was one of the first Pacific contexts in which large numbers of language community boundaries converged. Across social groups, regardless of any other markers of social similarity, calling someone <u>wantok</u> can evoke shared family or clan membership or ethnolinguistic affiliation. It is a major category of social solidarity that can legitimize one's participation in a social network in a larger system of exchange; using this term recognizes a social connection and signals distinction as well. The term continues to be socially and economically useful and symbolically charged as people increasingly move to new places and interact in wider social networks.

In addition to the centrality of language and talk in Pacific societies, the enormous diversity of languages also requires our attention. Linguistic diversity has in fact long characterized the Pacific. Linguists estimate that as many as thirteen hundred of the world's six thousand or so languages can be found in the Pacific (Foley 1986; Lynch 1998). The northern third of New Guinea alone (from the Bird's Head to the Sepik-Ramu Basin, an area no larger than Great Britain) is the most linguistically diverse part of the planet, with at least sixteen unrelated language families (Pawley 2007; Ross 2005). Diversity characterizes various dimensions of language. For example, within these thousand or so languages, there are differences in the size and density of language communities and their networks. This has social consequences for the distribution and meaning of communicative resources. There are also significant structural and genetic differences among Pacific languages, a topic that has been taken up from various cross-disciplinary perspectives—archaeological, biological, and linguistic—collaboratively seeking to unravel origins and contact using comparative methodologies, as with research on the ultimate origins of the Polynesians and their historical relations and contacts with peoples of Melanesia, Southeast Asia, and even South America.[13] These include investigating the life cycles of the few precolonial indigenous pidgin and creole languages that arose in the context of intergroup trading and social relationships (Foley 1988). More important than these indigenous contact languages per se was the multilingualism that evolved as speakers learned the languages of neighboring communities enabling kinship and trading relationships. Thus, various types of linguistic diversity were deeply connected to precolonial contacts between people across villages, islands, and continents.

The development of contact languages—pidgins and creoles—is itself a major linguistic consequence of colonial contact. Four major Pacific creole languages—Tok Pisin and Pijin (mentioned above), Bislama (Vanuatu), and Hawai'i Creole English—emerged out of plantation settings involving intense and sustained contact among laborers from multiple, mutually unintelligible language communities who had no previous relationships and were suddenly put in contact with each other. Because of the particular nature of the sociolinguistic and power dynamic in these plantation settings, these languages carry traces of their contact histories: they mix colonial languages with selected local vernaculars (e.g., Tok Pisin is primarily a mix of English and Tolai) but exhibit certain common structural properties. These four have become structurally complex and multifunctional, rooted in the social life of speech communities, while others may have been short lived.[14]

There have been different hypotheses about why there is such linguistic diversity and so many small language communities, particularly in parts of Melanesia. One explanation suggested is geographical isolation, but this idea is not widely supported because groups have maintained various (and in many cases extensive) forms of contact despite rugged mountainous terrain.[15] A second explanation is long-term human habitation (forty thousand years), which usually results in language change and diversification (Foley 1986: 8). The third proposal, based on social attitudes and linguistic ideologies, claims that linguistic diversity is a matter of choice, something which has been cultivated in order to highlight difference and maintain boundaries among groups that are otherwise culturally similar.[16] In the Pacific, as elsewhere, though multilingualism is valued, one's own language is a foremost marker of identity, whether it indexes one's local village or a larger social group.

The consequences of contact history for linguistic diversity in the Pacific have sparked considerable academic debate. Using the notion of "linguistic imperialism" to describe missionization and colonization, Mühlhäusler (1996) envisions a contemporary Pacific in which there is rapid, irreversible, and extensive disruption of precolonial linguistic ecologies. He claims that many vernacular languages have already become obsolescent or at least seriously damaged as English and associated literacy practices have spread. The result of these processes of language shift, decay, and death, he concludes, is linguistic homogeneity in terms of structure, meaning, and patterns of use. Certainly, as Mühlhäusler and others before him have argued, colonization and missionization, often linked, led the shift from precolonial or traditional egalitarian multilingualism or linguistic diversity in the Pacific to increased hierarchization of languages and linguistic hegemony (Sankoff 1980a). Consequential transformations of such hierarchical arrangements are detailed in this volume by Jourdan for urban Solomon Islanders (chap. 2), by Makihara for Rapa Nui (chap. 3), and by Riley for Marquesans (chap. 4).

Singling out literacy as a particularly potent technology, Mühlhäusler claims this introduced communicative technology and its associated practices have often led to "an almost total transformation of most Pacific societies and most languages spoken in the area" (1996: 212). While numerous scholars working in the Pacific view this assessment as exaggerated and overly pessimistic, all agree that the introduction of literacy and the institutions in which it was embedded has had significant cultural, sociopolitical, and epistemological impacts in previously nonliterate Pacific societies.[17]

Points of encounters

In the Pacific, literacy in vernacular or colonial languages was commonly introduced as part of a sustained program of missionization. Regimentation, surveillance, and the imposition of new institutional forms (churches, schools, and clinics) and worldviews characterized these colonial projects. As a number of ethnographic and sociolinguistic studies of literacy practices have shown, however, literacy is not an autonomous technology that, when imposed on a community, is taken up "as is."[18] When there are "discrepant intentions" between the introducers and the recipients of literacy, its control is up for grabs (Besnier 1995: 17). Like other new forms of knowledge, local people take up literacy, at least partially, according to their own ideologically and culturally informed purposes. These in turn shape local processes of indigenizing this technology, which is crucial to its integration in the community's communicative repertoire. These are both sites and signs of local agency and meaning-making, the consequences of which may or may not endure. Understanding them as contexts of dynamism offers insights into the linguistic and cultural processes involved.

Even when agents of colonization and missionization held a shared interest in changing local communities or appropriating indigenous souls or lands, encounters themselves were highly variable in terms of duration, intention, and scale. It was in such encounters, ranging in scope from a single instance to sustained contact, that different modes of communication, appearance, and assumptions about the world produced not only the possibilities for transformation, innovation, and reorganization, but new communicative practices and ideologies as well. Three short examples of different types of encounters and the short- and long-term consequences for particular literacy practices illustrate just a few of the possible scenarios that have been documented. Each exhibits different temporal organization regarding points or phases of contact, as well as manner, duration, and intensity.[19] They illustrate ways in which the incorporation of new modes (literacy) expand local communicative repertoires and give rise to new genres and registers along with new ideas about language itself. These examples also highlight the different types of evidence—historical, ethnographic, sociolinguistic, and linguistic—that are resources for understanding the nature of contact and issues of agency and interpretation.

Rapa Nui, like other Pacific societies, had no indigenous literacy prior to European contact. In 1770, a Spanish expedition made a six-day visit to the island which included signing an official deed annexing the island to Spain, or so the Spanish thought. It may have been this event that inspired the creation of an indigenous script, *rongorongo* incised on wood tablets, twenty-five of which survive today. One interpretation of the origin of *rongorongo* is that the inhabitants of Rapa Nui associated the act of making signs at this deed-making event with power and prestige and sought to emulate it in devising their own scripts based on indigenous motifs, rather than use the Roman alphabet. Though relatively little is known about the exact use or content of these tablets, they fostered social and political change, the emergence of literate ritual specialists, and the teaching of this script (Fischer 1997, 2005). The *rongorongo* embodies one kind of local response following exposure to a new technology, literacy. Local transformations unfolded on multiple levels. Rapa Nui seemed to have taken the *idea* of writing, invented their own script, and devised locally relevant uses for it. Less than a hundred years later, more enduring and intensive forms of European contact started to have a major influence on Rapa Nui language and social life (see Makihara 2004 and chap. 3 of this volume). The arrival of slavers led to a major population decline, and missionaries led the community to convert to Christianity. *Rongorongo* was abandoned, and its meanings obscured.

Analyses of contemporary literacy practices among the Nukulaelae islanders in Tuvalu, a Polynesian nation, provide our second example, an account of continuing indigenization and dynamism (Besnier 1993, 1995). Samoan pastors sent in the 1860s by the London Missionary Society introduced Christianity on this small atoll, and in the process restructured local social and political life. The islanders quickly learned how to read and write in Samoan, which remained the language of school, church, law, and government until the 1930s, when Tuvaluan began to replace it. While pastors encouraged Bible reading, at the same time local people quickly became letter writers, first in Samoan but later in Tuvaluan, adapting literacy for their own social purposes. The extensive letters written by both men and women are used to maintain contacts outside of Nukulaelae, including its diasporic communities, and perform affective, informational, moral, and economic functions. This early emergence and continuous use of letter writing may be viewed as a mild form of resistance as the local uses of literacy significantly went beyond those intended by the religious authorities who introduced it (Besnier 1995: 178). This locally important emphasis on personal writing stands in stark contrast to the commonly held view that "literacy has become a source of confusion and doubt in the oral societies of the Pacific, and . . . is contributing to cultural erosion" (Topping 1992: 30).[20]

Our final case focusing on the introduction of literacy and new language varieties comes from Erromango (southern Vanuatu), where, in the mid-nineteenth century, Presbyterian mission policy promoted one local language among many as a lingua franca, now known as Erromangan (Crowley 2001). Lacking ethnographic or linguistic documentation regarding precontact language and social life on Erromango or Erromangans' original response to missionization, Crowley compares mid-nineteenth- and early-twentieth-century missionary texts (a catechism and hymnal) with extensive samples of contemporary written and spoken Erromangan. His linguistic analysis demonstrates local peoples' sensitivity to the missionaries' written version of their spoken language. More specifically, Erromangans continue to use the early missionary hymns, which are structurally simplified and diverge radically from their spoken language. Moreover, they are also highly selective in which grammatical features they use, rejecting certain features when modeling contemporary hymns after these missionary versions. Crowley hypothesizes that the local community initially viewed this nineteenth-century missionary variety as "bad" Erromangan but later reevaluated it as "good" Erromangan, and it now functions as a written and sung register for religious purposes. Thus local people are constructing this "good" Erromangan, underlining their active and selective adaptation of literacy and its features as a register while resisting its influence into spoken registers (255). Outsiders such as missionaries can also shape the process of indigenization in local communities, for example, by selecting or "shaping" vernaculars (or trade or colonial languages) according to their own ideologies and purposes to make them more effective for proselytizing and literacy as well.[21] Handman (chap. 8, this volume) provides a detailed account of these processes currently in progress in Bible translation training at SIL International (formerly known as the Summer Institute of Linguistics) in Papua New Guinea. Philips (chap. 9, this volume) offers historical analyses of how missionaries collaborated with local Tongan elites in shaping secular nation-state formation through scholarly representations of chiefly language.

It is difficult to historically reconstruct the language ideologies of Pacific Islanders as both agents and recipients of change because written accounts of these contact encounters were relatively rare, and those that survived were biased in one direction. We often do not have the methods or means to trace the linguistic and cultural practices—the origins of which are easily lost—that create new vernacular forms and meanings. We have to search for linguistic and cultural traces of participants' voices. Fortunately, as part of the Western preference for writing letters and leaving records, we have documentation of what European and other missionaries thought they were doing, as well as reminders of what they were "planting" with their imperial languages and ideologies. In addition to records and letters, their translations of liturgical materials, often published, provide evidence for tracking contact-induced change in vernacular languages and their practices. Though language change over time can go unnoticed and undocumented, one (handy) consequence of the introduction of literacy and these publication practices is the creation of material artifacts—texts that can provide clues to language contact histories. Sources and types of evidence may already be the product of multiple contact and mediation, requiring analysts to be attentive to such heteroglossic voices in these texts. We see additional types of evidence for tracing linguistic and cultural change in transcripts as well as in missionary and scholarly documents and other materials in Schieffelin for Bosavi, Papua New Guinea (chap. 7 of this volume), and in Philips for Tonga (chap. 9).

We have selected examples of what happens to oral varieties of language when they are in contact with, or are translated or transformed into, literate varieties to illustrate a number of points about the sites and consequences of contact. For one, in mission and colonial contexts, writing is thought of as being more authoritative than speaking, and written documents (especially deeds and treaties) are among the first written texts that many groups new to literacy experience. These texts carry an authority of print, with the power of words enduring over time and space. But the power and meaning of such texts have been and continue to be challenged by, for example, Maori. Missionaries thought of the Bible and its translations as another type of verbal contract, one that promised salvation to those who abided by it. The notions of language, oral and written, that accompanied missionary and colonial regimes were embedded in particular language ideologies, ideas about language and their users that traveled with the very codes and projects that were the concerns of these agents of contact and change.

We turn next to the concept of language ideology as a theoretical framework as it provides a way to understand how participants on all sides of the cross-cultural interchange think about and use language. This provides a link between the sociocultural and linguistic processes emergent in contact situations. Though some expect language to be transparent—a list of vocabulary items containing meanings with largely functional equivalencies across code boundaries—this is not the case. It is often not only difference in codes and problems in translating between them that make understanding difficult, but ideas about the nature of language itself or its functions which, when taken for granted on one side and unimagined or even unimaginable on the other, lead to the misrecognition of meaning and even intentions. These issues are elaborated in this volume by Stasch for Korowai, West Papua (chap. 5), and by Robbins for Urapmin, Papua New Guinea (chap. 6).

Language ideologies and sites of contact and change

Though shaped by asymmetrical power relations, colonial encounters are dynamic and complex. There is rarely a clear "zero point" separating the times before and after contact. Language and the speech activities that give shape to both subjective and intersubjective social lives are themselves shaped by language ideologies and by conceptions about persons, worlds, and knowledge. Ways of feeling, thinking, and speaking about language (metalanguage), a property of human communication, are never neutral or ahistorical, but are closely tied to specific sociocultural and epistemological frameworks and processes. The chapters in this volume explore the nature and mechanisms of such cultural processes that not only transform languages but also social realities and relationships as they are linguistically constituted, encoded, and enacted. In this way, language ideologies and practices mediate consequences of cultural contact over time. The chapters exemplify various cultural conceptions of language, its uses, and users, which are made particularly salient and observable in contact across interactional and institutional settings.

Here, we offer a definition of language ideology that is broad enough to encompass the theoretical and methodological perspective dominant in linguistic anthropology.[22] We take language ideologies to be cultural representations, whether explicit or implicit, of the intersection of language and human beings in a social world. Mediating between social structures and forms of talk, such ideologies do not just concern language. Rather, they link language to identity, power, aesthetics, morality, and epistemology in terms of cultural and historical specificities. Through such linkages, language ideologies underpin not only linguistic form and use, but also significant social institutions and fundamental notions of persons and community.

In framing our discussion of language ideology, we draw inspiration from Raymond Williams's perceptive assertion that "a definition of language is always, implicitly or explicitly, a definition of human beings in the world" (1977: 21). This characterization, itself already ideological and interestingly ambiguous, captures a broad range of widely shared cultural ideas that have resonance not only in academic discussions but in local language communities.[23] In fact, Williams's observation becomes particularly germane in situations of contact between language communities within a broader multilingual speech community.[24] This conceptualization allows room for choice and change, which are always intertwined, both in terms of code(s) themselves and the indexical associations between language elements and social meanings. As history demonstrates, these associations may be recruited for various political, religious and other identity projects. When cultural and linguistic elements come into contact, systems that are already conventionalized and enshrined in institutions may be renewed as dominant or may persist as residual. At the same time, actors might innovate or at least experiment with these elements, formulating new articulations out of the mixture of both sets of resources.[25] As Williams reminds us, we are not talking about personal experience but rather "social experience which is still *in process*, often indeed not yet recognized as social, but taken to be private, idiosyncratic, and even isolating, but which in analysis...has its emergent, connecting, and dominant characteristics, indeed its specific hierarchies" (132).

Williams's emphasis on the processual nature of cultural formations is equally applicable to linguistic elements. Studies of linguistic and cultural contact often focus on norms and outcomes, relegating agency as manifested in attempts at establishing innovative forms and meanings to the back burner. Close attention to process, on the other hand, reminds us that both new social and linguistic elements must be collectively recognized as meaningful in order to join the category of potentially legitimate alternate forms of expression. Where contact is relatively recent or benign, there may be stances of apprehension best characterized as curiosity or disinterest. For innovated or introduced elements to enter a system, however, they must generate sufficient consensus among speakers in a given language community if choice among alternates is to be socially meaningful. If this does not occur, such innovated forms could be rejected or reinterpreted. The gradual emergence and recognition of new linguistic forms constitutes the mortar for language change more generally. The accumulation of many small choices may lead to unintended outcomes—for example, an increased linguistic diversity in Melanesia. Here we would add that the language ideology perspective demands nuancing the assertion that linguistic diversity in Melanesia is a matter of choice. Given the variety of contact histories and trajectories, individual linguistic choices may be more or less socially established and more or less conscious, synchronically (across speakers, genres, situations, and communities) and diachronically.

There are, thus, variable degrees of consciousness in contact settings regarding different elements of language and language change. Recognizing, and then incorporating elements from a new language as a form of embodiment connects this practice to Bourdieu's notion of habitus (1977). Contact often is the context that disrupts and possibly transforms one's habitual practices, or at least makes one aware that what was taken for granted is now subject to scrutiny. Voicing new forms, based either on mimesis or as a novel form to avoid such association, allows one to engage with the other, the previously unknown, and provides the potential for transforming one's self, language, and language ideologies.

Language ideologies materialize—but also naturalize—the linguistic status quo. When language users accept particular practices as the usual or dominant, there is no further need for explicit articulation of operative ideologies. The emergence of alternative possibilities in mission or colonial contact, however, often foregrounds the interaction between previously naturalized and newly available linguistic forms, creating a context for discussions of difference as well as for affective responses, such as desire. Contexts in which language ideologies are in conflict often give rise to a higher degree of explicitness about underlying views and beliefs. These are also the sites in which language ideologies are recalled or produced, made visible and audible, and their naturalness questioned, bringing us to what Giddens (1984) would call "discursive consciousness." This is where processes of reconfiguration are often initiated. Missionizers and colonizers sharing the goal of creating different types of persons often challenge the integrity and value of local cultural and linguistic practices by prohibiting certain words, genres, and languages and insisting on the use of others. Their rationalizations for such actions are usually expressed as "civilizing," "modernizing," and Christianizing native people. All parties, regardless of power dynamics, are motivated by affective and subjective dimensions of their actions and must have had a range of emotions affecting how interactions unfolded and concluded. The degrees of surprise, wonder, curiosity, fear, and uncertainty and of consequent transformation in European contact encounters vary greatly across communities and over time. Each of the numerous meetings and engagements between indigenous and European individuals and groups involves ambiguity and mismatch between what was intended and unintended. This conditions the points of articulation between the old/indigenous and the new/nonindigenous.

Often unnoticed and undocumented are moments of choice, compromise, adjustment, and outright opposition on the part of local community members facing introduced ideas and actions. In such encounters, not only are the imposed ideas taken under consideration, but traditional ones may be reevaluated and lead to syncretic cultural or linguistic forms. In some cases, even if communities subscribe to mission or colonial evaluation of their tradition, their reworking of what they desire to incorporate or change requires substantial cognitive, social, and linguistic reorganization.[26] This is often difficult to achieve and may exacerbate existing lines of social conflict and generate new ones. Homogeneity is rare in the way such moments are perceived, understood, talked about, and remembered.

From a methodological perspective, we need to be able to scrutinize such early and emergent formulations and their interactions with what are dominant and residual, and to seriously consider the role of agency in these processes. We value the notions of voicing and dialogism (Bakhtin 1981), paying careful attention to the actual linguistic forms that speakers use when in dialogue with various interlocutors in order to establish stance, as expressed through modality, pronoun choice, code selection, and the many pragmatic resources that language affords. It is in this sensitive and often ambiguous area between the privately felt and the socially recognized that speakers' voicings are especially relevant. Whether speakers are carrying out mundane routines or performing public political speech that stands for a group's location in the world, agency and utterance matter. We must attend to the details—such as who is able to or chooses to speak, the particular form of utterance, and its effect on the listeners—as part of any methodology that is concerned with language ideology and its place in analyses of linguistic and social change. By closely examining both the contexts of language use and the ideologies that give them meaning, we can see how particular social and cultural formations and linguistic forms arise, continue to be effective, or come to be associated in new ways (such as inversion) as consequences of contact, which themselves are available for further transformation.

Chapter overviews

In this introductory essay, we have sought to promote a perspective that highlights the importance of language ideologies in understanding the interconnectedness of linguistic and cultural processes in contact situations. In discussing contact and its consequences in the Pacific, we underscore the complexity of contact histories in the region, the centrality of language in its social life, and the diversity of languages and linguistic forms in its societies. We briefly introduce each chapter and then describe the salience of these issues in the individual chapters in this collection as a way of drawing connections across Pacific experiences. The map of the Pacific Islands indicates the location of each chapter.

In chapter 2, Christine Jourdan analyzes the changing urban modalities of language use by residents of Honiara, the multilingual capital city of the postcolonial Solomon Islands. The sociolinguistic order inherited from the colonial period—when English was at the top of the hierarchy, and local vernaculars and Pijin at the bottom— is undergoing reorganization. Jourdan argues that language selection is central to constantly redefining sociality, revealing speakers' agency and the situatedness of the urban self, and expressing ethnic, generational, social, and gender identities.

In chapter 3, Miki Makihara examines ideologies of code choice and language revalorization embedded in the political discourse of the bilingual, indigenous Polynesian community of Easter Island, Chile, where the local Rapa Nui language has in the past been marginalized and endangered by Spanish. Rapa Nui speakers have challenged this situation first by expanding syncretic Rapa Nui–Spanish speech styles into public and political domains and, more recently, by constructing purist Rapa Nui speech styles. She argues that Rapa Nui speakers deploy these speech styles as linguistic registers for political ends, voicing different but complementary sets of values—democratic participation, on the one hand, and primordialism and ethnic boundary construction, on the other. Makihara illustrates the ways that Rapa Nui have revalorized and maintained their language by establishing new linguistic registers, thereby adding extra sociolinguistic meanings to speech styles and increasing linguistic heterogeneity.

Chapter 4 focuses on the Marquesas (French Polynesia), where most adults use both Marquesan and a local variety of the colonial language, French, switching between them—sometimes intrasententially—in a number of contexts. Kathleen Riley explores the contradictions and effects of official discourses and everyday socializing practices in this multilingual community. Language socialization data from two time periods a decade apart evidence the ways in which Marquesans are rejecting in practice the diglossic separation of their two languages, producing and reproducing instead the officially lamented but covertly prestigious code-switched variety charabia/*sarapia* to index their identities as both French and Polynesian.

In chapter 5, Rupert Stasch charts an ideology of linguistic difference that shapes how Korowai of West Papua have evaluated and spoken an intrusive lingua franca over the first quarter-century of their contact with it. Calling Indonesian "demon language" (where "demon" contrasts paradigmatically with "human"), Korowai emphasize that the new language is simultaneously strange and parallel to their own. Stasch examines speech practices and evaluations of this new language as a perspective on the world that is alien to the community's geographic and cultural position, but that exists as a kind of displaced, deformed counterpart to that position. Bilingual Korowai increasingly make passing use of Indonesian in conversation with other Korowai, precisely because of the artful potential of the language for signifying strangeness and parallelism at the same time.

In chapter 6, Joel Robbins puts forth the idea that language ideologies stand in complex relationship to ideologies of material exchange, especially in Melanesia, where contemporary changes in language ideology have been in important respects shaped by transformations in traditional ideologies of exchange. Among the Urapmin of Papua New Guinea, the relationship between the two changing ideologies and wider ideologies of change that have developed in the wake of conversion to Christianity has been apparent in local debates over the practice of charismatic Christian rituals of Holy Spirit possession. Robbins discusses these rituals and the debates that surround them in detail to show how new ideologies of change have transformed how the Urapmin think about both material and linguistic exchange.

Bambi Schieffelin, in chapter 7, analyzes Tok Pisin Bible reading and vernacular translation practices introduced during missionization in Bosavi, Papua New Guinea. These are critical sites for studying linguistic and cultural processes that reshape the vernacular. Focusing on the metapragmatic domain of reflexive language, specifically reported speech and thought and the speech act of blasphemy, Schieffelin illustrates what happens when language ideologies and languages associated with fundamentalist missionaries, biblical scripture and Bosavi pastors come into contact over a twenty-year period (1975–1995). Reflexive language and the ideas that underlie its use are found to be culturally and sociohistorically specific and, as such, do not travel easily across texts and time in either Tok Pisin or Bosavi.

In chapter 8, Courtney Handman examines the role of linguistic versus cultural knowledge as it is theorized for Bible translation at the Summer Institute of Linguistics in Papua New Guinea. As part of a process of revising its training procedures, SIL has shifted from using its own expatriate member-translators to using Papua New Guineans, who are members of the Bible Translation Association and 'native speakers' of the languages into which the Bible is translated. Handman argues that their training regimes are based on a linguistically oriented notion of group identity, rather than native culture, that establishes 'heart' or native language as more central to authenticity and Christian commitment.

In chapter 9, Susan Philips proposes that Christian missionaries and the Tongan chiefly class collaborated over time in changing language ideology about Tongan lexical honorifics (lea faka-'eiki 'chiefly language') as one way of highlighting their concept of the political shift from a Tongan traditional hierarchy to a Tongan secular modern nation-state hierarchy. Based on careful examination of scholarly representations of these honorifics in descriptions of Tongan language over the past two hundred years, she shows the considerable stability over time in the number of levels of honorification described, and even in some of the specific lexical items associated with each level. In contrast, the conceptualization of the targets of the honorifics—that is, who is indexed by the particular honorifics (e.g., God or the King)—has changed significantly. In this way, the language ideologies of Christian missionaries and Tongan chiefly class have stressed continuity over rupture while repressing the sacred in Tongan nation-state formation.

In chapter 10, Joseph Errington provides a thoroughgoing commentary on these contributions. Here, we offer a few provisional, synthetic remarks to help orient the reader. The chapters in this volume share a perspective that highlights the dynamics of linguistic and cultural processes in contact situations brought about by historical and ongoing missionization and (de)colonization. Working with ethnohistorical, ethnographic and sociolinguistic data, they offer analyses of a range of sites in which multiple social and linguistic transformations have occurred and continue to unfold as a result of the types of contact we have discussed above. These sites enable the creation of new types of local actors, such as pastors, Bible translators, teachers, political activists, spirit mediums, and tour guides, some of whom introduce, innovate, legitimate, or resist new ideas and ways to express them through language. Local actors take their roles as agents in these societies creating new genres and registers to accommodate and participate in their changing social contexts, transforming local language communities. In the process, they have cultivated new cultural conceptions of language, for example, as a medium for communicating religious knowledge and truth (chapters by Robbins, Schieffelin, and Handman) and for (re)constructing social boundaries and transforming relationships of domination (chapters by Jourdan, Makihara, Riley, Stasch, and Philips).

In times of cultural contact, communities often experience language change at an accelerated rate. This is particularly so in small-scale communities where innovations and continuity routinely depend on the imagination, creativity, and charisma of fewer individuals. The essays in this volume provide evidence of this potential and a record of their voices. We can thus gain insight into the social history of a language because it is marked by the history of its users and by the contexts in which they transform and construct their ethnolinguistic landscape.

The chapters also provide examples of communities and their different contact histories of varying depth, highlighting different consequences for the multiple codes, styles, and modes of communication which are developing, competing, or coexisting simultaneously. Several focus on small-scale, relatively egalitarian communities that are in the earlier phases of sustained contact and newly experiencing the emergence of multiple linguistic ideologies and language varieties (e.g., chapters by Stasch, Robbins, and Schieffelin). Others underscore the effect of longer contact histories, emphasizing the subsequent and continuing transformation of heterogeneous linguistic ideologies and practices (e.g., chapters by Jourdan, Makihara, Riley, Handman, and Philips).

Contact settings constitute sites for producing new linguistic forms and practices drawing on different colonial, lingua franca, and local language varieties and ideologies. Speakers use linguistic processes such as addition, deletion, and modification, including reordering or reversal of elements for transforming codes (denotational and indexical). For example, Korowai incorporate Indonesian into their linguistic repertoire through loans, calques, and neologisms (Stasch, chap. 5) and Honiarans import their village vernaculars' phonologies and lexicons into their Pijin speech (Jourdan, chap. 2). Marquesans (Riley, chap. 4) and Rapa Nui (Makihara, chap. 3) alternate between colonial and vernacular codes, each creating a new style of speech. In addition, some Marquesan and Rapa Nui speakers consciously avoid previously borrowed elements from colonial languages. These linguistic processes and their resulting codes provide a lens for understanding yet another set of relationships between linguistic ideologies and practices and their role in the transformation of social relations over time.

Language ideologies are intricately attached to conceptions of person, community, and power. This becomes particularly apparent and consequential in cross-cultural contact settings—be they religious, governmental, colonial, or economic—that are inherently asymmetrical in terms of power relations. In such contact settings, these fundamental notions about person, community, and power cannot be assumed, and must be negotiated or at least articulated. These same notions inform speakers' and writers' linguistic choices and discursive strategies. Here we foreground the simultaneity and multiplicity of linguistic phenomena, addressing how and why new language varieties are created and how selection among multiple codes and forms transform languages and language communities. For example, urban Honiarans are expanding the social meanings of Pijin through the creation of dialects that signify social differentiation, ethnicity, gender, and generation, thus valorizing this creole language not only as a national language, but as their own. In the context of missionization, a new register, Christian talk, is emerging as Bosavi pastors read and translate the Tok Pisin Bible in church services. This new variety is not yet formally recognized and named. Similarly, Rapa Nui activists are developing registers of political discourse in which a purist style of speech is strategically deployed in particular, public interethnic contexts. Marquesans have created new genres for socializing children by combining French-style reprimands within Marquesan teasing frameworks. Innovated language varieties and practices reorganize semiotic associations and evaluations of languages and functions. These new articulations of cultural and social formations provide evidence of how speakers mobilize linguistic resources and how they are accommodated into the linguistic ecology, revising and enriching it.

Contact settings provoke opportunities for language users to consciously reflect on language at different levels. Even the nature of language itself may come to pose certain dilemmas. Urapmin in Papua New Guinea are struggling to enact a Christian conception of language as a vehicle of sincerity and social truth, which traditionally are demonstrated primarily through nonlinguistic acts and exchange. Bilingual in their vernacular and Tok Pisin, they do not seem preoccupied about code selection or code boundaries in their religious and secular communication as it is language itself that they find untrustworthy (Robbins, chap. 6). Bible translators at SIL, on the other hand, consider similar properties of language, sincerity and authenticity, as exclusive to the "heart" language of its native speakers. They advocate the sole use of vernaculars for translation and proselytizing, rejecting other languages, including Tok Pisin, a national language, which they claim is inadequate, not a real or true language (Handman, chap. 8). At SIL, language is conceptualized generally as a referentially and semantically transparent vehicle for the transmission of cultural knowledge, but one language, the heart language, is privileged for the purpose of Bible translation because it is thought to be inalienable, intimately linked to the notion of personhood. Furthermore SIL language ideology constructs cultural knowledge as alienable, substitutable with Christian knowledge. Australian missionaries in Bosavi subscribed to similar ideas about the separability of language and culture, but they were comfortable using Tok Pisin in

Bible translation. Though translation activities often lead to misunderstanding and misrecognition, they also provide opportunities for introducing ideas that previously had no linguistic expression. They also induce heightened awareness of code boundaries and differences between codes.

In other communities, it is the boundaries between different languages that draw explicit attention as markers of social difference to be recruited in the expression of new social identities (Jourdan, Stasch). In communities experiencing language shift or loss, such awareness of code boundaries may give rise to the ideas of language surveillance and techniques of language policing expressed as purist ideologies, which has consequences for power relationships (Makihara, Riley). We note an interesting set of contrasts organized around notions of the detachability of parts of language and alienation of language from its speakers. In different language communities, some parts of language are thought of as more detachable than others. These language elements may be more available as resources for playing, innovating, and experimenting with ways for marking affective and social stances and identities. Deploying accents and loanwords provide evidence of these flows among urban Honiarans and Korowai speakers. In circumstances of language shift in process, however, language community members may come to lament their detachment and alienation from their ancestral language, remembering its past with nostalgia. At the same time, they are also being pragmatic, and they work to recover what they can of their language, often disattending to the formal code boundaries of past varieties they no longer speak. The syncretic linguistic ideologies in Rapa Nui and Marquesan, though perhaps viewed as compromises, give life to their languages and underscore the inalienability and centrality of language in local language communities and add diversity to local speech economies.

One fundamental theme uniting these chapters is that in all communities, language is conceptualized, objectified, and manipulated to constitute new social realities. Drawing on and transforming linguistic ideologies, speakers actively reshape language. They add new language practices and are willing to give up or revise old ones. As the chapters that follow illustrate, all levels of language may be deployed, from lexical and grammatical through a range of metalinguistic and discursive strategies, by speakers who are mobilizing new social and political formations, as well as enacting new visions of themselves.

Notes

The idea of this collection grew out of our informal session on Language Ideologies and Social Change held at the Meetings of the Association for Social Anthropology in Oceania (ASAO) in 2003 in Vancouver, British Columbia. Over the next three years, various subsets of our group convened in Salem, Lihu'e on Kaua'i, Chicago, and San Diego to share ideas with each other and various audiences. The exchanges helped us rethink what has been important in societies undergoing cultural and linguistic transformation in the Pacific beyond such categories as Melanesia, Micronesia, and Polynesia. We wish to thank the ASAO and those who attended our sessions for their interest and support. We thank our collaborators for thoughtful and inspirational words that contributed to the completion of this volume. We also thank Graham Jones, Joel Robbins, and Rupert Stasch for comments on earlier versions of this essay and Meghan Harrington and Chantal White for assisting with the final bits.

We dedicate this volume to the people of the Pacific, who have assisted all of us in so many different ways in our years of fieldwork. We hope that these essays will contribute to the growing documentation and understanding of processes of change that are taking place in Pacific communities and their language(s).

1. For this discussion, we use "Pacific" to refer to Melanesia, Micronesia, and Polynesia in a broad geographic sense. The chapters in this volume, however, focus on communities generally categorized as Melanesian and Polynesian.

2. Bellwood and Renfrew 2003; Blust 1999; Kirch 2000.

3. Clifford 2001; Douglas 1998; Feinberg and Zimmer-Tamakoshi 1995; Gegeo 2001; Hanson 1989; Hobsbawm and Ranger 1983; Jolly and Thomas 1992; Kame'eleihiwa 1992; Keesing and Tonkinson 1982; Lindstrom and White 1994; Linnekin 1983, 1991; Linnekin and Poyer 1990; Trask 1991, [1993] 1999; Wagner 1975.

4. Clifford 2001; Robbins 2004; Robbins and Wardlow 2005; Rumsey 2006; Sahlins 1981, 1985.

5. See, for example, essays in Diaz and Kauanui 2001a; and in Teaiwa 2001.

6. Borofsky 1997; Obeyesekere 1992; Sahlins 1981, 1996; Tcherkézoff 2003.

7. This is illustrated in another academic debate in Pacific ethnography regarding the substance as well as the truthfulness of what was said to Margaret Mead in Samoa and how she interpreted it (see Acciaioli 1983; Brady 1983; Freeman 1984; Mead 1928). This suggests that there are always multiple views and layers of interpretation that complicate any event or encounter.

8. See Errington 2001 for a historical, comparative review of colonial linguistics and the role played by missionary and nonmissionary linguists.

9. See Besnier 2004; Brenneis and Myers 1984; Brison 1992; Duranti 1994; Goldman 1983; Keating 1998; Kulick 1992; Lutz 1988; Merlan and Rumsey 1991; Ochs 1988; Sankoff 1980b; Siegel 1987; Watson-Gegeo 1986; Watson-Gegeo and White 1990. This work was preceded by foundational anthropological scholarship on language in the Pacific, including the work of Bronislaw Malinowski, Ward Goodenough, Harold Conklin, Charles Frake, John L. Fischer, Michelle Rosaldo, and Anne Salmond.

10. See Mühlhäusler 1996: chap. 6, for an overview of mission language policies in the Pacific.

11. See Benton 2001; Harrison and Papa 2005; Hohepa 2000; Kapono 1995; Karetu 2002; King 2001; Mutu 2005; Pihama et al. 2004; Schütz 1994; Warner 2001; Wilson and Kamanā 2001.

12. For example, Maori, Hawaiian and other Polynesian languages share distinctive phonological systems that were not recognized by the Europeans. The early orthographies devised by Christian missionaries did not include symbols for a glottal stop or vowel length (in Hawaiian 'okina and kahakō respectively) which are part of the phonological inventories of these languages. In the case of Hawaiian, according to Kualono (n.d. cited in Romaine 2002: 198) "to omit 'okina and kahakō in print... is to do the language a great injustice... (and) in words where they do exist to be a misspelling of those words." Because of the variation in the use of these symbols, we follow the usage in the original publications in the references.

13. For example, see Friedlaender 2007; Kirch 2000; Pawley and Ross 1993. Thor Heyerdahl 1952 made it into more popular discourses.

14. It is beyond the scope of this discussion to detail the linguistic and social histories of Pacific pidgin and creole languages. The following studies provide a comprehensive overview. See Carr 1972; Crowley 1990; Jourdan 1991; Jourdan and Keesing 1997; Keesing 1988; Meyerhoff 2003; Reinecke 1969; Romaine 1995; Sakoda and Siegel 2003; Sankoff 1980b; Siegel 2000; Smith 2002; Tryon and Charpentier 2004.

15. Kulick 1992 provides a compelling argument and additional sources.

16. Foley 1986; Kulick 1992; Laycock 1982; Sankoff 1980a; Sumbuk 2006.

17. Mühlhäusler's arguments were based on secondary sources. A number of linguists who had done extensive empirical research on vernacular Pacific languages criticized his examples as highly selective and not generalizable to warrant his alarmist position. Additionally, Mühlhäusler was highly critical of linguists working in the Pacific, whom he claimed maintained an ideological neutrality and were not adequately concerned about language loss. A principal goal of his book was to expose what he believed was wrong about linguistics. Many found this critique both misdirected and unfounded (see Crowley 1999; Kulick 1999; Lynch 1996; Siegel 1997).

18. Kulick and Stroud 1993; Schieffelin 2000; Street 1984.

19. Silverstein 1996 outlines several dimensions of contact that are relevant to studying change in local language communities, including "periodicity."

20. Talking about literacy practices in Gapun, Papua New Guinea, Kulick and Stroud perceptively observe that they take place "with a characteristic Melanesian eye for the novel and the useful [as the villagers] have been active and creative in their encounter with literacy" (1993: 55).

21. See, for example, McElhanon 1979 and Rutherford 2005.

22. Several edited volumes and articles on language ideology review and explore this multidisciplinary area of inquiry. See Blommaert 1999; Gal and Woolard 2001; Joseph et al. 2003; Joseph and Taylor 1990; Kroskrity 2000; Schieffelin, Woolard, and Kroskrity, 1998; and Silverstein 1979.

23. We find it interesting that Williams's characterization of language can be read from a Chomskian, universalist notion of language as well as from a culturally relativistic one in which language is understood to be grounded in its sociohistorical context, thus subject to variation and change at all levels.

24. Here we are using Silverstein's (1996) distinction between "language community" (which is based on a single, shared denotational code [i.e., language X] and its norms of usage including grammar) and "speech community" (which is a more general term referring to a social group in regular interaction sharing norms of language usage). Many speech communities are composed of multilingual individuals belonging to multiple language communities, some of which are in contact with each other. Even if a speech community is isomorphic with a language community, thus having the label monolingual, this distinction allows us to examine the interaction of referential or denotational levels with social functions of language—for example, those that index social identities. As Silverstein 1998 reminds us, both membership in and allegiance to a language community and a speech community are matters of degree, thus allowing variation.

25. This notion of elements in contact reconfigured in novel formations resonates with discussions in creole studies (e.g., superstrate, substrate, and cognitive influences) and anthropological theories about continuity and discontinuity in cultural change. We emphasize the processual and transformative nature of these categories in producing new forms and practices through interaction.

26. See Sahlins 1985.

References

Acciaioli, Gregory, ed. 1983. *Fact and Context in Ethnography: The Samoa Controversy.* Special issue of *Canberra Anthropology* 6 (1, 2).

Bakhtin, Mikhail M. 1981. Discourse in the Novel. In *The Dialogic Imagination: Four Essays by M. M. Bakhtin*, pp. 259–422. Austin: University of Texas Press.

Bellwood, Peter, and Colin Renfrew, eds. 2003. *Examining the Farming/Language Dispersal Hypothesis.* Cambridge, UK: McDonald Institute for Archaeological Research, University of Cambridge.

Benton, Richard A. 2001. Balancing Tradition and Modernity: A Natural Approach to Maori Language Revitalization in a New Zealand Secondary School. In *Bilingual Education,* ed. Donna Christian and Fred Genesee, pp. 95–108. Alexandria, VA: Teachers of English to Speakers of Other Languages, Inc.

Besnier, Niko. 1993. Literacy and Feelings: The Encoding of Affect in Nukulaelae Letters. In *Cross-Cultural Approaches to Literacy*, ed. Brian V. Street, pp. 62–86. New York: Cambridge University Press.

———. 1995. *Literacy, Emotion, and Authority: Reading and Writing on a Polynesian Atoll*. New York: Cambridge University Press.

———. 2004. Diversity, Hierarchy, and Modernity in Pacific Island Communities. In *A Companion to Linguistic Anthropology*, ed. Alessandro Duranti, pp. 95–120. Malden, MA: Blackwell.

Biggs, Bruce. 1989. Humpty-Dumpty and the Treaty of Waitangi. In *Maori and Pakeha Perspectives of the Treaty of Waitangi*, ed. I. Hugh Kawharu, pp. 300–312. Auckland, New Zealand: Oxford University Press.

Blommaert, Jan, ed. 1999. *Language Ideological Debates*. Berlin: Mouton de Gruyter.

Blust, Robert. 1999. Subgrouping, Circularity and Extinction: Some Issues in Austronesian Comparative Linguistics. In *Selected Papers from the Eighth International Conference on Austronesian Linguistics*, ed. Elizabeth Zeitoun and Paul Jen-kuei Li, pp. 31–94. Taipei: Academia Sinica.

Borofsky, Robert. 1997. CA Forum on Theory in Anthropology: Cook, Lono, Obeyesekere, and Sahlins. *Current Anthropology* 38 (2): 255–282.

Bourdieu, Pierre. 1977. *Outline of a Theory of Practice* Translated by Richard Nice. New York: Cambridge University Press.

Brady, Ivan, ed. 1983. Speaking in the Name of the Real: Freeman and Mead on Samoa. Special section of *American Anthropologist* 85 (4): 908–947.

Brenneis, Donald L., and Fred R. Myers, eds. 1984. *Dangerous Words: Language and Politics in the Pacific*. New York: New York University Press.

Brison, Karen. 1992. *Just Talk: Gossip, Meetings, and Power in a Papua New Guinea Village*. Berkeley: University of California Press.

Carr, Elizabeth B. 1972. *Da Kine Talk: From Pidgin to Standard English in Hawaii*. Honolulu: University Press of Hawaii.

Clifford, James. 2001. Indigenous Articulations. *The Contemporary Pacific* 13 (2): 468–490.

Codrington, Robert H. 1885. *The Melanesian Languages*. Oxford: Oxford University Press.

———. 1891. *The Melanesians, Their Anthropology and Their Folk-Lore*. Oxford: Oxford University Press.

Crowley, Terry. 1990. *Beach-la-Mar to Bislama: The Emergence of a National Language in Vanuatu*. New York: Oxford University Press.

———. 1999. Linguistic Diversity in the Pacific. *Journal of Sociolinguistics* 3 (1): 81–103.

———. 2001. The Indigenous Linguistic Response to Missionary Authority in the Pacific. *Australian Journal of Linguistics* 21 (2): 239–260.

Diaz, Vincente M., and J. Kēhaulani Kauanui, eds. 2001a. *Native Pacific Cultural Studies on the Edge*. Special issue of *The Contemporary Pacific* 13 (2).

———. 2001b. Native Pacific Cultural Studies on the Edge. *The Contemporary Pacific* 13 (2): 315–341.

Douglas, Bronwen. 1998. *Across the Great Divide: Journeys in History and Anthropology*. Amsterdam: Harwood Academic.

Duranti, Alessandro. 1994. *From Grammar to Politics: Linguistic Anthropology in a Western Samoan Village*. Berkeley: University of California Press.

Errington, J. Joseph. 2001. Colonial Linguistics. *Annual Review of Anthropology* 30: 19–39.

Feinberg, Richard, and Laura Zimmer-Tamakoshi, eds. 1995. *Politics of Culture in the Pacific Islands*. Special issue of *Ethnology* 34 (2).

Fischer, Steven R. 1997. *Rongorongo: The Easter Island Script: History, Traditions, Texts*. Oxford: Oxford University Press.

———. 2005. *Island at the End of the World: The Turbulent History of Easter Island*. London: Reaktion Books.

Foley, William A., ed. 1986. *The Papuan Languages of New Guinea*. New York: Cambridge University Press.

———. 1988. Language Birth: The Processes of Pidginization and Creolization. In *Linguistics: The Cambridge Survey, IV Language: The Socio-Cultural Context*, ed. Frederick J. Newmeyer, pp. 162–183. New York: Cambridge University Press.

Freeman, Derek. 1984. *Margaret Mead and Samoa: The Making and Unmaking of an Anthropological Myth*. Cambridge, MA: Harvard University Press.

Friedlaender, Jonathan S., ed. 2007. *Genes, Language, and Culture History in the Southwest Pacific*. New York: Oxford University Press.

Gal, Susan, and Kathryn Woolard, eds. 2001. *Languages and Publics: The Making of Authority*. Manchester, England: St. Jerome.

Gegeo, David W. 2001. Cultural Rupture and Indigeneity: The Challenge of (Re)visioning "Place" in the Pacific. *The Contemporary Pacific* 13 (2): 491–507.

Giddens, Anthony. 1984. *The Constitution of Society*. Berkeley: University of California Press.

Goldman, Laurence R. 1983. *Talk Never Dies: The Language of Huli Disputes*. London: Tavistock.

Hanson, Allan. 1989. The Making of the Maori: Culture Invention and Its Logic. *American Anthropologist* 91 (4): 890–902.

Harrison, Barbara, and Rahui Papa. 2005. The Development of an Indigenous Knowledge Program in a New Zealand Maori-Language Immersion School. *Anthropology & Education Quarterly* 36 (1): 57–72.

Hau'ofa, Epeli. 1993. Our Sea of Islands. In *A New Oceania: Rediscovering Our Sea of Islands*, ed. Epeli Hau'ofa, Eric Waddell, and Vijay Naidu, pp. 2–16. Suva, Fiji: School of Social and Economic Development, University of the South Pacific.

Heyerdahl, Thor. 1952. *American Indians in the Pacific: The Theory behind the Kon-Tiki Expedition*. London: Allen & Unwin.

Hobsbawm, Eric J., and Terence O. Ranger, eds. 1983. *The Invention of Tradition*. New York: Cambridge University Press.

Hohepa, Pat. 2000. Towards 2030 AD (2) Maori Language Regeneration Strategies, Government, People. *He Pukenga Kōrero* 5 (2): 10–15.

Jolly, Margaret, and Nicholas Thomas, eds. 1992. *The Politics of Tradition in the Pacific*. Special issue of *Oceania* 62 (4).

Joseph, Brian D., Johanna Destefano, Neil G. Jacobs, and Ilse Lehiste, eds. 2003. *When Languages Collide: Perspectives on Language Conflict, Language Competition, and Language Coexistence*. Columbus: Ohio State University Press.

Joseph, John E., and Talbot J. Taylor, eds. 1990. *Ideologies of Language*. New York: Routledge.

Jourdan, Christine. 1991. Pidgins and Creoles: The Blurring of Categories. *Annual Review of Anthropology* 20: 187–209.

Jourdan, Christine, and Roger Keesing. 1997. From Fisin to Pijin: Creolization in Process in the Solomon Islands. *Language in Society* 26: 401–418.

Kame'eleihiwa, Lilikalā. 1992. *Native Land and Foreign Desires*. Honolulu: Bishop Museum Press.

Kapono, Eric. 1995. Hawaiian Language Revitalization and Immersion Education. *International Journal of the Sociology of Language* 112: 121–135.

Karetu, Timoti S. 2002. Maori—New Zealand Latin? In *Indigenous Languages across the Community*, ed. Barbara Burnaby and Jon Reyhner, pp. 25–29. Flagstaff: North Arizona University Press.

Kawharu, I. Hugh, ed. 1989. *Maori and Pakeha Perspectives of the Treaty of Waitangi.* Auckland, New Zealand: Oxford University Press.

Keating, Elizabeth. 1998. *Power Sharing: Language, Rank, Gender, and Social Space in Pohnpei, Micronesia.* New York: Oxford University Press.

Keesing, Roger M. 1988. *Melanesian Pidgin and the Oceanic Substrate.* Stanford, CA: Stanford University Press.

Keesing, Roger, and Robert Tonkinson, eds. 1982. Reinventing Traditional Culture: The Politics of Kastom in Island Melanesia. Special issue of *Mankind* 13 (4).

King, Jeanette. 2001. Te Kohanga Reo: Maori language revitalization. In *The Green Book of Language Revitalization in Practice*, ed. Leanne Hinton and Ken Hale, pp. 119–128. San Diego, CA: Academic Press.

Kirch, Patrick V. 2000. *On the Road of the Winds: An Archaeological History of the Pacific Islands before European Conquest.* Berkeley: University of California Press.

Kroskrity, Paul V., ed. 2000. *Regimes of Language: Ideologies, Polities, and Identities.* Santa Fe, NM: School of American Research Press.

Kualono. n.d. Hale Kuamoʻo. University of Hawaiʻi at Hilo Hawaiian Language Webpages. Electronic document, http://www.olelo.hawaii.edu, accessed March 2007.

Kulick, Don. 1992. *Language Shift and Cultural Reproduction: Socialization, Self, and Syncretism in a Papua New Guinean Village.* New York: Cambridge University Press.

———. 1999. Review of *Linguistic Ecology: Language Change and Linguistic Imperialism in the Pacific,* by Peter Mühlhäusler. *Anthropological Linguistics* 41 (8): 404–406.

Kulick, Don, and Christopher Stroud. 1993. Conceptions and Uses of Literacy in a Papua New Guinean Village. In *Cross-Cultural Approaches to Literacy*, ed. Brian V. Street, pp. 30–61. New York: Cambridge University Press.

Laycock, Donald C. 1982. Melanesian Linguistic Diversity: A Melanesian Choice? In *Melanesia: Beyond Diversity*, ed. R. J. May and Hank Nelson, Vol. 1, pp. 33–38. Canberra: Australian National University Press.

Levinson, Michael, R. Gerard Ward, and John W. Webb. 1973. *The Settlement of Polynesia: A Computer Simulation.* Minneapolis: University of Minnesota Press.

Lindstrom, Lamont, and Geoffrey M. White, eds. 1994. *Culture, Kastom, Tradition: Developing Cultural Policy in Melanesia.* Suva, Fiji: Institute of Pacific Studies.

Linnekin, Jocelyn S. 1983. Defining Tradition: Variations on the Hawaiian Identity. *American Ethnologist* 10 (2): 241–252.

———. 1991. Cultural Invention and the Dilemma of Authenticity. *American Anthropologist* 93 (2): 446–449.

Linnekin, Jocelyn S., and Lin Poyer, eds. 1990. *Cultural Identity and Ethnicity in the Pacific.* Honolulu: University of Hawaiʻi Press.

Lutz, Catherine. 1988. *Unnatural Emotions: Everyday Sentiments on a Micronesian Atoll and Their Challenge to Western Theory.* Chicago: University of Chicago Press.

Lynch, John. 1996. Review of *Linguistic Ecology: Language Change and Linguistic Imperialism in the Pacific,* by P. Mühhäusler. *Language in Society* 26 (3): 461–464.

———. 1998. *Pacific Languages: An Introduction.* Honolulu: University of Hawaiʻi Press.

Makihara, Miki. 2004. Linguistic Syncretism and Language Ideologies: Transforming Sociolinguistic Hierarchy on Rapa Nui (Easter Island). *American Anthropologist* 106 (3): 529–540.

Malinowski, Bronislaw. [1935] 1978. *Coral Gardens and Their Magic.* 2 vols. New York: Dover Publications.

McElhanon, Kenneth A. 1979. Some Mission Lingue Franche and Their Sociolinguistic Role. In *New Guinea and Neighboring Areas: A Sociolinguistic Laboratory*, ed. Stephen A. Wurm, pp. 277–289. The Hague: Mouton.

McKenzie, Don F. 1987. The Sociology of a Text: Oral Culture, Literacy and Print in Early New Zealand. In *The Social History of Language*, ed. Peter Burke and Roy Porter, pp. 161–198. New York: Cambridge University Press.

Mead, Margaret. 1928. *Coming of Age in Samoa: A Psychological Study of Primitive Youth for Western Civilization*. New York: William Morrow.

Merlan, Francesca, and Alan Rumsey. 1991. *Ku Waru: Language and Segmentary Politics in the Western Nebilyer Valley, Papua New Guinea*. New York: Cambridge University Press.

Meyerhoff, Miriam. 2003. Formal and Cultural Constraints on Optional Objects in Bislama. *Language Variation and Change* 14 (3): 323–346.

Mühlhäusler, Peter. 1996. *Linguistic Ecology: Language Change and Linguistic Imperialism in the Pacific Region*. New York: Routledge.

Mutu, Margaret. 2005. In Search of the Missing Māori Links—Maintaining Both Ethnic Identity and Linguistic Integrity in the Revitalization of the Māori Language. *International Journal of the Sociology of Language* 172 (1): 117–132.

Myers, Fred, and Donald Brenneis. 1984. Introduction: Language and Politics in the Pacific. In *Dangerous Words: Language and Politics in the Pacific*, ed. Donald Brenneis and Fred Myers, pp. 1–30. New York: New York University Press.

Obeyesekere, Gananath. 1992. *The Apotheosis of Captain Cook: European Mythmaking in the Pacific*. Princeton, NJ: Princeton University Press.

Ochs, Elinor. 1988. *Culture and Language Development: Language Acquisition and Language Socialization in a Samoan Village*. New York: Cambridge University Press.

Pawley, Andrew. 2007. Recent Research on the Historical Relationships of the Papuan Languages: or, What Does Linguistics Say about the Prehistory of Melanesia? In *Genes, Language, and Culture History in the Southwest Pacific*, ed. Jonathan S. Friedlaender, pp. 36–60. New York: Oxford University Press.

Pawley, Andrew, and Malcolm Ross. 1993. Austronesian Historical Linguistics and Culture History. *Annual Review of Anthropology* 22: 425–459.

Pihama, Leonie, Kaapua Smith, Mereana Taki, and Jenny Lee. 2004. *A Literature Review on Kaupapa Māori and Māori Education Pedagogy*. The International Research Institute for Māori and Indigenous Education, University of Auckland.

Pike, Kenneth. 1947. *A Technique for Reducing Languages to Writing*. Ann Arbor: University of Michigan Press.

Reinecke, John E. 1969. *Language and Dialect in Hawaii: A Socio-linguistic History to 1935*. Honolulu: University of Hawaii Press.

Robbins, Joel. 2004. *Becoming Sinners: Christianity and Moral Torment in a Papua New Guinea Society*. Berkeley: University of California Press.

Robbins, Joel, and Holly Wardlow, eds. 2005. *The Making of Global and Local Modernities in Melanesia: Humiliation, Transformation and the Nature of Cultural Change*. Burlington, VT: Ashgate.

Romaine, Suzanne. 1995. Birds of a Different Feather: Tok Pisin and Hawai'i Creole English as Literary Languages. *The Contemporary Pacific* 7 (1): 81–123.

———. 2002. Signs of Identity, Signs of Discord: Glottal Goofs and the Green Grocer's Glottal in Debates on Hawaiian Orthography. *Journal of Linguistic Anthropology* 12(2): 189–224.

Ross, Malcolm D. 2005. Pronouns as a Preliminary Diagnostic for Grouping Papuan Languages. In *Papuan Pasts: Cultural, Linguistic, and Biological Histories of Papuan-Speaking Peoples*, ed. Andrew Pawley, Robert Attenborough, Jack Golson, and Robin Hide, pp. 15–66. Canberra: Pacific Linguistics, Australian National University.

Rumsey, Alan. 2006. The Articulation of Indigenous and Exogenous Orders in Highland New Guinea and Beyond. *Australian Journal of Anthropology* 17 (1): 47–69.

Rutherford, Danilyn. 2005. Frontiers of the Lingua Franca: Ideologies of the Linguistic Contact Zone in Dutch New Guinea. *Ethnos* 70 (3): 387–412.

Sahlins, Marshall. 1981. *Historical Metaphors and Mythical Realities.* Ann Arbor: University of Michigan Press.

———. 1985. *Islands of History.* Chicago: University of Chicago Press.

———. 1996. *How "Natives" Think: About Captain Cook, for Example.* Chicago: University of Chicago Press.

Sakoda, Kent, and Jeff Siegel. 2003. *Pidgin Grammar: An Introduction to the Creole English of Hawai'i.* Honolulu: Bess Press.

Sankoff, Gillian. 1980a. Political Power and Linguistic Inequality in Papua New Guinea. In *The Social Life of Language,* pp. 5–27. Philadelphia: University of Pennsylvania Press.

———. 1980b. *The Social Life of Language.* Philadelphia: University of Pennsylvania Press.

Schieffelin, Bambi B. 2000. Introducing Kaluli Literacy: A Chronology of Influences. In *Regimes of Language: Ideologies, Politics, and Identities,* ed. Paul V. Kroskrity, pp. 293–327. Santa Fe, NM: School of American Research Press.

Schieffelin, Bambi B., Kathryn A. Woolard, and Paul V. Kroskrity, eds. 1998. *Language Ideologies: Practice and Theor+ y.* New York: Oxford University Press.

Schütz, Albert J. 1994. *The Voices of Eden: A History of Hawaiian Language Studies.* Honolulu: University of Hawai'i Press.

Siegel, Jeff. 1987. *Language Contact in a Plantation Environment: A Sociolinguistic History of Fiji.* New York: Cambridge University Press.

———. 1997. Review of Linguistic Ecology: Language Change and Linguistic Imperialism in the Pacific Region. *Australian Journal of Linguistics* 17: 219–244.

———, ed. 2000. *Processes of Language Contact: Studies from Australia and the South Pacific.* Montreal: Les Editions Fides.

Silverstein, Michael. 1979. Language Structure and Linguistic Ideology. In *The Elements: A Parasession of Linguistic Units and Levels,* ed. Paul R. Clyne, William F. Hanks, and Carol L. Hofbauer, pp. 193–247. Chicago: Chicago Linguistic Society.

———. 1996. Encountering Language and Languages of Encounter in North American Ethnohistory. *Journal of Linguistic Anthropology* 6 (2): 126–144.

———. 1998. Contemporary Transformations of Local Linguistic Communities. *Annual Review of Anthropology* 27: 401–426.

Smith, Geoff P. 2002. *Growing up with Tok Pisin: Contact, Creolization, and Change in Papua New Guinea's National Language.* London: Battlebridge.

Street, Brian V. 1984. *Literacy in Theory and Practice.* New York: Cambridge University Press.

Sumbuk, Kenneth. 2006. Papua New Guinea's Languages: Will They Survive? In *Language Diversity in the Pacific: Endangerment and Survival,* ed. Denis Cunningham, D. E. Ingram, and Kenneth Sumbuk, pp. 85–96. Tonawanda, NY: Multilingual Matters.

Summerhayes, Glenn. 2007. Island Melanesian Pasts—A View from Archaeology. In *Genes, Language, and Culture History in the Southwest Pacific,* ed. Jonathan S. Friedlaender, pp. 10–35. New York: Oxford University Press.

Tcherkézoff, Serge. 2003. The Unwarranted Encounter between the Etymology of Papalagi and the Apotheosis of Captain Cook. *Journal of the Polynesian Society* 112 (1): 65–73.

Teaiwa, Teresia K. 2001. Militarism, Tourism and the Native: Articulations in Oceania. Ph.D. diss., University of California, Santa Cruz.

Topping, Donald M. 1992. Literacy and Cultural Erosion in the Pacific Islands. In *Cross-Cultural Literacy: Global Perspectives on Reading and Writing*, ed. Fraida Dubin and Natalie A. Kuhlman, pp. 19–33. Englewood Cliffs, NJ: Regents/Prentice-Hall.

Trask, Haunani-Kay. 1991. Natives and Anthropologists: The Colonial Struggle. *The Contemporary Pacific* 3 (1): 159–177.

———. [1993] 1999. *From a Native Daughter: Colonialism and Sovereignty in Hawai'i*. Revised ed. Honolulu: University of Hawai'i Press.

Tryon, Darrell T., and Jean-Michel Charpentier. 2004. *Pacific Pidgins and Creoles: Origins, Growth, and Development*. Berlin: Mouton de Gruyter.

Wagner, Roy. 1975. *The Invention of Culture*. Englewood Cliffs, NJ: Prentice-Hall.

Ward, R. Gerard. 1989. Earth's Empty Quarter? The Pacific Islands. *Geographical Journal* 155 (2): 235–246.

Warner, Sam L. No'eau. 2001. The Movement to Revitalize Hawaiian Language and Culture. In *The Green Book of Language Revitalization in Practice*, ed. Leanne Hinton and Ken Hale, pp. 133–146. San Diego, CA: Academic Press.

Watson-Gegeo, Karen A. 1986. The Study of Language Use in Oceania. *Annual Review of Anthropology* 15: 149–162.

Watson-Gegeo, Karen A., and Geoffrey M. White, eds. 1990. *Disentangling: Conflict Discourse in Pacific Societies*. Stanford, CA: Stanford University Press.

White, Geoffrey M., and Karen A. Watson-Gegeo. 1990. Disentangling Discourse. In *Disentangling: Conflict Discourse in Pacific Societies*, ed. Karen A. Watson-Gegeo and Geoffrey M. White, pp. 3–49. Stanford, CA: Stanford University Press.

Williams, Raymond. 1977. *Marxism and Literature*. Oxford: Oxford University Press.

Wilson, William H., and Kauanoe Kamanā. 2001. "Mai loko mai o ka 'i'ni: Proceeding from a Dream." The 'Aha Pūnana Leo Connection in Hawaiian Language Revitalization. In *The Green Book of Language Revitalization in Practice*, ed. Leanne Hinton and Ken Hale, pp. 147–176. San Diego, CA: Academic Press.

CHRISTINE JOURDAN

Linguistic Paths to Urban Self in Postcolonial Solomon Islands

Introduction

I think in many languages, therefore I am. This pastiche of one of the most famous quotes of Western thought encapsulates the linguistic state of affairs in Honiara, the 50-year-old capital city of the Solomon Islands. For it is true that the everyday linguistic practice in this city of sixty thousand people requires most inhabitants to be at least bilingual if they want to have a place in this urban linguistic maze. Carrying the pastiche further, we could transform it into *I think in many languages because I am.* Thus doing, we would capture one of the inescapable aspects of Honiara sociality, namely that one's urban self is predicated on one's many identities, a number of them being experienced through different languages.

The interplay of languages in the linguistic repertoire of individuals and groups has a long and rich history in the Solomon Islands, as in all of Melanesia. Yet the relationships in which speakers have kept all these languages have changed over the years and reveal the place that languages have in the construction of the social self and in the creation and reinforcement of multiple identities. From the precolonial period to the postcolonial period, the effects of cultural and linguistic contact have been felt in different ways. This is particularly true of the linguistic scene of Honiara, where multilingualism rules and where individuals have had to negotiate otherness daily.

Contact, cultural and linguistic, has important consequences for the cultural groups at play. Whether it is sporadic or sustained over a long period of time, whether it is limited to trade or chance encounters or takes the form of colonization, contact has the inevitable result of change. Cultural groups and individuals are exposed to new ideologies and practices that may challenge or corroborate people's ways of being and thinking. In many cases, contact leads to a reevaluation of the relationships that people entertain with cultural and linguistic diversity and difference and may lead groups and individuals to redefine how they see themselves. In the best cases, this plays out in accommodation of difference through bilingualism and multilingualism, borrowing, cultural hybridity, and linguistic creolization. In the worst cases, it plays out in conquest and genocide.

The history of cultural contacts in the Solomon Islands predates colonial times, but its trajectory took a dramatic turn when colonization challenged the more egalitarian ethos of Solomon Islands sociality. Christianization, urbanization, and globalization in turn also brought about ideologies that had direct bearing on the shaping and defining of self in the contemporary Solomon Islands. Nowhere is this more obvious than in Honiara, where cultural and linguistic contact is a way of life. Together with ideologies of change and "progress," contact has forced a definition of urban identity that feeds on ideologies of *kastom* (custom practices, often reified), tradition, modernization, and social roles and options, and is revealed through language choice and practice.

In this chapter, I sketch the urban modalities of language use by residents of Honiara with the goal of showing how contact has affected the urban definition of self and identity. Part of the argument involves paying attention to language selection not simply as an expression of the speaker's agency, but also as the road to a constantly redefined sociality and to the situatedness of the social self in situations of cultural contact. What better than the inescapability of language to index one's places in a social world that one contributes to create? A central theme running throughout the various arguments presented here is that of the legitimacy conferred to languages by the culture that sustains them. The chapter starts with some background information on the effects of contact on the general linguistic situation of the Solomon Islands prior to colonization, and on postcolonial Honiara in particular. It moves to the analysis of four important loci of the expression of identity through language: social differentiation, ethnic affiliation, generation, and gender.

Background

As with other parts of Melanesia, the Solomon Islands is the site of a great number of spoken languages. With as many as sixty-four ethnic groups and as many languages, language diversity and attendant multilingualism has been part of the cultural soundscape of the place. As Sankoff (1980) has shown for Papua New Guinea, multilingualism is the rule rather than the exception in the Solomon Islands and is not limited to urban life. This needs to be qualified, however, because in the rural areas of the Solomon Islands, the knowledge and use of several vernaculars is probably more typical of the linguistic behavior of adult men than of children and women. Enmeshed as they have been in trade and kinship relationships with neighboring groups, men especially have commonly made use of their linguistic repertoire in order to posture, reinforce their ethnic identity, establish links with people from other linguistic groups, or simply to strike good deals. Caught between pragmatism and symbolism, people practiced a linguistic modus vivendi that reflected the relative cultural significance and relevance of all the vernaculars for the cultural world at hand.

The prevalence and importance of multilingualism in the linguistic practice of Solomon Islanders is revealed by the absence of local lingua francas. Curiously, and despite trading networks that covered vast expanses of land and sea, no regional lingua franca seem to have surfaced prior to colonization. It might be argued that Roviana in the western part of the archipelago (Edvard Hviding, private communication, February 2004) and Lau in northern Malaita (Pierre Maranda, private communication, February 2004) could have aspired to the status of a small regional lingua franca, but the record is not conclusive.

From a pragmatic point of view, knowing many languages brings many advantages to a speaker. We will not repeat them here. From a symbolic point of view, the advantages are not negligible either: speaking many languages anchors the speakers in the social worlds they seek to be associated with, just as sociolects do. Active bilingualism or multilingualism is an exercise in identity creation and affirmation. In the Solomon Islands, and until colonial time, multilingualism seems to have been reciprocal among language groups. It often took the form of chain multilingualism and was made possible by the proximity in which the groups lived and by regular social and economic contacts. The result was a language practice that functioned more or less like so: I know the languages of my immediate neighbors and they know the languages of their immediate neighbors, mine included. Linguistic groups located at the ends of the multilingual chain would not know the languages of each other, but within the chain all groups would know the language of their close neighbors. What we know of social life of these cultural groups, particularly with regard to gender distribution of social responsibilities, leads us to assume that not all members of a cultural group were multilingual to the same extent. Again, as with trade, it seems that active, rather than passive, multilingualism was practiced more by men than by women. Nevertheless, the question that we should ask is: Why opt for multilingualism where a lingua franca could have helped bridge the language gaps? It could be argued that this linguistic practice has at its heart a concern for reciprocity that extends beyond the linguistic sphere, a concern that we find often associated with exchange networks or clan obligations. Reciprocal multilingualism, or balanced multilingualism as I like to call it, may be construed as yet another form that exchange between groups takes (see also Robbins, chap. 6 of this volume). It is the linguistic incarnation of balanced reciprocity. We can also argue that reciprocal multilingualism may stem from a more encompassing ideology of egalitarianism between ethnolinguistic groups: By learning the language of the other, we recognize the other; we also acknowledge their difference and, more important, their right to this difference. It plays a central role in the crystallization of identity in that it reinforces one's sense of difference. Yet we observe that reciprocal multilingualism can take place only when coevality has been achieved between the speakers of different languages (Fabian 1983). We have here interesting tensions between inclusion and exclusion, belonging or not, self and other, cultural proximity or distance, all expressed through the languages one knows and uses. As we know from the studies dealing with exchange in Melanesia, reciprocal multilingualism may also stem from the mutual dependence of social groups for the acquisition of traded goods. As with exchange, it is a social act, therefore a constructing act, and as such it indexes and paves the way for particular types of intergroup relations that reveal the extent, nature, and depth of contacts established among neighboring cultural groups. In Melanesia, language does not seem to have been an object of discord. As Wardaugh (1987) cited by Tengan (1994: 13) states about pluralism in Africa: "Many Africans are indeed multilingual, but language itself seems never to have been a divisive issue." Melanesian multilingualism offers a sharp contrast to unbalanced and nonreciprocal types of multilingualism typically associated with situations of cultural and linguistic hegemony.

But colonization (annexation by England took place in 1893) and its various phases and incarnations and subsequent urbanization and postcolonial politics have altered this state of affairs. In the first instance, regional missionary lingua francas were introduced, or established and recognized as such by some churches. This is the case for Mota, the language of the Banks Islands[1] (Hilliard 1978) in the New Hebrides (now Vanuatu), which served as the language of Christianization for the Anglican Church in the eastern part of the archipelago through its Melanesian Mission. This is also the case for Roviana, which became the language of evangelization of the Methodists in the western part of the archipelago. In the early twentieth century, two new languages, English and Pijin, were introduced on the language scene. English, the language of the colonial administration, was imposed from above. British administrators and colonial residents thought of the languages at hand in the Solomon Islands in terms of "quality" and "value" and in terms of a hierarchy: the horizontal linguistic mosaic featuring reciprocal multilingualism was transformed into a vertical linguistic order based on hierarchy. As might be expected, English occupied the top position in that hierarchy. Pijin was put at the bottom, and the local Melanesian languages somewhere in the middle, but closer to the bottom than to the top. As was common in colonial linguistic ideology (Calvet 1974), the latter were thought and spoken of as "dialects"[2] and not as "true languages." Such a labeling, resting as it did on racial categories, contributed to signal and reinforce the social and intellectual distance the colonials sought to establish between themselves and local populations. Colonial worlds set the stage for linguistic regimes to collide and be transformed. It was true also in the Solomon Islands (Jourdan 1990; Keesing 1990). Except for some missionaries and the odd planter, British colonials never bothered learning the local languages; and if some tried to learn Pijin, it was with a sense that this "childish" and "debased" form of speech was not a true language. The result was that the great majority of them never learned it well.[3]

Pijin, known initially as Pisin, belongs to the family of Pacific pidgins known as Melanesian pidgins that were lexicalized from English. Introduced in the Solomon Islands in the later part of the nineteenth century by indentured workers returning from Queensland, Pijin spread through grass-roots networks during the colonial period (1898–1975). It served as an interethnic language of communication in social settings in which traditional chain multilingualism would not be adequate. Typical contexts included plantations and contacts with British administrators and overseers, who despised it (Keesing, 1990). Despite the advantages that it brought to its speakers, Pijin's cultural life was limited: it was nobody's language insofar as no one used it as a mother tongue, and speakers always made use of their vernacular ancestral language when discussing cultural matters pertaining to the village's everyday social life. As a result, nobody developed an emotional attachment toward this new language. One needs to remember that over the course of its social history in the Solomon Islands, Pijin became the most important language of the country in terms of number of speakers and variety of contexts in which it was used. Anchored as they were in the culture of colonial relationships, English and Pijin coexisted but were clearly of different social worlds. Their cultural rooting was also different. And not surprisingly, the introduction of these languages in the Solomon Islands and the subsequent role they played in colonial and postcolonial relationships were destined to change radically the balance of power that existed among Solomon Islanders because of the language they knew. The situation came to the fore in Honiara, where English and Pijin quickly became central to the daily language practice of many urbanites.

With the increasing importance of Honiara in the cultural and political life of the country, and particularly after independence in 1975, the balance of power of these languages shifted. Pijin is now spoken as a second language in the Solomon Islands and has become the main language of the capital city and the mother tongue of two generations of urbanites. It is the de facto national language of the country despite not having been given such a status in the constitution of the country at the time of independence. In the rural areas, early childhood formal education now often takes place in Pijin because it is often difficult to qualify enough teachers from each language area to ensure that early childhood education will take place in the local vernacular. With 80 percent of the Solomon Islands population still living in rural areas, the vernacular languages have remained strong. However, people rely increasingly on Pijin for interethnic communications, and knowledge of multiple vernaculars seems confined mostly to people who learn the language of a spouse who belongs to a different ethnic group. The expansion of Pijin as a lingua franca was aided by the fact that it could not be associated with any particular ethnic group. Through formal schooling, English has spread in the population: it is a requirement for employment in the public sector and for white-collar work. It is the official language of the country and is the language used in the newspapers.

Multilingualism still exists in the Solomon Islands, but its linguistic and social parameters have changed, particularly in towns: more often than not it involves Pijin and vernaculars, and in Honiara it includes English as well. I will show below how Honiarans make use of the different varieties of language they know to index their position in the urban world, claim membership in ethnic relationships, and illustrate their social sophistication. Their choice of language and how they use language reveals their urban experience and the construction of their social selves.

One of the interesting facets of the recent history of the Solomon Islands has been the development of cultural worlds that are seen by the population as being essentially urban and are seen as necessarily involving complex forms of social relations, emphasis on nuclear families, reliance on wage employment, redefinition of social propriety, and reanalysis of cultural practice. These ways of being and of thinking social life are anchored in and reveal social differentiation.

Urban living and social differentiation

It is hard to reconcile Honiara with the images in tourist brochures advertising the Pacific. The city is crowded, noisy, and dusty, and the sea that graces its shore is dirty. Its attractive power does not rest on its physical attributes but rather on its economic opportunities (possible employment, schooling, shopping). From the moment of its establishment around 1952 on what was left of the U.S. Army base on Guadalcanal, people were quick to respond to the beckoning calls of Honiara. It was a hub through which hundreds of laborers passed looking for work, and as a colonial capital, it was the seat of the British protectorate; it was also the main port of entry into the country. As economic opportunities developed, Solomon Islanders increasingly settled in town to pursue paid employment. After independence in 1975, the town grew even faster and quickly became one of the faster growing towns of the Pacific Islands.

As Jourdan (1996), Gooberman-Hill (1999), and Berg (2000) have shown, many Honiarans have progressively developed middle-class values of cosmopolitanism and individualism that increase the cultural distance between their sociality and that of village folk. This, in turn, creates tensions within families with regard to traditional forms of exchange and obligations. Village folk are sometimes referred to as burdens who come to town uninvited and never leave. Reciprocally, urban folk are perceived by villagers as selfish if they refuse to pay or entertain their visiting *wantoks* (members of one's lineage or ethnolinguistic group);[4] they can also be accused of being morally loose if they fail to uphold *kastom*. Yet some of the moral constructions that underlie urban social life, however reified or folklorized they may be (see Babadzan 1988; Keesing 1982) still connect urbanites to those of their home village (Akin 1999; Gegeo 1994). They are often at the core of a construction of their urban identity analyzed in moral terms (Jourdan 1994; Stritecky 2001). The link between towns and villages is never fully severed. As urbanites participate in forms of sociality that are further removed from that of their forebears and become the exponents of values that are seen contrary to *kastom*, they are challenged by their village folk: How can one be an urbanite and yet remain a Kwaio, a Rannongga, or a Bellona? How does one belong to the larger world and remain connected and, most important, *worthy* of the local scene? Clearly, this challenge does not rest on an appropriation by Solomon Islanders of the tenets of Orientalism. It rests on a local construction of what is at the core of local forms of sociality and expression and that villagers recognize as central to their definition of self: exchange, reciprocal obligations, membership in clans.

Looking in from the outside, vernaculars may seem to have become marginal in the life of many city people, particularly for the younger elite who seem to function mainly in Pijin and English. Yet vernaculars keep their status as "true" languages even in the eyes of those who do not know them. Nostalgia plays an important role here: for many older urban people, the local languages are the languages they associate with their "true" identity, defined as it is by the experiential world of the village. Some members of the older educated urban elite will alternate comfortably between English, Pijin, and vernaculars. This is particularly true of politicians.

Though Pijin has made distinct practical and symbolic gains in town, it is clear that these gains are concomitant with its own acquisition of cultural depth. The culture that sustains Pijin is both familiar and foreign to village people, who are quick to criticize it. The city has existed for over fifty years, and two generations of urbanites have made their mark on it. They have done their own readings of the lifestyles, ideologies, and popular culture that they inherited from the colonial world, and they have transformed the cultural world they inherited from village-based sociality. The result is a creolized cultural world that has given Pijin the cultural legitimacy it lacked for so long. Pijin has gone from being no one's language (emotionally) to everyone's language, succeeding linguistically and socially. At the same time, all varieties of Pijin do not carry equal symbolic value with speakers, and one finds, in addition to the well-established geographical dialects, social dialects that are measured in terms of their distance from vernaculars. Variation in Pijin was always recognized and acknowledged by speakers, who could immediately identify the ethnic origin of speakers by paying attention to phonology. This is still the case, but variation is also evaluated against an urban form that is increasingly homogeneous among the young and that serves as the standard for the definition of good Pijin for the young. These varieties coexist in Honiara, and they measure speakers' location on the social scale. The result is that two competing sociolinguistic norms have developed in Pijin. One is based on nostalgia and uses the rural varieties as the yardstick of acceptability (Bourdieu 1982). The other is based on an ideology of the *moden* (modern, sophisticated) and measures acceptability against the variety used by the young urban crowd. It is a lesson for this anthropologist who, having made an effort to learn what was recognized then by her mentors as the "good" variety of Pijin, to now be told by young people that her Pijin reminds them of their grandmother's. The remark was not meant as a compliment (far from it) and signaled the lumping of the anthropologist, symbolically and practically, with the older crowd. It served also as a social commentary on the existence of dialects in Pijin, on the increasing social differentiation they index, and on speakers' awareness.

English reigns as the language of social advancement, the language of schooling, and is associated with professional success. Most Honiarans who have finished primary school have a rather good understanding of it, and a great number speak it well. The elite are, in general, fluent, of course, and many among them alternate easily between English, Pijin, and, if the speaker is older, vernaculars. Others will intersperse their Pijin with English and create a linguistic continuum that is sometimes hard to define. The term "acrolectal" comes to mind. Young people who do not master English will try to sprinkle their Pijin with a few words of English to establish their level of social sophistication. In most cases, urbanites will be at least bilingual, but with different combinations of languages: vernaculars and Pijin for the majority of the older people; Pijin and English for the younger ones born in town;[5] vernacular, Pijin, and English for a number of well-educated older city people and for some younger adults. Language shift has been in progress since the early 1980s (Jourdan 1985).[6] At first, it was the result of pragmatic language choices made by young urban parents, who recognized that Pijin was the language of the town and that vernaculars were not essential to urban life. The following quote from an interview I conducted in 1983 is enlightening in this regard: *Mi laek hem save Pijin bikos bae hem had fo hem taem hem go lo skul. So mi laekem hem save fastaem Pijin; langgus bae hem save bihaen* (I want him to know Pijin, otherwise it will be hard for him when he goes to school. So I want him to learn Pijin first; he will learn vernacular later). For this family, speaking Pijin is not only the consequence of living in a multilingual environment; it is a deliberate choice made in light of the importance they recognize and attribute to Pijin in such a milieu. The child in question was four years old at the time. Now in his late twenties, he still does not know any of the vernaculars of his parents, save a few prototypical words of address for friends and grandparents. He is, however, fluent in Pijin and in English. Today, language shift is even more prevalent among the younger crowd and is driven by an ideology of language that focuses on the importance of the present and on social change as a moral imperative (see also Makihara, chap. 3 of this volume).

As with Calvet (1994), we recognize that urbanization takes place in phases that have linguistic effects. His model proposes a dual-phase model contrasting a period of radical expansion, during which urban migrants come from the provinces, with a period of stabilization, during which they come from foreign countries. This contrast does not quite work for the Solomon Islands. Yet the linguistic effects Calvet associates with the first phase (multilingualism and the reinforcement of a lingua franca) are quite relevant for Honiara. Says he: "A la période de croissance maximale correspond à la fois le plurilinguisme et l'émergence véhiculaire" (To the period of maximal growth [of the town], multilingualism and an emerging lingua franca coexist) (61). At this stage, it is hard to predict whether what he associates with the phase of stabilization (national status for the lingua franca and a resurfacing of vernacular languages) will be borne out in Honiara.

The ethnic self

In Honiara, the coexistence of almost all of the country's sixty-four ethnic groups and separate vernaculars has created a form of exacerbated otherness that leads residents to be almost obsessively interested in knowing people's cultural origins. Nicknames using vernacular labels are used to refer to various ethnic groups: some are disparaging, and others are simply indexical. In all cases, they reveal the importance of alterity in Honiara's social landscape. To know who the other is matters. Honiarans have become extremely skilled at identifying the vernacular phonemes that smatter people's Pijin and reveal the ethnolinguistic origin of the speaker (Jourdan 1985; Gooberman-Hill 1999; Jourdan and Selbach 2004). The *wantok* networks, which are central to the social life of ethnic groups in town, function as support groups but also as pressure and interest groups and as a system of reciprocal obligation and exchange. They function as a matrix within which the ethnic self is enacted and given meaning. Most young people born in town have a secondhand knowledge of their parents' home culture, or *kastom,* for whom the village-defined version is the point of reference. Often, they have not experienced this cultural world firsthand beyond summer vacations in the village, and they know only the most salient elements that their parents have kept alive in town. *Kastom* has become part of the rhetoric of urban life and central to the discourse of ethnicity redefined locally. As has been well analyzed,[7] these salient elements—such as bridewealth payments, compensation payments, respect due to elders, music and dance, cooking in the *motu* (stone oven, from Roviana)—have become symbols of ethnic identity for urban people, sometimes in a folklorized way. Singled out as they are, these symbols are often endowed with legitimacy-bearing qualities that reinforce their status as markers of cultural integrity, authenticity, and morals (see also Jourdan 1996; Gooberman-Hill 1999; Stritecky 2001). Along with bridewealth exchanges and compensatory payments, local languages are central to a discourse about a form of identity rooted in the past or rooted in an imagined village cultural world, even if one does not know them. For some of the younger Honiarans, the rhetoric of nostalgia involves elements that many of them have not experienced firsthand but that allow a projection of identity into a world still perceived, "in fragments," as meaningful (see Hill 1998: 69). Interestingly, when asked where they are from, young people born in town will continue to identify themselves by the name of the ethnolinguistic group to which their parents belong (to that of their fathers' when the parents are from different ethnolinguistic groups). Yet, for almost all young people ages twenty-five and under who were born and raised in town, social life will be built in Pijin. And, kinship and ethnic (*wantok*) ties notwithstanding, they will also associate through church activities, neighborhood organizations and workplace relationships with people from different ethnolinguistic groups.

The urban ethnic self lies at the crossroads between urban social networks, which are established away from any reference to the "home" culture and emphasize social links across ethnic boundaries, and cultural networks fostered within the *wantok* system, which people in cities tend to redefine at their convenience. To belong to and be recognized by one's own ethnic group, one has to conform to the social pressures exerted by members who reside in town and by those who do not. People in urban settings navigate these tensions with varying degrees of ability and frustration, at times leaning more toward their urban self, and at others toward their ethnic self. Flexibility, adaptability, playing the system, and recognizing that the self is contextual and multifaceted are essential for someone trying to make a life in town. Linguistically, this is easier for the urban adults, whose language repertoire almost always includes the vernacular of their parents, than it is for the younger crowd, whose repertoire usually does not (which I will discuss in more detail below).

In 1998, an ethnic crisis developed in Honiara. Often understood as a conflict between the people of Malaita and those of Guadalcanal over land usage around Honiara, the crisis was linked to the overwhelming presence of Malaitans in government and economic affairs. It degenerated into a coup that toppled the government, established a climate of violence and fear on the island of Guadalcanal, and led to the repatriation of ten thousand Malaitans. The linguistic outcome of this so-called ethnic crisis (Kabutaulaka 2000) has been a renewed interest in vernaculars in Honiara. Even though the transformation of Pijin into the de facto national language of the country and the language of the towns is a fait accompli, vernaculars have resurfaced as symbols and anchors of ethnic identities. As with other cultural matters, the symbolic power of languages is very often contextual and relational: historical events may trigger the crystallization of group consciousness. As is happening in Honiara, it is often manifested in a renewed interest in vernacular language and culture.

Generation gap

In Honiara, one can easily observe that the basic linguistic repertoire of younger people is increasingly different from that of older ones. Though people forty and older who were born in rural areas usually speak their own vernacular and one or two others plus Pijin and (among those who are educated) English, this is not the case for the younger population, particularly those born in town. The linguistic repertoire of the younger people, those age thirty and younger, is often limited to Pijin (their

mother tongue) and some English. Sometimes, it may include a very limited passive knowledge of a vernacular (a few words only, in many cases). As we have seen
in the previous section, the degree of proximity or separation from the vernacular
languages is paralleled by a comparable degree of proximity or separation from the
vernacular cultures.

For the young segment of the population, these tensions and cultural distanc-
ing translate into contradictions that shape their linguistic practice. First, there is a
reification of vernaculars: the few words they have picked up from their parents are
sprinkled here and there in their Pijin or English. Using the vernacular establishes
their ethnic identity through practice (here, linguistic) and not only through descent
(Linnekin and Poyer 1990), however limited this practice is. This is very reminis-
cent of the situation of young second-generation migrants in Grenoble, France, as
reported by Jacqueline Billiez (1993).[8] Her research shows that second-generation
youth voluntarily sprinkle vernacular terms in vehicular language (French, in that
case) for the purpose of creating links between speakers. Also, as a sociolinguistic
norm of Pijin grammar and usage develops, this norm acts as a criterion of differentiation between the urban and rural segments of the population and, within the
urban segment, between the younger and the older generations. Rural varieties, heavily accented in the direction of vernaculars and shaped by vernacular grammar, are
looked down upon by the young, urban Pijin speakers, who are quick to mock rural
varieties and their speakers, whom they often pejoratively qualify as *lokol* (hillbilly).
Their own variety of Pijin they see as sophisticated and *moden* (modern). Yet careful
analyses show that the linguistic differences between the speech of the urban adults
and urban youth are more a matter of degree than of substance. They mostly consist
of a phonological distance from the vernaculars (drop of interconsonantal vowels
typical of Oceanic languages, for instance) and adoption of phonological traits associated with English (consonant clusters, among others), increased borrowing from
English vocabulary to meet the demand of urban living and technology, development
of complex morphology (morphological plural, for instance), and further development of syntax (e.g., more systematic usage of relative markers). Many of these linguistic traits are also part of the speech patterns of older urban adults, but what makes
young people's practice so noticeable is the consciousness they have of being able to
put their own imprint on the language. Young people see this linguistic change as an
index of their own social sophistication.

The generation gap is paralleled by a social gap. Young urbanites, particularly
those born and brought up in town, are testing the limits of the cultural worlds they have
inherited from their parents. Direct cultural transmission between generations is now
challenged by a form of transmission mediated by schooling and popular culture (videos
and music particularly). *Respekt* (respect) due to elders and family members used to be
the social cement between generations; younger people who seek to redefine the rules
of intergenerational exchange on their own terms now question it. More important, the
young urban people, those who were born in town particularly, are shaping for themselves an identity that does not make automatic reference to the world of the village
and to ancestral land. Their primary spatial reference is the neighborhood in which they
live, in which most of them own nothing; their sense of place is anchored through
people in their networks. Pijin terms of address and reference for family members still

largely make room for affectionate terms such as *smolmami* (mother's younger sister), *anti* (female older relative or fictive kin), *grani* (reciprocal terms of address for grandparent/grandchild), and more. But one notices an increasing number of terms of address that seek to establish a difference between members of the nuclear family, members of the extended family, and members of the peer group. Thus for many young people in the city, terms such as *mami*, *dadi*, *brata* and *sista* (mommy, daddy, brother, sister) refer strictly to the members of the inner nuclear family and do not apply to aunts, uncles, and male and female cousins, as is the case in the varieties of Pijin spoken by older urban people and rural family members. I have made the case elsewhere (Jourdan 2000, but see also Berg 2000) that this state of affairs is a direct reflection of the changes of the value system that is associated with urbanization: households composed around the nuclear family become the norms in some social realms of Honiara, and traditional obligations toward the extended family become more tenuous. In other parts of the lexicon, young people's Pijin has increased in semantic fields that until then had been handled through vernaculars. As a result of cultural rooting, young speakers now make use of a large number of terms relating to domains of knowledge and practice that their parents did not know or, because of social control, did not talk about. New words or expressions relating to sex and varied sexual practices (Buchanan-Aruwafu, Maebiru, and Aruwafu 2003), consumption of drugs and alcohol, new technology and new ways of being a social subject are now part of the common vocabulary of young urban people. Young people can effect these sociolinguistic and cultural changes all the more easily because the town is the locus of a cultural flux that gives them much freedom. The sociolinguistic norm that they contribute to developing is not yet so stringent that it would curb creativity or expressivity. Yet it clearly indexes the development of cultural identities that are flexible, multiple, and increasingly complex. And given their number (more than 60 percent of the town population) and their higher levels of education, young people are in a position to drive this change.

In her study of the linguistic practice of young Kanaks in Nouméa, New Caledonia, Sophie Barnèche (2005) proposes that their not knowing the ancestral language of their parents weakens the ethnic positioning of the young and creates what she calls "linguistic guilt" (translation mine). She says:

> This situation is a source of suffering for these young people, and particularly for those who adopt an identity building strategy based entirely on their ethnic belonging, so much so that at times it is hard for them to acknowledge how limited is the knowledge they have of their vernacular. The data allow us to speak of a real linguistic guilt that, for some of them, can be very intense and destructive. (2, translation mine)

One might wonder whether the young people in Honiara are rendered fragile in the same way by their lack of knowledge of the vernaculars. My research with young people in the 1990s in Honiara shows that they are often the object of resentment on the part of the adults because of the way they flout *kastom*. At the same time, the loss of vernacular by the young generation was felt by the adults, who in most cases were responsible for this loss because they did not teach their own ancestral languages to their children, as an inevitable effect of social change. Adults may lament this situation, but most of the young urban people I spoke to did not. What was important to them was to know that *kastom* was a frame of reference that served as the background to an affirmation of the urban self. The vernaculars were part of it, but it was more important for young urbanites to be able to talk about the languages and the *kastom* that sustained them than to actually use them. The ethnic tensions I mentioned above may have created in the young people a renewed interest in the vernacular languages of their parents. Yet the situation in Honiara is significantly different from that found by Barnèche in Nouméa if only because of two factors. The first one is linked to the political status of the two entities we are considering: the Solomon Islands are an independent country, whereas New Caledonia is still under the domination of France. The second is more properly linked to the language scene. In New Caledonia, two sets of language are at play: French, the colonial language, and the Melanesian languages.[9] Caught up as they are in a political context that marginalizes Melanesians, young residents of Nouméa experience their lack of knowledge of their ancestral language as more than a loss: it is a moral failing. Lamenting the loss of the vernacular may be akin to lamenting the presence of the colonial power and one's inability to change the situation.

In the Solomon Islands, Pijin is the interstitial language that has inserted itself between English, the colonial language, and the Melanesian languages. The young people in Honiara have now appropriated Pijin as their language, and as the language of the interstitial culture of the town, which is neither colonial nor typically Melanesian. For them, Pijin plays the role that the Melanesian languages played for their parents: the language through which cultural and social life is lived.

The Gendered Self

Mi Mere by Jully Makini (1986: 8)

I am a woman, born in the village
Destined to spend my life
In a never ending vicious circle
Gardening, child-bearing, house-keeping
Seen and not heard.

I am a woman, born in town
Educated, dedicated to a career
Making a name for myself in government
Seen and not heard.

I am the echo heard in the jungle
The conch shell heralding a bonito catch
The reporter writing articles in the Star
The announcer in Radio Happy Isles
At long last! Heard but not seen!

When it was first published in 1986, this poem by famed Solomon Island author Jully Makini was hailed as bold and as the vanguard of demands by women in Solomon

Islands for more social recognition. The title became the eponymous name of an association of women. It is particularly interesting for us here in that it suggests that there exist different models of women's roles in the Solomon Islands. Not all women fit the same model: we need to move away from the archetypal Melanesian woman who would raise pigs as part of the prestige economy on which rests her husband's political life. There are more models, of course, that Aruhe'eta Pollard (2000) describes in her book on women in the Solomon Islands. She suggests that in addition to the village woman (itself a reductionist category), urban women come into three main types: (1) unemployed urban women; (2) wage-earning women; and (3) professional women. One can also propose that men in Solomon Islands come also in different types and are not limited to the artificial dichotomy of village men versus town men. For our purpose here, and for the sake of clarity, each of these types, however reductionist they may be, can be associated with particular language practices.

In rural areas, it is still quite common to find men, women, and younger children who do not speak Pijin, let alone English. This is increasingly rare in Honiara, aside from some older people who have come to town to visit with their children, or younger children who come for the first time. In general, urban women have a linguistic repertoire that is as complex as that of the men for the corresponding age group, but it will vary with their degree of insertion in various urban social circles.

Once again, various criteria such as age, length of residence in Honiara, place of birth, and level of education and social class must be taken into account in order to understand the language practice of women in this new town. Women thirty and younger usually do not know a vernacular if they have been raised in town. They almost always use Pijin as the main language of social interaction. In general, English is less prevalent among women who have arrived in town recently or among those who are not educated. Typically, knowledge of English is associated with education or with long-term residence in town and exposure to that language through work, church, or other social networks. Yet there exists an increasing number of women, either well educated professional women or skilled wage earners, who are fluent in English. Their education made it possible, and their professions requires it. On the other hand, Pijin is an important language for the vast majority of urban women because it has been liberating in many ways. First, it has allowed them to establish neighborhood and church links across linguistic boundaries. For urban women in general and for unemployed women in particular, these are the most important social networks they can be part of. Second, it has been an avenue to paid employment in, for instance, shops. It has brought some measure of independence that many women had lost once they were transformed into homemakers, whereas they had traditionally been the feeders of their families (Jourdan 1985; Pollard 2000). Third, it has freed them from the danger associated with particular word taboos in their husband's vernacular, a danger that had rendered many of them mute or the brunt to constant recriminations from in-laws. To these women, Pijin has become a language of empowerment. Some of them have confided in me that their husband had explicitly forbidden them to speak *langgus* (Pijin: local languages, as opposed to English or Pijin) so as to avoid the pitfalls of word tabooing. The case of Tafui is particularly enlightening in that regard. A Malaitan from Kwara'ae, she has lived in town since her marriage to Peter, a Malaitan from Kwaio. In addition to her own mother tongue, Kwara'ae, and as is common for people who have been raised away from towns, she speaks some of the languages spoken by the neighboring cultural groups: Kwaio, Baelelea and Langa Langa. She and her husband routinely speak either Kwara'ae, which he had picked up when both lived in Kwara'ae country, or Pijin. When her in-laws visit, all speak Pijin. Tafui would like to be able to speak Kwaio with them, but her husband forbids it because, so she says, he fears that she, not knowing the language well, might break some language taboos. This is how she phrases it (translation mine):

> I am afraid to speak because their custom is like that. If a woman says something, sometimes she swears or misspeaks, then her husband will have to give money to my husband's family. Because of the word taboo she broke, he will seek compensation. In the Kwaio way. This is why my husband prevents me from saying something wrong. I do not speak [Kwaio]. For us it is very dangerous. Eventually my husband said: "No, you will not speak in [Kwaio]; you will not speak my language anymore."[10]

Truly, Pijin does contain words that are not socially acceptable, and women will avoid them according to rules of propriety that seem to be impressed by colonial and missionary ideologies of proper women's behavior. But these words are not at all of the same realms as the words that have become taboo in vernaculars, such as names of ancestors and sacred places, for instance (Keesing and Fifi'i 1969): the latter call for expensive social and economic redress. Because of word tabooing associated with cultural rooting, vernaculars are understood to be potentially dangerous. Pijin remained free of such connotations. The situation is different for the current generation of children who have appropriated it and for whom Pijin in the mother tongue. Yet, beyond swear words and sexual innuendos, Pijin is still perceived as a language that will not bring about cultural danger. The more they are educated and the longer they live in town, the more women are likely to master English. Professional women use it as a regular medium of communication with expatriates, but they may resort to using Pijin with their coworkers.

The relationship that men entertain with the languages they master is also both instrumental and symbolic. Typically, men have picked up Pijin on plantations where young men from the rural areas, as part of a quasi rite of passage, have made a habit of going before getting married and settling down in the villages. From plantations to town, however, the mental and cultural distance is short, and many of them, having picked up working skills at the plantations, have opted to settle in Honiara. As with the women, their degree of knowledge of English will vary with their level of education and their degree of exposure to it. The significant difference lies in the role played by vernaculars in the life of adult urban men. In addition to my own work and that of Aruhe'eta Pollard, research done in Honiara by Berg (2000), Feinberg (2004), Frazer (1974, 1985), Gooberman-Hill (1999) and Stritecky (2001) reveal that adult men tend to attach greater importance to their *wantok* network. Within these networks, in which issues relating to *kastom* are continual objects of discussion, negotiation, and arbitration, vernaculars are the primordial medium of communication. The word *wantok* itself reveals the central importance of vernaculars in cultural groupings. One wonders how the *wantok* system will become redefined now that so many young urban men do not know the vernacular that is central to the life of their cultural networks. Will it lose its role of cultural buffer between village and town? Will it lose its importance to the profit of other types of social groupings? Will its significance be limited to the recently arrived urban migrants or transient? Will Pijin become its main medium? Some of these developments are already taking place.

Conclusion

If thinking and acting in multiple languages is common to most Honiarans, the repertoire of languages that people use differs mostly according to age group and social class. As city people become removed from the vernacular cultures, they also become removed from the vernacular languages. In the process, Pijin, the local lingua franca, has become the main language of the town and the de facto national language, and English, the language of the former colonial power, has become the language of choice of the upwardly mobile. Building on colonial ideologies about language, Honiarans have established differences between the languages at play on the urban scene. The hierarchy they construe, itself an important departure from pre-colonial language relations, differs markedly from that which was dominant during colonial times. It is flexible and varies with individuals and contexts: the ethnic self puts vernaculars at the top, whereas the gendered self puts Pijin and vernaculars at the top, depending on gender and age. Young urban people put Pijin at the top as the language of daily interaction, but they know that English is the language of social advancement. The hierarchy constitutes a linguistic market in which people express their various identities by making a selective use of the languages available to them. The linguistic ideology that was dominant during precolonial times (reciprocal multilingualism) and the one associated with the colonial order (linguistic hegemony and hierarchy) have been replaced by multiple and competing linguistic ideologies. In the situation I have described, languages have ceased to mark ethnicity alone, as was the case in precolonial times; they now index social class, age group, gender, and urban identity. They also index social proximity or distance from social values associated with village life. Language choice represents an acknowledgment of the speakers' multiple connections to a wider social world that is perceived as increasingly complex. Each language connects the speakers to different layers of their cultural experiences.

As is the case everywhere else, languages in the Solomon Islands have always been constitutive of the person. In Honiara, they are constitutive of multiple person-hoods in an increasingly complex web of social relationships. By using one language rather than another, individuals create and reinforce relationships that are essential to the recognition of their individuality, subjectivity, and agency. Using language x or y, rather than z demonstrates a social positioning but also a consciousness that one is linked to social worlds that preexist the speaker and frame the speech event. Using one language rather than another generates social meaning and creates new social worlds that frame the speech event. The language scene speaks to the richness of the social scene and to its complexity. It also speaks to the strength of the community of linguistic practice in that each of them represents an interest group within which language produces and indexes identity creation. "In a world composed of multiple different perspectives, the very claim to a perspective is flattening," says Marilyn Strathern (1991: 31). I contend that this is quite applicable to the urban actors I have presented above. Beyond the symbolic and pragmatic advantages brought to their ability to use multiple languages or multiple dialects of the same language, multilingualism brings about a form of exhilaration. Homo Ludens is at play here, using language to create herself. Caught up in a world where different ideologies coexist and often confront one another, people play with languages to modulate their urban selves and to express their individuality.

Yet people do not exist outside of the relationships they have built and are enmeshed in. Thus through language, Honiarans can also express their location in the relationships that constitute them. They speak in many languages because they *are*. They speak in many languages, therefore they *are*.

Notes

1. Bishop Selwyn had made English the lingua franca of the Melanesian Mission. Bishop Patterson, who succeeded him, found English unsuited to the task and preferred Melanesian languages. By 1867, Mota had replaced English as the language of instruction of the Melanesian Mission in the Pacific. By 1931, the language debate came to an end when English replaced Mota as the language of instruction in the Melanesian Mission schools in the Solomon Islands. See Hilliard 1978: 34 and 271.

2. In western Africa and in Vietnam, the French colonials referred to local languages as *dialectes*: those *dialectes* were thought to have no grammar, and the fact that they were not written was taken as a proof of the lack of it. The term quickly took a pejorative connotation and was contrasted with *langue*, which referred to the European languages (Ginette Devy, personal communication, August 1999). I grew up in Senegal and Ivory Coast and remember distinctly the disparaging comments made by French nationals about the local languages. In Honiara, I heard some expatriates make similar comments about the Melanesian languages in the Solomon Islands.

3. The British colonial administration had caught on early to the advantages that a lingua franca could bring to the running of the country. In 1950, they commissioned George Bertram Milner, then professor of linguistics at the School of Oriental and African studies, to look into the feasibility of adopting a lingua franca in the Solomon Islands. In his 1951 report to the Secretary for Development and Native affairs, he considers in turn Pijin and English and finds them unsuitable (Milner 1951: 3). The grammar of Pijin (he spells the word pidgin) is too fluid, and the variation within the archipelago too great to allow for a comprehensive grammar to be written. English is culturally and linguistically too foreign and too strange to Solomon Islanders and may trigger some form of nationalist resistance. Vernacular languages are better choices, and he proposes that the language of Nggela (which he spells Gela) be used if ever the colonial administration wishes to pursue the idea of establishing a second official language in the country alongside English (Milner 1951: 6).

4. From English "one talk." The word initially referred to members of one's language group, and appeared in the social context of plantation work, characterized by multiethnicity.

In Honiara, the term is now also used increasingly as a term of friendship and endearment with people who are not part of one's ethnic group. It is essentially a male form of address.

5. See Sankoff (1980) for a similar situation in Papua New Guinea, even though young people in towns started to shift away from vernaculars earlier than in the Solomon Islands. For a description of similar phenomena in contempary Papua New Guinea, see Smith (2003).

6. For a discussion of code-switching in the Marquesas, see Riley, chap. 4 of this volume.

7. See Keesing and Tonkinson 1982; Linnekin and Poyer 1990; Babadzan 1988.

8. For a Polynesian example of a similar situation, see Makihara, chap. 3 of this volume, and Makihara 2005.

9. For a similar situation in Polynesia, see Riley, chap. 4 of this volume.

10. *Mi fraet fo talem, bikos kastom blong olketa olsem ia. Uans wuman hem talem samting, samtaem hemi tok sue o olsem tok nogud, hasban nao bae hem givim mani long saed long hasban blong mi noa. Long Kwaio. Hem nao hasban blong mi hem stopem mi fo rong. Mi no toktok. Long mifala hemi dadieres tumas ia ... Gogo, olo blong mi hem se: Nomoa, iu stop foa spikim long toko blong mi nao.*

References

Akin, David. 1999. Cash and Shell Money in Kwaio, Solomon Islands. In *Money and Modernity: State and Local Currencies in Melanesia*, ed. David Akin and Joel Robbins, pp. 103–130. Pittsburgh: University of Pittsburgh Press.

Babadzan, Alain. 1988. *Kastom* and Nation Building in the South Pacific. In *Ethnicities and Nations: Processes of Interethnic Relations in Latin America, Southeast Asia, and the Pacific*, ed. Remo Guidieri, Francesco Pellizzi, and Stanley J. Tambiah, pp. 199–288. Austin: University of Texas Press.

Barnèche, Sophie. 2005. De l'identité ethnique à l'identité ethno urbaine: pratiques linguistiques et dynamiques identitaires des jeunes Mélanésiens à Nouméa (Nouvelle-Calédonie). Paper presented at the meetings of the Canadian Anthropology Society. Merida, Mexico, May 4.

Berg, Cato. 2000. Managing Difference: Kinship, Exchange and Urban Boundaries in Honiara, Solomon Islands. Master's thesis, University of Bergen.

Billiez, Jacqueline. 1993. Le parler véhiculaire interethnique de groupes d'adolescents en milieu urbain. In *Des langues et des villes, Actes du colloque international (Dakar, 15–17 décembre 1990)*, ed. Gouarni Elhousseine and Ndiasse Thiam, pp. 117–126. Paris: ACCT-Didier Érudition.

Buchanan-Aruwafu, Holly, Rose Maebiru, and Francis Aruwafu. 2003. Stiki lole: Language and the Mediation of Desire in Auki, Malaita, Solomon Islands. *Culture, Health, and Society* 5 (3): 219–236.

Bourdieu, Pierre. 1982. *Ce que parler veut dire: l'économie des échanges linguistiques*. Paris: Fayard.

Calvet, Louis Jean. 1974. *Linguistique et colonialisme: Petit traité de glottophagie*. Paris: Bibliothèque Payot.

———. 1994. *Les voix de la ville: Introduction à la sociolinguistique urbaine*. Paris: Payot.

Fabian, Johannes. 1983. *Time and the Other. How Anthropology Makes its Object*. New York: Columbia University Press.

Feinberg, Richard. 2004. *Anuta: Polynesian Lifeways for the Twenty-First Century*. 2nd ed. Long Grove, IL: Waveland Press.

Frazer, Ian. 1981. Man Long Taon: Migration and Differentiation amongst the To'ambaita, Solomon Islands. Ph.D. diss., Australian National University.

———. 1985. Walkabout and Urban Movement: A Melanesian Case Study. *Pacific Viewpoint* 26 (1): 185–205.

Gegeo, David. 1994. Kastom and Bisnis: Towards Integrating Cultural Knowledge into Rural Development in the Solomon Islands. Ph.D. diss., University of Hawaii.

Gooberman-Hill, Rachel. 1999. The Constraints of "Feeling Free": Becoming Middle Class in Honiara (Solomon Islands). Ph.D. diss., University of Edinburgh.

Hill, Jane. 1998. 'Today's There Is No Respect: Nostalgia, Respect, and Oppositional Discourse in Mexicano (Nahuatl) Language Ideology. In *Language Ideologies: Practice and Theory*, ed. Bambi Schieffelin, Kathryn Woolard, and Paul Kroskrity, pp. 68–86. New York: Oxford University Press.

Hilliard, David. 1978. *God's Gentlemen. A History of the Melanesian Mission, 1849–1972*. Santa Lucia: University of Queensland Press.

Jourdan, Christine. 1985. Sapos iumi mitim iumi: Creolization and Urbanization of Solomon Islands Pijin. Ph.D. diss., Australian National University.

———. 1990. Solomons Pijin: An Unrecognized National Language. In *Language Planning and Education in Australasia and the South Pacific*, ed. Richard Baldauf and Allan Luke, pp. 166–181. Clevedon, UK: Multilingual Matters.

———. 1996. Where Have All the Cultures Gone? Sociocultural Creolization in Solomon Islands. In *Melanesian Modernities*, ed. Jonathan Friedman and James Carrier, pp. 34–52. Lund: Lund University Press.

Jourdan, Christine, and Rachel Selbach. 2004. Phonology of Solomon Islands Pijin. In *Varieties of English*, ed. Bernd Kortmann and Elizabeth Closs Traugott, pp. 690–710. Amsterdam: Mouton de Gruyter.

Kabutaulaka, Tarcisius, T. 2000. Beyond Ethnicity: Understanding the Crisis in the Solomon Islands. *Pacific News Bulletin,* May 5–7.

Keesing, Roger. 1982. *Kastom* in Melanesia: An Overview. In Reinventing Traditional Culture: The Politics of Kastom in Island Melanesia, ed. Roger Keesing and Robert Tonkinson. Special issue of *Mankind* 13 (4): 297–304.

———. 1990. Solomons Pijin: Colonial Ideologies. In *Language Planning in Education, in Australasia and the South Pacific*, ed. Richard Baldauf and Allan Luke, pp. 149–165. Clevedon, UK: Multilingual Matters.

Keesing, Roger, and Jonathan Fifi'i. 1969. Kwaio Word Tabooing in Its Cultural Context. *Journal of the Polynesian Society* 78 (2): 154–177.

Keesing, Roger, and Robert Tonkinson, eds. 1982. Reinventing Traditional Culture: The Politics of Kastom in Island Melanesia. Special issue of *Mankind* 13 (4).

Linnekin, Jocelyn, and Lyn Poyer, eds. 1990. *Cultural Identity and Ethnicity in the Pacific*. Honolulu: University of Hawai'i Press.

Makihara, Miki. 2005. Rapa Nui Ways of Speaking Spanish: Language Shift and Socialization on Easter Island. *Language in Society* 34 (5): 727–762.

Makini, Jully. 1986. *Praying Parents: A Second Collection of Poems by Jully Sipolo*. Honiara, Solomon Islands: Aruligo Book Centre.

Milner, George Bertram. 1951. Notes on the Languages of the British Solomon Islands (with reference to the question of adopting a lingua franca). Archives of the British Solomon Islands Protectorate, Honiara. BSIP I/III F 73/10.

Pollard, Alice Aruhe'eta. 2000. *Givers of Wisdom, Labourers without Gain: Essays on Women in Solomon Islands*. Suva, Fiji: Institute of Pacific Studies, University of the South Pacific.

Sankoff, Gillian. 1980. Multilingualism in Papua New Guinea. In *The Social Life of Language*, pp. 95–132. Philadelphia: University of Pennsylvania Press.

Smith, Geoff. 2003. *Growing up with Tok Pisin: Contact, Creolization and Change in Papua New Guinea National Language*. London: Battlebridge.

Strathern, Marilyn. 1991. *Partial Connections*. Savage, MD: Rowman & Littlefield.

Stritecky, Jolene Marie. 2001. Looking through a Moral Lens: Morality, Violence, and Empathy in Solomon Islands. Ph.D. diss., University of Iowa.

Tengan, Alexis. 1994. European Language in African Society. In *Language Contact, Language Conflict,* ed. Martin Pütz, pp. 125–138. Amsterdam: John Benjamins.

MIKI MAKIHARA

Linguistic Purism in Rapa Nui
Political Discourse

In recent years, new discourses and ideologies of language rights and endangerment have emerged in the context of increasingly effective indigenous and minority movements around the world. A growing pride in and appreciation for local histories, cultures, and languages have led communities to devote effort and resources to recovering, documenting, and revitalizing cultural traditions and languages and to establishing and improving bilingual and multicultural education programs.

Though these changes have generally been viewed as positive, some observers express concern that some approaches to language valuation and revitalization might inadvertently do harm, for instance by overly objectifying language in ways that arouse apprehension and opposition from locals or possibly even accelerate language loss in communities where a shift to a colonial or national language is already advanced. For example, Peter Whiteley argues that the rise of literacy-based and logocentric language ideologies in the discourse of language revitalization in Hopi and other small-scale orality-oriented societies had the unfortunate consequence of undermining spoken language use in culture and society. Despite the possibility of revitalization offered by the relatively large functioning language community that the Hopi have, he claims that recently constructed ideas of Hopi as a reified, secularized, and written language led to conflicts between generations and ambivalence and even resistance to language preservation projects by some in the community. Other studies have pointed to similar social dynamics leading to, or resulting from, language objectification.[1] This raises questions of when and why language might become so objectified and how objectification shapes the course of language and social change.

This chapter presents a study of political discourse in the bilingual, indigenous Rapa Nui community (known to outsiders as Easter Island), where the local language has in the past been marginalized and endangered by the spread of Spanish, the national language of Chile, but where recently a large number of people have become actively engaged in indigenous and political movements. I describe and analyze the ideologies of code choice and language revalorization that have emerged and become embedded in the discourse of the Rapa Nui indigenous movement, which has focused on demands for land and political decision-making power, but not, until very recently, on language maintenance per se. I describe the recent development of linguistic purism and in particular the ways that new purist codes and ideas have been constructed by political leaders and accommodated within the community's speech style repertoire. Linguistic purism can be defined as an insistence on purity or correctness of linguistic forms and, in the case of Rapa Nui, on an avoidance of Spanish influence. I identify and contrast two salient speech styles found in Rapa Nui political discourse—syncretic and purist—and relate these discursive strategies to the contexts in which they are deployed. Syncretic speech is characterized by the simultaneous presence of multiple varieties of Rapa Nui and Spanish within and across individual utterances. I argue that Rapa Nui speakers have not only constructed syncretic, and more recently purist, speech styles, but also deploy these as *linguistic registers*[2] for political ends to perform stances in ways that have served to reconcile different but not necessarily mutually exclusive sets of values—those of democratic participation and those of the politics of ethnicity. The Rapa Nui case illustrates how an endangered language community has contributed to revalorizing and maintaining its language by reexpanding the domains of language use, in particular by establishing new linguistic registers, which have added extra sociolinguistic meanings to speech styles and increased the linguistic heterogeneity of their language. This case stands as a counterexample to the findings of many studies that languages tend to exhibit declining variability under the dominating influence of a spreading language.[3]

Joseph Errington (2003) has highlighted three salient approaches or rhetorical strategies in the discourses of language endangerment and has pointed out how they each draw on different traditions of thought about language and society—comparativist, localist, and language rights approaches. "Comparativist" approaches value linguistic diversity as an aggregate of human universal capacities, and they draw on nineteenth-century comparative philology and contemporary linguistics. "Localist" approaches draw on late-eighteenth- and nineteenth-century Romanticist thought and portray language in nature, closely tied to a place, culture, and an indigenous community. Finally, an emerging approach to language valuation focuses on the concept of "language rights" and builds on the discourse of the politics of recognition with its notions of human rights, indigenous property rights, and a multicultural civic society. Though different in their reasoning and strategy, all three approaches can reify or objectify language in ways that may remove it from the context of language use. The danger that has been pointed out is that this may smother linguistic liveliness and flexibility by, for example, imposing purist standards and devaluing language-internal variation, including both synchronic and diachronic and especially variation induced by language contact.[4]

The emerging linguistic purism on Rapa Nui evokes the localist approach to language and identity and other incipient ideas about language rights. Linguistic purism can, at one level, be viewed as consistent with language status planning objectives aimed at establishing local and national recognition of Rapa Nui as a legitimate *language* whose use should be authorized and privileged in extended spheres of the island speech community. The ideology of language ownership and rights finds its energy in a monolingual concept of language, in which collective ownership depends crucially on imagining a historical continuity of language from a time prior to contact with outsiders. Such monolingual localist conceptions have inspired emerging practices such as language policing and the elimination of Spanish elements in Rapa Nui speech. As in other contexts, one might fear that such language policing and language revitalization efforts informed by the logic of linguistic purism could have the unintended effect of generating linguistic insecurities within the ethnic community—especially among non-speakers or nonfluent speakers and learners of the Rapa Nui language (a large group in the Rapa Nui situation)—by overly objectifying the language and restricting its use to the realms of self-conscious performance.[5]

Yet in Rapa Nui this danger has remained contained. The political activists who most commonly practice purist speech have been quite deliberate and effective at shifting between purist and syncretic speech styles in flexible and strategic ways that have, thus far at least, limited the danger of such unintended consequences. Purist styles have been used mostly to enhance Rapa Nui claims over symbolic and material resources, for instance by drawing ethnolinguistic boundaries between Chileans (referred to locally as "Continentales") and Rapa Nui in ethnically mixed contexts. Purist linguistic choice has mainly had the effect of strengthening Rapa Nui unity vis-à-vis Continental Chileans rather than marking or creating differences within the Rapa Nui community. Syncretic styles continue to dominate everyday use and political discourse among the Rapa Nui in the charged debates about staking out new claims and defining new rights as an indigenous people. Purist speech is not displacing syncretic speech styles, nor has it been aimed at that. The Rapa Nui's choice to strategically mobilize linguistic resources according to interactional contexts has served them well. Syncretic Rapa Nui serves as an effective code for everyday and political discourse with its inclusive appeal in a language community with a wide range of bilingual competences and preferences.[6] Rapa Nui stands in contrast to communities in which linguistic purism has exacerbated social differentiations or intensified conflicts. Two important factors allowed or fostered this divergent development: the transformation of linguistic ideologies and the relatively low level of social and economic differentiation within the Rapa Nui community. As will be described in the next section, the low level of social differentiation within the Rapa Nui community is a result of the island's particular history of contact.

Sociolinguistic and political context

The early 1990s marked the beginning of a period of resurgent political activism and rapid social change on Rapa Nui. This was fed by long-standing demands for political representation and rights and catalyzed in part by democratization and political decentralization projects and the continued rapid expansion of the heritage tourism economy following the end of military rule in Chile in 1989. The struggle for land has long been central to the Rapa Nui, who were formally stripped of their land rights when Chile annexed the island in 1888.[7] Since 1989, the Rapa Nui have succeeded in remarkably reshaping the political landscape of the island by gaining new local decision-making autonomy, land titles, and vast expansions of representation and employment in local government. The meanings of Rapa Nui identity and language and interethnic social relations have been extensively reshaped by the struggles and successes of this indigenous movement in a relatively short period of time.

Throughout its contact history, the Rapa Nui people have had to adapt and fight to survive as a people with a distinct culture and language in the face of frequently daunting odds. Most dramatically, in the 1870s the Rapa Nui were tragically reduced to only 110 survivors from an estimated population of 3,000 to 5,000, as a result of Peruvian blackbirders' slave raids and the spread of new diseases.[8] This demographic devastation, coupled with intensified contact with outsiders, created a significant cultural and social discontinuity, including a flattening of internal social differentiation within this community. European Catholic missionaries who stayed on the island for several years after the slave raid led a community-wide conversion to Christianity among the survivors.[9] Chile, a young independent nation brimming with new maritime ambition following its victories over Peru and Bolivia in the War of the Pacific, sent a navy ship to annex the island in 1888.[10] After failed attempts to establish a settler colony and to administer the distant island directly, the Chilean government decided to lease the entire island to a Scottish-owned company to be run as a sheep ranch. Without apparent irony or shame, this commercial venture aptly named itself the "Easter Island Exploitation Company." "La compañía," as Rapa Nui still refer to it today, transformed the devastated island into a "company state" (Porteous 1981), monopolizing resources and territorially confining Rapa Nui for more than sixty years starting in 1895 to the village lands of Hanga Roa (Haŋa Roa). Over this period, the Chilean government gradually increased its control over the island's affairs, establishing a civil registry in 1915, commencing primary school instruction in 1934, and promoting cultural and linguistic assimilation. Starting in 1956, Rapa Nui was administered as a colony under Chilean navy rule, but in 1966 a nonviolent political revolt led Chile to grant islanders citizen rights.

The arrival of a new civil administration and the opening of regular air travel in the mid-1960s expanded economic opportunities and improved lives for most Rapa Nui. It also, however, had the immediate effect of further establishing Spanish as the dominant language of the public domain, particularly after the influx of a large number of Spanish-speaking government functionaries and their families and the introduction of new Spanish-language radio. In this period, the Rapa Nui language came to be devalued by its speakers vis-à-vis Spanish and was increasingly restricted to private, in-group, and family domains; this accelerated a community-wide language shift to Spanish. As a result, a majority of Rapa Nui children and teenagers are not fluent Rapa Nui speakers.

Language shift on the island has not always been a uniform or one-directional process, however. Though the community became increasingly integrated into Chilean economic and social life, the Rapa Nui also greatly expanded their speech style repertoire with formal and informal varieties of Chilean Spanish and Rapa Nui ways of speaking Spanish.[11] New syncretic ways of speaking Rapa Nui have become the clear dominant unmarked code choice for everyday communication among Rapa Nui adults. Although syncretic Rapa Nui speech was originally mostly confined to in-group private settings, by the early 1990s it was fast being adopted as an emblem of modern Rapa Nui identity and solidarity in the context of a rising indigenous movement and new Rapa Nui assertiveness in both the political and economic spheres.[12]

Today, almost three-fourths of the island remains state property (as a state farm, a national park, and other public service lands). Land disputes on Rapa Nui have consequently involved direct confrontations and negotiations between the indigenous community and the government.[13] Rapa Nui political activists have strategically worked to increase local political and economic control by mobilizing their kin-based networks, operating within the national political party system, and forming shifting alliances with Chilean and international nongovernmental organizations.

Public debates regarding the drafting and implementation of Chile's 1994 Indigenous Law engaged the island residents as never before in questions of who is indigenous, who represents the community, and whether and how the new law should be modified and applied. Today, the island has about thirty-eight hundred residents, about one third of whom are Continental Chileans, including many who are married to Rapa Nui. Most Rapa Nui objected to the law's very broad original definition of "indigenous" as all who habitually practiced "life styles, customs or religion" of the "ethnic group," "whose spouse is indigenous" or who "self-identified" as indigenous.[14] After much debate and agitation, the Rapa Nui succeeded in having the law redrafted in 1998 to restrict Rapa Nui ethnic membership to the "right of the blood."

By the mid-1990s, large numbers of Rapa Nui were participating in local politics to such an extent that in a 1999 race to select five ethnic representatives to the Development Commission of the government, forty-five Rapa Nui (6 percent of eligible voters) competed as candidates. Oratory and kinship are two important resources in these political contests. Hundreds of people turned out regularly for meetings and other public events, and the church grounds overlooking Hanga Roa became the site for near-permanent displays of signs and protest encampments. As a result of Rapa Nui political campaigns, the Chilean Congress approved special territory status for the island, and the government's legislative proposal was discussed on the island in 2006. Syncretic speech styles became increasingly prevalent in new public forums such as village meetings. Elsewhere, I have argued that the rise and spread of syncretic speech in the context of improvements to Rapa Nui economic and political fortunes have contributed to the maintenance of the Rapa Nui language (Makihara 2004). Over a relatively short time, the Rapa Nui succeeded at remaking their language into a public language by asserting syncretic Rapa Nui and Rapa Nui Spanish as legitimate language choices in public spaces where Spanish (and in particular formal Chilean Spanish) had dominated. It is only more recently that some Rapa Nui—particularly political leaders and intellectuals—have begun to develop linguistic purism, selectively using the purist register in public speeches in lieu of syncretic Rapa Nui or Spanish.

As in many other ethnolinguistic minority group contexts, the Rapa Nui often actively sought to incorporate themselves into the contact zones created by their colonial and postcolonial encounters with others. They constructed their ethnic identity and their language first in relation to, and only recently increasingly in opposition to, outsiders and their languages. The construction of ethnolinguistic identity and community has been not only about imagining and building solidarity and homogeneity but also, at times, about selectively identifying with or differentiating from social categories in the contact zones.

The changes in language ideology that have taken place over a decade and a half on the island are remarkable. During my first visit in 1991, it was still not uncommon to hear islanders describe Rapa Nui as "only a dialect," limited in expressions and "not a language," even among people involved in local politics. Such views partly reflected the internalization of still prevalent Chilean paternalistic, assimilationist, and discriminatory attitudes, which had been widely expressed in popular

and academic writings and discourse over the earlier but still recent history of Chilean–
Rapa Nui contact. A particularly jarring expression of such views can be found in a
1954 article published in Santiago in the journal *Occidente* by E. Martínez Chibbaro.[15]
The article stated that the Rapa Nui language was a "Polynesian dialect... conserved
only for special circumstances by an indigenous group of no more than 800 individuals, considerably isolated from external beneficial influences and from our country."
The author also stated bluntly that "the Rapa Nui lexicon does not seem to be enough
in itself" and is "eminently affective, and for the most part onomatopoeic," going
on to argue that the "conceptual content of Rapa Nui, being necessarily poor, reveals
incipient forms of many illogical categories," and that the speakers' "mental world
is extremely reduced," as they "do not know verbal termination, even the notion of
verbal time, employing simply the words 'before', 'after', and 'now' to determine
their forms of preterit, future and present" (31–33, 35, my translations).

Linguistic syncretism in political discourse

In the 1990s, political debates and other public displays of political expression
became recognized as important speech events, and syncretic Rapa Nui soon became
the common code choice at these events. Syncretic Rapa Nui speech is characterized
by Spanish–Rapa Nui bilingual mixtures such as code-switching and interference.
Rapa Nui speakers often use the term *ture* 'fight' or 'demand' to describe their political movement, especially in the context of their demands for the return of ancestral
land (*henua*) as in *ture henua* 'land fight'.[16] To outsiders, *ture henua* political events
and debates often seem lively, even chaotic. Many discussions, particularly when
they involve large numbers of Rapa Nui participants, are characterized not only by
linguistic syncretism but also direct, often confrontational styles of argument. Speakers address each other using nicknames, kin terms, and first names without titles.
Bystanders and self-appointed spokespeople often make their way into supposedly
closed meetings. Even though there is a general appreciation of the rules of debate,
participants often speak simultaneously, jockeying to control the speaking floor.
Rapa Nui have made informality and directness in speech, dress, and other aspects of
self-presentation a tradition of their own that has strongly challenged the Continental
Chilean institutional dominance and the formality and respect for social hierarchy
that Chilean authorities had previously found easier to uphold.

The following excerpts taken from a three-hour forum to debate aspects of the
Indigenous Law provide a vivid example of the use of syncretic speech at such political events. The meeting brought together the island's Rapa Nui governor and representatives of a self-proclaimed new Council of Elders, which was challenging the
existing council. Several dozen Rapa Nui attended. In Text 1, Juan Chávez, the president (C.) of the newly proclaimed Council (which many came to refer to as "Consejo
Dos" or 'Council II') expresses his demand that his group should play a formal role
in ongoing negotiations with the Chilean government concerning the modification
of the Indigenous Law. After several minutes of debate with many interruptions and
catcalls, the Rapa Nui governor (G.) rose to address the crowd and clarify the circumstances surrounding the government's proposal.[17]

TEXT 1. Use of Syncretic Rapa Nui in Political Debate

	Translation
01 C: *E tiaki ena a mātou, ki tū* <u>*compromiso*</u> *era o te* <u>*gobierno*</u> *pe nei ē he aŋa mai e rāua i te* declaración. *Ko kī 'ana ho'i e A. ko garo'a 'ā e koe pe nei ē, mo tu'u* 05 *mai o ra* <u>*decracione*</u> (declaración), *ki u'i atu e mātou 'ana titika he* <u>*buka*</u> (<u>busca</u>) *a tātou i te* <u>*manera*</u>, *he aŋa te* <u>*rey*</u> (<u>ley</u>) *āpī*, <u>o que se yó</u>, *o he* <u>*junta*</u> *ara-rua* <u>*rey*</u>, <u>no sé</u>. *Entonces, ko rā* 10 *me'e te me'e nei o mātou e tiaki atu ena,* <u>*incluso*</u> *ko ma'u mai 'ā a mātou* <u>por escrito</u> *mo ai o te me'e pahe* <u>acta</u> *o vānaŋa tahaŋa o puhia te vānaŋa i te tokerau.* 15 ... G: <u>No</u>, *ko* <u>*acuerdo'ā*</u> *pa'i a tātou.* <u>Mira, el problema</u> *i te* <u>*hora*</u> *nei to'oku mana'u* <u>es el siguiente......</u> *Te me'e o te* <u>sub-secretario</u> *i* <u>*pía*</u> *mai ki a au,* "<u>mire señor,</u> 20 <u>usted vaya a la Isla de Pascua y materialize este acuerdo." ¿Cuál es el acuerdo? Primero, el gobierno va a estudiar una declaración de voluntad</u> *o mo* <u>*rectifica*</u> *i te* <u>inscripción fiscal</u> *pe nei* 25 *ē i aŋa ai te ha'aura'a mo* <u>*protege*</u> *i te* <u>*derecho*</u> *o te Rapa Nui,* <u>bueno eso, la declaración que van a estudiar</u> *i kī mai ena.* <u>Eso lo están estudiando, ese es el primer compromiso del gobierno.</u> 30 <u>Segundo, dentro del plazo de treinta dias,</u> *ka oho a kōrua ki Rapa Nui,* <u>dentro el plazo de treinta dias, póngase de acuerdo</u> *ka haka-ma'u mai te* <u>modificacione</u> (modificación), *mo haŋa* 35 *o kōrua mo* <u>*modifica*</u> *i te* <u>artículo segundo letra C,</u> *he to'o mai he haka-ma'u* <u>urgentemente</u> *ki roto i te* <u>Congreso</u> *mo* <u>*aprueba*</u> *e te* <u>Cámara de Diputados y Senadores,...</u>	C: *We (excl.) are waiting for the* <u>commitment</u> *by the* <u>government</u> *that they would elaborate a* declaration. *A. (his fellow participant) told you and you heard that when the* <u>declaration</u> *arrives, and when we (excl.) see that it is correct, we (incl.) would* <u>look for</u> *the* <u>way,</u> *to make a new* <u>law,</u> <u>or what do I know,</u> *or* <u>combine</u> *together two* <u>laws,</u> <u>I don't know.</u> <u>Therefore,</u> *that is what we (excl.) are waiting for. We (excl.)* <u>*even*</u> *brought* <u>in writing</u> *(petition for the declaration) for the* <u>act,</u> *so not just to talk for talking sake and have the words get blown away in the wind* ....[several turns of expositions by other participants] G: <u>No,</u> *(it's that) we (incl.)* <u>agreed.</u> <u>Look, the problem</u> *of the moment in* <u>my opinion is the following......</u> *(This is) what the* <u>sub-secretary</u> <u>*asked*</u> *me* "<u>look sir, you go to Easter Island and materialize this agreement." What is the agreement? First, the government will study a declaration of will</u> <u>*or*</u> *to* <u>rectify</u> *the* <u>fiscal inscription</u> *which indicates the intention to* <u>protect</u> *the* <u>rights</u> *of the Rapa Nui,* <u>well, that,</u> *the* <u>declaration that they will study,</u> *(that's what) they said.* <u>They are studying that, that is the first commitment from the government.</u> <u>Second, within the period of thirty days,</u> *you go to Rapa Nui,* <u>within the period of thirty days, get in agreement</u> *to send us back the* <u>modifications,</u> *if you want to* <u>modify</u> *the* <u>second article Letter C,</u> *take it and* <u>urgently</u> *send to the* <u>Congress</u> *so that it would be* <u>*approved*</u> *by the* <u>House of Deputies and Senators,...</u>

The text illustrates the "bilingual simultaneities" (Woolard 1998b) which characterize the syncretic Rapa Nui speech style, in particular the frequent inter- and intrasentential code-switching between Rapa Nui and Spanish, Rapa Nui interferences, and the frequent use of Spanish borrowings. Except for the numerous Spanish political and legal terms, the syncretic speech in political discourse is very similar to everyday Rapa Nui speech. In both cases, there can be considerable heterogeneity in the amounts of Spanish (or Rapa Nui) elements found in utterances across individual speakers or across contexts, indexing the Chilean–ness (or Rapa Nui–ness) of the discourse segments and the characteristics of interactional contexts such as topics and conversational participants' bilingual competences and preferences. In this example, the governor's syncretic speech is more Hispanicized than is his own speech in other contexts or the challenging leader's speech. Besides code-switching and interference, other forms of bilingual simultaneities such as convergence are also observed in syncretic Rapa Nui speech. Consider, for example, the following utterance, taken from a similar political meeting.

1)   Se mantiene *pahe* Consejo de Anciano *'ā*.
     'It's kept (*nonetheless/still*) *as* Council of Elders'.

Though most of the morphemes are in Spanish, the utterance is syntactically congruent in both Rapa Nui and Spanish and can be interpreted as a case of convergence of Spanish and Rapa Nui morphosyntactic frames. The utterance starts with the Spanish reflexive verb, followed by the Rapa Nui adverbial and the Spanish noun phrase, and ends with the Rapa Nui postverbal particle *'ā*. This particle is normally used within the Rapa Nui verbal phrase in combination with a preverbal particle to either indicate progressive or resultative aspects,[18] and its presence in this utterance adds an emphasis to the continuing status of the Council of Elders.

Syncretic Rapa Nui speech in public domains was at first considered non-standard or a reflection of imperfect Spanish skills, but over time it evolved into an oppositional linguistic strategy that challenged the institutional dominance of Spanish (Williams 1977). By extending syncretic Rapa Nui from in-group and private settings into the public arena as they pressed for political demands and wider representation, the Rapa Nui contributed to eventually breaking down the previously established "colonial diglossia"—a sociolinguistic hierarchy and associated diglossic compartmentalization of the functions of the two languages (Makihara 2004). Syncretic Rapa Nui speech in political discourse partly reflects the rising democratic participation by Rapa Nui who were, in large numbers, taking part in local politics, challenging and often taking the place of Continental Chilean administrators and appointees. Syncretic Rapa Nui in such local political domains stands in contrast with the use of Spanish, which had at that point come to be viewed as an act of accommodation on the part of bilingual Rapa Nui toward monolingual Spanish-speaking Continentals and their authority. The more recent emergence of purist Rapa Nui speech in political discourse, which I detail below, is a further development transforming the ecology of political discourse on Rapa Nui.

Development of purist Rapa Nui registers
in political discourse

The use of the Rapa Nui language in public and political discourse contexts where Spanish dominated was previously mostly limited to Rapa Nui greetings. Most commonly used is the versatile one-word greeting, *'Iorana*, originally of Tahitian provenance (Tahitian *Iaorana*), which has been widely adopted in daily interactions and is typically the first Rapa Nui word that outsiders learn. Continental officials have also frequently adopted the Rapa Nui greetings, *'iorana* or *'iorana kōrua* in initiating and *maururu* 'thank you' (also of Tahitian provenance) in terminating their speech otherwise conducted in Spanish.

Rapa Nui speakers have recently begun to address the community members in public and political speeches as *mahiŋo* in opening formulas of address such as the following:

2) *E*   *te*   *mahiŋo,*   *'iorana*   *kōrua.*
   VOCATIVE   the   kinsfolk   greetings   you (plural)

3) *E*   *te*   *mahiŋo,*   *'iorana*   *te*   *mahiŋo*   *o*   *te*   *kāiŋa.*
   VOCATIVE   the   kinsfolk   greetings   the   kinsfolk   of   the   territory

The term *mahiŋo* refers to an organized group of kin people. Broadly, it could refer to all community members or, more restrictively, to Rapa Nui unilineal descent groups and the non–Rapa Nui who are now associated with them. Social anthropologist Grant McCall observed that the term denoted "a group of persons under the dominance of a particular person" and was rarely heard during his fieldwork between 1972 and 1974 (1977: 37). During my stays between 1991 and 2007, I heard the term frequently, but exclusively at public speeches. The revitalized term has been used with a sense of inclusiveness congruent with the democratization of the political climate. The term *kāiŋa* originally denoted an estate occupied by a descent group, but increasingly is used to refer to the entire island. Both *mahiŋo* and *kāiŋa* evoke the unity of the Rapa Nui and continuity in the strong connection between the land and its people.

Over time, Rapa Nui leaders and intellectuals came to make speeches in what I call a purist Rapa Nui speech style. Purist Rapa Nui is not an archaic or older form of Rapa Nui but rather a newly constructed Rapa Nui speech form characterized by speakers' purging of Spanish elements and by the conscious Polynesianization of talk. By limiting use of this speech form to carefully chosen occasions, they have been establishing this not only as a new speech style but also as a new linguistic register. In the context of the recent indigenous and political movement, Rapa Nui purist speech styles are emerging as one of a few new registers associated with the politics of ethnicity and as a code for the speech genre of public and political oratory. The values motivating the politics of ethnicity are "enregistered" (Agha 1999) into purist speech styles by speakers and socially recognized by the community. Through the purist register, therefore, speakers voice values and stances of the ethnolinguistic group's self-conscious reflexive authentification and differentiation from other groups.

The recent creation of purist Rapa Nui registers constitutes a second set of discursive strategies whose deployment, along with syncretic speech, has been displacing monolingual Spanish speech, particularly in political and public discourse. Unlike the syncretic speech styles whose use was extended from informal and in-group contexts to political and public settings, purist speech is a more recent style that has been constructed as a register originating within political and public contexts. The development of the purist register has involved a markedly more conscious construction and deployment on the part of the speakers. The process of negotiation and acceptance through which this new style has been diffused and circulated in the community has taken place in contexts that have been highly charged with emotional and political sentiments.

One of the earliest striking examples of the use of purist Rapa Nui as a register that I witnessed took place at a 1994 meeting between the previously mentioned Council II and an official delegation of visiting Chilean senators, with a large Rapa Nui observing audience (see Text 2). At the start of the meeting, Juan Chávez, the president of the second council (the same speaker as in Text 1), pointedly and ceremoniously addressed the monolingual Spanish-speaking Continental officials in Rapa Nui. Chávez was a successful Rapa Nui businessman who could and regularly did also speak Spanish.[19] He began by explaining the wishes of the Rapa Nui community, consciously limiting himself to Rapa Nui words and pausing every couple of sentences to allow another leader of the group (T)—also a successful businessman in the local tourist industry—to translate his words into formal Chilean Spanish.

TEXT 2. Use of purist Rapa Nui at a Meeting with Continental Government Official

	Translation
01 C: *Maururu te vānaŋa o te taŋata rarahi i oho mai ai ki te roa nei o tātou, hakaroŋo mai ia tātou ture.*	C: *Thank you for the words of the many persons who have come far to us (incl.), to listen to our (incl.) demands.*
T: <u>Muchas gracias, honorables Senadores</u> 05 <u>por habernos dado la oportunidad, vuestra</u> <u>visita y así poder expresar nuestras</u> <u>inquietudes.</u>	T: <u>Thank you very much, honorable</u> <u>senators for having given us the</u> <u>opportunity, your visit and so that we can</u> <u>express our concerns.</u>
C: *Te mātou me'e haŋa, he hakanoho i te me'e ta'ato'a nei o te <u>hora</u> nei e makenu* 10 *mai ena, 'ina he aŋiaŋi mai. Te rua, te henua ko hape 'ā. <u>Tiene que</u>[20] hakatitika rāua i te rāua me'e, he hakahoki mai i te tātou henua.*	C: *What we (excl.) want is to stop all that is moving at this <u>moment</u>, that we don't understand. Secondly, the land (arrangement) is incorrect. They <u>have to</u> straighten out their deed and return our (incl.) land.*
T: <u>Nosotros solicitamos como legítimos</u> 15 <u>representantes del pueblo de Rapa Nui</u> <u>que por intermedio de ustedes, ver la</u> <u>posibilidad de parar todo proyecto que</u> <u>esté destinado al desarrollo de Isla de</u> <u>Pascua. Pues nos falta una cosa muy</u> 20 <u>principal que es la tierra, por eso estamos</u> <u>aquí para que ustedes trasmitan al</u>	T: <u>We solicit as legitimate representatives</u> <u>of the Rapa Nui people, that through your</u> <u>intermediation, to see the possibility of</u> <u>stopping every project that is destined to</u> <u>the development of Easter Island. Because</u> <u>we need one very principal thing, which is</u> <u>the land, that is why we are here so that</u> <u>you transmit our concern to the supreme</u>

supremo gobierno nuestra inquietud, para
que vean la solución de reconocer y
restituir nuestra propiedad a la tierra que
25 es la base de todo el desarrollo de la isla.
Sin la tierra no podemos hacer nada.
C: *O te vānaŋa era e kī era hoko rua*
tātou, he pia atu au ki a kōrua ta'ato'a, te
hakatere nei o te hora nei e oho nei, mai
30 *te matamu'a 'ā, mai te hora era o*
Policarpo Toro i tu'u mai ai ki nei
ararua ko reva tuai era 'ā. Ko tū me'e
'ā te me'e nei e aŋa e oho nei, 'ina he
me'e i kamiare. Mo rāua e u'i mai e
35 *hakatitika tako'a mai.*

T: Los quiero invitar a todos los presentes
para que viajemos al pasado, situarnos en
el día ocho de septiembre de mil
40 ochociento ochenta y ocho. Justamente la
iglesia que existe en Pascua, ahí fue el sitio
donde se inició toda esta historia. Cuando
don Policarpo Toro tomó posesión de la
isla, con la voluntad de un
45 pueblo libre, soberano, lo entregó a otro
pueblo libre y soberano. Ya existía
nuestra bandera. La bandera que tenemos
izada, solamente es para recordar lo que
pasó en esa época.
50 C:[21] *'O ira, vānaŋa ta'e rahi ta'aku, ko te*
vānaŋa mau nei 'ā te tātou vānaŋa,
potopoto i ha'a'au ai o roaroa te aŋa. I
ruŋa i te puka nei te tātou me'e ta'ato'a,
mai te matahiti ho'e ta'utini e ono
55 *hānere, e va'u hānere e ono 'ahuru ma*
piti, mai ira ki te hora nei te tātou me'e o
ruŋa o te puka nei.
T: Por eso, quiero aclarar que mi
exposición va a ser corta, porque es
60 tiempo. Porque la historia lo dice así
desde mil ochociento sesenta y cinco y
que esperamos una buena disposición por
parte de ustedes, honorables Senadores, y
lo que queremos es que el gobierno tenga
65 la bondad de reconocer. Y eso es todo.
C: *Maururu.*

government, so that they see the solution
to recognize and return our property to the
land, which is the base for all
development of the island. Without the
land we cannot do anything.
C: *Regarding what has been said about*
how there are two (groups) of us (incl.), I
ask you all, the way of doing things and
thinking which we carry on at this time,
since the antiquity, since when (Chilean
Captain) Policarpo Toro arrived here,
with the ancient flag that had already
existed. What we're doing now is the same,
nothing has changed. They should look
after us and also straighten things for us.

T: I want to invite all those present so that
we travel to the past, to situate ourselves
in the day 8 of September of eighteen
hundred eighty-eight. Exactly the church
that exists on Easter. That was the place
where all this history started. When Don
Policarpo Toro took possession of the
island, with the will of one free sovereign
people, who handed to another free and
sovereign people. Our flag already
existed. The flag that we have raised is
only to remember what happened in that
period.
C: *Therefore, it is not a lot that I want to*
say. What I have said is all our (incl.)
words, briefly stated so not to prolong the
work. In this book are all our (incl.) things
(information), from the year one thousand
six hundred, eight hundred sixty-two,
since that time until now our (incl.) thing
(information) is in this book.
T: That is why, I want to clarify that my
exposition will be brief, because it is time.
Because history says so since eighteen
sixty-five and that we are waiting for a
good disposition on your part, honorable
senators, and what we want is for the
government to have the goodness to
recognize. And that is all.
C: *Thank you.* (applause)

The delivered bilingual speech had two intended audiences: the Continental Chilean senators and the Rapa Nui participants and audience. The message to the senators in purist Rapa Nui speech was largely symbolic, aimed at highlighting the cultural differences between the representatives of the state and the Rapa Nui, and at adding weight to Rapa Nui claims to self-representation and ancestral rights over their land. The propositional content of the main leader's Rapa Nui speech, however, also targets his fellow Rapa Nui as explicitly addressed recipients of the message. The speaker frequently uses the inclusive first-person pronoun *tātou* ('we' or 'our', including you) to refer to Rapa Nui (except for one occasion where the exclusive pronoun *mātou* ['we' or 'our', excluding you] was used, line 8), and he refers to the senators and Chileans in general as *rāua* 'they'. He presents claims and requests addressed at the Chilean government by explaining them to the Rapa Nui audience, and he calls on the Rapa Nui to unite (especially lines 27–35) in pressing these claims. Of course the message content and the shift in "footing" (Goffman 1981) were fully intelligible only to the Rapa Nui–speaking audience, particularly as it was not translated literally by the other member (T.) of the group. In his translation, T. in fact goes well beyond the original in establishing the identities of the parties involved and the relationships between them: (1) the speakers as "legitimate representatives of the Rapa Nui people" (lines 14–15); (2) the addressees as "honorable senators" (lines 4 and 63), intermediaries who should "transmit our concern to the supreme government" (lines 21–22) and whose "good disposition" (line 62) would lead "the government to have the goodness to recognize" our concerns (lines 64–65); and (3) the Rapa Nui audience as the "free sovereign people," who had voluntarily agreed to a treaty with another free sovereign people (lines 45–46). Through the use of these "contextualization cues" (Gumperz 1982) and politeness markers, T. skillfully establishes a horizontal alignment between Chileans and Rapa Nui, and between the senators and the leaders of his organization.[22]

The juxtaposition of the speaker and the translator and of two clearly separated languages, and especially the choice of purist Rapa Nui, contributed greatly to the communicative effectiveness of the performance. Rapa Nui purist speech is a highly marked and stylized form of speech that stands in clear contrast to the syncretic speech forms common in everyday usage. Mistakes that the speaker made and self-corrected in the use of Rapa Nui numerals (lines 54–55) may have pointed to the extent to which Rapa Nui terms for large numbers had fallen into disuse in favor of Spanish numerals, and the highly self-conscious nature of his speech act. The resulting linguistic code symbolically erases traces of Spanish and Chilean influence while indexing an autonomous Rapa Nui language and community.

The debates regarding the Indigenous Law have led to a sharply raised awareness regarding the definition of indigenous persons and the status of Continental residents married to Rapa Nui. In recent times, some Rapa Nui have blamed the increasing number of migrants and temporary workers from the Continent for a loss of local culture and employment, and many have argued for restricting immigration to the island. The logic of ethnic distinction is now at times also being recursively applied to the area of language. Notions of correctness are emerging that identify Spanish elements in contemporary Rapa Nui speech as inappropriate and to be erased and replaced by Rapa Nui or Polynesian elements. This resembles what Judith

Irvine and Susan Gal (2000) call "register-stripping," referring to the replacement of Turkish words by Slavic forms in the remaking of Bulgarian and Macedonian literary languages.

By choosing to use purist Rapa Nui and erasing Spanish elements in public speeches where the audience includes monolingual Spanish-speaking Continentals, the speakers are able to fortify the ethnic boundaries between Chileans and Rapa Nui by metaphorically deploying linguistic boundaries. Though only a fraction of Rapa Nui would have full competence in purist Rapa Nui speech or would choose to use it, many Rapa Nui would be able to understand much of the semantic content and certainly the metapragmatic meaning of this type of speech. The use and acceptance of a purist Rapa Nui register relies on the shared political demands of the Rapa Nui community and the view that this form of speech symbolizes and unifies the Rapa Nui, despite significant heterogeneity in individual linguistic competence. At the same time, the new register constructs and reinforces ethnic boundaries in ways that establish new internal distinctions or hierarchies by conferring discursive authority onto the political activists, who can now claim to represent the ethnolinguistic community. By virtue of their cultural and linguistic expertise, they have illustrated and established a symbolically recognized continuity between the past and present.

Language ideologies and language maintenance on Rapa Nui

The language ideology perspective[23] views language as dynamically connecting the individual to the social. It offers a useful framework with which to understand linguistic change and the ways that heterogeneity and variability in language use emerge and are maintained or are transformed as results of the choices of individuals and social groups motivated by language ideologies. Elements of the communicative context, such as who has discursive authority, are established out of a process of negotiation.

The Rapa Nui political movements and discourse that emerged in the 1990s strongly challenged and overturned older views—particularly those devaluing Rapa Nui culture and language—and fostered a new culturalist formulation of indigenous identity and rights. The remaking of the Rapa Nui language as a public language and the expansion of the syncretic Rapa Nui in political and public arenas are important reflections of this ideological change. Leaders and participants in political movements claimed and gained discursive authority for themselves, as well as increased symbolic value for their language, through the expanded use of the Rapa Nui language—albeit in syncretic styles—in domains previously dominated by Spanish.

Some Rapa Nui advocates today argue for new language maintenance projects using the rhetoric of the politics of territory, treating language as another indigenous right.[24] Like their ancestral land, language is described as a resource and a form of cultural property whose inherited ownership must be recognized by, and wrestled back from, the state. Like the local Rapa Nui lobster which is threatened by extinction, language has to be protected, and local, national, and international projects for this purpose should be managed and planned by its rightful owners, but financed by the national government as a form of restitution. Elsewhere, I have elaborated on these ideas and reproduced and discussed an allegorical account to describe the Rapa Nui language situation related to me by the late elder, Nico Haoa.[25] Choosing his words carefully but eloquently in purist Rapa Nui in front of an impromptu gathering of Rapa Nui bystanders, he explained how the ancestral Rapa Nui language still existed in an essential form but that it had been displaced to the top of Punapau mountain just as the island's native grasses had been driven there by the spread of foreign grasses brought in by outsiders. Just as the native grass wanted to return to grow again in its birthplace, the Rapa Nui language would return and prosper. Elaborating on this botanical metaphor connecting people, territory, language, and history, he painted an image that depicted the language as enjoying an autonomous existence and agency that stood apart from everyday language use.[26] His choice of purist Rapa Nui, which contrasted with the syncretic speech style of the surrounding conversations, resonated iconically with this image.

Instances of language objectification and linguistic purism in particular can be also observed outside of political meetings. The most frequent targets are Spanish lexical items, such as numbers, names of seasons, and cultural borrowings. During a 2003 visit, I observed several cases of Rapa Nui speakers commenting on the use of Spanish loanwords and Rapa Nui replacements, including lively discussions regarding the use of terms such as *roro uīra* 'brilliant brain' for 'computer' coined by a local radio announcer. Corpus planning efforts have also been launched by the Council of Elders and local schoolteachers, which yielded dictionaries and a reference grammar.[27] Nevertheless, many Rapa Nui find Polynesianization and de-Hispanization unnatural. As one local fisherman summarized his views, "It is perfectly fine to speak in half Chilean and half Rapa Nui; we prefer to speak so that people can understand." A popular song composed by a Rapa Nui singer in his early forties openly mocks the practice of *haka Rapa Nui*, or Rapanuization, by political and cultural leaders, as a form of 'brain washing' (*tata puoko*).[28]

Partly because of these positive attitudes toward linguistic syncretism, the use of purist Rapa Nui registers has largely remained restricted to interethnic and public settings where the association between linguistic codes and ethnic identity remains highly salient. Speakers in such public and political events are thus very self-consciously deploying purist speech as a linguistic resource and as a register to adopt specific stances. In cultivating and using purist registers, Rapa Nui speakers are constructing and participating in new political rituals.[29] These serve to claim and protect the newly captured political spaces and to represent the Rapa Nui as a unified ethnolinguistic community with an ancestral right to land and other resources.

A multiplicity of language ideologies can often be found within a community, reflecting the divergent perspectives associated with social groups that hold differing interests and positions within a society. An important contribution of recent work on language ideologies is the emphasis it places on recognizing the social origins of ideologies in power relations. Kathryn Woolard writes that language ideologies are "derived from, rooted in, reflective of, or responsive to the experience or interests of a particular social position" and exist "in service of the struggle to acquire or maintain power" and organize social relations (1998a: 6, 7).[30]

It is from characterizations such as these—which connect different ideologies to different social positions—that several observers have generalized to warn of the potential dangers of purist linguistic ideologies in communities where local languages are being lost. As I mentioned at the beginning of the chapter, the concern is that purism might further polarize social groups within communities and create negative associations or insecurities among people who do not speak Rapa Nui or do not speak it well. Though this concern is a real one on Rapa Nui, I have sought to illustrate how ideologies can also be evoked in taking a stance or in voicing certain situationally grounded registers. This suggests that observed variability in ideology may reflect not only the positions of social groups with differing interests within a society but also political ideas variously emphasized or enacted by the same individuals across different communicative contexts. Individuals hold, order, and hierarchize linguistic ideologies or ideas in ways that may be sensitive to context. Linguistic purism on Rapa Nui has so far been accommodated into the larger and more dominant linguistic ideology of syncretism.

One of the important historical factors that may have fostered the development of this configuration is the relatively low level of social differentiation—along tribal, generational, gender, and class lines—of Rapa Nui society compared with other communities undergoing language shift. Ever since the leveling effects of the late nineteenth-century population crash, the Rapa Nui community has remained with relatively little vertical differentiation. Over the course of most of its contact history, the differentiation that developed was between the Rapa Nui and outsiders. Notwithstanding some class differentiation that has emerged in recent decades, the relatively low level of internal social differentiation has meant that there has been little evident advantage to politicizing language use or highlighting language differences within the ethnic group. This has served as the context for the transformation of linguistic ideologies and practice that I have discussed above.

In the recent postcolonial period, hierarchical language boundaries between Rapa Nui and Spanish were at first established but then challenged and blurred by the rise of syncretic linguistic practices which spread in part with the politics of democratization and the indigenous movement. The very success of the movement has now led some local leaders to develop forms of linguistic purism. If developed further, Rapa Nui linguistic purism could lead to a functional re-compartmentalization of language boundaries, with either Rapa Nui or Spanish chosen according to the situation. The question for the future is: Will this situation lead to a new form of diglossia—a form in which the Rapa Nui language is reified to approximate the superposed "high" variety in terms of its position in the sociolinguistic hierarchy, but objectified and encircled by purist language boundaries, with the consequent danger of contributing to language insecurity and hastened language loss? Or will purist Rapa Nui continue to be used selectively in mostly ritualized performances that help to preserve and recover Rapa Nui?

I am not able to predict how things will turn out. I have, however, tried to characterize the ways that different ideas about language and language use characterize modern Rapa Nui political discourse. This is not a case of two or more groups within a community with divergent socioeconomic positions holding diverse opposed ideas and expressing conflicts through language use (as in the Mexicano case described by Hill and Hill 1986). Rather, this is a case of individuals, often the same individuals, deploying and managing purism as one of several discursive strategies. Purist Rapa Nui speech is used almost exclusively in contexts in which its participants are highly aware of a Chilean and other non–Rapa Nui audience, and mostly for the purpose of highlighting symbolic claims of Rapa Nui cultural autonomy. Yet it is syncretic Rapa Nui that continues to dominate everyday life and through which the real discussions of substance in political discourse take place. Instead of targeting purism at creating sociolinguistic boundaries within the ethnic community, for example along generational or class lines, the Rapa Nui have deployed purist registers in ways that have mostly worked to symbolically unify the ethnolinguistic community against outsiders.

Notes

Field research was supported by the National Science Foundation and the Wenner-Gren Foundation for Anthropological Research. Ivonne Calderón Haoa provided invaluable research assistance. Bambi Schieffelin, Susan Philips, and Riet Delsing offered extensive comments on earlier versions of this chapter. I am also grateful for the encouragement and comments of the participants at the Association for Social Anthropology of Oceania and at the Interdisciplinary Workshop on Language Ideology and Minority Language Communities at the University of California, San Diego, and of the other contributors to this volume.

1. Some of these studies have described the development of competing models and varieties of minority, previously vernacular, languages such as "unified Quichua" in Ecuador and "neo-Breton" in France, borne out of language maintenance or revalorization efforts in postcolonial contexts (King 2001; Kuter 1989; Timm 2003). These newly constructed varieties have tended to be standardized, based in formal schooling and literacy, and modeled after the European colonial and national languages. They have been preferred by the urban, educated, and younger bilingual speakers (or learners of the minority language). Community-internal disagreements have emerged regarding the evaluations of these varieties and their normalization efforts (Collins 1998).

2. The recent sociolinguistic and linguistic anthropology literature has struggled to define the concepts of linguistic style and register (see Agha 1998; Bell 1997; Biber and Finegan 1994; Chambers 1995; Eckert and Rickford 2001; Ferguson 1994; Halliday 1978; Labov 1972; and Wolfram and Schilling-Estes 1998). For the purpose of this essay, I employ the term "style" as a more general category covering linguistic varieties including what in some literature may be distinguished into "dialects" and "registers"—or user-based and use-based varieties. Choice of the term "style" rather than "linguistic variety" reflects my emphasis on the speakers' roles in creating their orientations toward the world and the situatedness of performance through the use of linguistic varieties rather than on linguistic structure. Syncretic speech on Rapa Nui is characterized by the juxtaposition of Rapa Nui and Spanish in conversational discourse. Though co-occurring linguistic features are important for characterizing styles, the development of a style has more to do with differentiation within a system of possibilities, linking co-occurring linguistic features to social meanings, and constituting and indexing social formations such as the distinctiveness of individuals and groups in specific communicative situations (Irvine 2001). I use the term "register" to denote a more specific type of style when linguistic styles are or have become associated with social activities or practices and with persons engaged in them, and possibly with certain social stances and values.

3. See Dorian 1981, 1994b; Fishman 1965, 1967; Mougeon and Beniak 1991; and Schmidt 1985a, 1985b. The decline in variability noted in these studies refers not only to grammatical structure and domains of usage, but also to stylistic or register variation.

4. See Hill 2002; Jaffe 1999; and Maurer 2003.

5. Coulmas 1989 highlights a similar problem of "alienation of the language from the masses" when describing Sanskritization and purist Hindi language policy in India. See Dorian 1994a for a comparative discussion of the ways that conservative and purist attitudes have hampered efforts to revitalize endangered languages.

6. Makihara 2005 describes how the Rapa Nui extended-family language socialization context has contributed to maintain and cultivate Rapa Nui knowledge among dominantly Spanish-speaking children via linguistically syncretic interactions. See also Riley, chap. 4 of this volume, for an analysis of similar language socialization practices and positive attitudes toward linguistic syncretism in the Marquesas, where there has been resistance to official purist discourse.

7. See El Consejo de Jefes de Rapanui and Hotus 1988, a Rapa Nui genealogy book that provides descriptions of tribal territorial arrangements before European contact and a Rapa Nui account of the history of contact with outsiders.

8. See Maude 1981; McCall [1980] 1994; and Routledge [1919] 1998.

9. A French missionary first stayed on the island for nine months in 1864 and returned with others in 1866 to continue mission work in the midst of the population collapse. Aided by three Mangarevan Christians, they used Tuamotuan language and the Tahitian sermons while learning Rapa Nui and developing a Rapa Nui catechism. The missionaries eventually left the island in 1871, as a result of their rivalry and confrontations with a French planter. By the end of the 1870s, the missionaries and the planter had taken or sent more than half of the remaining Rapa Nui to the islands of Mangareva, Tahiti, and Mo'orea, where many were indentured to work on plantations (Anguita 1988; H. Fischer 2005; S. Fischer [1999] 2001). The Rapa Nui catechists returning from their training in Mangareva and Mo'orea continued the work of European missionaries until the arrival from Chile in 1935 of a German Capuchin missionary Sebastian Englert, who also served as the naval chaplain until 1969.

10. The Chilean annexation of Easter Island took place the same year that Germany, Britain, and France added Nauru, the Cook Islands, and the Futuna Islands, respectively, as colonies under their control. Ten years later, the United States would annex Hawai'i and, as a result of the Spanish-American War, gain control over Guam and other territories. France, which had earlier annexed the Marquesas in 1840s (see Riley, chap. 4 of this volume), proceeded through the 1880s to annex other eastern Polynesian island groups such as the Society Islands (e.g., Tahiti, Mo'orea), the Gambier Islands (Mangareva), and the Tuamotus Islands.

11. See Makihara 2005.

12. This situation contrasts, for example, with language use and ideology in the trilingual (Tewa, Navaho, and English) speech community of Arizona Tewa (described by Kroskrity 1993, 2000), where the indigenous practices of strict compartmentalization and purism have been largely maintained.

13. This stands in contrast to the case of the Mapuche, the largest indigenous group in Chile, with approximately one million people, where the struggle to recover native lands has been complicated by the fact that many lands in dispute are now held by private individuals and forestry and electricity companies. The high rates of Mapuche dislocation and rural-to-urban migration over many decades has also complicated collective action to reclaim land. Aylwin and Castillo 1990 provide a useful and detailed discussion of Chilean laws affecting indigenous communities including the Mapuche and Rapa Nui (see also, e.g., Aylwin 2002 and FIDH 2003 on the Mapuche).

14. Ministerio de Planificación y Cooperación [1993] 1998: 31–33, 35, my translation. In community meetings, some Rapa Nui complained, for example, that such a law would make a Continental person Rapa Nui because "he goes fishing, cooks on fire [*tunu ahi* style], or goes to the local [Catholic] church" or "eats *taro*, knows how to say '*iorana koe* [a greeting], dances *tamurē*, and lives here [on the island]."

15. E. Martínez Chibbaro's father was part of a twelve-day Chilean scientific expedition to Easter Island in 1911, then spent a year and a half on the island as the resident observer at the meteorological station and published a Rapa Nui word list. See Martínez Y. 1913.

16. The local courthouse, which was established on the island in 1966, is also referred to as *hare ture*. The word *ture* is thought to have been first introduced to refer to 'law' (from Hebrew *torah* 'sacred law') into Tahitian, the first Polynesian language to have been given a written form by European missionaries (Ellis [1833] 1859: 3:176).

17. Rapa Nui elements are in italics, transcribed using a single closing quote ['] for the glottal stop, [ŋ] for the velar nasal, and a macron for the five long vowels. Spanish elements are underlined and a close-to-standard Spanish orthography is used except where forms significantly diverge from standard Spanish, which are provided in parentheses. Relatively well assimilated Spanish borrowings are in italics and underlined, non-Spanish borrowings are italicized and dot underlined. Translations are also italicized or underlined to reflect the original code choice. The following abbreviations are used in this chapter: excl. for exclusive pronoun, incl. for inclusive pronoun.

18. One of two preverbal articles can be used with the postverbal article *'ā: e* for a progressive aspect and *ko* for a resultative aspect.

19. His political organization was later transformed and renamed as the "Rapa Nui Parliament." In addition to being a political leader and successful businessman, Chávez also contributed to language and cultural educational programs at the local school. He passed away in 2006.

20. See Makihara 2001 for a discussion of the mechanisms of adaptation of Spanish elements in Rapa Nui speech, which includes that of the introduction of a modal construction of obligation (tiene que) and its syntactic adaptation.

21. *Puka, ta'utini, hānere,* and *hora* are derived from English for book, thousand, hundred, and hour.

22. See Schieffelin, chapter 7 of this volume, for a discussion of translation as a metapragmatic activity involving differing cultural assumptions about personhood, power, identity, and theory of mind.

23. See Makihara and Schieffelin, chapter 1, for a discussion of this perspective.

24. In contrast, the leaders of the 'Maya movement' in Guatemala and of the Corsican nationalist movement in France focused on language at the early stages of their activism. England 2003 describes the strategic choice that Maya leaders made to focus on language rather than on political issues in order to depoliticize language issues in the face of severe military government repression in the mid-1980s (see also Brown 1998). Jaffe 1999 describes the rather different configuration of political economic and cultural contexts that led Corsican activists to make language the primary focus of their political discourse beginning in the late 1960s and 1970s.

25. Nico Haoa ran one of the largest local tourist inns, and was also a member of the second Council of Elders. He was also a key participant in the local language documentation projects. He passed away in 2003 (see Makihara 2004).

26. See Stasch, chapter 5 of this volume, for a discussion of the Korowai worldview, which links language, land, and categories of people, and of how Korowai speakers attribute physical and metaphysical force to linguistic forms. Handman, chapter 8, discusses the SIL notions of "people groups," each of which has a (local vernacular) "heart language" that the SIL thinks is crucial to the success of missionary activities in Papua New Guinea.

27. Comisión para la Estructuración de la Lengua Rapanui 1996, 2000; Hérnandez Sallés et al. 2001.

28. Emerging awareness of language boundaries concerns more than the conceptual differentiation between Rapa Nui and Spanish. For example, the same Rapa Nui singer declared to me that there were four language varieties on the island: (1) Rapa Nui, (2) Pascuense

(Sp. 'Easter Islander' for Spanish spoken on the island), (3) _Tire_ (Sp. borrowing from Chile for Chilean Spanish), and (4) Español (Spanish 'Spanish'). This illustrates awareness of local versus Chilean versus supranational varieties of Spanish.

29. Steven Lukes defines ritual as "rule-governed activity of a symbolic character which draws the attention of its participants to objects of thought and feeling which they hold to be of special significance" (1975: 291).

30. See Hill and Hill 1986 and Hill 1998 for relevant discussions on internal social hierarchies, language ideologies, and the development of code differentiation in the Malinche towns of central Mexico.

References

Agha, Asif. 1998. Stereotypes and Registers of Honorific Language. _Language in Society_ 27 (2): 151–193.

———. 1999. Register. _Journal of Linguistic Anthropology_ 9 (1–2): 216–219.

Anguita, Patricia. 1988. L'insertion des Rapanui à Tahiti et Moorea (1871–1920). _Bulletin de la Société des Etudes Océaniennes_ 20 (8): 21–39.

Aylwin, José. 2002. _Tierra y territorio Mapuche: Un Análisis desde una mirada histólico jurídica._ Mapu Territoriality Project, Institute for Indigenous Studies, University of La Frontera.

Aylwin, José, and Eduardo Castillo. 1990. _Legislación sobre indígenas en Chile a través de la historia._ Programa de Derechos Humanos y Pueblos Indígenas, Comisión Chilena de Derechos Humanos.

Bell, Allan. 1997. Language Style as Audience Design. In _Sociolinguistics: A Reader_, ed. Nikolas Coupland and Adam Jaworski, pp. 240–250. New York: St. Martin's Press.

Biber, Douglas, and Edward Finegan, eds. 1994. _Sociolinguistic Perspectives on Register._ New York: Oxford University Press.

Brown, R. McKenna. 1998. Mayan Language Revitalization in Guatemala. In _The Life of Our Language: Kaqchikel Maya Maintenance, Shift, and Revitalization_, ed. Susan Garzon, R. McKenna Brown, Julia Becker Richards, and Wuqu' (Arnulfo Simón) Ajpub', pp. 155–170. Austin: University of Texas Press.

Chambers, Jack K. 1995. _Sociolinguistic Theory: Linguistic Variation and Its Social Significance._ Cambridge, MA: Blackwell.

Collins, James. 1998. Our Ideologies and Theirs. In _Language Ideologies: Practice and Theory_, ed. Bambi Schieffelin, Kathryn Woolard, and Paul Kroskrity, pp. 256–270. Oxford: Oxford University Press.

Comisión para la Estructuración de la Lengua Rapanui. 1996. _Gramática fundamental de la lengua Rapanui._ Santiago, Chile: La Nación.

———. 2000. _Diccionario etimológico Rapanui-Español._ Valparaíso, Chile: Puntángeles Universidad de Playa Ancha Editorial.

Coulmas, Florian. 1989. Language Adaptation. In _Language Adaptation_, ed. Florian Coulmas, pp. 1–25. New York: Cambridge University Press.

Dorian, Nancy C. 1981. _Language Death: The Life Cycle of a Scottish Gaelic Dialect._ Philadelphia: University of Pennsylvania.

———. 1994a. Purism vs. Compromise in Language Revitalization and Language Revival. _Language in Society_ 23: 479–494.

———. 1994b. Stylistic Variation in a Language Restricted to Private-Sphere Use. In _Sociolinguistic Perspectives on Register_, ed. Douglas Biber and Edward Finegan, pp. 217–232. New York: Oxford University Press.

Eckert, Penelope, and John R. Rickford, eds. 2001. _Style and Sociolinguistic Variation._ New York: Cambridge University Press.

El Consejo de Jefes de Rapanui, and Alberto Hotus. 1988. *Te mau hatu 'o Rapa Nui: Los soberanos de Rapa Nui; Pasado, presente y futuro*. Santiago, Chile: Editorial Emisión; Centro de Estudios Políticos Latinoamericanos Simón Bolívar.

Ellis, William. [1833] 1859. *Polynesian Researches during a Residence of Nearly Eight Years in the Society and Sandwich Islands*. 4 vols. 2nd ed. London: Henry G. Bohn.

England, Nora C. 2003. Mayan Language Revival and Revitalization Politics: Linguists and Linguistic Ideologies. *American Anthropologist* 105 (4): 733–743.

Errington, Joseph. 2003. Getting Language Rights: The Rhetorics of Language Endangerment and Loss. *American Anthropologist* 105 (4): 723–732.

Ferguson, Charles A. 1994. Dialect, Register, and Genre: Working Assumptions about Conventionalization. In *Sociolinguistic Perspectives on Register*, ed. Douglas Biber and Edward Finegan, pp. 15–30. Oxford: Oxford University Press.

FIDH, International Federation for Human Rights. 2003. *The Mapuche People: Between Oblivion and Exclusion*. Paris: FIDH (International Federation for Human Rights).

Fischer, Hermann. [1999] 2001. *Sombras sobre Rapa Nui: Alegato por un pueblo olvidado* Translated by Luisa Ludwig. Santiago, Chile: LOM Ediciones.

Fischer, Steven R. 2005. *Island at the End of the World: The Turbulent History of Easter Island*. London: Reaktion Books.

Fishman, Joshua A. 1965. Who Speaks What Language to Whom and When. *La Linguistique* 2: 67–88.

———. 1967. Bilingualism with and without Diglossia; Diglossia with and without Bilingualism. *Journal of Social Issues* 23 (2): 29–38.

Goffman, Erving. 1981. *Forms of Talk*. Philadelphia: University of Pennsylvania Press.

Gumperz, John J. 1982. *Discourse Strategies*. Cambridge: Cambridge University Press.

Halliday, M. A. K. 1978. *Language as Social Semiotic: The Social Interpretation of Language and Meaning*. Baltimore: University Park Press.

Hernández Sallés, Arturo, Nelly Ramos Pizarro, Kava Calderón Tuki, Viki Haoa Cardinali, Lina Hotu Hey, Catalina Hey Paoa, Christian Madariaga Paoa, Jacqueline Rapu Tuki, David Teao Hey, Alicia Teao Tuki, and Carolina Tuki Pakarati. 2001. *Diccionario ilustrado: Rapa Nui, Español, Inglés, Francés*. Santiago, Chile: Pehuén Editores.

Hill, Jane H. 1998. "Today There Is No Respect": Nostalgia, "Respect," and Oppositional Discourse in Mexicano (Nahuatl) Language Ideology. In *Language Ideologies: Practice and Theory*, ed. Bambi Schieffelin, Kathryn Woolard, and Paul Kroskrity, pp. 68–86. New York: Oxford University Press.

———. 2002. "Expert Rhetorics" in Advocacy for Endangered Languages: Who Is Listening, and What Do They Hear? *Journal of Linguistic Anthropology* 12 (2): 119–133.

Hill, Jane H., and Kenneth C. Hill. 1986. *Speaking Mexicano: Dynamics of Syncretic Language in Central Mexico*. Tucson: University of Arizona Press.

Irvine, Judith T. 2001. "Style" as Distinctiveness: The Culture and Ideology of Linguistic Differentiation. In *Style and Sociolingusitic Variation*, ed. Penelope Eckert and John R. Rickford, pp. 21–43. New York: Cambridge University Press.

Irvine, Judith T., and Susan Gal. 2000. Language Ideology and Linguistic Differentiation. In *Regimes of Language: Ideologies, Polities, and Identities*, ed. Paul V. Kroskrity, pp. 35–83. Santa Fe, NM: School of American Research Press.

Jaffe, Alexandra. 1999. *Ideologies in Action: Language Politics on Corsica*. New York: Mouton de Gruyter.

King, Kendall A. 2001. *Language Revitalization Processes and Prospects: Quichua in the Ecuadorian Andes*. Tonawana, NY: Multilingual Matters.

Kroskrity, Paul V. 1993. *Language, History, and Identity: Ethnolinguistic Studies of the Arizona Tewa*. Tucson: University of Arizona Press.

————. 2000. Language Ideologies in the Expression and Representation of Arizona Tewa Ethnic Identity. In *Regimes of Language: Ideologies, Polities, and Identities*, ed. Paul Kroskrity, pp. 329–359. Santa Fe, NM: School of American Research Press.

Kuter, Lois. 1989. Breton vs. French: Language and the Opposition of Political, Economic, Social, and Cultural Values. In *Investigating Obsolescence: Studies in Language Contraction and Death*, ed. Nancy C. Dorian, pp. 75–89. New York: Cambridge University Press.

Labov, William. 1972. *Sociolinguistic Patterns*. Philadelphia: University of Pennsylvania Press.

Lukes, Steven. 1975. Political Ritual and Social Integration. *Sociology* 9 (2): 289–308.

Makihara, Miki. 2001. Modern Rapanui Adaptation of Spanish Elements. *Oceanic Linguistics* 40 (2): 191–222.

————. 2004. Linguistic Syncretism and Language Ideologies: Transforming Sociolinguistic Hierarchy on Rapa Nui (Easter Island). *American Anthropologist* 106 (3): 529–540.

————. 2005. Rapa Nui Ways of Speaking Spanish: Language Shift and Socialization on Easter Island. *Language in Society* 34 (5): 727–762.

Martínez Chibbaro, E. 1954. El Rapa-Nui, lengua pascuense. *Occidente* May: 31–35.

Martínez Y., Edgardo. 1913. *Vocabulario de la lengua Rapa-Nui*. Santiago, Chile: Instituto Central Meteorológico y Geofísico de Chile.

Maude, Harry E. 1981. *Slavers in Paradise: The Peruvian Slave Trade in Polynesia, 1862–1864*. Stanford, CA: Stanford University Press.

Maurer, Bill. 2003. Comment: Got Language? Law, Property, and the Anthropological Imagination. *American Anthropologist* 105 (4): 775–781.

McCall, Grant. 1977. Reaction to Disaster: Continuity and Change in Rapanui Social Organization. Ph.D. diss., Australian National University.

————. [1980] 1994. *Rapanui: Tradition and Survival on Easter Island*. 2nd ed. Honolulu: University of Hawaii Press.

Ministerio de Planificación y Cooperación. [1993] 1998. Ley N° 19.253 Ley Indígena. Modified in Ley 19.587 (Nov. 13, 1998, ed.).

Mougeon, Raymond, and Edouard Beniak. 1991. *Linguistic Consequences of Language Contact and Restriction: The Case of French in Ontario, Canada*. New York: Oxford University Press.

Porteous, J. Douglas. 1981. *The Modernization of Easter Island*. Victoria, B.C.: Department of Geography, University of Victoria.

Routledge, Katherine P. [1919] 1998. *The Mystery of Easter Island: The Story of an Expedition*. Kempton, IL: Adventures Unlimited Press.

Schmidt, Annette. 1985a. The Fate of Ergativity in Dying Dyirbal. *Language* 61 (2): 378–396.

————. 1985b. *Young People's Dyirbal: An Example of Language Death from Australia*. New York: Cambridge University Press.

Timm, Lenora A. 2003. Breton at a Crossroads: Looking Back, Moving Forward. *E-Keltoi* 2: 25–62.

Whiteley, Peter. 2003. Do "Language Rights" Serve Indigenous Interests? Some Hopi and Other Queries. *American Anthropologist* 105 (4): 712–722.

Williams, Raymond. 1977. *Marxism and Literature*. Oxford: Oxford University Press.

Wolfram, Walt, and Natalie Schilling-Estes, eds. 1998. *American English: Dialects and Variation*. Malden, MA: Blackwell.

Woolard, Kathryn A. 1998a. Introduction. Language Ideology as a Field of Inquiry. In *Language Ideologies: Practice and Theory*, ed. Bambi B. Schieffelin, Kathryn A. Woolard, and Paul V. Kroskrity, pp. 3–47. New York: Oxford University Press.

————. 1998b. Simultaneity and Bivalency as Strategies in Bilingualism. *Journal of Linguistic Anthropology* 8 (1): 3–29.

KATHLEEN C. RILEY

To Tangle or Not to Tangle

*Shifting Language Ideologies and
the Socialization of <u>Charabia</u>
in the Marquesas, French Polynesia*

After a century and a half of French colonial rule, inhabitants of the Marquesan archipelago of French Polynesia still daily use distinctive regional varieties of their eastern Polynesian language as well as a local variety of French. In the 1970s, a cultural revival movement coalesced, motivated in part by the fear that the indigenous language would soon be lost (Le Cléac'h 1987). Over the past twenty-five years, an ideological discourse familiar in language-shift studies has been articulated by the movement leaders: the youth are accused of no longer acquiring standard French or "pure" 'Enana,[1] but replacing these with an emergent code-switching code referred to as <u>charabia</u>, a French term meaning 'confused, unintelligible, and incorrect speech'. This chapter explores the tensions and effects of communicative practices and emotional registers derived from both official discourses and everyday socialization interactions in a context of shifting language ideologies.

Shifting language ideologies—shifts in language socialization and practice

The phrase "shifting language ideologies" has three potential readings: (1) shifts in language ideologies, (2) ideologies about language shift within a community, and (3) ideologies about how speakers shift languages while speaking. As is demonstrated in this chapter, all three of these shifts in language and ideology have an interwoven effect via language socialization on the production of new linguistic varieties and practices.

Any speech community may over time experience shifts in their "language ideologies,"[2] but such shifts are expected particularly in situations of language/culture contact (e.g., Hill and Hill 1986; Kulick 1992). Linguistic varieties take on new contrastive values when juxtaposed within new political economic structures. Similarly, ideologies about how languages are acquired and/or lost and how they ought to be used or abused are shaped by new cultural juxtapositions and power dynamics. A particular type of shift in language ideology highlighted in such a context of language/culture contact concerns ideologies about shifting languages.

The phrase "shifting languages" is used here to coreference "language shift" (i.e., the ways in which languages displace each other within some or all domains within a given community [Fishman 1964]) and "code-switching" (i.e., the ways in which speakers shift between linguistic varieties within a conversation [Blom and Gumperz 1972]). Errington proposes this ambiguous reading of the term to signal "a dynamic tension between...institutional and interactional perspectives" (1998: 4–5).

The practice of interactional language shifting (or code-switching) only occurs within a sociohistorical context of institutional language shifting in which distinctive linguistic varieties are being made newly available and/or newly salient to speakers in new domains. Similarly, shifting between languages within a given interaction can in and of itself also be considered a form of institutional language shifting in that new linguistic forms are being used and associated with new domains. However, in neither case does code-switching necessarily entail language shift in the narrowest sense of the term: the total replacement in all societal domains of one language by another, sometimes called "language death" (see, for example, the chapters by Makihara, Jourdan, and Stasch in this volume).

Nonetheless, many speech communities marked by shifting languages tend to assume that code-switching is a harbinger of language shift unto death, rather than an indication of language shift in the sense of a new and creative form of language use (see Makihara's discussion of the literature on endangered languages in chap. 3). The assumption of a teleological progression from language shifting in the interactional sense to language shifting at the institutional level (Errington 1998: 185) is worth examining in detail in specific communities precisely because ideologies that presuppose a certain eventuality may well have an effect but not always in the self-fulfilling direction anticipated. How does this happen?

Shifting language ideologies affect language use via language socialization. As Ochs and Schieffelin have formulated it (1984), language socialization is the process by which cultural practices and understandings shape the way people acquire linguistic resources and strategies, while verbal interactions transmit and shape the cultural knowledge and behaviors that people acquire. As a result, culture and language are subject to ongoing dialogic negotiation and transformation. Ideologies of any sort (dominant or covert) shape and are shaped by language; thus, shifting language ideologies influence the mix in particularly rich and reflexive ways.

First of all, language ideologies (whether about the origins, strengths, or futures of particular linguistic varieties or about the relative legitimacy of "pure" versus "mixed-up" codes) will be transmitted but also negotiated and transformed via daily interactions, whether public or private. The language ideologies themselves will shift as a result of the socialization process: dominant ideologies may be subverted, and covert ideologies may lose their subversive "cool." Second, contextualized and instantiated by daily socializing discourses, specific ideologies about shifting languages will affect the language practices being simultaneously acquired and transformed; that is, shifts in language use (the preference for and production of one language over another or the mixing of more than one) will also be generated. Thus, language practices will shift simultaneously as a result of the shifts in ideology about them.[3]

In the following sections, language socialization data collected in 1993 and 2003 are used to examine the ways in which 'Enana are rejecting in practice the diglossic separation of their two codes, producing and reproducing instead the officially lamented but covertly prestigious <u>charabia</u> to index their identities as both French and Polynesian.

Colonialism, language use, and language ideology in the Marquesas

The Marquesan archipelago consists of six inhabited islands lying approximately 900 miles northeast of Tahiti. France claimed these remote islands as part of their Pacific protectorates in 1842 and had reorganized them by 1880 into their colonial <u>Etablissements français d'Océanie</u>. Following WWII, the islands were incorporated into a larger grouping of <u>Territoires d'Outre-mer</u>, and in the mid-1970s French Polynesia, with Tahiti as its capital, increasingly gained political autonomy, signaled most recently by its transformation from a <u>territoire</u> into an autonomous <u>pays</u> 'country'.[4]

As a result of their central position, Tahiti and the Society Islands have historically leveraged more social, economic, and political clout than have the other archipelagos of the far-flung territory. Concomitantly, the Tahitian language early on acquired considerable symbolic capital through its use as the territorial lingua franca. The Marquesas, however, are culturally and linguistically distinct from the Society Islands[5] and have struggled for many years to make these distinctions apparent to both French and French Polynesian governments (see, for instance, the insurrectionary use of 'Enana in the Territorial Assembly in 1978 [Henningham 1992: 162–163]). Especially tricky has been the 'Enana's attempt to articulate their distinctive ethnolinguistic identity while also cementing their alliances with the French state in order to bypass the growing hegemony of Tahitians within the increasingly autonomous <u>pays</u>.

During the first century of colonial control, language use and language ideologies in the Marquesas underwent significant but fairly predictable transformations. Although the population declined sharply during the nineteenth century because of disease, warfare, and societal disarray, rebounding only to eight thousand by the end of the twentieth century, the inhabitants were never overwhelmed by colonists (Dening 1980). The invasive languages (French, Tahitian, and English), valued for their symbolic capital, were acquired by a small but not insignificant portion of the population as a result of various educational, religious, and political economic forces. Nonetheless, 'Enana (in several regional dialects) remained the language of everyday discourse in most domains in the islands (Riley 2001).

Since the 1960s, the use of the available linguistic varieties, and local ideologies concerning their value and use, have shifted in complex ways (Lavondès 1972).

As of 1993, many children and adolescents in the archipelago's three towns (with a combined population of approximately two thousand) manifested only a very limited competence in any dialect of 'Enana, speaking instead the restructured variety of French that has developed in French Polynesia (Gobern 1997). Nonetheless, as of 2003, many valley-specific varieties of 'Enana (though grammatically simplified and replete with French, English, and Tahitian loans) continued to be spoken by people of all ages in every village of the islands as well as among older 'Enana living in Tahiti. By 1993, when I began doing research in the Marquesas, shifting among linguistic varieties (French, Tahitian, other regional varieties of 'Enana, as well as bits of English) at intrasentential, intersentential, and intercontextual levels was an everyday norm in even some of the most remote villages (Riley 2001). An extended illustration of this form of conversational switching among French, 'Enana, English, and Tahitian can be found in the appended transcription data (B42–53[e]).[6]

However, from the perspective of many 'Enana, especially those engaged for the past quarter-century in a still-burgeoning cultural revival movement, shifts in linguistic structures and practices over the past century and a half are cause for alarm. For them, interactional language shifting indicates that institutional language shift is occurring and presaging imminent language death. This ideological fatalism can, I propose, be tied to the fact that most of the leaders of the cultural revival movement are well-socialized products of the French educational system. They apply French purist ideologies for critiquing their decadent language, have founded French-style institutions for its recuperation, and have engaged in French-style emotional registers to instill in the population pride in their traditional culture and shame over their muddied linguistic heritage.

Identifying the "problem"

The "problem," according to the elite, is twofold: 'Enana has been sullied by contact with Tahitian, English, and French, and it has been simplified by lazy, ignorant "youth"[7] who refuse to learn it correctly. The French roots of this logic and the use of the French term charabia and its 'Enana-ized counterpart sarapia[8] to index the problem can be traced in the public and everyday discourse of both the elite and the nonelite.

Charabia, possibly derived from Provençal charrá 'to chat', was first applied in the nineteenth century to a stigmatized dialect in Paris, that of the coal sellers from Auvergne, perhaps ascribable to their shibboleth replacement of /s/ with /š/, in a manner interpreted as a form of lisping (Imbs 1977). Presumably, the term first appeared in the Marquesas in the late nineteenth or early twentieth century in the mouths of French missionaries and educators who used it to castigate young 'Enana for their "mixed-up" French. For example, one young mother reported in 1993 that her French teacher had used the term to scold her class for constantly introducing mea, an 'Enana filler meaning 'thing', into every French phrase.

The haka'iki 'chief, mayor' of Hatiheu used the term consistently in 1993 and 2003 to discuss the linguistic incompetence of the children who come to purchase items at her store. Her typical example is the phrase maka manini 'big candy' which should, she prescribes, be manini maka 'candy big'—the normal noun-adjective order should not be reversed in 'Enana as it would be in French in this case.[9] Very few 'Enana of the *haka'iki*'s generation attended secondary school; nonetheless, she did attend for several years the Catholic boarding school for girls which was established in the archipelago in the 1880s. Additionally, as an adult she has enjoyed friendly relations with French administrators, teachers, and doctors who reside on the island and come to her restaurant and bungalows for weekend getaways. Thus, I hypothesize that she learned her prescriptivist attitudes from the nuns as a child and had them reconfirmed over many years of contact with French professionals.

Similarly, in 1993, the four women who assisted me in transcribing their families' interactions regularly used the term charabia/*sarapia* to critique the recorded utterances of their children. None of these young women were members of the elite, but three of them had completed a couple of years of secondary education. The utterances they critiqued were either gibberish —instances of phonological play or other incomprehensible utterances deemed willful—or grammatically "incorrect." For example, one mother criticized her daughter for the following utterance: Elle ne veut pas donner le livre à elle 'She doesn't want to give the book to her'. In this case, the position of the indirect object is not the preferred one, but it is not ungrammatical in French; however, it is clearly a structural calque from 'Enana. My assistants' sensitivity to and desire to label calques as "incorrect" probably derives from French-language normativist attitudes acquired in school settings concerning not only the rules of grammar but also their inherent inflexibility.[10]

However, the term charabia/*sarapia* was most commonly employed, both in 1993 and in 2003, to complain about both the longtime integration of loanwords in 'Enana as well as the practice of conversational code-switching. In 1993, movement leaders focused primarily on the lexical level, bemoaning the loss of words recorded in the nineteenth-century dictionary (Dordillon 1904) and the addition of borrowings from French, Tahitian, and English. The 'Enana elite evidently adopted not only the word but also the French purist and prescriptivist ideologies underlying it, especially those associated with notions of romantic nationalism and rational enlightenment. Chief among those is the belief that a people's language must manifest ungrafted and unmixed roots deeply embedded in land and blood to clearly and reasonably articulate their ethnic/national identity (Grillo 1989).

But by 2003, I found that the elite had also created an indigenous phrase of critique for the conversational form of mixing: *kohi'i te 'eo* 'tangling the languages'. In 'Enana, *kohi'i* can be used to refer to constructive forms of entanglement, such as nest building, but when the term was applied to *'eo* 'language', the critical connotation was that people were tangling threads of language as they spoke, whether intentionally or not, to no good effect. Once, I suggested during a radio interview with one of the cultural revival leaders that *kohi'i* might be used more positively to refer to a creative 'braiding' of the two languages (as the interview was conducted in French, I chose the verb tresser to capture this notion, a term also used for the culturally relevant art of weaving palm fronds). His response was lukewarm at best as he complained that the youth in particular were simply incapable of keeping their languages apart.

Given this attention to French language ideologies for identifying and labeling the "problem," it is no wonder that 'Enana's movement leaders have also followed French models for dealing with it.

Rectifying the "problem"

Since the sixteenth century, French has been maintained, purified, and codified via official language policies, via institutions such as the Académie française that create dictionaries and grammars, and via schooling and the creation of pedagogical materials. Following the lead of their imperial oppressors, many of the regional movements in France in the 1970s used much the same means to address their own language maintenance problems.[11] That the revival movement in the Marquesas bears a resemblance to these movements is not merely a matter of osmosis: the association named *Motu Haka* (meaning 'assembly' or 'troop', e.g., of dancers), formed in 1978 to safeguard 'Enana cultural patrimony, was spearheaded by the Breton bishop of the archipelago.[12] LeCléac'h made the parallels explicit in interviews and speeches: he did not want to see happen in the Marquesas what had happened to Brittany when he was a boy.

Motu Haka's first project was that of changing the long-standing colonial rules concerning the use of 'Enana at school. As of 1980, students were still being punished for using 'Enana, whether in the classroom or on the playground (experiences of this kind were still fresh in the minds of young parents in 1993). In an abrupt reversal, the Territorial Assembly adopted in 1981 a policy requiring that local languages be taught in schools for two hours a week. Teacher training programs were instituted and some pedagogical materials for primary and secondary school teachers were created; however, real implementation of the policy has been left even now to the abilities and energies of the more creative teachers.

In 2000, the Territorial Assembly decreed the formation of the Académie marquisienne. Their most ambitious project, that of creating a definitive monolingual dictionary and grammar, has been stymied by predictable conflicts concerning orthography and dialectal variation.[13]

However, small steps have been taken. For instance, in 2003, the academy produced and distributed to school teachers a document titled *Mou pona tekao hou* 'Some New Words', which is a list of acceptable loans and neologisms for the expression of Western notions and objects. The academy has also been attempting to encourage literacy in 'Enana through a series of writing competitions for children and adults.

In 2004, the French government officially accorded 'Enana the same status as Tahitian. Though Article 57 identified French as the only official language, it also (a) recognized Tahitian as "a fundamental element of cultural identity," (b) accorded respect and support to three of the other Polynesian languages spoken in the pays ('Enana, Paumotu, and Mangarevian), and (c) stipulated that provisions be made for the teaching and maintenance of all four languages.

These language maintenance efforts are ensconced within other revival initiatives having to do with song, dance, sculpture, and tattooing. Song and dance festivals and arts and crafts exhibitions have attracted lots of media attention and clearly succeeded in instilling pride in indigenous identity, while also providing cultural commodities that are appealing to tourists. However, there are some obvious differences between the ways in which language and the other cultural genres are being revived.

First of all, only in language is the notion of syncretism rejected. In the other cultural genres, old forms are recycled and transformed; they are produced using many modern techniques and equipment; and they are freely mixed with other pan-Polynesian and Western motifs, movements, sounds, and so on. In the case of language, the revival movement elite insist on the necessity of instituting a state of functional diglossia in which only 'Enana will be spoken at home and proper French will be taught at school.

Second, when children are taught to perform and produce other more high-profile aspects of their indigenous culture, their teachers encourage them with compliments and liberally apply the prized indigenous descriptor *kanahau* 'amazing, beautiful'. By contrast, the analysis of the language "problem" and the registers used to socialize new linguistic habits have borrowed heavily from critical French registers and genres.

Critiquing the "problem"

According to Cartesian notions of rationalism (in which the 'Enana are well schooled), problems have root causes that can be rectified via analysis and critique. In the case of social problems, criticism directs attention to the causal behaviors, which concerned individuals are then expected to change, thus resolving the problems. With respect to charabia, students are challenged in school to be self-consciously aware of their grammar and to correct it, thus producing clarified statements. When applied to the "problem" of language shift, the resolution has been sought in first analyzing the root causes and then criticizing the responsible parties and directing them to change their ways.

For instance, movement leaders (many of them teachers and mayors) have criticized 'Enana mothers at public meetings and behind their backs (in ways that got back to the mothers) for speaking French "incorrectly" with their children in the home. The *haka'iki* of Hatiheu routinely accused the newly educated generation of mothers in 1993 of being conceited over their mastery of French and of falling into 'Enana midsentence out of incompetence. Instead of passing on this charabia, these caregivers have been instructed (for instance at Parents-Elèves meetings) to use only 'Enana with their children. These same caregivers, however, also hear that their 'Enana is of questionable merit.

These French corrective registers have been learned at school where French Catholic methods, which generally include more punishment than praise, are still used. In 2003, disciplinary measures in the classroom included ear pulling and fingernail slapping, which the teacher said were gentle by comparison with her own childhood experiences. By contrast, any praise was administered primarily as an example to others. These methods, once used to belittle children's inadequate French, were used to drill and reward them in their minimal (lexicon-based) lessons in 'Enana. As will be analyzed below, these French techniques for "forming" children have also trickled into the home and are used by older siblings, parents, and grandparents.

Thus, the movement leaders have not only analyzed the problem according to classic French models of language maintenance; they have also adopted a style of scolding critique in public discourse with which to implement the cure, that of stamping out the use of charabia in the home. But whereas most parents were aware of these reprimands from on high and reported them to their local anthropologist, few actually corrected their behavior. This is for several reasons. First, the dominant language ideology until the 1980s was that French clearly carried the most symbolic capital and ought therefore to be learned at all costs. After all, most elite families had acquired their status early on in part through giving their children a head start in French before they went to school. As a result, using French with children in the home had developed even in less elite households into an unconscious (and therefore intransigent) habitus. Second, even if they could change their habits, many caregivers were aware that they lacked everyday competence in the "authentic" 'Enana recorded in Dordillon's nineteenth-century dictionary and displayed during the revival movement's song-and-dance performances. Third and finally, these caregivers were simply not as concerned about this as the elite wished them to be. As one caregiver said with a shrug (neither obviously proud nor ashamed): <u>On parle les deux</u> 'We speak the two'.

Given this florescence of ideologies, institutions, and emotional registers stemming from French colonialism, one might reasonably anticipate a total breakdown in the actual transmission of even a much-transformed variety of the indigenous language. The codified literary version of 'Enana would be left to academics, whereas children would give up all attempts to speak the shameful *sarapia* of their elders, preferring instead to perfect a variety of school-taught French that, though "substandard" by Parisian standards, would feel adequate for local usage. This code, passed on to their children and supported by 'Enana teachers, would then gain currency in most contexts and for most functions from home to school to street life to business and administration.[14] But in the Marquesas, that has not so far been the result of these shifting language ideologies.

Shifting language ideologies and the socialization of everyday praxis

In 1993, my analysis of why children were speaking far less 'Enana than were the youth (adolescents and young adults) mostly confirmed the 'Enana elite's fears: 'Enana had apparently arrived at the "tipping point" (Dorian 1989) in which the youngest generation was failing to acquire the productive competence necessary to model and reproduce the language in their own children (Riley 1996a, 1996b). However, informal data collected during my trip in 2000 led me to question this teleological model of inevitable language death. I discovered that the children who had preferred French in 1993 were as youth in 2000 manifesting an increased competency in and valuation of 'Enana as well as *sarapia*.

I returned in 2003 to explore two possible explanations for this state of affairs: (1) the cultural revival movement had managed to nip language shift in the bud; or (2) a variety of conditions were supporting the adolescent reacquisition of 'Enana. Following my analysis of these new data, I have now concluded that the maintenance of a variety of 'Enana is occurring partly because of the valorization of *te Henua 'o te 'Enana* and the 'Enana lifestyle but also partly in spite of twenty-five years of cultural revival work and ideological haranguing on the part of the movement elite.

In this section, I examine two sociocultural factors that frame the socialization process: the maintenance of indigenous household structures and the return migration patterns that are having a transformative effect on language use and ideology.

I then use two transcribed episodes from the Pahuatini family in 2003 to illustrate the ways in which shifting language ideologies and use patterns are established via specific language socialization processes. I look first at issues of code choice—which linguistic varieties are employed by whom in which contexts and how this may affect children's acquisition of linguistic resources and of strategies for shifting between them. Second, I explore the origins of several socializing techniques and communicative genres and their influence on shifting language ideologies in the Marquesas.

Socialization contexts

Indigenous household structures take the form of extended family compounds, which promote multigenerational interaction and thus help to maintain indigenous language use patterns and ideologies. A typical example, the Pahuatini compound in 1993 spanned three generations: the elderly couple Meama and Kooua, their four youngest offspring (Teiki, age 18, Huki, age 17, Tahia, age 16, and Rafa, age 10), and one of their grandchildren (Siki, age 2). By 2003, Meama and Kooua still headed a multigenerational family consisting now of Tahia, Rafa, his wife, Georgina, and their daughter, Titikua (age 4), as well as Teiki, his wife, Lorenza, and their son, Ludovique (age 3). Thus, the youngest children at both periods were privy to and engaged in the interactions of kin ranging from adolescents to middle-aged grandparents, most of whom spoke 'Enana or *sarapia* much of the time. All of the other families in Hatiheu demonstrated much the same structural tendencies, and these had been reproduced or even strengthened by the time I returned for fieldwork in 2003.

By contrast, the return migration patterns of Hatiheu's adolescents and young adults have had a transformative effect on the household and village contexts in which both children and returning youth have been socialized. Not only do returnees speak differently than do villagers who have never left; they also provoke and produce contradictory language ideologies.

For several generations, increasing numbers of children and adolescents have left the village for schooling elsewhere in the islands. Now most Hatiheu children complete primary school in Hatiheu, many move on to secondary school at one of the three towns in the Marquesas, and some continue to higher degrees in Tahiti or even France. Beginning in the 1960s, some villagers (men in particular) used their secondary education or military service to find employment in Tahiti, elsewhere in the French Pacific, or in France. Usually, they found blue-collar work, but a few found jobs as civil servants, some even returning to teach in the Marquesas or to go into politics (the original revival movement elite). Of those who did not return, many married non-'Enana and moved to their spouse's archipelago. In keeping with this pattern, all but one of Meama and Kooua's older children had dispersed as a result of schooling, military service, employment, and/or marriage; but none had lost contact with the village. For example, the eldest son in France brought his French wife and daughter to Hatiheu for several weeks every summer.

However, beginning in the early 1990s, employment opportunities began to dry up elsewhere in French Polynesia as a result of the curtailed nuclear testing industry; by contrast, civil service jobs in the Marquesas were opened up to 'Enana with sufficient education. By 2003, a return migration pattern was evident, with some people coming home after decades away and others after only recently finishing (or not) their secondary degrees.

Some even returned with domestic partners that reversed earlier patterns of out-migration; for instance, Teiki's wife, Lorenza, was Tahitian, and Rafa's wife, Georgina, came from an elite 'Enana family (she had been raised in Tahiti, had completed her university-level teaching degree, and was presently teaching at the village school). Both of these women were clearly making attempts to integrate into village life by acquiring (or, in Georgina's case, reacquiring) 'Enana, as illustrated by their use of 'Enana and *sarapia* (see Appendix A 106–124[r] and Appendix B 41[d]).

In 1993, people who had been working in Tahiti or France returned in some sense with their tails between their legs, and though they had gained some prestigious fluency in Tahitian and/or French, they found on returning that they had to reacquire 'Enana or be ostracized in the village. In particular, they would be mocked for mixing up 'Enana with Tahitian. However, by 2003, *te Henua 'o te 'Enana* was no longer perceived as a savage backwater to return to in defeat; instead, the people returned articulating a back-to-the-land ideology about the allure of life in these remote islands where one did not need to make money to live. Knowledge of 'Enana was certainly a membership card, but fluency in unmixed 'Enana was no longer required. Instead, *sarapia* was becoming an unconscious index of a kind of hybrid "cool": the integration of traditional and cosmopolitan identities.

The traditional indigenous households peopled in part by these returning migrants provide a richly transformative socialization context for children and adolescents, who are acquiring and reacquiring linguistic varieties as well as language ideologies about their uses.

Socializing code choice in Hatiheu

The interactions in which children are engaged in village life provide them with both the social contexts and the linguistic access needed for at least a passive acquisition of the grammar and phonology of 'Enana (if a somewhat limited lexicon) as well as an understanding of the value and uses of *sarapia*. Their comprehension of the semantic and pragmatic meanings proves that the linguistic input is not falling on deaf ears, as does their competent production of many 'Enana forms, some as young children and others as returning adolescents.

In both 1993 and 2003, women tended to use something approximating standard French more than men did, whereas men manifested a wider range of registers in 'Enana, from crass joking to political oratory. However, generally speaking, adults and adolescents primarily used 'Enana or *sarapia* among themselves in village settings—at home or at church, while gardening or doing copra, playing bingo or partying—that is, in all but the most obviously French-defined contexts such as schools, administrative offices, or public meetings. Thus, most of the interactions among adults and adolescents in the presence of children tended to be in 'Enana or *sarapia*, providing them with plenty of exposure to these codes even when utterances were not directed at them. For instance, the sixty-six-year-old Meama and her twenty-six-year-old daughter, Tahia, always spoke to each other in 'Enana (see A 20–23[f]), and this pattern was also followed with her twelve-year old grandson, Siki (A 84–86[o]), although this was not always the case in 1993, when he was two years old (as it was also not true of her interactions with the four-year old Titikua in 2003—see below). Even the most French-oriented Georgina would switch to *sarapia* and 'Enana to speak with Meama (A 106–124[r]).

Also, during both time periods, almost all caregivers over the age of twelve used both French and 'Enana with children. The oldest males were the least likely to use French with the children, whereas even the oldest females would sometimes use French, especially for socializing commands concerning politesse (e.g., Meama scolding Titikua for making a farting noise as in A 132[u]) or to quote their grand-children (e.g., A 112–116[s]). In 2003, the well-educated Georgina used substantially more French with her daughter (e.g., A 1–19[a], 75–88[l]) than did the mothers in 1993. However, the three other young mothers in 2003 displayed a usage that much more closely resembled that of all the mothers in 1993: they used a generous mix of both languages for all types of speech acts from commands to teases.[15]

In general, all female caregivers sometimes used 'Enana to address children, especially for household commands and reprimands or in front of children to tease them, as when Tahia used 'Enana to say that she and Georgina would accompany me home in a way that excluded Titikua (A 10–11[c]). In general, younger males or male-identified women (both Tahia and Titi fit into this category)[16] were most likely to use 'Enana to tease or engage playfully with children, as did Titi with Titikua in B 16–21[a].

As a result of this extensive exposure to 'Enana, all of the children in the stud-ies showed that they understood utterances in 'Enana by answering appropriately, whether or not they did so in 'Enana and whether or not they themselves were being directly addressed. For instance, the four-year-old Titikua, who had been living in the Marquesas for less than a year, sometimes responded in French, as in her rebuttal (A 12–13[d]) to Tahia's teasing threat (A 10–11[c]) to exclude her, and sometimes in 'Enana, as when she inserted herself into Titi and Siki's discussion of what was for dinner by insisting it was not chicken, but pork (B 54–56[g]).

However, the children displayed a wide range in their interests and abilities to produce utterances in 'Enana, from early competent production of a variety of multi-word utterances to minimal production of routinized phrases or selected lexical items for locally significant objects. For example, Siki at the age of two produced a large number of multiword utterances in 'Enana, far more than he produced in French, while Titikua's abilities at the age of four were limited to a few stock phrases such as the mantras from her 'Enana-language class at school: *Tekao 'enana tatou... 'A 'e tekao hao 'e* (A 46–52[i]), and some culturally laden words such as *puaka* 'pig' (B 54–56[g]). However in A 79[m], she apparently whispered in her mother's ear the epithet *karaihi* (a multivalent word meaning not only 'rice', but also 'uncircumcised penis' and 'stupid foreigner') in reference to the stupid researcher (me) who had misheard her phrase gros mon 'big my' as gros mot 'bad word'. In other words, she was not only in command of the rich spectrum of semantic connotations of the actual gros mot *karaihi*; she also knew how to use it in a culturally complex and appropriate way (i.e., as an insulting aside) to index the visiting anthropologist's incompetence by contrast with her own linguistic competence, a competence she persisted in dis-playing despite her mother's attempts to silence her (A 79–87[m]).

Finally, returning adolescents and young adults used both 'Enana and *sarapia* among themselves, as the exchanges among Siki, Titi, and even the Tahitian Lorenza aptly display in appendix B. Some of the very same individuals who had as children in 1993 expressed a preference for and used more French were by 2003 displaying in practice and explicitly articulating a preference for 'Enana. For instance, Rafa used a lot more 'Enana with his daughter Titikua than he had with Siki when they were younger. And one adolescent reported to me in 2003 that she used 'Enana now at school in Tahiti, whereas as a child she never uttered more than single words and did even that only to prove to me that she knew some 'Enana. Finally, some youth expressed transgressive beliefs about shifting languages (i.e., about both mixing them up in conversation and having them change over historical time) that directly contradicted the elite ideology. One who had just returned from working at the nuclear testing facility on Moruroa in 1993 articulated elegantly (if drunkenly) his pleasure over the mixed-up and ever-changing state of his language, which would make it impossible for foreigners to ever learn, understand, or fix in their notebooks.

Thus, shifts in language use and ideology between 1993 and 2003 were less apparent in the repertoires and ideologies associated with particular social categories (e.g., women and men, children and adults) than in the usage and beliefs of particular individuals. Men generally still used more 'Enana than women, who used somewhat more French. Similarly, children still spoke more French than 'Enana, whereas adults in general spoke both French and 'Enana with children and more 'Enana and *sarapia* with other adults. However, individuals who had as children in 1993 preferred French were as adolescents in 2003 manifesting pride in and an ability to speak 'Enana as well as a more or less conscious engagement in the production of *sarapia*.

How had this happened? Aside from the maintenance and transformation of certain language ideologies and usages, there was also the reproduction of socialization genres, both French and 'Enana, which allowed for this shift in the linguistic repertoire of the community.

Socialization techniques, communicative genres,
and shifting language ideologies

In both 1993 and 2003, caregivers used a recognizable repertoire of French correction methods which were frequent, direct, and punitive for children's behaviors. These included slaps, threats to slap, and threats to tell Papa (who would slap). Additionally, verbal commands and reprimands borrowed the phrase il faut into 'Enana, indicative of the French origin of this directive speech act. In playing with Titikua, Titi reproduced these methods in teasing mode as when she threatened to pull the little girl's ears (B 16–17[a]) or used (il) faut to "reprimand" her for the misdemeanor (by French standards) of sticking her tongue out (B 27[b]). By 2003, young mothers (by contrast with those in 1993) were beginning to provide rationales for why a child should or should not do something in ways that recall the Cartesian influences discussed above. For instance, Georgina told Titikua to eat her manioc because it would be "good" for her (A 6–8[b]).

By contrast, indigenous techniques for socializing preferred behaviors and dealing with misbehaviors were far less direct. The most common 'Enana way of inhibiting undesirable behaviors was teasing, whether directly to someone or indirectly in front of them but not to them. For example, in response to Titikua's disapproved eating behavior, Georgina's direct critique (A 1–8[a]) seems decidedly French by contrast with Tahia's indigenous teasing (A 10–16[c]), an effective ploy, which Georgina freely exploits a few lines later (A 18–19[e]). This speech genre known as *keu* is used in all sorts of situations both by caregivers with children and by children and adolescents among themselves—note the way Titi *keu*s with both Titikua throughout appendix B and with the older Siki (B 46–48[f])—and functions in psychosocial ways to socialize persons into a certain flexibility of character. For example, Meama, Kooua, and Georgina join together to tease Titikua for how much she talks in A 94–128[q], but the precocious Titikua attempts to have the final *keu* with her farting joke (A 129–135[t]).

Rather than explain to a child how something ought to be done, the 'Enana way is to model correct behaviors and request that they be mimicked as in the *pe'au* 'say-it' routines. For example, Meama not only told Titikua to mock her grandfather for having said he speaks American; she also gave Titikua the precise phrase and tone with which to say: 'You don't know the American language' (A 54–55[j]). In this example, Titikua is being shown how to *keu* with her grandfather, a behavior that would probably not be encouraged in most French families, certainly not modeled by the grandmother. And given Titikua's other jokes during this short dinner segment, it is clear that the coaching has already had the desired results (though she did not in this instance perform as Meama directed her).

Combinations of French and 'Enana socialization genres also occurred. Caregivers would use a French-style reprimand within a teasing framework (e.g., Titi threatening to pull Titikua's ears while tickling her in B 16–17[a]). Alternatively, caregivers may first reprimand a child for teasing another child and then tease that child to make him or her stop teasing.

French education and socialization methods have not been entirely detrimental to the development and manifestation of cultural pride. French education teaches children to display knowledge via talk. Thus, French-influenced children such as Titikua spoke much more and more publicly than did children immersed in village life, such as Siki in 1993. Meama was always commanding Siki to speak for my tape recorder (Siki and Tahia allude to this in A 42–44[h], as do I more explicitly in A 91–92[p]), whereas Titikua could not be shut up throughout both of these taping sessions. French-influenced parents encouraged very young children to report and explain things, unlike more traditional parents, who did not expect 'Enana children to speak much before the age of five. And the French-influenced children appeared most interested in displaying even their very limited knowledge of 'Enana (e.g., Titikua's display of the school mantra and her discussion of *karaihi* in appendix A). Thus, the pride in indigenous culture encouraged by the revival movement was exhibited using French-style elicitation and performance methods.

French genres used by the local elite to criticize villagers for not maintaining 'Enana in the home could also have hurt cultural pride. However, the indigenous teasing genre *keu* and the flexibility of character that it engenders have played an important role in counteracting the elite critique. Youth returning home from school, whether for brief vacations or more permanently to take up family life and village employment, have engaged children and each other via *keu* in ways that overcome the linguistic shame impressed upon the population by French pedagogy at school and by the French-influenced rhetoric of their *haka'iki*.

Not only has *keu* socialized a subversive playful pride in being 'Enana; it has also allowed adolescents and young adults to repossess their sense of competence in 'Enana. Primarily performed in 'Enana and/or *sarapia*, this indigenous genre has allowed for the activation of the youth's passive knowledge of 'Enana and the extension of their vocabulary through practical use. It has also engaged them in the appropriate (if not prescriptively "correct") 'entangling' of 'Enana, French, Tahitian, and English. The exchange between Titi and Siki in B 30–63[c] provides an excellent illustration of the interplay of this joking style and the use of what the elite would consider *sarapia*.

In other words, whereas the elite use French-style modes to criticize the youth for their 'Enana, the intention being to reinstate the "pure" code and extinguish the "mixed-up" one, the youth employ the traditional genre of *keu* to transform the ideology and reconstitute the code.

Conclusion

Building on Joseph Errington's application of the phrase "shifting languages" to refer not only to language shift at the societal level but also to code-shifting at the discourse level (1998), the present chapter investigates how ideologies concerning language shift at the macro level may interact productively with the ideologies that influence agents' code-switching strategies in particular contexts. Though shifts in the dominant language ideology may establish overt prestige for two distinctive "pure" codes and promote their diglossic separation, a subversive ideology may simultaneously emerge which engenders a more or less covert prestige for a code-switching code used by speakers to index their heteroglossic identities (see Makihara 2004 and chap. 3 of this volume for an analysis of some similar issues in Rapa Nui).

Language ideologies are undeniably shifting in the Marquesas—especially ideologies about how shifting languages (whether in midsentence or across generations) occurs and about whether it has any value. In the late 1970s, official ideology shifted. 'Enana went from being of little value, best left out of all civilized enterprises, to having enough symbolic capital to be used in the Territorial Assembly. It became the launching pad of a reasonably well subsidized revival movement at least so long as the 'Enana was kept "pure." However, the official word took longer to trickle down to caregivers in the villages, who were already speaking <u>charabia</u>. And in the 1990s, when adolescents and young adults returned from secondary school and unemployed from jobs in Tahiti speaking *sarapia*, ideologies shifted once again, if at a covert level.

Since then, the indigenous communicative system (consisting of local speech genres and socializing routines) has interacted productively with the imported one to produce and maintain an identity-marking state of heteroglossia. From this *karaihi*'s perspective, entangling the languages may yet prove to serve a strategic, nest-building function.

Appendix A

Setting: Evening meal (1/16/03), participants seated around kitchen table.

Participants: Titikua (female/4.9), Siki (m/11.9), Georgina (f/20), Tahia (f/26), Meama (f/66), Kooua (m/70), and Kate (researcher)

L#	G(eorgina)	Ti(tikua)	Ta(hia), S(iki), Ka(te), Ko(oua), M(eama)
1	**[a]** <u>Bé, mange</u>		
2	<u>correctement. Mange ton</u>		
3	<u>pain.</u> *Titikua!* [Babe, eat		
4	correctly. Eat your bread.	<u>Je veux pas. Je veux pas.</u> [I	
5	Titikua!]	don't want. I don't want to.]	
6	**[b]** <u>Tu manges que de</u>		
7	<u>bananes? Mange les</u>		
8	<u>maniocs. C'est bon.</u>		
9	[You eat only bananas?	<u>Je veux pas.</u> [I don't want to].	
10	Eat the manioc. It's		**[c]** Ta (to G): *Na taua e*
11	good.]		*kave.* [It's for us two to take
12	(makes affirmative	**[d]** <u>Eh quoi? Qu'est-ce</u>	(Kate home).]
		<u>qu'on va</u>	
13	eyebrow flash at Ta)	<u>amener</u>? [What? What is it we	
14		are going to take?]	Ta: <u>Tu restes.</u> [You're
15		<u>Non!</u> [No!]	staying.]
16			Ta: <u>Si!</u> [Yes!]
17		<u>Non, je viens.</u> [No, I'm	
		coming.]	
18	**[e]**<u>Eh ben, tu manges,</u>		
19	<u>eh?</u> [Well, you eat,		
20	okay?]	(begins to eat)	**[f]** M: *'Enā me ta ia*
21			*okaoka?.* [Does she (Kate)
22			have a fork?]
23			Ta: *'O ia, me ta ia okaoka.*
24			[Yes, she has her fork.]
25	…	…	…
26	<u>Siki, donne-moi un peu le</u>		
27	<u>saladier.</u> [Siki, give me		

28	please the bowl.]		
29	Le saladier. [The bowl.]		
30			(S passes the bowl of
31	Merci. [Thanks.]		chicken and papaya to G)
32		Comment? On dit "De rien."	
33		"De rien," on dit. "De rien."	
34		"Merci." Dis chez Maman.	
35		[What? One says "You're	[g] M: Tu manges pas bien.
36		welcome." "You're welcome,"	Tu manges pas bien, bébé.
37		one says. "You're welcome."	On regarde. On te filme.
38		"Thanks." Say to Mama.]	[You're not eating well.
39			You're not eating well,
40			babe. One's watching.
41			One's filming you.]
42			[h] S: Parlez! [Speak!]
43		Parlez, parlez en français.	
44		[Speak, speak in French.]	Ta: En marquisien [In
45		Français. [French.]	'Enana.]
46		[i] Tekao 'enana tatou [We all	
47		speak 'Enana.]	M: Voilà! [There!]
48	...	...	...
49		'A 'e tekao hao 'e. [We don't	
50		speak foreigner (language).]	Ko: Tekao menike. Tekao
51			menike. [(We) speak
52		Tekao 'enana tatou. [We all	American. (We) speak
53		speak 'Enana.]	American.] (laughs)
54			[j] M: Pe'au 'oe "'A'e 'oe
55			'ite te 'eo menike." [You
56			say 'You don't know the
57			American language.']
58			S: What's your name?
59		XXX (trying to mimic S)	(ENG)
60	...	...	...

(contd.)

Appendix A   (contd.)

L#	G(eorgina)	Ti(tikua)	Ta(hia), S(iki), Ka(te), Ko(oua), M(eama)
61		C'est gros mon *kopu*	
62		maintenant. [My stomach is big	
63		(full) now.]	**[k]** Ka: <u>Ah oui? Qu'est-ce</u>
64			<u>qui est un gros mot?</u> [Oh
65		(explaining to Kate) <u>Le</u> *ma'a*	yeah? What's a bad word?]
66		(TAH). [(Big with) the food	M: (laughs)
67		(TAH).]	Ta: *Kaikai.* [Food.]
68			Ka: <u>Oui. Pas un gros mot,</u> le
69			*ma'a* (TAH). [Yes. Not a
70	<u>Non, c'est</u> *kaikai* <u>en</u>		bad word, the *ma'a.*]
71	<u>tahitien, le</u> *ma'a* (TAH).		
72	[No, it's food in		
73	Tahitian, the *ma'a.*]		
73	<u>C'est grand, son</u> *kopu.*		
74	[It's big, her stomach.]		
75	**[l]** (to Ti) <u>Tu as rien</u>		
76	<u>mangé. Il y a rien dans</u>		
77	<u>ton ventre.</u> [You've eaten		
78	nothing. There's nothing		
79	in your stomach.]	**[m]** (whispers in G's ear)	
80	**[n]** <u>Tu es bête.</u> [You're		
81	an idiot.]	<u>Non.</u> (laughs) <u>J'ai bien</u> <u>appris le</u>	
82		<u>marquisien.</u> *Karaihi* <u>c'est</u> <u>le riz.</u>	(S. passes between the table
83		[No, I've learned 'Enana well.	and the camera.)
84	<u>Tu veux manger du riz?</u>	*Karaihi* is rice.]	**[o]** M: (to S.) *Hano kaukau*
85	[You want to eat some	<u>Non, je veux pas manger</u> <u>du riz.</u>	*'i te vai. Ti'ohi te'ā ha'ina.*
86	rice?]	*Karaihi,* <u>c'est le riz, riz.</u> [No, I	*'Ua tu to 'oe 'ima.* [Go take
87		don't want to eat any rice.	a shower. Watch that thing
88	*Kua! Kua,* <u>tu arrêtes!</u>	*Karaihi* is rice, rice.]	(camera). Your hand hit it.]

89	[Kua! Kua, you stop!]	J'en traine de parler, toute seule.	
90		[I'm speaking, all alone.]	
91			[p] Ka: C'est le contraire à
92			Siki. [It's (she's) the
93			opposite of Siki.]
94			[q] M: Tekao, tekao, tekao.
95	Desfois, desfois tu es	(begins singing theme from	[Talk, talk, talk.]
96	fatigué de l'entendre	Mexican TV show, correctly	
97	parler. [Sometimes,	pronouncing some of the	
98	sometimes you're tired	Spanish words, inventing	
99	of hearing her talk.]	others)	Ka: Oui. [Yes.]
100	C'est fatigant. Si elle		
101	parle pas, elle crie. Si		
102	elle crie pas, elle chante.		
103	[It's tiring. If she doesn't		M: Ti'ohi au ta ia, ma'akau
104	talk, she yells. If she		ia tekao kanea pu ia ta ia
105	doesn't yell, she sings.]		tekao. [When I look at her, I
106	[r] Mea au oko 'ia		think she's just making up
107	amerder te 'enana. Il faut		her talk.]
108	hano ha'ateakao 'ia ia.		
109	[She likes a lot bothering		
110	people. (She) has to go		
111	after making (them) talk	Attention! [Listen!]	
112	to her.]		[s] M: Kaponei pe'au 'ia u
113			"Regarde mon papa. Voilà,
114			dans la mer. Regarde."
115			Ma'akau nei au eia na te
116		(her puppy is underfoot)	tua ha'e. [Before she said to
117		Noni, mon petit chien. Noni,	me "Look at my Papa.
118		mon grand chiot. Maintenant	There, in the ocean. Look!"
119		mon petit chiot, il est grand.	I thought he was behind the

(contd.)

Appendix A   (contd.)

L#	G(eorgina)	Ti(tikua)	Ta(hia), S(iki), Ka(te), Ko(oua), M(eama)
120	*Kua,* assis-toi, assis-toi.	[Noni, my little dog. Noni, my	house.]
121	[Kua, sit down. Sit	big puppy. Now my little puppy	M: *'Ia noho ia ma 'i'a va'e*
122	down.]	is big.]	*ia ta'a 'enana.* [When she
123	*Kaponei va'e ta'a 'ia 'ua*		stays outside, she calls to
124	*Dadu 'ia Philipo.*		people.]
125	[Before she was calling		Ko: *Va'e pe'au "Dadu,*
126	to those two, Dadu and		*memai."* [(She) was saying
127	Phillipo (neighboring		"Dadu, come here."]
128	children).]		M: *Pa'opa'o Dadu.* [Dadu
129		**[t]** Non, j'ai dit à *Dadu* "Faut	was tired.]
130		faire le pétard." [No, I said to	
131		*Dadu* "Must make the little	
132		fireworks/farts."]	**[u]** M: Nooon. [Nooo.]
133		(makes fireworks/ farting noise	
134		with tongue between teeth)	Ta: *Iii!* (scolding)
135		C'est qui a pété? [Who farted?]	
136			M: (laughs)
137			Ta: C'est toi, *ho'i!* [It's you,
138			really!]

Appendix B

Setting: Going-away party for Titi (1/10/03); in the kitchen, women are preparing food; outside, men are grilling, drinking, and setting food out on table under an open-air, tin-roofed area.

Participants: Ludovique (m/3.3), Titikua (f/4.9), Siki (m/11.9), Titi (f/20), Tahia (f/26), Lorenza (f/25?), Taiara (m/43?).

L#	Titikua (Tk)	Titi (Ti)	Lud(ovique), Lor(enza), K(ate), S(iki), Ta(hia)
1	(seated on K's lap on	(seated on floor talking to Ta.)	
2	floor, looking at Ti in		K: (reverses screen so Ti can
3	video screen)		see herself) Titi peut regarder.
4	*Titi nnnn!* (sticking		[Titi can look.]
5	tongue out at Ti,	*E a?* Eh bon! [What? Oh good!]	
6	laughing)	(seeing herself in screen)	
7	C'est en bas. [It's		
8	down.] (trying to		K: (shifts camera down)
9	point camera down)	(wiggles thumb and pinky,	Voilà! [There!]
10		laughing)	K: Tu vas par là. Tu vas par
11			là. Tu vas chez Titi. [You go
12	(goes and gets in Ti's		there. You go there. You go
13	lap; wiggles thumb		sit with Titi.]
14	and pinky, laughing)	(nibbles Tk's thumb)	
15	*Ai ai ai ai!*		
16	[Ow ow ow ow!]	[a] *E moi e kere. To'o 'ia 'e au*	
17		*tenā puaika 'o 'oe.* [Don't fight.	Lud: (trying to come in door)
18	(opens the door for	Your ears will be pulled by me.]	Titi, ouvre la porte. [Titikua,
19	Lud, dances a few		open the door.]
20	steps, and returns to	*Tenā vaevae 'o 'oe. Tenā vaevae*	(Lud comes in, hides from the
21	Ti's lap)	*'o 'oe.* [That foot of yours. That	camera)

(contd.)

Appendix B   (contd.)

L#	Titikua (Tk)	Titi (Ti)	Lud(ovique), Lor(enza), K(ate), S(iki), Ta(hia)
22		foot of yours.]	
23	(foot in the air) <u>Y a</u>		
24	<u>plus mon pied.</u> [No		
25	more my foot.]	*Aaaa!* (grabsTitikua's foot)	
26	*Ai ai!* (sticks out her		
27	tongue)	**[b]** <u>Faut pas tirer la langue.</u>	
28		[Mustn't stick out your tongue.]	
29	…	…	…(Siki enters the kitchen)
30		**[c]** (to Siki) *Sea Faio?* [Where's	
31		Faio?]	S: *Sea 'oti.* [Don't know.]
32		*'A he mea 'uka 'ā?* [Not up there	
33		(at Tehono's)?]	S: *Aa.* (shrugs)
34		*Enā ha'ana me te kio'e mate 'i*	
35		*'uka me Ara – me Faio.* [There's	
36	(looking at food on	maybe a dead rat up there with	S: *Ae?* [Yeah?]
37	counter) <u>Moi, je veux</u>	Ara – with Faio.]	
38	<u>les œufs.</u> [<u>Me</u>, I want		
39	the eggs.]		T: (to Tk) *Sea?* [Where (are
40			the eggs)?]
41	*Sea 'oti.* [Don't		**[d]** Lor: *'I 'uka 'iō* <u>Mami.</u>
42	know.]	**[e]** <u>Eh, tu me tapes</u>	[(The eggs are) up there at
43	<u>Non! Ow! Okay okay</u>	<u>seulement?</u> [Hey, you're spanking me?]	Grandma's.]
44	<u>okay.</u> [No! Ow! Okay	(begins pinching Tk again)	Lud: (calling Tk) *Titi!*
45	okay okay.]		S: *'A 'i ve'a te kaikai?* [The
46		**[f]** *Ha tenā! 'Ua 'oke?* [What's	food's not ready yet?]
47		that! (You're) hungry already?]	S: *'Ua au 'oke.* [I'm hungry.]

48		Go to hell you! (ENG)	
49			S: *'A'o'e. 'A'i 'oke.* [No.
50		*Mitipeu* (TAH) *'a'o'e, enā me te*	(I'm) not hungry.]
51		*tapu kaikai 'i vaho.* [If not (TAH)	
52		no, there's a table of food outside.]	S: *E aha, moa?* [What's it,
53		*Ma'akau* <u>oui</u>. [Maybe yes.]	chicken?]
54	[g] *'A'o'e. Puaka!*		
55	[No. (It's) pig!]	(pinches Titikua)	
56	*Aaai! Puaka!*		
57	[Owww! Pig!]		S: *Heke maka nei na maua me*
58			*Huki.* [(I'll) go down and get
59		*Uu?* [Huh?]	some for Huki and me.]
60			*Na maua me Huki.* [For Huki
61		*Uu? 'A'i – 'a'e heke mai* <u>Tonton</u>	and me.]
62		*Huki?* [Huh? Uncle Huki hasn't –	
63		isn't coming down?]	S: *'O ia.* [Yes (he will).]

Notes

The National Science Foundation and Wenner-Gren generously supported my doctoral fieldwork in 1992–1993, and Wenner-Gren provided a subsequent postdoctoral write-up and follow-up research grant in 2002–2003. The long list of those who have aided me in the field and beyond will always be incomplete but must include at least the following: Pierre, Vaha, Heidy, Robert, Denise, Yvonne, Moi, Noella, Manu, Tapu, Teresi, Georgina, Perena, Caroline, and the many children. Thanks to all and to Neil and Anna, without whose support neither the research nor the stamina to write it up would have been possible. I am grateful to Miki Makihara and Bambi Schieffelin for exceptionally insightful editorial support. This essay is dedicated in fond memory to Meama Pahuatini (1937–2004).

1. Indigenous terms for the Marquesas, its people, and its language vary by region. In the south, the archipelago is referred to as *te Fenua 'o te 'Enata* and in the north as *te Henua 'o te 'Enana*—literally 'the Land of the People'—and their language is designated as *te 'eo 'enata* and *te 'eo 'enana,* respectively. Though use of the French terms <u>les Marquises</u> and <u>marquisien</u> avoids the necessity of choosing between the regional variants, it also undermines the people's initiative to index their cultural identity with an indigenous term. Thus, for publications

and institutional names, a choice is made; I use '*Enana* because I worked in the north. As discussed at more length below, orthography is also an issue in the Marquesas; I follow the standard pan-Polynesian linguistic practice of using apostrophes for glottal stops and macrons for long vowels.

2. As elaborated in all of the chapters in this volume, "language ideologies" (Irvine and Gal 2000; Kroskrity 2000; Schieffelin, Woolard, and Kroskrity 1998; Silverstein 1979) refers to ideologies about the forms, functions, and meanings signaled by language in general as well as to ideologies about the value and uses of specific linguistic varieties.

3. For more about the socialization of communicative resources and cultural values in multilingual/multicultural contexts, see Garrett 2005, Garrett and Baquedano-López 2002, Kulick 1992, Paugh 2005, Zentella 1997.

4. The TOM of DOM-TOM (Départements d'Outre-mer-Territoires d'Outre-mer) was transformed into the more diversified COM (Collectivités d'Outre-mer) in March 2003. Within this collectivity, French Polynesia was reclassified from territoire into pays in early 2004 by way of a many-articled statute (Loi organique no 2004-192 du 27 février 2004 portant statut d'autonomie de la Polynésie française). This, building on the local powers granted by earlier statutes in 1976, 1984, and 1996, extended once again the powers of the French Polynesian government in preparation for eventual independence.

5. Substantial research devoted to understanding the prehistoric and early colonial periods in the Marquesas has been undertaken by both archaeologists (Suggs 1960; Rolett 1998; Ottino-Garanger 2006) and ethnohistorians (Thomas 1990; Dening 1980). Ethnographic research began in the late nineteenth century with the work of von den Steinen ([1925–1928] 2005), and continued with that of Handy (1923) and Kirkpatrick (1983). Linguistic, sociolinguistic, and ethnolinguistic work has been undertaken by Cablitz (2002), Lavondès (1972), and Tetahiotupa (2000).

6. In 1993, research took the form of a ten-month ethnographic study of language socialization and cultural identity in Hatiheu, a village of approximately a hundred persons on one of the larger islands of the Marquesan archipelago. Subsequently, two short field studies were undertaken in 2000 and 2003 involving three-week stays in Hatiheu. All three studies were contextualized by several weeks of sociolinguistic research in Tahiti and a number of other Marquesan villages and towns. Both the 1993 and 2003 periods of fieldwork incorporated the methodology first formulated by Schieffelin and Ochs for the study of language socialization (Ochs 1979, 1988; Schieffelin 1979, 1990), in which caregivers (usually mothers) assisted me in transcribing the recorded discourse of children and their caregivers (see Riley 2001 for a detailed description of this methodology). Transcribed data from the latest fieldwork period are used to illustrate points in this chapter using the following code:

italics = utterances in 'Enana or Tahitian

underlined = utterances in French or English

[ ] = loose translations provided in square brackets

( ) = contextual or implicit information placed in parentheses

(TAH) = preceding word was in Tahitian (noted in the utterances and the translations)

(ENG) = preceding utterance was in English, so no translation is provided

XXX = unintelligible syllables

– = self-correction

... = section of dialogue elided

Information about the age and gender of participants at the time of the taping is coded in parentheses: e.g., Titikua (f/4.9) means that Titikua was a girl, age four years and nine months.

All references in the chapter to interactions from these transcripts cite the appendix (A or B), the line number(s), and a letter in brackets indicating the spot in the transcripts where the referenced interactions begin.

7. As used in this chapter, "youth" is intended to correlate with the French term les jeunes, which is employed in the Marquesas to refer to young people ranging in age from thirteen to thirty years, and thus encompasses both adolescents and parents of several children. See Riley 2001 for a discussion of the French term's relationship to the indigenous category taure'are'a, analyzed at length in Kirkpatrick 1987.

8. I use the distinction between charabia and sarapia to label utterances that would be considered "incorrect" French or "incorrect" 'Enana, respectively. However, 'Enana do not apply these terms in this way. Instead, they choose the pronunciation based in part, but not exclusively, on which language they are apparently in the midst of speaking.

9. A similar complaint—that the normal French ordering of noun-adjective phrases is being reversed because of the influence of English—is also made in France.

10. As early as 1993, 'Enana was learned at secondary school by memorizing rules from Zewen's 1987 grammar. However, most 'Enana do not discuss grammatical structures. Instead, grandparents use pe'au commands, the local 'say it' routines (see Schieffelin 1990), to model and elicit grammatically correct structures (Riley 2001). Nonetheless, one mother who finished school around the time the cultural revival movement was beginning reported that she had, while at school, used French verbal conjugations as a model in trying to schematize the system of spatial deictics in 'Enana.

11. Recent struggles over marginalized language rights both in mainland France (Basque, Alsace-Lorraine, and Corsica) and in the Départements d'Outre-mer-Territoires d'Outre-mer (Martinique, Guadeloupe, and New Caledonia) have tested France's abilities to accept and celebrate linguistic and cultural diversity within its borders while nonetheless retaining the ideology that French itself is the best language on earth for articulating the Republican values of liberty, equality, and fraternity (Grillo 1989; Ager 1999).

12. See also the history as related by Toti Teikiehuupoku (Sivadjian 1999: 47–50).

13. Dialectal differences lead to arguments over which dialects will be represented where and in what order in titles, word lists, and so on. Orthographic debates arise out of tensions over ethnic identification (Polynesian versus Tahitian versus French) and over the authority of particular texts and "experts." LeCléac'h's recently published French-'Enana dictionary (1997) is a good example of the tensions and confusions that may ensue from dictionary making in a context of extreme dialectal diversity marked by a long history of orthographic variation. The title on the cover represents the northern dialect (Pona Tekao) and the title on the inside title page represents the southern dialect (Pona Te'ao). LeCléac'h also clearly outlined his decision to use the standard orthography employed by linguists of Polynesian languages and yet he left all long vowels unmarked.

14. Such a pattern of language shift has been repeated over and over in other corners of the colonial world, including the Brittany of M. LeCléac'h's youth.

15. For extensive examples of code-switching patterns from 1993, see Riley 2001. One short example to illustrate the similarity between the two time periods is provided here. In 1993, thirty-year-old Noella instructed her eleven-year-old daughter, Perena:

> 'A va'e ta 'oe lecture tatau…. 'A hano haka'ua tatau 'a 'oe. Vas lire ta lecture.
> 'Do your reading reading…. Go get again your reading. Go read your reading.'

In 2003, Perena, now twenty-one, scolded her four-year-old daughter, Amélie:

> Ue keu. Ça va abimer. 'Don't play (with the camera). It'll ruin (it)'.

16. See Riley 2003 for a discussion of gender categories in the Marquesas.

References

Ager, Dennis. 1999. *Identity, Insecurity, and Image: France and Language.* Clevedon, England: Multilingual Matters.

Blom, Jan-Petter, and John Gumperz. 1972. Social Meaning in Linguistic Structures: Code-switching in Norway. In *Directions in Sociolinguistics*, ed. John Gumperz and Dell Hymes, pp. 407–434. New York: Holt, Rinehart, & Winston.

Cablitz, Gabriele Heike. 2002. Marquesan—A Grammar of Space. Ph.D. diss., Christian Albrechts University.

Dening, Greg. 1980. *Islands and Beaches: Discourse on a Silent Land: Marquesas 1774–1880.* Honolulu: University of Hawaii Press.

Dordillon, Ildephonse René. [1904] 1999. *Grammaire et dictionnaire de la langue des Iles Marquises.* Tahiti: Société des Etudes Océaniennes.

Dorian, Nancy C. 1989. *Investigating Obsolescence: Studies in Language Contraction and Death.* Cambridge: Cambridge University Press.

Errington, Joseph. 1998. *Shifting Languages: Interaction and Identity in Javanese Indonesia.* Cambridge: Cambridge University Press.

Fishman, Joshua. 1964. Language Maintenance and Language Shift as a Field of Enquiry: A Definition of the Field and Suggestions for Its Further Development. *Linguistics* 9: 32–70.

Garrett, Paul B. 2005. What a Language Is Good For: Language Socialization, Language Shift, and the Persistence of Code-Specific Genres in St. Lucia. *Language in Society* 34 (3): 327–361.

Garrett, Paul B., and Patricia Baquedano-López. 2002. Language Socialization: Reproduction and Continuity, Transformation and Change. *Annual Review of Anthropology* 31: 339–361.

Gobern, Roselyne. 1997. Le français parlé à Tahiti. In *Polynésie, Polynésiens, hier et aujourd'hui*, ed. Guy Fève, pp. 13–36. Paris: L'Harmattan.

Grillo, Ralph. 1989. *Dominant Languages: Language and Hierarchy in Britain and France.* Cambridge: Cambridge University Press.

Handy, E. S. Craighill. 1923. *The Native Culture in the Marquesas (Bishop Museum Bulletin 9).* Honolulu: Bishop Museum.

Henningham, Stephen. 1992. *France and the South Pacific: A Contemporary History.* Honolulu: University of Hawaii Press.

Hill, Jane, and Kenneth Hill. 1986. *Speaking Mexicano: Dynamics of Syncretic Language in Central Mexico.* Tucson: University of Arizona Press.

Imbs, Paul, ed. 1977. *Trésor de la langue française: Dictionnaire de la langue du XIXe et du XXe siècle (1789–1960).* Tome Cinquième. Paris: Editions du Centre National de la Recherche Scientifique.

Irvine, Judith, and Susan Gal. 2000. Language Ideology and Linguistic Differentiation. In *Regimes of Language*, ed. Paul Kroskrity, pp. 35–83. Santa Fe, NM: School of American Research Press.

Kirkpatrick, John. 1983. *The Marquesan Notion of the Person.* Ann Arbor: UMI Research Press.

———. 1987. Taure'are'a: A Liminal Category and Passage to Marquesan Adulthood. *Ethos* 15 (4): 382–405.

Kroskrity, Paul, ed. 2000. *Regimes of Language: Ideologies, Polities, and Identities.* Santa Fe, NM: School of American Research Press.

Kulick, Don. 1992. *Language Shift and Cultural Reproduction: Socialization, Self, and Syncretism in a Papua New Guinean Village.* New York: Cambridge University Press.

Lavondès, Henri. 1972. Problèmes sociolinguistiques et alphabétisation en Polynésie Française. *Cahiers ORSTOM, Series Sciences Humaines* 9: 49–61.

Le Cléac'h, Hervé. 1987. Préface du Premier Bulletin de l'Association "Motu Haka." *Bulletin de l'Association Motu Haka o te Henua Enana* 1: 3–5.

———. 1997. *Pona Tekao Tapapa 'Ia –Lexique Marquisien-Français.* Papeete, Tahiti: STP Multipress.

Makihara, Miki. 2004. Linguistic Syncretism and Language Ideologies: Transforming Sociolinguistic Hierarchy on Rapa Nui (Easter Island). *American Anthropologist* 106 (3): 529–540.

Ochs, Elinor. 1979. Transcription as Theory. In *Developmental Pragmatics*, ed. Elinor Ochs and Bambi Schieffelin, pp. 43–72. New York: Academic Press.

———. 1988. *Culture and Language Development: Language Acquisition and Language Socialization in a Samoan Village*. New York: Cambridge University Press.

Ochs, Elinor, and Bambi B. Schieffelin. 1984. Language Acquisition and Socialization: Three Developmental Stories and Their Implications. In *Culture Theory: Essays on Mind, Self, and Emotion*, ed. Richard Shweder and Robert LeVine, pp. 276–320. New York: Cambridge University Press.

Ottino-Garanger, Pierre. 2006. *Archéologie chez les Taïpi: Hatiheu, un projet partagé aux îles Marquises*. Tahiti: Au Vent des Iles.

Paugh, Amy. 2005. Multilingual Play: Children's Code-switching, Role Play, and Agency in Dominica, West Indies. *Language in Society* 34 (1): 63–86.

Riley, Kathleen. 1996a. Engendering Miscommunication in the Marquesas, F. P. In *Gender and Belief Systems: Proceedings of the Fourth Berkeley Women and Language Conference*, ed. Natasha Warner et. al. Berkeley: Berkeley Women and Language Group.

———. 1996b. Langue perdue ou gardée aux Iles Marquises. *Bulletin de la Société des Etudes Océaniennes* 271: 58–67.

———. 2001. The Emergence of Dialogic Identities: Transforming Heteroglossia in the Marquesas, F.P. Ph.D. diss., CUNY Graduate Center.

———. 2003. The Marquesans. In *Encyclopedia of Sex and Gender,* Vol. 2, ed. Carol Ember, pp. 635–644. New York: Kluwer Academic/Plenum.

Rolett, Barry. 1998. *Hanamiai: Prehistoric Colonization and Cultural Change in the Marquesas Islands (Eastern Polynesia)*. Yale University Publications in Anthropology, Vol. 81.

Schieffelin, Bambi B. 1979. Getting It Together: An Ethnographic Perspective on the Study of the Acquisition of Communicative Competence. In *Developmental Pragmatics*, ed. Elinor Ochs and Bambi Schieffelin, pp. 73–108. New York: Academic Press.

———. 1990. *The Give and Take of Everyday Life: Language Socialization of Kaluli Children*. Cambridge: Cambridge University Press.

Schieffelin, Bambi, Kathryn Woolard, and Paul Kroskrity, eds. 1998. *Language Ideologies: Practice and Theory*. New York: Oxford University Press.

Silverstein, Michael. 1979. Language Structure and Linguistic Ideology. In *The Elements: A Parasession on Linguistic Units and Levels*, ed. Paul Clyne, William Hanks, and Carol Hofbauer, pp. 193–247. Chicago: Chicago Linguistic Society.

Sivadjian, Eve. 1999. *Les Iles Marquises: Archipel de mémoire*. Paris: Editions Autrement.

Suggs, Robert C. 1960. *The Island Civilizations of Polynesia*. New York: Mentor Books.

Tetahiotupa, Edgar. 2000. Bilinguisme et scolarisation en Polynésie Française. Ph.D. diss., Université Paris I.

Thomas, Nicholas. 1990. *Marquesan Societies: Inequality and Political Transformation in Eastern Polynesia*. Oxford: Clarendon Press.

von den Steinen, Karl. [1925–1928] 2005. *L'art du tatouage aux îles Marquises*. Illustrations and texts chosen and translated by Denise and Robert Koenig and Julia Nottarp-Giroire. Papeete, Tahiti: Editions Haere Po.

Zentella, Ana Celia. 1997. *Growing Up Bilingual: Puerto Rican Children in New York*. Malden, MA: Blackwell.

Zewen, François. 1987. *Introduction à la langue des Iles Marquises*. Papeete, Tahiti: Editions Haere Po No Tahiti.

5

RUPERT STASCH

Demon Language

The Otherness of Indonesian in a Papuan Community

To use language is to participate not only in a semiotics of talking referentially "about" subjects outside of language, but also in a metasemiotics of reflection on codes. In the midst of speaking and listening, language users recognize codes that are being used, associations of those codes, and relations that different persons have to the codes. For example, to different persons in particular interactional contexts, specific codes are "mine," "yours," "ours," "theirs," or "foreign." Overlapping with this metasemiotics of relations to codes, speakers and hearers of languages have ample contact with forms of linguistic otherness, such as multilingualism; language-learning; dialectal and idiolectal variation; speech errors; register differences; innovations; tropic artistry; and interaction with children, nonspeakers, and semi-speakers. Thus the relation between a code and its users is not seamless, in the manner of the famous pronoun-centered models of code "interpellating" subjects in its image through its call of "Hey you!" (Althusser 1971), or of code and subjectivity melding through language users identifying alternately with first- and second-person grammatical forms (Benveniste 1971). Acts of language are surrounded by people's diverse judgments of not only identification but also estrangement in relation to linguistic forms.

Given these broad points, we might expect the mediation of linguistic practice by linguistic ideology to rest partly in ideologies of otherness, language users' cultural sensibilities about what linguistic heterogeneity is and how they should relate to it. To illustrate the importance of this side of linguistic ideological processes, this chapter explores a sensibility about linguistic otherness prominent in a small Pacific community at one historical moment. I look at how Korowai speakers in the southern lowlands of Papua, Indonesia, have categorized and evaluated the Indonesian language during their first quarter-century of direct involvement with it. I show that Korowai approach Indonesian with an ideology of linguistic otherness that emphasizes the strangeness of the foreign code, but that simultaneously emphasizes this code's association with a coherent sociocultural perspective parallel to Korowai people's own position in the world. This ideology contributes to a pattern of language contact and incipient bilingualism in which the intrusive code is incorporated as an alternately fearful and fascinating supplement to people's linguistic repertoire, analogous to their own proper language but not hierarchically superior or subordinate to it. At least, these were the general tendencies in the years 1995–2002, the ethnographic present of this chapter.

Following an overview of the sociohistorical context of Indonesian's presence in Korowai people's lives, my starting point in giving an account of Indonesian's meaning will be Korowai metalanguage for talking about whole languages. Korowai call Indonesian 'demon language' *(laleo-aup)*, underscoring the alienness of the intrusive code. I show that built into this categorization is a model of the close link between the foreignness of a language, the territorial belonging of its speakers, and its speakers' inhabitance of a deformed perspective in the world that Korowai can imagine and artfully take on. Korowai acts of emphasizing a language's strangeness also open the possibility of embracing the perspective of that strange language and its world, to comment on their own world and its place in an expanded cultural sphere. I end this chapter with examples of ways that Korowai now avidly incorporate the demonic language of Indonesian into the demotic of their lives.

Questions of linguistic otherness are synecdochic of an even more general theoretical problem of otherness and culture. Everywhere, culturally situated actors interact with strangers, learn about alien cultural forms, make some of those forms their own, and navigate cultural disparities or contradictions in their lives. There is an "internal alterity" (Santner 2001: 9) to cultural processes: cultural forms are not only reductions of other possibilities into something conventional and familiar, but also media through which people engage with what is strange to them.[1] By documenting a sensibility about linguistic otherness that Korowai have applied to Indonesian, I aim in this chapter also to provide a sketch of one distinctive cultural approach to cultural alterity, a specific way certain people conceptualize social action across margins of cultural strangeness.

Indonesian in Papua and in the Korowai lands

Indonesian has a formidable presence across the region currently known as Papua, the western half of the island of New Guinea.[2] About the size of California, this land in 2000 had a population approaching 2.3 million persons (Badan Pusat Statistik Provinsi Papua 2003: 87–88). Of these, about 65 percent, roughly 1.5 million, were indigenous Papuans, and about 35 percent, a little less than 800,000, were settlers from elsewhere in Indonesia such as Java and Sulawesi, including Papua-born children of migrant parents (Munro 2002; McGibbon 2004: 25). Most settlers have migrated to Papua (at their own initiative or in formal state population transfer programs) since 1963, when Indonesia wrested sovereignty over the territory from the Netherlands. The indigenous Papuan population includes speakers of about 270 local languages, most of which are, like Korowai, non-Austronesian. According to the 2000 census, about 85 percent of indigenous Papuans lived in "village" settings, whereas settlers made up about two-thirds of the territory's 600,000 town-dwellers (McGibbon 2004: 26). Almost all settlers speak Indonesian fluently, and many speak it as their first language. Knowledge of Indonesian is also widespread among indigenous Papuans. Almost all town-dwellers, including Papuans, can speak Indonesian (Biro Pusat Statistik 1983: 34, and 1992: 40), and most Papuans raised in or near towns speak it as their first language.[3] The 1990 census reported that 87 percent of village-dwelling people in Papua, meanwhile, were native speakers of a language other than Indonesian, but that 72 percent of village dwellers nonetheless "could speak" Indonesian (Biro Pusat Statistik 1992: 34–45). These figures do not differentiate indigenous from nonindigenous rural populations (in 2000, there were roughly 1.3 million rural indigenous Papuans and 350,000 rural settlers).[4] Also, indigenous Papuans who do not speak Indonesian are particularly likely to be undercounted. Nonetheless, the numbers give a rough sense of the intensity of the lingua franca's contact and coexistence with indigenous languages in Papua today.

The diversity of Indonesian varieties spoken in the territory and settings in which they are spoken defies summary and is poorly known to scholars. Papua's burning issue is Indonesian economic, military, and political domination of indigenous Papuans, and indigenous Papuans' nationalist opposition to Indonesian rule.[5] Given the international prominence of this conflict, and the prominence in scholarship of the idea of the Indonesian language's identification with Indonesian nationalist consciousness (through works such as Anderson 1991 and Siegel 1997), I should clarify at the outset that most indigenous Papuans do not associate use of Indonesian with political integration in Indonesia. Nor do they exclusively associate the language with settlers. In arguments for or against Papuan national independence or other possible changes in the nature of Indonesian rule, few people focus intensively on Indonesian language issues (but see Rutherford 2005 for one counterexample). Violence, landownership, resource expropriation, racism, economic inequality , and the international geopolitical history that led to the territory's integration in Indonesia (Saltford 2003) are much more prominent as overt subjects of contention in the politics of Papua's relation to Indonesia.

This partial delinking of Indonesian from separatist and ethnic politics is ascribable in some measure to the historical depth of Indonesian's presence in many areas of Papua, far predating the language's designation as "Indonesian." As is well known, "Malay" was the name of a language or set of language varieties spoken unevenly across the Dutch colonial territories; it was eventually renamed "Indonesian" by protagonists of the nationalist, anticolonial movement that culminated in the Indonesian state's founding in 1945.[6] Some Papuans in coastal and riverine locations spoke dialects of Malay for decades if not centuries prior to Indonesian takeover in 1963, thanks to processes of trade, suzerainty, missionization, or Dutch colonization in which the lingua franca figured prominently.[7] The relative independence of Indonesian from contemporary lines of political fracture also follows from Papuans often knowing the language as much as a lingua franca for communication with other Papuans as one for communication with settlers and with functionaries of the Jakarta-centered government (compare Romaine 1992: 54). Symptomatically, in many locations, including the Korowai area, Papuans call the language <u>bahasa umum</u> 'General Language, Lingua Franca' more readily than they call it <u>bahasa indonesia</u> 'Indonesian'.[8] Differences of dialect, register, interactional style, and fluency *within* Indonesian—such as contrasts between government-promulgated Standard Indonesian and non-Standard "Papua dialect"—routinely do take on emblematic, charged status in relations between Papuans and Indonesians, and these political dimensions of linguistic difference badly need further documentation and analysis.[9] Many Papuans are mindful of the loaded political significance that promulgation of Standard Indonesian had in the "development"-couched authoritarianism of the long dictatorial rule of the second Indonesian president, Suharto, who stepped down in the crises of 1998. Yet rural Papuan parents who do not identify nationally with Indonesian nonetheless strongly consider their children's prospects of social advancement to depend on fluency in Indonesian acquired through schooling (compare Sankoff 1980: 23). Also, Indonesian varieties do not map in any simple way onto differences of ethnic identity. For example, performance genres such as class-marked stories of interaction between town dwellers and country bumpkins are common icons of Papuanness in daily conversation as well as in newspapers and other media. These stories rely heavily on dialect and register features for expressive force, but the stories are as often about social heterogeneity within Papuan populations as they are about relations with settlers.

Korowai people's political and linguistic situation is at once highly exceptional and highly exemplary in the wider Papuan context. A few thousand speakers of Korowai dialects live dispersed across several hundred square miles of lowland forest, twenty miles south of New Guinea's highland ranges and a hundred miles inland from the Asmat coast. They make their livelihoods by gardening, sago processing, fishing, and hunting. What is exceptional about their situation is their relative autarky. Their location far from centers of governance, transport, and resource extraction has meant that they have only recently become subject to powers of the Indonesian state and Indonesian settlers, and their involvement with those powers remains quite tenuous.[10] Korowai started interacting regularly with Indonesian speakers only around 1980, when Dutch and Papuan personnel of the missionary organization Zendings Gereformeerde Kerken began traveling to the southwest edges of their lands and then built a mission post. Processes of village formation stimulated by initial missionary projects of the 1980s have taken major hold, despite the fact that from about 1990 to 2002 no expatriate missionaries lived in the area.[11] Many southwestern Korowai families now maintain part-time residences in the new multiethnic villages, alternating between these settlements and dispersed houses on forest territories. Numerous Korowai who do not live in villages are nonetheless intently interested in village spaces and the objects, people, and social norms encountered in them. The coexistence of 'village' and 'forest' as whole contrastive arrangements of living is today a central preoccupation of Korowai consciousness. What is exemplary about Korowai involvement with Indonesian, in the broad sweep of Papuan linguistic histories, is Indonesian's strong association with specific kinds of social spaces (the multiethnic villages) and with close involvement with people and institutions marked as culturally strange.

In forest living, Korowai uphold strong cultural commitments to autonomy and egalitarianism, while also intensely valuing social attachment. They uphold these commitments in part through spatial practices of living thinly dispersed across the land on separate patriclan-owned territories, while also constantly traveling across margins of belonging and ownership to pursue ties with others, such as their affinal and matrilateral kin. Patterns of speaking are also marked by relative egalitarianism. Men, women, and children take successive or overlapping turns of speech with little sense of intrinsic hierarchies of speakers. There are no forms of specially marked oratory. People's subjects of discourse, the views they express, and their decisions to speak or stay silent are generally conditioned much more by relation-specific qualities of who belongs together with whom or who is strange to whom than by stable categories of status position.

As of 2002, about 5 percent of Korowai spoke Indonesian well enough that they would do so regularly in the presence of more than just one other person, and the number of Indonesian speakers was growing quickly. Interaction with people who do not speak Korowai but do speak Indonesian is the main way Korowai learn Indonesian and is the main context in which they speak it. To underscore this major contextual association of Indonesian as a code with interlocutors *who do not speak Korowai,* I borrow Lüdi's distinction between "endolingual interaction" in which conversationalists have shared language backgrounds, and "exolingual interaction" in which they do not have coextensive language backgrounds (Lüdi 1987, cited in Milroy and Muysken 1995: 10). Indonesian is marked as a language of exolingual interaction, in which interlocutors share partial access to Indonesian, but pointedly do not share other codes, such as the Korowai vernacular. The linguistic otherness of Korowai people's Indonesian-language interlocutors is thoroughly bound up with those strangers' cultural, spatial, and political otherness.

The vast majority of interactions with Indonesian speakers occur in villages. Most Korowai who speak Indonesian with some fluency are men and youths whose clan lands lie near villages, and who have had at least fleeting careers as social mediators involved in village institutions of commodity commerce, wage labor, government, church, school, tourism, and coresidence with Papuans of neighboring ethnolinguistic affiliation (such as Kombai and Citak). The link between village space and the activity of speaking Indonesian is so clear that people who do not speak Indonesian often spontaneously explain their lack of knowledge of the language with statements like "I have only just started to approach the village."

A few villages with Korowai-owned houses are home to small numbers of Indonesian-speaking Papuan church personnel and schoolteachers and their relatives from the highlands or from the Digul region to the east of the Korowai area. Non-Papuan government personnel and traders, many of them based at commercial and administrative centers (kecamatan) forty miles to the southeast and southwest, occasionally stay in the larger villages. Since 1992, several of the most stable settlements have been made official 'villages' (desa) in the government administrative hierarchy, which involves local persons taking on bureaucratic titles. Korowai increasingly travel to the regional centers for government business, medical care, schooling, and (above all) shopping. Their foothold in cash commerce is largely owed to tourism. Several thousand international tourists have visited the Korowai area since the early 1990s, motivated by fantasies of first contact and the opportunity to photograph forest-dwelling Korowai people's impressive "tree-house" homes. It is a paradox of economic and cultural globalization that Korowai live at the outermost fringes of motorized transport and mass-commodity trade in Papua, yet for this reason tourists bring them chances for cash income unknown in other areas.

The Indonesian speech of bilinguals shows heavy interference from their vernacular. For example, following Korowai phonology, most bilinguals do not have a phonemic contrast between [l] and [r], as in Standard Indonesian. Dozens or hundreds of Indonesian words are used in Korowai-language semantic patterns that depart from Standard Indonesian lexicography. For example, Standard Indonesian tikus 'mouse, rat' is used as a translation equivalent of Korowai nduo 'mammal'. Indonesian tidak bisa 'not possible, cannot' and orang 'person' occur in bilinguals' speech as self-standing utterances, calquing the Korowai interjections bamondinda 'impossible' and mayox 'people'. The Indonesian phrase dari itu 'from that' is used as a calque for Korowai clause-final switch-reference suffixes, meaning 'following that' or 'because of that'. Korowai Indonesian also shows many dialect characteristics of Papuan Indonesian (see note 5), as well as dialect features of Papuan southern lowlands Indonesian more locally, such as the regionally distinctive verb mayangi 'perform festival dance.'

Beyond the growing set of active speakers, other Korowai across the forest landscape all have a relation to Indonesian. They might speak it disfluently. They might passively understand some connected speech, and actively command a small vocabulary. Or they might merely be aware of the foreign code's existence, and command a small number of foreign-marked but phonologically assimilated borrowings, such as platəli for 'plastic bag' (from Indonesian plastik). Differences of generation, gender, and geography tend to be major influences on people's fluency in Indonesian, alongside the main factor of degree of direct participation in village life. People who live close to villages, or who live with other Korowai who once lived in villages, learn more Indonesian than others. Young adults tend to be conspicuously attracted to speaking Indonesian, whereas some elderly men and women (who were already well into middle age when Indonesian entered the Korowai world) are not just indifferent to the new language, but actively averse to contact with it. Women tend not to travel long distances as often as men, and they tend to be more restrained than men in seeking interaction with strangers, so that few female Korowai speak Indonesian. Many women who live in villages stay away from parts of villages where non-Korowai dwell and communication in Indonesian is normative. By contrast, women are sometimes particularly associated with multilingualism in languages other than Indonesian, because intermarriage between Korowai and neighboring people is common, and it is usually women who change residence.

Korowai people's evaluative judgments about Indonesian are closely intertwined with their evaluative judgments of the new spaces, people, and social norms they have become involved with in the recent period. Their involvement with these new phenomena and with Indonesian speech has taken thousands of forms, and thousands of different, unstable evaluative shadings, so any generalizations will necessarily be partial. Even so, one clear pattern in Korowai approaches to Indonesian is ambivalence, or the dialectical coexistence of contrary evaluations. On the one hand, the language is strange and repulsive. On the other, it is familiar and attractive. In the remainder of this chapter, I document these contradictory judgments, and try to understand their conjunction as a cultural form. How do contrary evaluations coexist? What is the nature of their co-articulation and interdependence?

Human and demon

One prominent Korowai view about the recent linguistic encounter is summed up in people's use of the compound word *laleo-aup* 'demon-language' as the Korowai term for Indonesian. In Korowai speech, the word *laleo* occurs in close paradigmatic contrast with words for 'human' (*yanop, mayox*), and it prototypically signifies a type of markedly nonhuman monster that humans become after death. These intensely feared monsters have the appearance of walking corpses. To meet one of these monsters face-to-face, people think, would cause a person to die. Yet the monsters themselves are thought to miss their living relatives. They try to intrude in the lives of humans, even desiring their relatives' deaths. The monsters' malign nature is the main reason I take 'demon' as a good English gloss for *laleo*.

The 'demon language' label for Indonesian is based on a more general categorization of all new types of strange people as 'demons' (pl. *laleo-alin*). This term is routinely applied to Dutch missionaries; Papuan mission and church workers; other Indonesian-speaking Papuans from faraway places; Indonesian and European tour guides; European, North American, and Japanese tourists; Indonesian police and civil government agents; traders or other itinerant Indonesian visitors; and academic researchers. By fitting an existing image of repulsive monstrosity to these new outsiders, Korowai have expressed how alien they find the people to be. Korowai fear the demonic dead and want to stay separate from them. So too calling Indonesian 'demon language' summarizes an estrangement-dominated evaluation of that language. One very basic initial Korowai response to the new categories of radical strangers, and to their strange language, is repulsion. Hearing Indonesian spoken, Korowai who lack much experience of that language often fall markedly silent, and may say they are scared (*ŋgolo*) of the unfamiliar speech.

Before discussing in more detail the aesthetic and emotional judgments of repulsiveness summarized in the label 'demon language', though, I want to look at another layer of people's ideological expectations about languages. Alongside bald emphasis on radical strangeness, categorization of Indonesian as demon language also subtly draws upon certain Korowai understandings of what a "language" is to begin with.

The linking of land, language, and category of being

Korowai assume that a language, like a type of people, is a territorial entity. A language is defined by and associated with the lands of its speakers.[12] In Korowai speech, language names are formed by modifying the word *aup* 'language, talk, voice' with ethnonymic proper names like *kolufo* 'Korowai', *aim* 'eastern Kombai', *nabexa* 'western Kombai', and *banam* 'Citak'. Each ethnonym also participates in a paradigm of further compound words closely linked to the language name. Besides being prefixed to *aup* 'language', the ethnonyms are prefixed to *-anop* 'people' and *bolüp* 'territory, place'. Thus *kolufo-aup* is 'Korowai language', *kolufo-anop* is 'Korowai people', and *kolufo-bolüp* is 'Korowai territory, Korowai place'. The concept of a distinctive language overlaps with concepts of owning a distinctive expanse of land and being a distinctive category of human.[13]

Korowai ethnonyms denote types rather than groups. No person has knowledge of the whole Korowai population, territory, or dialect continuum. Nor does anyone have knowledge of the whole population, land, and linguistic range of any neighboring ethnic type. Ethnic populations are not units of coordinated action and decision-making. Specific ethnoterritorial and linguistic boundaries that people experience directly are often fuzzy. When Korowai speak of whole ethnolinguistic territories and populations, they do so in notional, contrastive terms. In most social contexts, people are preoccupied with relations between specific persons or networks within the Korowai-speaking population or across its outer margins rather than with relations between large named social totalities. The Korowai model of an alignment of land, language, and people in this way differs somewhat from the European, Herderian nation-state model. The Korowai landscape is itself internally differentiated. It consists of a patchwork of hundreds of 'places' (*bolüp*) owned by small, named patriclans. The term for clan-owned places, *bolüp*, is the same one used for much larger whole ethnolinguistic territories, and the smaller spatial level is by far the term's dominant sense. People's social lives are organized in terms of spectrums of belonging and estrangement in relation to different places and the people on them. Symptomatically, besides being an ethnic self-designation meaning 'Korowai', the word *kolufo* is more frequently used with a different meaning. It is an other-designating term for 'upriver people', who are usually feared as 'angry' and antisocial. Although Korowai are quite cognizant of phonological and lexical shibboleths that make geographically separated speakers of the vernacular linguistically strange to each other's ears, other social issues like kinship distance and land-focused belonging stand out even more strongly than dialect differences as dimensions of otherness across which social relations unfold. Perhaps the relative muteness of dialectal difference among Korowai speakers as a focus of social grouping follows from the way relations between even linguistically close people are often ones of estrangement. Nonetheless, a notion of a large-scale unit of human type does coalesce around language at the scale of total linguistic unintelligibility. The notion of a 'territory, place' associated with a broad ethnolinguistic identity is a wider, weaker version of the experience-near phenomenon of small clan-owned places.

The assumption of a metaphysical link between land and language can also be seen in the fact that Korowai call themselves collectively by a second ethnonym besides *kolufo-anop* 'Korowai people', namely *bolü(p)-anop* 'place people, place owners', and that they call their language *bolü(p)-aup* or *bolü(p)-an-aup* 'place language.' The word *bolüp* 'place' strongly entails 'belonging', in the sense of both ownership and comfortable familiarity. Asked why they call themselves 'place people', Korowai typically answer that it is because they all speak the language that they do. They take the land-focused ethnonym to be self-evidently explained by their linguistic code. People also explain that calling themselves 'place people' is a sequitur to the fact that people of other places, on all sides of them, have other languages. The

category 'place' carries a reflexive meaning of 'here in the middle space of belonging, where our language is spoken.' To be speakers of a particular language is to be
centered in a place of belonging, and centered in a category of human.

Korowai have readily applied the model of a close bundling of language, place,
and type of person to the new categories of actors intruding on their world. Encountering speakers of Indonesian, Korowai have initially assumed them to be a unitary type
of people, all of whom speak Indonesian as their first language and come from a single
land where that language is spoken, perhaps even all knowing each other there (compare Kulick 1992: 83; Romaine 1992: 53).[14] 'Demon' as an ethnonym for the strangers
harmonizes with these assumptions. In their beliefs about demons as a type of monster
(predating use of the term to speak of social foreigners), Korowai understand the dead
to be an ethnoterritorial grouping. The idea that the monstrous dead are a society parallel to the human one extends to describing these dead as having their proper 'demon
territory' (*laleo-bolüp*), distantly downriver from Korowai lands (compare A.-C.
Taylor 1993: 654). Calling new outsiders 'demons' is a way of categorizing them as
ethnolinguistic others comparable to the human ethnic others at the edges of Korowai
lands. The 'demons' come from farther away in geography and in category of being,
beyond the pale of humanity but still recognizable as a territorial, ethnic population.

In sum, Korowai have an ideology of linguistic heterogeneity according to
which difference of linguistic code is figurally associated with difference of place
and difference of being. This saturation of people's idea of a linguistic code with an
idea of connection to land and to category of being is consistent with another strand
of Korowai linguistic ideology, a view that uttering certain words can physically
damage people or objects (Stasch 2002). For example, many objects and all people
are thought to have a truer identity underlying their present appearance ('crocodile'
is the secret identity of canoes, the name of some dead male predecessor is the secret
identity of a particular living boy, and so on). Verbalizing this identity should be
avoided in the presence of the object or person, because the word would physically
damage its secret referent.[15] Korowai recognize word avoidance to be so common
that it is a major cause of linguistic heterogeneity, through proliferation of synonyms
and indirections. These practices of linguistic avoidance share with the model of
language-to-territory correspondence a notion that a creator demiurge put them in
place. Also common to both strands of thinking about language is an attribution of
physical and metaphysical force to linguistic forms, whether whole codes or particular avoided registers within them. Language links up substantially and causally to the
lifeworld of land, objects, and bodily persons that the code is used in.

An allied point emerges from the metalanguage of fluency. People most commonly speak of whether someone knows a particular language by saying whether the
person 'hears' (*dai-*) the language, consistent with general focus on effect-on-hearers
as speech's meaning. Korowai sometimes put the subjective experience of disfluency
in terms of having a 'heavy tongue.' The idiom of greatest interest, though, is that
people also describe fluency by prefixing a possessive pronoun to *aup* 'language,
talk.' For example, it is a common turn of speech to say to a nonnative speaker that
Korowai "has become your language" (*g-aup tə-lo-bo*), as a way of saying the person has acquired fluency.[16] In other words, people's relations to languages, like their
relations to places, are relations of belonging or alienness. To acquire knowledge

of a language is to become native to that language and have that language become native to oneself. One is at home in relation to it. This question of belonging versus alienness might seem an obvious, universal dimension of people's relations to languages cross-culturally, but Korowai give it a particular thickness and affective color, and they link it up with other questions of personal being such as where one belongs on the land and what kinds of speech one should or should not hear spoken.

Parallelism and deformity: difference of language as difference of world

What does 'demon' actually signify when used to speak of new strangers, and what does 'demon language' mean as a label for Indonesian? Assimilation of whites or other radical strangers to nonhuman spirits, dead kin, ancestors, or divinities has been widely reported in the histories of various New Guinea and Pacific societies, but obviously this assimilation has had different meanings in different contexts. Many Korowai spontaneously remark that calling outsiders 'demons' is a figure of speech ("[They are] not true demons, it's just for naming"), or that 'demon' now has distinct senses. To these speakers, though the metaphor of foreigners as demons is far from dead, so to speak, it is moving toward the status of a routinized, communicatively expedient cliché, comparable to Cantonese *gweilo* 'ghost man, foreign devil' or Indonesian bule 'albino' (but see Fechter 2005). One indication of the increasingly nonliteral quality of the 'demon' usage is that through involvement with tourism and regional ethnic discourses, many Korowai are experimenting with dozens of new ethnonyms made by borrowing Indonesian-language ethnonyms into the Korowai paradigm of ethnic compounds, to form such designations as *amerika-anop, jerman-anop, jawan-anop, indonesia-anop*, and *papua-anop*. The compound *turis-anop* operates in this same paradigm as a word for all 'tourists', also conceived as an ethnic population.[17] All the new ethnic categories work in discourse alongside 'demon', as hyponyms of it rather than as replacements.[18] Yet the growth of a nuanced Korowai anthropology of different types of ethnic foreigners (at least among a subset of speakers), and the routine application of the root *-anop* 'human' to them, marks a departure from a notion that the radical strangers actually are nonhuman walking corpses. Nowadays laleo might just mean 'foreigner.'

Nonetheless, it is important to acknowledge the severe intellectual and emotional shocks that Korowai have experienced in their involvement with the new foreigners. Some Korowai who have not interacted much with foreigners continue to posit a relation of literal identity between foreigners and the demonic dead. Ethnohistorical narratives assert clearly that this full identification of newcomers with dead monsters was a matter of wide, commonsense agreement among Korowai at the time of the foreigners' initial intrusions into the region. As one person put it of Korowai people's earliest interactions with radical foreigners, "At first their thoughts were that they were grave-pit demons [*mebol-laleo*, i.e., monsters from the actual dead]." Even explicitly figurative or semantically frozen uses of 'demon' to denote foreigners stand in an "intertextual series" (Hill 2005) with uses involving full identification of new strangers and the dead. Frozen or explicitly figurative uses call into view an idea of foreigners' monstrosity while also allowing whimsical, ironic disavowal of that same idea, somewhat in the manner that (in Hill's account) putatively nonracist uses of mock Spanish in the United Stated depend on interdiscursive relations with overtly racist uses for their indexical value of "easygoing persona."

Across the range of relatively figurative versus literal uses of 'demon' for foreigners, the category's core idea is one of conjoined disparity from and parallelism to Korowai humanity. This idea is again richly precedented by the imagery of the demonic dead, as this imagery existed prior to the new foreigners' intrusion. Those dead are said to perceive human night as day and day as night. They occupy a perceptual and moral world that is in many further ways a chiasmus of the human one. Using the monstrous dead to understand the language and culture of outsiders puts into play a model of coexisting parallel, reciprocally strange cultural worlds. Korowai frequently imagine that the territory of light-skinned strangers is atmospherically bizarre. Perhaps there is no sun there, and it is very cold. They often suggest that the cities of the new outsiders would be like a dream to them, a displaced and otherworldly world. Sometimes Korowai see these cities *in* dreams.

The most routine practice of positing simultaneous cultural deformity and parallelism between Korowai people's own world and the world of new foreigners is productive use of *laleo* 'demon' as a prefix for forming Korowai-language compound words to designate unfamiliar objects by analogy to familiar precedents. Rice, for example, is *laleo-ndaü* 'demonic sago', matches are *laleo-məlil* 'demonic fire', clothes are *laleo-xal* 'demonic skin', guns are *laleo-bai* 'demonic bows', instant noodles (ramen) are *laleo-len* 'demonic intestinal worms', metal roofing is *laleo-lel* 'demonic thatch', and so forth. For contrastive emphasis, endogenous objects can be called by counterpart compounds prefixed with a word meaning 'people, human', giving 'people sago', 'people bows', 'people thatch', and so forth.[19] Here, too, 'human' and 'demon' are construed to be at once contrastive and parallel, the world of the one apprehended as a systematic deformation of the world of the other. In this tropic elaboration on the logic of dead monsters, demons also have a culture in the sense of a coherent array of kinds of objects that are native to them. The expression laleo-aup 'demon talk, Indonesian' is the only intangible entity in this paradigm.

The paradigm of neologisms highlights how 'demon' is a paradoxical category for expressing and apprehending that which is refractory to categorization. In this respect, the category is highly metasemiotic and figurative even in its most basic denotation, such that it is probably a mistake to speak of *any* use of 'demon', even for the dead, as "literal." As an image of deformity, the monsters are protean. They are expected not to conform to type, since they are deformations of type. Symptomatically, 'demon' is also an interjectional swearword in Korowai comparable to English "damn." People blurt it out upon stubbing their toes or hearing preposterous suggestions. The category is an element of cultural sense-making that is reflexive about the limits and possibilities of sense-making itself, whether it is applied in trying to understand what happens to humans after death or, more widely, in trying to understand what it is to stub one's toe or encounter radical strangers. The demonic is also inherently open and flexible. Every use of the word is interdiscursive and exploratory, pointing to other differently figurative uses and other attempts at making sense of what is foreign to human normalcy. The open paradigm of demon compounds underscores deformity, and this quality of deformity is more basic than the question of actual deadness. In a similar way, the internal diachrony of the 'demon' category as an ethnonym (the ongoing shift in the sense in which 'demon' is applied to foreigners, which is also an ongoing shift in the strangeness or familiarity of those foreigners) aligns with the term's denotation of monstrousness, rather than contradicts it. Much as death is an event of intense discontinuity, so too the monstrous dead are apt figures not just of an epochal break but of historical change as such. The demonic is *supposed* to change, such as by revealing points of common ground with 'human' denied at an initial moment of othering what is unfamiliar. Korowai speakers' pleasure taken in proliferating 'demon' compounds for new objects, using Korowai language words, supports a looking-glass sensibility of the parallelism of codes. People cultivate ways of expressing Indonesian items in Korowai categories, enacting a cultural "intimation of underlying commonality that is directly proportional to the degree of apparent difference" (Rumsey 2006: 62).

A similar process occurs in the other linguistic direction when persons who are not capable of connected Indonesian speech, and who have little passive comprehension of the language, nonetheless use certain Indonesian words that designate focal figures of anxiety, pathos, or value in Korowai life. Prominent examples include the Indonesian words mama-tua 'old woman', which monolingual old women often use as descriptions of themselves, suangi 'witch', and the verb mati- 'die'.[20] This circulation of highly iconized categories and word forms poses use of Indonesian terms as a demonstration of deep cultural or transcultural salience of Korowai categories calqued by those terms. Using bits of Indonesian, speakers make the point that the other tongue, too, has the category under discussion. In another portrayal of codes as parallel counterparts, the act of translating is itself expressed by the reduplicated verb phrase *lefu-di-lefu-di-* 'say one part, say one part'. A few Korowai speakers who worked as language teachers to missionaries have readily adopted interlinear translation as a way of speaking with language-learning foreigners. They spontaneously break conversational text into measured segments, and repeat each segment once in Korowai and once in Indonesian (compare Schieffelin, chap. 7, on Bosavi pastors).

The idea of paired, antipathetic but parallel populations is not limited to the demon model but widely informs Korowai social relations (Stasch, n.d.), including relations between living ethnolinguistic populations. The model of the coordination of language, land, and category of human being outlined in the previous section itself involves a notion that an encounter with speakers of a different language is an encounter with another centered perspective on the world. A language, an ethnic category of human, and an owned place are perspectival positions. People of different linguistic places meet each other as strange counterparts. In one representation, for example, pairs of geographically counterposed ethnic populations are held to be each other's unutterable secret identities. For example, 'Korowai' and 'Citak' (the next people downriver) are each other's hidden names: the one ethnonym is not supposed to be uttered in the other type of people's presence. The perspectives of ethnic populations are at once interchangeable and incompatible.

Another indication of how Korowai regard a language as amounting to a situated, coherent position in the world existing separately from and parallel to other positions is people's use of the suffix -gop 'via, by the vehicle of', combined with a language name, to describe people as having conversed in that language. This form's main other uses are in combination with terms for 'canoe' or 'oar' to say that people traveled by boat, with a loan for 'airplane' to say that people traveled by plane, with words for 'torch' or 'flashlight' to say that people traveled by the light of these objects, or with terms for 'dream', 'spirit mediumship', or 'witchcraft' to say that someone gained knowledge or took action through one of these experiential channels removed from waking-life visible reality. Differences of linguistic code are analogous to differences of how people move toward their goals, and differences of how they experience the world.

The sense of Indonesian as a code linked to a parallel, discrete cultural world is supported by Indonesian use's strong association with village space, by contrast with Korowai use's association with spaces of dispersed residence on clan-owned forest places. People commonly put their reasons for visiting or avoiding villages in linguistic terms: they go there to hear Indonesian, or they stay away so they do not have to hear or speak it. Persons who live in villages commonly categorize different lanes or buildings in terms of linguistic codes, and they approach or avoid those spaces out of attraction or antipathy to the codes spoken there. Many people's main motive for attending Sunday church services is to listen to Indonesian. Even without villages on the land, Korowai have long associated spatial difference with linguistic difference. Travel, marriage, feasting, and diverse events of residential displacement within the Korowai-speaking area bring people into close interaction with speakers of hard-to-understand dialects. Particular households practice locality-specific word avoidance, and social relations across households often involve people learning these negative linguistic practices as well as positive uses, such as local stream names. Almost all current villages are sited on interstitial lands where Korowai have long interacted with speakers of neighboring language groupings, and where multilingualism was common prior to Indonesian's presence. Now Indonesian as a distinct code and villages as a distinct multiethnic type of cultural space are strongly associated with each other. 'Village' and 'forest' are prominent not only as contrasting spaces but as parallel, contrastive whole modes of life. The Indonesian language is metonymic of the temporally new, culturally foreign pole of a two-style world.

Strangely attractive: Indonesian's indexical and iconic values

Indonesian's status of being at once disparate from and parallel to Korowai is not only a matter of pure classification. This status also has an evaluative, aesthetic, and emotional side. Having explored the dialectical coexistence of deformity and analogy in the Indonesian-Korowai relationship, I turn now to documenting an allied unity of opposites: the coexistence of estrangement and attraction in speakers' relations to Indonesian. Paradoxically, the same judgments of deformity through which speaking selves experience Indonesian as alien are also spurs to experiencing the language as sublimely fascinating and useful. The more people link Indonesian to the idea of a strange perspective analogous to their own, the more too they open up the possibility of taking on that alternative perspective themselves.

Dealing with this evaluative dimension of Korowai ideologies of linguistic otherness brings me back to the empirical state of Korowai bilingualism, which I sketched earlier in this chapter without offering causal generalizations beyond the broad link of Indonesian-learning to villagers and exolingual social engagement. It is well established in literature on language contact and multilingualism that language choice reflects and expresses what can broadly be termed indexical-iconic values of different codes. By this, I mean the meaningful associations that a code per se carries, independently of the meanings that are denoted semantically through that code. For example, Kulick (1992) shows in detail that in one Papua New Guinea village, patterns of code-switching between villagers' vernacular and the exogenous language Tok Pisin, as well as the overall shift to socializing children as monolingual speakers of the exogenous language, are motivated by indexical-iconic associations of the lingua franca with possibilities of self-transcendence like economic development, religious success, or a cooperative social persona. Similarly Woolard (1989) shows that in Barcelona, bilinguals' choices of Castilian versus Catalonian are shaped by their judgments of their interlocutors' ethnicity, not necessarily for reasons of comprehension but because of the codes' indexical-iconic standing in a cultural formation of Catalonian boundary maintenance. So, too, Catalan's historical prosperity, in numbers of speakers, is shaped by *economic* prosperity, or the language's association with a national minority ethnicity that is materially dominant in the subnational region. Chapters by Riley, Makihara, and Jourdan in this volume also exemplify the general finding. Indexical-iconic processes have clearly mediated Korowai speakers' bilingualism in Indonesian, too, including their learning of the language in the first place.[21]

The 'demon language' label asserts that Indonesian is indexical and iconic of a condition of ontological monstrosity with which people should avoid contact.[22] Fear of Indonesian is a response that comes up in many concrete contexts. Alongside persons describing themselves as ill at ease in villages and wanting to stay away from them, it is also common to encounter monolingual Korowai who describe themselves as 'scared' of Indonesian speech or as finding Indonesian 'unpleasant' (bə-six-da). Although only tacitly involving the contrast between Korowai and Indonesian linguistic codes, initial responses to Christian preaching are a specific area where Korowai have portrayed outsiders' linguistic practices as both parallel and antipathetic to their own. A handful of Korowai have converted to Christianity or are interested in doing so. Recognizing biblical narratives to be 'cosmology' (*lamol-aup*, lit. 'world talk'), though, the Korowai population's overall response has thus far been to assert that they have preexisting talk of this genre, and therefore they are not supposed to be involved with the openly spoken Christian talk. People say such things as "They [church personnel] are speaking talk on the top. Our talk underneath is sufficient/identical [*kül*]," or "It's not as though it's different talk. We're not going to listen." Some youths with wide travel experience have picked up Indonesian-language Papuan string-band lyrics and melodies, and sometimes sing them at night to the accompaniment of carved fishing-line guitars. Persons unaccustomed to the sound of these instruments and songs, such as feast visitors from a long distance upstream, routinely report that being within earshot of the songs makes them sleepless with fear. In these kinds of responses, Indonesian as a whole code has the status of an avoided object, something like avoided registers within the Korowai code, such as the 'transgressive underlying identity' register mentioned above.

Yet fear, demonization, and avoidance are themselves stances of engagement. They are ways of taking the measure of an object and naming its effect in one's life. Some Korowai experiences of fear are also clearly experiences of what should also be translated as 'wonder'. Attraction frequently accompanies fear as a response to foreign objects, or it supersedes fear. Village-experienced youths' attraction to string-band songs is a case in point, as is the intense desire of many Korowai to possess a radio cassette player, despite the poor supply chain, the machines' high price and short life, and the cost and difficulty of obtaining batteries. Desire to listen to tape players is often as keenly felt by monolingual Korowai as by those who understand Indonesian. Bare human voices, unintelligible and invisible but musical, are a stimulus of great beauty. People with extensive experience of the machines value Papua New Guinean tapes as more pleasurable than the commoner Indonesian-language ones, explicitly because there is less chance of making out words. Similarly, when I have been in the presence of tourists or other light-skinned people visiting the Korowai area, Korowai acquaintances who speak Indonesian and are aware that the outsiders and I share another code altogether have frequently urged me to strike up conversations in my language with the visitors, or they have after the fact expressed aesthetic satisfaction at overhearing such conversations.

Attraction to inscrutable speech is not new. Across much of the Korowai area, the most appreciated feast performance songs are sourced to the downriver Citak linguistic community. (The songs are called *laleo-gom*, literally 'demon song', but speakers say there is no connection between this name and the 'demon' category.) The songs' lyrics are often unintelligible even to persons singing them, though the most acclaimed singers usually have some Citak speaking ability. More mundanely, it is common for persons who can speak a neighboring language, or who know a few words of that language, to use single foreign words humorously amid Korowai-language interaction, typically words designating highly emblematic human objects or acts such as 'tobacco' or 'to drink'. Conversely, Korowai speakers themselves often complain that "Korowai is distasteful" (*kolufo-aup bə-six-da*). This is part of a wider pattern of deprecating what is familiar, as in statements that one's own body is 'ugly, bad' (*ləmbul*) or that one is 'bored' (*ŋgawel*) with one's own clan territory and the people and food there.

Indonesian's strangeness, summarized in the 'demon language' label, is an important part of why Korowai are learning the language and why they are using it in the ways they do. To put the matter in the non-Korowai idiom of the case described in Handman's chapter 8 of this volume, Indonesian is not 'heart language', but Korowai often think that is what is good about it.

The value of strangeness is intertwined with political and economic reasons to learn the language. The dominant indexical-iconic fact about Indonesian for Korowai is the language's association with exolingual interaction with social others who control forms of wealth, institutional order, and spatial practice that are historically new to people's experience. In becoming involved with traders, tourists, government personnel, and Papuans from elsewhere, and often growing to value some aspects of that involvement, Korowai develop a reflexive interest in learning to understand and speak Indonesian. Many youths deliberately work at learning Indonesian because they understand this will serve them instrumentally in travel to villages and towns away from the Korowai lands, and in their efforts to make money through tourism, sale of forest commodities, and the like.[23] Even to Korowai who do not travel to villages, Indonesian is strongly associated with paper money ('demon tree leaves') and store-bought commodities such as rice and cotton clothing. Money denominations are some of the Indonesian expressions that monolingual Korowai most commonly know and use (reanalyzing them as monomorphemic in the process). Korowai avidly appreciate material objects, and they appreciate the moral force of possessing, lacking, or being given objects. Access to steel tools, cotton clothing, and other valued 'demonic articles' (*laleo-misafi*) is now a dominant Korowai preoccupation. Indonesian's prestige and instrumental value has risen on the tide of interest in imported objects. An illustrative case is the wide circulation of the loanword *obase* 'pill' (<*obat* 'medicine'). Korowai intensely value the perceived effectiveness of pills in making sick people healthy or in relieving their pain. To monolingual Korowai, knowing and uttering the foreign-marked word is a step of putting a request in foreigners' own terms, a kind of cultural outreach suited to eliciting from foreigners an act of health-giving generosity in return.

Many Korowai have also had experiences of being politically hectored in Indonesian by visiting police or other government functionaries, or by other strangers whose postures of social superiority to Korowai were readily perceived despite linguistic obstacles. Indonesian is associated with forms of authority and verbal practices of command that are alien to endogenous Korowai norms and frequently unwelcome, but also impressive and sometimes appealing.

On Korowai speaking Indonesian to one another

The contours of these mixed indexical-iconic associations of power, status, wealth, and otherness are most richly visible in the endolingual echoes of Indonesian's exolingual life: Korowai use of Indonesian with other Korowai interlocutors. In Indonesian-language conversations with non-Korowai speakers, use of Korowai elements does not make sense, except in asides between the Korowai speakers present. In conversations between Korowai speakers, by contrast, many figurative interactional effects can be produced through use of elements of the two codes together. It is in talk between Korowai speakers themselves that people juxtapose Korowai and Indonesian codes with greatest semiotic reflexivity. Makihara (chap. 3 of this volume) describes purist Rapa Nui talk as a "highly marked and stylized form of speech that stands in contrast to the syncretic speech common in everyday usage." An Indonesian utterance between Korowai is a marked, stylized act of much this same quality. The act's markedness here involves staking a claim to alien new historical horizons, rather than to a recoverable ancestral heritage (as in the Rapa Nui case).

A few days into my Korowai fieldwork, I recorded a bilingual youth's Korowai-language history of the opening of a village and then played it back to him. He said that he was 'embarrassed, ashamed' (malu, *xatax*), and he asked to re-record the narrative in Indonesian. Having his talk repeated by the machine drew attention to him as a speaker to be heard, violating a Korowai ideal of self-effacement. To be recorded speaking in Indonesian, though, would be prestigious. This feeling that speaking Indonesian is prestigious or, at least, embarrassment-canceling, is far from constant for Korowai, and the particular example is shaped by my and the recorder's presence. But Korowai bilinguals do sometimes hold status or power by speaking Indonesian with other bilingual Korowai, or even by speaking Indonesian *at* uncomprehending monolingual Korowai. These are performances in which much of what is signified is the activity of speaking Indonesian itself, and the speakers' bilingualism as such, since the choice of this code baldly departs from the unmarked norm of speaking the shared vernacular when interacting endolingually. Besides sheer linguistic access versus linguistic exclusion, social connections and capacities are also iconically indexed by Indonesian-language talk between Korowai. Bilinguals put on display their own histories of involvement with non-Korowai places and people. Indonesian-language conversations play with the idea that the speakers are as though foreigners themselves, and that the speakers' identities as masculine mediators who work with foreign structures of government bureaucracy, commodity commerce, or tourism are as fundamental as their identities as speakers of the Korowai language.

Not too much overt emphasis is put on superiority, though. The positive effects of Indonesian do not all rest on excluding and derogating other persons and other norms. A specific site of Indonesian forms' increasing endolingual salience is the way men and youths with village connections have taken to half-humorous, half-serious use of conventional Indonesian greetings and valedictions with meanings like 'good morning', 'good evening', or 'travel safely'. Korowai generally cross the thresholds of entering or leaving one another's presences in silence, or with conversational exchanges that do not explicitly mark that conversation and interaction are beginning or ending. By contrast with this norm, the new fashion for Indonesian greetings is also a fashion for a style of more freewheeling presumptuousness toward one another in interaction, associated with villages and youths. The greetings are most commonly uttered by Korowai in villages when entering each other's houses. In those settings, they strongly index village living as a new, multiethnic social form, in a wider Indonesian-speaking world of Papuan villagers and village locations. But in forest spaces, too, some youths readily use these salutations toward each other, figuratively drawing village sociability into forest social contexts.[24]

In village and forest locations alike, Korowai are also very enthusiastic in their use of borrowed or calqued Indonesian categories for reckoning time (compare Schieffelin 2002). Even monolinguals widely take interest in a village-associated cycle of seven numbered days that are Korowai-language calques for the Indonesian days of the week. Many people recognize this unprecedented system of cardinal time coordination as being very useful for organizing activities of their forest lives. They also take intellectual pleasure in mastery of the system. Keeping track of the day category in this way means orienting to certain village spaces, where Sunday church services are the cycle's most consistent anchor. So, too, many people are intently interested in the idea of knowing and expressing diurnal time in terms of numbered hours. With a recent boom in extraction of eaglewood (kayu gaharu), an internationally valuable aromatic resin deposit in some fungus-infected specimens of a tree, people are also widely using the Indonesian weight measures kilo and on 'ounce', the latter calqued by the Korowai form *lüp-tə-bo-xa* 'weightiness, that which is heavy'.[25] Use of various fragments of Indonesian speech, as well as Korowai loan translations of patently Indonesian semantic categories, expresses alongside of denotation a positive valuing of Indonesian as a code, and a positive valuing of the exogenous social and categorical orders it is associated with.

Personal naming is another area where Indonesian's attractiveness even to monolingual Korowai is increasingly registered. By the late 1990s, it was increasingly common for persons to have both Indonesian and Korowai names, and to be referred to by an Indonesian name even in Korowai-language speech. Some children were being given only Indonesian-derived names. Sometimes a person's widely used Indonesian name is a translation-equivalent of his or her previously conferred Korowai-language name, as when a man whose Korowai name means 'fish' is called by the Indonesian term for fish, ikan. The trend more recently has been to give children Indonesian names without semantic content and thus without Korowai-language equivalents. Many people value the names because of their exoticness of phonological form and their association with links to strange and desirable objects, places, people, and powers. To adopt foreign words as the names of persons is to forcefully "exogenize the endogenous" (Rumsey 2006: 22) and to portray language's basic relation to people as one of alienness. A similar fashion is the interest that monolingual Korowai have in saying names of distant towns they have never seen. Papua's political and economic capital, Jayapura, is particularly prominent in Korowai speech (*ajafula, jajafula, ajafulan, ajapula*), in reference not only to the distant urban center itself and the crowds there, but also to fearfully strange and desired objects associated with the epoch of connection to that city. The gourami fish arrived in Korowai rivers shortly before missionaries came to the area and was lexicalized in Korowai as *ajafula*. Store-bought tobacco is called, among other things, *ajafula dəlem mail* 'Jayapura steel drum water', building on endogenous metaphorization of tobacco as 'water', and novel sensory experience of steel drums full of water at the corners of missionary houses. People's explicit evaluations of Indonesian are often not instrumentalist ones about what the language is good for, but aesthetic ones about whether it is 'pleasant' (*six*, lit. 'delicious').

The increasing popularity of Indonesian names to designate persons, like the other endolingual uses of Indonesian I have sketched, reflects a cultural principle of the aesthetic fascination and pleasurability of foreign forms. Sometimes inscrutability is exactly why a foreign linguistic code is not only attractive but socially efficacious (compare Rutherford 2003). Korowai have long taken interest in letters (surat, *suras*) for their effect of causing recipients to do what senders tell them to do. Korowai who have attended any grades of school are often asked by relatives to write Indonesian-language letters requesting payments from other Korowai who have wronged them. I was frequently asked if I could send letters to tour guides in Jayapura or overseas to make them come to a particular clan place. On one occasion, a Korowai friend requested that I write a letter to a Papuan woman elsewhere who had once lived in his village as a health nurse trainee. The young woman, now married, had expressed romantic interest in my friend at the earlier time, and I was now supposed to write to her, *in my own language*, to demand monetary payment on my friend's behalf, in compensation for the indignity (as he saw it) of her having made open romantic advances and then gone on to marry someone else. My first argument against doing this was that there was no way the recipients would be able to understand a letter written in English, but my friend said this was his goal: a letter's unintelligibility would make the demand for payment all the more compelling. Similarly, in 2002, landowners in one locality posted an Indonesian-language wooden sign ordering residents of a nearby village to stop seeking food on their land. They thought that the unintelligibility of Indonesian and of writing, associated with state authority (peraturan 'regulations, laws'), would strengthen the force of their demands.

There is a related transformation under way from using the Korowai category 'demon' as a figure to say things about outsiders toward embracing the exogenous linguistic code as an icon for commenting reflexively on being Korowai, in the now-expanded social field. An example that I encountered in 2002 again involved literacy, which bears strong associations with schools, villages, and exogenous technical know-how. A rumor circulating before a feast had it that feast owners planned to make all comers to their event write on a blackboard, and that only those who knew how to write could wear clothes at the feast instead of traditional dress. This was a complex self-deprecatory gesture. Korowai have formed a stereotype that tourists want imported articles, including clothes, to be kept off-camera. The chalkboard rumor took literacy as an emblem of new technology and material culture, and it asserted that if people could not write, then they had no business wearing clothes either. In starting this rumor, the feast owners sought to persuade their guests to manage appearances in a way that would make tourists happy with the feast event and would lead them to pay the feast owners well.

A somewhat different example of using Indonesian to comment on being Korowai, also in the highly reflexive cultural context of feasting, occurred one morning in 1996 when other feast sponsors initiated a stage of work by whimsically hoisting an Indonesian flag they had on hand. The flag possessors were youths involved in the bureaucratic offices of a nearby village.[26] Regarding feast preparations under way that morning, one of the young men who had just raised the flag then said in Indonesian, toward no one in particular, kami bikin upacara sendiri 'we are conducting a ceremony of our own'. The term upacara 'ceremony' here drew on experience of small government rituals in regional bureaucratic centers, such as Independence Day celebrations or development policy workshops. Other men on the scene jokingly described the feast activities as their tugas 'duty, assignment', and as matters that they were working to urus 'arrange, administer', again using signature lexemes of Indonesian state bureaucratic discourse. The men's utterances posed Korowai feast ritual as a worthy, recognizable parallel to the rituals of government bureaucrats. The speakers wryly borrowed Indonesian rhetoric and a foreign perspective to say what the feast owners were up to on this morning.

Conclusion

The situation I have sketched runs somewhat at right angles to stereotypes of colonially subjugated peoples acquiring an intrusive lingua franca because they are forced to do so to have access to even the limited possibilities of political and economic agency the colonial social formation allows them. Certainly there are elements of this pattern in the Korowai linguistic field, but they are intertwined with other elements, such as extraordinary local aesthetic reflexivity about codes and their cultural associations. The picture I have given may also run somewhat at right angles to foreign academics' images of on-the-ground political conditions in Papua today. I should emphasize again that the Korowai situation is highly exceptional in regional political geography. One reason I have written this chapter (despite not having conducted truly in-depth field research on Korowai bilingualism) is that there is so little existing linguistic-anthropological work on Indonesian in Papua. Variation, rather than homogeneity, is sure to be the dominant question of studies of Indonesian in this region, and description of an exceptional case can be taken as a starting point for further theorization of the regional situation rather than as an isolated aberration from that regional situation. The case documented here also points to a possible aporia in studies of multilingualism generally, not just multilingualism in Indonesia—a scarcity of detailed documentation of the cultural processes at work in what Diebold (1961) decades ago labeled "incipient bilingualism," during which the terms of codes' coexistence may be particularly unstable and multiform. Above all, though, this chapter's intended contribution has been to document the complex otherness-saturated understanding of interlinguality that is shaping bilingualism in one speech community, in order to suggest that distinctive ideologies of otherness probably shape people's evaluations of codes in other multilingual settings as well.

The examples of Korowai evaluations of Indonesian mentioned in this chapter go in many different directions, but that is part of my point. The language's significance is unstable and is richly susceptible to innovation, reversal, and elaboration. I have specifically sought to show that Korowai evaluate Indonesian contradictorily: it is both good and bad, attractive and repulsive, usefully one's own and irreducibly strange.

Sometimes the different evaluations are expressed by different people. One illuminating disparity along gender lines that I encountered involves two married couples in Yaniruma, the only village in the area with an airstrip (and hence a major economic and social center). The respective husbands in these couples are among the most skilled Indonesian speakers of their generation in the Korowai population, and they are also among the Korowai men most experienced in cooperating with foreigners. Each man has repeatedly told his wife that she should try speaking Indonesian with him so that when non-Korowai speakers come by their house when he is away, she will be able to understand the visitors and converse with them. Otherwise, the husbands say, the visitors will mock them for their silence and their unfitness for village living, and the couples will be embarrassed. The two wives, unimpressed by their husbands' views, have consistently rebutted them with such statements as "It's not as though it's our mother's language; it's not as though it's our father's language." To these women, parent-child relationships are the last word in linguistic belonging. It is communication with one's mother and father that defines the code one should know and speak, not pressures to conform to norms of village living or answer to the communicative expectations of foreigners.

But single speakers also alternate between these two sorts of poles, or orient toward both simultaneously. Whatever the felt power, prestige, or pleasurability of

Indonesian some of the time to some persons, Korowai experience a much more formidable and stable power, prestige, and pleasure in being 'owners' of land, belonging at a place, and speaking the language of that place. The imagined, embarrassing scene of foreigners approaching a village house and addressing a Korowai woman in it who is unable to converse with them is mirrored by another kind of scene I have often witnessed: Korowai asserting their status as landowners and, among themselves in the Korowai language, mocking tourists and other foreigners as lacking standing in the place. Categorization of outsiders as 'demons' remains a light act of mockery in this mode, counterposed to the act of speaking Korowai, people's own language.

The nature of the demon category's contrast with 'human' is open to revision. Some Korowai joke ruefully that it has turned out that they themselves are demonic, and it is the outsiders who are human, not the reverse (as everyone formerly thought). This is a way people disparage their own technologies and social manners. It may be in part a half-wry, half-serious adaptation of narratives Korowai have heard from government and church functionaries.[27] It also represents judgments some Korowai are entertaining through their own perceptions, and it is supported by a broader cultural tendency to value representations of oneself as existing in a condition of lack and degradation. At present, though, the overall standing of Korowai as speakers' "own" language, and Indonesian as the "alien" language, is straightforward to most Korowai. If anything, the 'demon' categorization seems to be supporting a situation of deepening but still highly unstable linguistic contact in which bilingualism is understood as a matter of participating in two disjunct, parallel cultural orders. One order does not evaluatively subordinate the other.

In monolingual Korowai talk, speakers can use a small sprinkling of Indonesian forms as icons of a strange otherworld and their access to it, or of their awareness of it as an alternative scene peripheral to their lives. In connected Indonesian speech, they can iconically signify the activity of communicating with cultural aliens itself. This seems to be the force, for example, of youths yelling out advice, instructions, or threats at European or American tourists in Indonesian, knowing very well that the tourists do not understand, but that other Korowai bystanders see the speech as appropriately reaching out toward the cultural others. In underscoring Indonesian's status as foreign, Korowai incorporate this code as a supplementary addition to their linguistic repertoire, rather than engage it as a code that displaces or devalues their own more familiar languages. Even as they speak it, Korowai hold the other language at arm's length, as a parallel code to their proper one.

In a pair of important papers, Gal and Irvine identify iconization, fractal recursivity, and erasure as three main semiotic processes by which ideologies construct and construe linguistic difference (Gal and Irvine 1995; Irvine and Gal 2000). Korowai involvement with Indonesian has included many developments that can be understood in these terms. I have broadly argued, for example, that Indonesian speech and Indonesian words have become icons of foreignness and social involvement with foreign institutions and people. The language is felt to be an image of these foreign entities, whatever happens to be said through that language. The Korowai word *laleo* and the productive paradigm of 'demonic' compounds is probably experienced as iconic of an ability to express exogenous categories in familiar terms: the foreign and familiar are inside each other, not mutually exclusive. Numerous emergent social and linguistic differences *within* the Korowai-speaking population are recursively reinscribed versions of differences between Korowai at large and the exolingual world of Indonesian talk, foreign spaces, and foreign people. These new divisions include the difference between 'village people' and 'forest people' as it is now sometimes drawn among Korowai speakers, the difference between a bilingual husband who advocates being able to converse with non-Korowai people in village space and his monolingual Korowai wife who devalues Indonesian as not her people's, and even the difference between a single Indonesian word and its surrounding co-text in a predominantly Korowai-language conversation. Finally, Korowai generalizations about 'demon language' erase differences of dialect and competence among foreigners whom Korowai encounter, and also erase the increasing intimacy with which some Korowai inhabit Indonesian speaking positions as their own normal voice.

Yet the overall ideology of linguistic difference that I have documented in this chapter exceeds these three sorts of processes. It seems highly likely that typologies of major processes by which linguistic difference is made and unmade will grow more elaborate as the study of linguistic ideologies further intensifies. I have argued that Korowai themselves have a distinctive reflexive understanding of what "difference" even is. They understand linguistic difference as a combination of strange disparity and close parallelism. This reflexive approach to difference of code is deeply shaping Korowai people's practical involvement with Indonesian in the early decades of their contact with it.

Notes

I wish to thank all Korowai persons who spoke with me during my sixteen months of fieldwork in 1995–1996, 1997, 2001, and 2002. I also want to single out for special thanks Wayap Dambol and Fenelun Malonggai, the two Korowai persons with whom I have had by far the greatest number of conversations in and about Indonesian. Research and writing for this article was supported by a Fulbright-IIE fellowship, the Wenner-Gren Foundation for Anthropological Research, the Luce Foundation (through its Fellowships in Southeast Asian Studies program at the Australian National University), and Reed College. I also warmly acknowledge the help of Miki Makihara, Bambi Schieffelin, Joe Errington, Laura Hendrickson, Courtney Handman, Paul Manning, Sue Philips, and Joel Robbins, whose encouragement and comments have been critical to my work here.

1. Studies addressing this problematic of internal alterity are enormous in number. One classic is Basso 1979. Interesting recent statements include Robbins 2003, 2004; Bashkow 2004; and Hastings and Manning 2004. Rutherford 2003 is an important ethnography of the significance of the foreign among Biak people of northern Papua.

2. The territory's names have included Netherlands New Guinea, Irian, Irian Jaya, and West Papua, all linked to different historical periods, speech communities, or political programs. In early 2000, Abdurrahman Wahid, Indonesia's fourth and least authoritarian president, announced that *Papua* would replace *Irian Jaya* as the territory's official name. This was an unusual act of recognition of Papuan political aspirations, and within the territory as well as internationally the change took rapid hold in popular, governmental, and academic usage. The change was initially rejected in Jakarta by the national assembly but became national law in 2001.

3. Elmslie 2002: 76–84 is wrong to assume that Papuans do not speak Indonesian as their first language, and that non-Papuan settlers do speak it as their first language. It also bears

emphasis that the "settler" and "Papuan" populations are heterogeneous, that there are many persons interstitial or peripheral to these two categories, and that the categories are far from natural or disinterested but have become subjectively and politically real through a contingent history. All generalizations about the existence, size, and characteristics of these populations should be treated skeptically. So, too, with generalizations about "town" and "village" populations. The state's label 'village' (desa), for example, is applied to quite varied nonurban ways people occupy space.

4. My mixing of 2000 and 1990 census data here stems from differences between the questionnaires in those respective years. The 2000 Indonesian census was the first to document "ethnicity," enabling differentiation of Papuan and non-Papuan populations. McGibbon 2004 reports results from that census that are based on direct inquiry at census offices and are more useful than the state-published results (Badan Pusat Statistik 2001: 64–75). However, the 2000 census protocol dropped the questions about language, so, unlike the earlier censuses, its results no longer offer any information about the sociolinguistics of Indonesian.

5. See Vlasblom 2004 for a general history, and Timmer 2005 for one effort to chart the current situation.

6. See Hoffman 1979 for a history of Dutch debates over colonial language policy in prenationalist times.

7. See, for example, Seiler 1983; Swadling 1993; Rutherford 1998, 2005; Shiraishi 1996; and Overweel 1998.

8. In this chapter, Indonesian words are underlined, and Korowai words are italicized.

9. 'Papua dialect' (logat Papua; in previous decades, logat Irian) differs from Standard Indonesian and overlaps with some other regional Indonesian dialects in making heavy use of the distinctive third person plural pronoun dorang and numerous other distinctive pronouns and person-designating nouns, heavy use of the Standard verb punya 'have' (or non-Standard pu) to form genitive noun phrases, and little use of Standard Indonesian derivational verb morphology (meN-, etc.). Glazebrook 2004: 7–8 gives a brief account of dialect features' prominence in the politically charged artistic performances of anthropologist Arnold Ap and his associates, leading up to Ap's killing by Indonesian soldiers in 1984. There are no detailed studies of varieties of Indonesian spoken anywhere in Papua, but for fragments on regional dialect features, see especially van Velzen 1995, as well as Roosman 1982; Suharno 1983, and references in van Baal, Galis, and Koentjaraningrat 1984: 30; and Carrington 1996 (s.v. "Indonesian," "Malay"). For one overview of the history and sociolinguistics of Indonesian-Malay varieties in the Indonesian archipelago at large, see Sneddon 2003. See also Voorhoeve 1983 and Taylor 1983 for sketches of Moluccan Malay varieties having many features in common with Papuan Indonesian.

10. In essays complementary to this one (Stasch 2001, 2003, 2005), I discuss other major strands of the recent Korowai history of intercultural engagement, namely the strands of violence, village formation, and nationalism. My arguments in those articles run broadly parallel to this chapter's findings: the current processes of cultural change and intercultural engagement are organized by Korowai people's own distinctive sensibilities about otherness as an intrinsic aspect of social life, and by their distinctive practical techniques for managing otherness and making social ties around it.

11. Gerrit van Enk and Lourens de Vries, who worked in the region for the Calvinist missionary organization in the 1980s, later published a very substantial book on the Korowai language (1997) consisting of a grammar sketch, word list, and selection of texts. A Dutch Summer Institute of Linguistics (SIL) family moved to the Korowai lands in 2002.

12. This model of a language being linked to land, and to its speakers' position of belonging on land, can appropriately be understood as an aspect of Korowai "metapragmatics," in the same sense that Schieffelin (chap. 7 of this volume) uses the term, albeit a very

broad-scale aspect: the model is a culturally distinctive set of assumptions and understandings about language use, and about what it is to be a speaker of a language, in a situation of speaking it. More generally, the various facts of Korowai talk about languages, translation, ethnolinguistic being, and so on that I describe in this chapter should all be read from the perspective of the understanding of reflexive language's significance set forth in Schieffelin's chapter and works cited there.

13. Korowai assumptions resemble some Australian Aboriginal peoples' positing of direct links between languages and segments of country, such that relations between people and language or between people and country are even thought to be derivative of the language-to-country link (e.g. Merlan 1998: 125; Merlan 1981 and citations there; and Rumsey 1993. See also Kulick 1992: 80, 85, and Robbins 2006 on land-language links in two Papua New Guinea societies, and Handman's chap. 8 of this volume on SIL's assumptions of discrete language-people units). The assumption of language's relation to land received passing expression in one Korowai man's way of explaining that the village he and I were in was sited on Kombai land. He said the site "is not territory of our language" ("not our-language-COMITATIVE territory").

14. Thus the Korowai association of Indonesian with exolingual interaction has initially *not* involved understanding the language itself as a lingua franca without native speakers. This contrasts with the pronounced understanding of Indonesian as "unnative" (Errington 1998) in many other parts of the archipelago.

15. This lexical substitution register is described more fully in Stasch (forthcoming).

16. Similarly, speakers can predicate of some person a language name modified by the comitative suffix *-man-xa*, in constructions like "[person X] is Korowai-having, [person X] is one-who-has-Korowai." Here, too, the relation of possession describes an *attribute* of the speaker, defining the type of entity he or she is, rather than describing an external object the independently existing person happens to have collected as an appendage (which is perhaps more the force of the otherwise similar English construction "[person X] has [language Y]").

17. Tourists too are partly defined linguistically, albeit by a linguistic lack: a *turis-anop* is a foreigner who does not speak Indonesian.

18. Also newly salient in this field are the phenotype-focused Korowai-language labels 'light-skinned people' (i.e., whites), 'long-haired people' (i.e., Javanese people, or non-Papuan Indonesians generally), and 'short-haired people' (i.e., Papuans).

19. Compare Lee 1943 on a similar pattern historically in Wintu.

20. Borrowed Indonesian words are routinely used as inflectable verbs in Korowai by addition of the Korowai verbalizing suffix *-moxo* 'do, install' (compare van Enk and de Vries 1997: 86; de Vries 1993: 15; Gardner-Chloros 1995: 78–79; Kulick 1992: 77; Romaine 1995: 131–141).

21. Whereas Kulick 1992 offered a detailed analysis of why and how a New Guinea community is dropping its vernacular from its repertoire in favor of an exogenous language, this chapter is a brief study of what it has meant for a community to begin adding the exogenous lingua franca to its repertoire in the first place. Compare Kulick 1992: 67–73, 280–281 n. 7 on the first Gapun generations to learn Tok Pisin.

22. One way Korowai categorization of foreigners as 'demons' contrasts with assimilation of whites to spirits or the dead in many other New Guinea societies is that the Korowai demon category is thoroughly a figure of horror, and meeting demons is a nightmarish event. See Leavitt 2000 for a discussion of a more hopeful side to some people's categorization of whites as dead relatives.

23. In a similar way, a few Korowai, aware that English is the language of most talk between international tourists and Indonesian or Papuan tour guides, now want to learn English so they can guide tourists themselves, rather than merely working as subordinates for nonlocal guides who bring tour groups to the area.

24. The greetings are examples of what Garrett 2005 terms "code-specific communicative practices."

25. On the boom in this product and its social ramifications, see Momberg 2000; Gunn et al. 2004; and Sekretariat Keadilan dan Perdamaian 2004.

26. Around 2000, during a period when separatist sentiment was suddenly expressible and expressed in public spaces across Papua to an unprecedented degree, many village-connected Korowai became familiar with the Papuan separatist Morning Star flag and the symbolism of its hoisting. Their sympathies are such that raising an Indonesian flag for fun is now an unlikely event.

27. The Indonesian term manusia 'human, humanity' is often used across Papua (and elsewhere) to mean 'civilized, culturally and economically dignified'. It occurs in state functionaries' discourses (variously paternalistic or berating) urging 'backward', 'isolated', and less-than-human subject populations to turn themselves into cultured humanity. Papuans also speak in parallel terms. In Korowai villages as across much of Papua, people often use the expression menjadi manusia 'become human' to mean quite specifically 'become a salaried civil servant', such as a schoolteacher (akin to English "become somebody"). They typically use the expression to explain why they work so hard to send their children to grades of school taught only at distant administrative and commercial centers, where (among other things) they become more thoroughly skilled in speaking Indonesian. Many Papuans who use the idiom in this way are hostile to Indonesian settlers, or think that the state's development initiatives have failed, so their use of the idiom does not index quite the same political views as were held by government functionaries who might have initially promoted the idiom's circulation. Although Korowai are at an unusual remove from direct, constant governmental domination—more so since the state's 1998 fiscal and political retrenchment—they have had plenty of encounters with these discourses (such as in one incident when police visiting a Korowai village criticized residents as living like "animals," not humans), and they frequently quote and debate the outsiders' evaluations. This is part of the context of the 'demon' versus 'human' categories' meanings now and may be one of the pressures prompting people to entertain the idea that they are themselves 'demonic'.

References

Althusser, Louis. 1971. Ideology and Ideological State Apparatuses. In *Lenin and Philosophy and Other Essays*, pp. 123–173. Translated by Ben Brewster. London: Monthly Review Press.

Anderson, Benedict. 1991. *Imagined Communities: Reflections on the Origin and Spread of Nationalism*. London: Verso.

Badan Pusat Statistik, Jakarta. 2001. *Penduduk Papua: Hasil Sensus Penduduk Tahun 2000.* Series L2.2.30. Jakarta: Badan Pusat Statistik.

Badan Pusat Statistik Provinsi Papua. 2003. *Papua Dalam Angka 2002.* Jayapura: Badan Pusat Statistik Provinsi Papua.

Bashkow, Ira. 2004. A Neo-Boasian Conception of Cultural Boundaries. *American Anthropologist* 106: 443–458.

Basso, Keith. 1979. *Portraits of "the Whiteman": Linguistic Play and Cultural Symbols among the Western Apache.* Cambridge: Cambridge University Press.

Benveniste, Emile. 1971. Subjectivity in Language. In *Problems in General Linguistics*, pp. 223–230. Translated by M. E. Meek. Miami: University of Miami Press.

Biro Pusat Statistik. 1983. *Penduduk Propinsi Irian Jaya: Hasil Sensus Penduduk 1980.* Jakarta: Biro Pusat Statistik.

———. 1992. *Penduduk Irian Jaya: Hasil Sensus Penduduk 1990.* Jakarta: Biro Pusat Statistik.

Carrington, Lois. 1996. *A Linguistic Bibliography of the New Guinea Area*. Pacific Linguistics Series D–90. Canberra: Australian National University.

de Vries, Lourens. 1993. *Forms and Functions in Kombai, an Awyu Language of Irian Jaya*. Pacific Linguistics Series B–108. Canberra: Australian National University.

Diebold, A. Richard. 1961. Incipient Bilingualism. *Language* 37: 97–112.

Elmslie, Jim. 2002. *Irian Jaya under the Gun: Indonesian Economic Development versus West Papuan Nationalism*. Honolulu: University of Hawai'i Press.

Errington, J. Joseph. 1998. *Shifting Languages: Interaction and Identity in Javanese Indonesia*. Cambridge: Cambridge University Press.

Fechter, Anne-Meike. 2005. The 'Other' Stares Back: Experiencing Whiteness in Jakarta. *Ethnography* 6: 87–103.

Gal, Susan, and Judith Irvine. 1995. The Boundaries of Languages and Disciplines: How Ideologies Construct Difference. *Social Research* 62: 967–1001.

Gardner-Chloros, Penelope. 1995. Code-switching in Community, Regional, and National Repertoires: The Myth of the Discreteness of Linguistic Systems. In *One Speaker, Two Languages: Cross-disciplinary Perspectives on Code-switching*, ed. Lesley Milroy and Pieter Muysken. Cambridge: Cambridge University Press.

Garrett, Paul B. 2005. What a Language Is Good For: Language Socialization, Language Shift, and the Persistence of Code-Specific Genres in St. Lucia. *Language in Society* 34: 327–361.

Glazebrook, Diana. 2004. Teaching Performance Art Is Like Sharpening the Blade of a Knife. *The Asia Pacific Journal of Anthropology* 5: 1–14.

Gunn, B., P. Stevens, M. Singadan, L. Sunari, and P. Chatterton. 2004. *Eaglewood in Papua New Guinea. Resource Management in Asia-Pacific Working Paper No. 51*. Canberra: Resource Management in Asia-Pacific Program, Research School of Pacific and Asian Studies, Australian National University.

Hastings, Adi, and Paul Manning. 2004. Introduction: Acts of Alterity. *Language & Communication* 24: 291–311.

Hill, Jane H. 2005. Intertextuality as Source and Evidence for Indirect Indexical Meanings. *Journal of Linguistic Anthropology* 15: 113–124.

Hoffman, John. 1979. A Foreign Investment: Indies Malay to 1901. *Indonesia* 27: 65–92.

Irvine, Judith T., and Susan Gal. 2000. Language Ideology and Linguistic Differentiation. In *Regimes of Language: Ideologies, Polities, and Identities*, ed. Paul V. Kroskrity, pp. 35–83. Santa Fe, NM: School of American Research Press.

Kulick, Don. 1992. *Language Shift and Cultural Reproduction: Socialization, Self, and Syncretism in a Papua New Guinea Village*. Cambridge: Cambridge University Press.

Leavitt, Stephen C. 2000. The Apotheosis of White Men?: A Reexamination of Beliefs about Europeans as Ancestral Spirits. *Oceania* 70: 304–323.

Lee, Dorothy D. 1943. The Linguistic Aspect of Wintu' Acculturation. *American Anthropologist* 45: 435–440.

Lüdi, Georges. 1987. Les marques transcodiques: regards nouveaux sur le bilinguisme. In *Devenir bilingue—parle bilingue. Actes du 2e colloque sur le bilinguisme, Université de Neuchâtel, 20–22 Septembre, 1984*, ed. Georges Lüdi, pp. 1–21. Tübingen: Max Niemeyer Verlag.

McGibbon, Rodd. 2004. *Plural Society in Peril: Migration, Economic Change, and the Papua Conflict. Policy Studies 13*. Washington, DC: East-West Center Washington. Downloaded from www.eastwestcenterwashington.org.

Merlan, Francesca. 1981. Land, Language, and Social Identity in Aboriginal Australia. *Mankind* 13: 133–148.

Merlan, Francesca. 1998. *Caging the Rainbow: Places, Politics, and Aborigines in a North Australian Town*. Honolulu: University of Hawai'i Press.

Milroy, Lesley, and Pieter Muysken. 1995. Introduction: Code-Switching and Bilingualism Research. In *One Speaker, Two Languages: Cross-disciplinary Perspectives on Code-switching*, ed. Lesley Milroy and Pieter Muysken, pp. 1–14. Cambridge: Cambridge University Press.

Momberg, Frank, Rajindra Puri, and Timothy Jessup. 2000. Exploitation of Gaharu, and Forest Conservation Efforts in the Kayan Mentarang National Park, East Kalimantan, Indonesia. In *People, Plants, and Justice: The Politics of Nature Conservation*, ed. Charles Zerner, pp. 259–284. New York: Columbia University Press.

Munro, Catharine. 2002. Count Reveals 312 Tribes in Indonesian Province. In *Australian Associated Press Newsfeed* Available at: http://www.westpapua.net/news/02/07/160702-population.htm.

Overweel, Jeroen. 1998. "A Systematic Activity": Military Exploration in Western New Guinea, 1907–1915. In *Perspectives on the Bird's Head of Irian Jaya*, ed. Jelle Miedema, Cecilia Odé, and Rien A. C. Dam, pp. 455–478. Amsterdam: Rodopi.

Robbins, Joel. 2003. On the Paradoxes of Global Pentecostalism and the Perils of Continuity Thinking. *Religion* 33: 221–231.

———. 2004. *Becoming Sinners: Christianity and Moral Torment in a Papua New Guinea Society*. Berkeley: University of California Press.

———. 2006. On Giving Ground: Globalization, Religion, and Territorial Detachment in a Papua New Guinea Society. In *Territoriality and Conflict in an Era of Globalization*, ed. Miles Kahler and Barbara F. Walter, pp. 62–84. Cambridge: Cambridge University Press.

Romaine, Suzanne. 1992. *Language, Education, and Development: Urban and Rural Tok Pisin in Papua New Guinea*. Oxford: Oxford University Press.

———. 1995. *Bilingualism*. 2nd ed. Oxford: Blackwell.

Roosman, Raden S. 1982. Pidgin Malay as Spoken in Irian Jaya. *The Indonesian Quarterly* 10: 95–104.

Rumsey, Alan. 1993. Language and Territoriality in Aboriginal Australia. In *Language and Culture in Aboriginal Australia*, ed. Michael Walsh and Colin Yallop, pp. 191–206. Canberra: Aboriginal Studies Press.

———. 2006. The Articulation of Indigenous and Exogenous Orders in Highland New Guinea and Beyond. *The Australian Journal of Anthropology* 17: 47–69.

Rutherford, Danilyn. 1998. Trekking to New Guinea: Dutch Colonial Fantasies of a Virgin Land, 1900–1940. In *Domesticating the Empire: Race, Gender, and Family Life in French and Dutch Colonialism*, ed. Frances Gouda and Julia Clancy-Smith, pp. 255–272. Charlottesville: University of Virginia Press.

———. 2003. *Raiding the Land of the Foreigners: The Limits of the Nation on an Indonesian Frontier*. Princeton, NJ: Princeton University Press.

———. 2005. Frontiers of the Lingua Franca: Ideologies of the Linguistic Contact Zone in Dutch New Guinea. *Ethnos* 70: 387–412.

Saltford, John. 2003. *The United Nations and the Indonesian Takeover of West Papua, 1962–1969: The Anatomy of Betrayal*. London: RoutledgeCurzon.

Sankoff, Gillian. 1980. *The Social Life of Language*. Philadelphia: University of Pennsylvania Press.

Santner, Eric L. 2001. *On the Psychotheology of Everyday Life: Reflections on Freud and Rosenzweig*. Chicago: University of Chicago Press.

Schieffelin, Bambi. 2002. Marking Time: The Dichotomizing Discourse of Multiple Temporalities. *Current Anthropology* 43 (S4): S5–S17.

Seiler, W. 1983. The Lost Malay Language of Papua New Guinea. In *Studies in Malay Dialects, Part II. Nusa, Linguistic Studies of Indonesian and Other Languages in Indonesia, Vol. 17*, ed. James T. Collins, pp. 65–72. Jakarta: Badan Penyelenggara Seri NUSA, Universitas Atma Jaya.

Sekretariat Keadilan dan Perdamaian, Keuskupan Agung Merauke. 2004. *Bisnis Gaharu dan Dampaknya Terhadap Kehidupan Orang Awyu dan Wiyagar di Distrik Assue, Kabupaten Mappi — Papua Selatan [The Gaharu Business and Its Impact on the Lives of Awyu and Wiyagar People in Assue District, Mappi Regency, South Papua]*. Merauke: Office of Justice and Peace, Archdiocese of Merauke. Downloaded from http://www.hampapua.org/skp/indexe.html.

Shiraishi, Takashi. 1996. The Phantom World of Digoel. *Indonesia* 61: 93–118.

Siegel, James T. 1997. *Fetish, Recognition, Revolution*. Princeton, NJ: Princeton University Press.

Sneddon, James. 2003. *The Indonesian Language: Its History and Role in Modern Society*. Sydney: University of New South Wales Press.

Stasch, Rupert. 2001. Giving Up Homicide: Korowai Experience of Witches and Police (West Papua). *Oceania* 72: 33–55.

———. 2002. Joking Avoidance: A Korowai Pragmatics of Being Two. *American Ethnologist* 29: 335–365.

———. Forthcoming. Referent-Wrecking in Korowai: A New Guinea Abuse Register as Ethnosemiotic Protest. *Language in Society* 37(2).

———. 2003. The Forest, the Village, and the Subdistrict Seat: Rural-Urban Articulations in the Politics of Sovereignty in West Papua. Paper presented at the American Anthropological Association annual meeting, Chicago.

———. 2005. Heterogeneity of Spatial Experience Before and After Village Formation: Shifting Geographies of Belonging among Korowai of West Papua. Paper presented at the Association for Social Anthropology in Oceania annual meeting, Lihue.

———. n.d. Society of Others: Kinship and Mourning in a West Papuan Place. Unpublished manuscript.

Suharno, Ignatius. 1983. The Reductive System of an Indonesian Dialect: A Study of [the] Irian Jaya Case. In *Papers from the Third International Conference on Austronesian Linguistics, Vol. 4: Thematic Variation*, ed. Amran Halim, Lois Carrington, and Stephen A. Wurm. Pacific Linguistics C–77. Canberra: Research School of Pacific Studies, Australian National University.

Swadling, Pamela. 1993. *Plumes from Paradise: Trade Cycles in Outer Southeast Asia and Their Impact on New Guinea and Nearby Islands until 1920*. Boroko: Papua New Guinea National Museum.

Taylor, Anne-Christine. 1993. Remembering to Forget: Identity, Mourning, and Memory among the Jivaro. *Man* 28: 653–678.

Taylor, Paul M. 1983. North Moluccan Malay: Notes on a "Substandard" Dialect of Indonesian. In *Studies in Malay Dialects, Part II*, ed. James Collins, pp. 14–27. NUSA Monograph Series, Vol. 17. Jakarta: Badan Penyelenggara Seri NUSA.

Timmer, Jaap. 2005. *Decentralisation and Elite Politics in Indonesian Papua*. State, Society, and Governance in Melanesia, Discussion Paper 2005/6. Canberra: Research School of Pacific and Asian Studies. Downloaded from rspas.anu.edu.au/papers/melanesia/discussion_papers/05_06_dp_timmer.pdf.

van Baal, Jan, K. W. Galis, and R. M. Koentjaraningrat. 1984. *West Irian: A Bibliography*. Dordrecht: KITLV.

van Enk, Gerrit J., and Lourens de Vries. 1997. *The Korowai of Irian Jaya: Their Language in Its Cultural Context*. Oxford: Oxford University Press.

van Velzen, Paul. 1995. Some Notes on the Variety of Malay Used in Serui and Vicinity. In *Tales from a Concave World: Liber Amicorum Bert Voorhoeve*, ed. Connie Baak, Mary Bakker and Dick van der Meij, pp. 311–343. Leiden: Department of Languages and Cultures of South-East Asia and Oceania, Leiden University.

Vlasblom, Dirk. 2004. *Papoea: Een Geschiedenis*. Amsterdam: Mets & Schilt.

Voorhoeve, C. L. 1983. Some Observations on North-Moluccan Malay. In *Studies in Malay Dialects, Part II*, ed. James Collins, pp. 1–13. NUSA Monograph Series, Vol. 17. Jakarta: Badan Penyelenggara Seri NUSA.

Woolard, Kathryn A. 1989. *Double Talk: Bilingualism and the Politics of Ethnicity in Catalonia*. Stanford, CA: Stanford University Press.

6

JOEL ROBBINS

You Can't Talk behind the Holy Spirit's Back

Christianity and Changing Language Ideologies in a Papua New Guinea Society

It is not news that part of what makes language ideologies such a productive area of research is the fact that they are always about much more than just language (Woolard 1998). They connect up with everything from notions of personhood, gender, and agency to those of inequality, social structure, and the nature of knowledge. Given this, one promising way forward in this area of research is to look for cultural domains in which the links between language and other ideologies have not been fully examined. This is the point of departure for this chapter—for from the point of view of Melanesia, it is hard to miss the fact that language ideologies stand in complex relationship to ideologies of exchange in ways that linguistic anthropologists, especially those working elsewhere, have only begun to explore. In Melanesia, both language ideologies and ideologies of exchange tend to be highly elaborated, and both are in important ways shaping and being shaped by the changes of the contemporary postcolonial era. In this chapter, I explore how changes in language ideology can be related to and to some extent constrained by persistent ideologies of exchange.

Although linguistic and material exchange are not placed in the same analytic framework as often as one might expect,[1] it is not difficult to see that it makes some sense to do so. The range of meanings of the English "communicate"—which refers to both material and linguistic exchanges—argues as much, as does the rather obvious sense in which material gifts carry socially important information. Yet to go beyond such general observations, we require the formulation of some models of how the two orders of exchange can interrelate in particular ethnographic cases. I want to focus here on the formulation of two such models.

Bambi Schieffelin (1990: 110–111), who has in important respects pioneered research on the relation between language and exchange, discusses one of these models in her study of language socialization among the Kaluli. "Talk is not only instrumental," she writes, "but is also a metaphor for what happens in exchange: Meaning is offered and taken, asked for and given. Children through…exchanges of mediated or assisted talk are learning about reciprocity as well. They are learning about the form and functions of giving and taking, that reciprocity and social relationships are bound to one another." In this model, linguistic and material exchanges serve as analogues for one another. Issues that are important in one—the role of turn taking, for example, or of providing an appropriate response, or of making sure that appropriate meaning is conveyed—are also salient in the other. For this reason, people are given to thinking about the two orders of exchange in terms of one another, and ethnographers can, as Schieffelin indicates, draw on how people relate them to develop a rounded ethnography of the broad ideologies of communication and interaction that are important to particular groups (see also Munn 1986).

Along with serving as models for one another, the two orders can also, as it were, compete and/or cooperate to do similar communicative work. Levi-Strauss (1963: 296) long ago suggested that society could be seen as comprising systems of communication operating on three levels: communication of people on the level of kinship (he infamously referred here to the "communication of women," but the difficulties with this understanding of the level of kinship need not concern us in the context of the present argument), communication of goods and services on the economic level, and communication of messages on the linguistic level. When society is thought of this way, one question that immediately arises is how the levels are interrelated. I have suggested elsewhere that in societies where ideologies of communication see material exchange as the most reliable or weighted level of human intercourse, speech may be seen as relatively unreliable and that the opposite will be true where speech is seen as most important (Robbins 2001b). Keane (1997) has similarly analyzed in detail an Indonesian case in which the two orders of linguistic and material exchange are seen to complement one another. More generally, this model of the two orders as of necessity interrelated stresses the need for analysts to look at how, in various cultures, people think of the two as doing similar or distinctive types of work in the construction of social life (Weiner 1984).

Beyond focusing our attention on the social work these two orders are seen to do, this model also directs us to attend to the ways people move between the two orders in practice—how they relate linguistic and material exchange in the flow of their daily lives. Schieffelin's (1990) account of the Kaluli is again illustrative, for she shows in numerous ways that a good deal of children's socialization is aimed at teaching them how to interrelate speech and exchange—how to shift between spoken and material circuits and work through both to construct social relations.

With these two models in hand, I argue in this chapter that changes in language ideologies have to be analyzed not only in themselves but also in their relation to what is happening to ideologies of material exchange and to the rules that guide movement between spheres governed by each of these ideologies. The relations between these two ideologies—both their "real" relations and those of analogy that people draw on in constructing their understandings of them—are important moving targets to keep in view in any account of cultural change in Melanesia.

My ethnographic focus here is on some of the ways the Urapmin of Papua New Guinea have worked to create a new role for speech and a new kind of speaker in the wake of their conversion to a charismatic form of Protestant Christianity. The Protestant linguistic ideology to which this form of Christianity has introduced them regards speech as an important means for conveying truth and demands that people speak sincerely and truthfully at all times (Keane 1998; Robbins 2001a). Such a positive evaluation of speech and the demands for sincerity and truthfulness that go with it played no part in traditional Urapmin language ideology, which figured speech as having no reliable capacity to convey truth and assumed that sincerity was impossible to achieve in spoken communication. Traditional Urapmin thinking thus left issues of sincerity out of account altogether and left those of truthfulness to be settled at the level of material exchange. Since traditional ideologies of language and of material exchange are still very much in play in Urapmin life, tensions regularly arise between traditional Urapmin ideas about the nature of speech and speakers and the ideals held out by the Protestant language ideology to which they have become committed.

One place in which these tensions have come to a head is a controversy that has developed around the speech of female Spirit mediums (<u>Spirit</u> <u>meri</u>,[2] 'Spirit women') who are held to report things the Holy Spirit has shown or told them and who sometimes in the midst of such reports call for people to carry out traditional kinds of sacrificial material exchange. People generally see these Spirit women as the paradigmatic example of modern truth speakers, since it is held that all that they say while occupying their Spirit woman role is true. Yet others, generally those scandalized by the Spirit women's calls for traditional sacrifices, are inclined to doubt the veracity of some of what they say. In the body of this chapter, I show that to understand why the speech of the Spirit women has proven controversial, one has to understand how linguistic and material exchange are serving both as analogues of one another and as levels of exchange that are in effect competing to do the same work in Urapmin life. Analyzing how this controversy unfolds on both of these levels brings us to the heart of language ideological change in contemporary Urapmin.[3]

Christianity, cultural change, and the rise of mediumship among the Urapmin

The Urapmin of Papua New Guinea are a group of 390 people living in the West Sepik Province. First colonized at the end of the 1940s, the entire Urapmin community converted to a form of charismatic Protestant Christianity in the late 1970s during a revival movement that was important in many parts of Papua New Guinea. As the revival gained influence, the Urapmin dismantled their traditional religion, 'throwing out' the bones of their ancestors, tearing down their cult houses, and abrogating the extensive system of taboos on food, intersexual contact, and land use that had until that time structured many aspects of their lives. Since 1978, when the revival reached its height, the Urapmin have seen themselves as a completely

Christian community in which no one in any important sense practices traditional religion.

As with charismatic and Pentecostal Christians in many parts of the world, the conversion of the Urapmin does not mean that the ontology of spiritual powers that underpinned their traditional religion has disappeared (Robbins 2004b). The Urapmin continue to contend with a host of nature spirits (*motobil*) who own all of the natural resources people use and often make people sick in retaliation for what they perceive to be disrespectful treatment. The Urapmin now see these spirits as unambiguously evil, and they enlist God's support in their effort to be rid of them, but at this time the spirits remain a prominent feature of their world. The meaning of these spirits in the Urapmin view of things is complex, but one way to see them is as a stubborn reminder of the persistence of the past among a group of people who like to understand themselves as having quite decisively broken with it. Referring to the coming of the whites, colonization, and, most important, Christianity, the Urapmin often say, "Before was before, and now is now" (bipo em i bipo, na nau em i nau) expressing as they do so their sense of having effected a profound rupture in their way of life. But the persistence of the spirits, a persistence that is quite literally sickening, indicates that in some respects their break with the past has not been complete, and that it continually needs to be remade.

It is in relation to the Urapmin commitment to a model of temporal rupture in the face of the difficulty of fully effecting such radical change that I want to examine the transformation of ideologies of language and exchange in their community. The most obvious aspect of linguistic change in Urapmin, one that is apparent even before one considers issues of language ideology, has been the widespread adoption of Tok Pisin, the most prominent lingua franca in Papua New Guinea, as a second regularly used code. Though no Urapmin learn Tok Pisin as their first language, all children older than twelve or so, men younger than forty-five, and women younger than thirty are fluent in it. The Urapmin desire to distinguish the present from the past is evidenced in the extent to which the Urapmin have embraced Tok Pisin, for they very much regard it as a language that is connected with the present and with the Western world to which they are working to connect (cf. Kulick 1992). Their sense of Tok Pisin as a 'modern' language decisively effects usage, as it has become most widely used within new institutions such as the courts, local government meetings, and, most important in the present context, the church. The relatively frequent reliance on Tok Pisin in church settings and the extensive use of Tok Pisin loanwords when Urap is spoken in them and in other Christian contexts also follow, at least in part, from the Urapmin tendency to avoid finding or using Urap analogues for items from Tok Pisin's elaborate Christian vocabulary. Such attention to preserving the boundary between the Tok Pisin lexicon and that of the vernacular has not been evident in all cases of conversion in Papua New Guinea (cf. Renck 1990).[4] Urapmin efforts to preserve the boundary, I would suggest, are rooted in their more general effort to distinguish the Christian present from the past, in this case by outfitting the present with its own code.

The link between Tok Pisin, the present time, and Christianity is widely accepted in Urapmin and is not a source of controversy. Yet it is also the case that Tok Pisin has not brought with it, as it were, an elaborated language ideology and set of linked practices that would enable the Urapmin to construct themselves as the sincere speakers their Christianity requires them to become. People are not understood, for example, to be able to speak more sincerely in Tok Pisin. Instead, it has been left to Christianity to make sincerity desirable and possible, both by fostering a language ideology that promotes and facilitates it and, crucially, by developing a number of linguistic practices in which such speech can be produced and interpreted. By contrast to the spread of Tok Pisin as a code, a process that has produced little strife in Urapmin, the installation of a Christian linguistic ideology of sincerity has been a tense one. As I indicated above, a productive way of exploring the tensions its introduction has generated is to consider the controversy that has arisen over the work of Urapmin Spirit women. This controversy not only reveals the difficulties that beset language ideological change in Urapmin, but also makes clear how such change is linked to changing ideologies of exchange.

Spirit women are a class of adult women in Urapmin who can in most cases become possessed by the Holy Spirit at will. Clients come to Spirit women and entreat them to pray over them and to ask the Holy Spirit to help them discover which nature spirits are making them or their children sick (and, less often, to help them find lost or possibly stolen items or to discern whether a given time is an auspicious one to undertake a planned trip). When they are possessed, Spirit women shake and speak in tongues as the Holy Spirit speaks in their hearts and shows them pictures ('like showing them videos,' say those who have seen videotape programs in towns). Once their trances subside, Spirit women interpret what they have heard and seen for their clients, telling them the names of the nature spirits who are troubling them (or the answers to the other kinds of questions they ask) and passing on the Holy Spirit's recommended course of action, which is usually to pray to God to chase the nature spirits from the sufferer and bind them far from the Urapmin world.

Spirit mediumship of the sort the Spirit women practice is new to the Urapmin; it came with Christianity and stands, by virtue of the way it demonstrates the power that God has made available to them, as an important index of their ability to fashion the wholly new, Christian world in which they aspire to live. The diagnostic tasks the Spirit women now perform were formerly undertaken by male diviners who did not see or hear the nature spirits directly but rather relied on putting questions to leaves floating in bowls of water to determine the causes of people's suffering. Since such divination is now seen as a sinful traditional practice, the Urapmin have found it important that God has provided a new, acceptable way to meet the needs it once met. Further, with the Spirit women's power to pray effectively for healing or other good outcomes, they bring new skills to the role of seer that the older diviners did not possess. As with many new Christian aspects of their culture, the Urapmin do not see Spirit women so much as a substitute for a traditional religious form but as a vast improvement upon it.

One striking aspect of the way the Urapmin talk about the practice of Spirit women is that they believe them to be unimpeachable truth speakers. Whatever they say about what they have heard and seen in trance, people hold to be true. In fact, to doubt them is tantamount to doubting God himself, who through his Spirit has told and shown the Spirit women what they know and has guided their reports. One should not, the Urapmin say, 'talk behind the Holy Spirit's back' (tok baksit long Holi Spirit) by casting doubt on what the Spirit women say. In this respect, among the Urapmin the Spirit women are paradigms of a new kind of speaker—a Christian speaker who consistently speaks the truth.

Yet despite people's often-expressed opinion that Spirit women can always be trusted to speak truthfully when acting in their role as medium, near the end of my fieldwork a controversy began to develop that indicated that their reputation for truthful speech might not be completely secure. This controversy centered on the Spirit women's tendency, particularly in cases in which spirits were thought to threaten a child with death, to report that the Holy Spirit had recommended not only prayer, but also the sacrifice of a pig (*kang anfukelang*) by the child's parents to the nature spirits so the spirits will release the child.[5] People always regard such sacrificial prescriptions as somewhat awkward. Urapmin routinely claim that Jesus was the last sacrifice, and they recognize further that similar sacrifices were regularly ordered by the male diviners of the pre-Christian order, making the ones the Spirit women demanded obvious throwbacks to a pre-Christian religious life that in all other respects people see themselves as happily done with. Indeed, pig sacrifice is the only traditional ritual that is still practiced (at least publicly) in Urapmin.[6] To be sure, the Urapmin now surround sacrificial ritual with Christian prayer, and theological sophisticates argue that it really isn't sacrifice in the old sense. But even they cannot erase the core structure of the old ritual that provides the basis for the newer one, and for most people contemporary sacrifice stands as a morally suspect survival from the ritual life of the past. But as ambivalent as the Urapmin are about sacrifice, no one wants to spare any effort when the life of a child is at stake, and in my experience parents, regardless of their qualms, tend to follow through when the Spirit women, purportedly speaking on behalf of the Holy Spirit, order them to perform the ritual.

Toward the end of 1992, however, I began to hear rumblings from some men that Spirit women had been ordering sacrifice too often of late. Sacrifice really is a sinful practice, they argued, one in which people in effect enter into exchange relations with spirits with whom they should be at war in a fight in which God should be their only spiritual ally. Perhaps, they suggested, these Spirit women were actually in fact possessed by evil spirits who tricked them into thinking that it was the Holy Spirit who was guiding them to call for these rituals. If either of these was the case, their prescriptions should not be followed.

I have called this a controversy, but perhaps it was more like a small trend; a kind of talk a few men were trying out on a regular basis, waiting to see if it might catch on with others and develop into a full-fledged critique of the Spirit women's practice.[7] I left Urapmin before it was clear if this trend would fade away or develop a strong public presence, but the signs pointed to it sputtering out before it had any real influence. Both its existence and its relative weakness as a trend left me with several questions. What was the attraction in promoting a model of evil spirit possession in which the Spirit women's reputation for truth would lose its grounding? Why would men who, along with others, had always articulated for me the idea that one can't talk behind the Holy Spirit's back possibly be doing just that now, and quite self-consciously (though if evil spirits were the possessing agents, they of course would not be doing so, which is why I say "possibly"). And at the same time, why was the rather easy resort to evil-spirit inspiration as a challenge to the Spirit women so rarely taken, and why did it register so weakly on public discourse when it was? Examining some potential answers to these questions gets us to the issues at the core of the kinds of changes currently transforming language and exchange ideologies in Urapmin.

Spirit women and the relationship between linguistic and material exchange

Answers to some of the questions just posed become clear when we recognize that the Spirit women have been caught up in a series of transformations in the way the Urapmin think about the relationship between the orders of linguistic and material exchange. One of these transformations, to be examined in detail later, is being effected by the Spirit women themselves and turns on the way Urapmin understand the relationship of analogy that holds between linguistic exchanges and material ones. The other transformation, the focus of this section, is one in which all Urapmin are taking part and involves shifting the ways Urapmin understand linguistic and material exchange to shape social life. This second transformation is thus far incomplete and has been an important site of struggle between traditional and Christian ideas. In the midst of this struggle, the Spirit women find themselves working on both sides, and it is their contradictory positioning that makes their practice so potentially controversial. In understanding their position, then, it is useful to lay out the terms of this struggle over the proper roles of different kinds of exchange.

In important ways, the Urapmin see the move they are trying to make from the traditional past to the Christian present as one from a regime in which what I will call 'social truth' is most often established through ritualized exchange involving primarily material objects to a regime in which ideally it can be established through speech. By social truth, I mean simply the truth of people's social relationships: the extent to which people are in accord or conflict with one another, committed or only casually connected to one another, thinking about or disregarding one another. The sense of ontological security people in any culture have regarding their social world depends upon the constant augmentation and adjustment of such truth. Traditional Urapmin ideas about the nature of language and its use—their language ideology—does not hold that speech is an effective instrument for establishing social truth. In common with many Melanesian peoples, Urapmin generally hold that it is impossible to determine a person's intentions, thoughts, or feelings by listening to what they say (see Robbins 2001a; Schieffelin 1990, chap. 7 of this volume). Too much can happen between the heart (*aget*—the seat of thought and feeling) and the mouth, Urapmin say, for speech to be a reliable index of what people think and feel. Because they distrust speech in this way, they hold that it cannot reliably evidence people's feelings for and commitments to one another and thus cannot dependably establish social truth.

Instead of relying on speech to establish social truth, Urapmin turn to the exchange of material goods. When things are going well, they establish the truth of their mutual involvements by exchanging everyday things like food—things which no adults need from anyone else but which they almost always give to and get from other people anyway as a way of marking their connections to one another. When people give, they are said to be 'thinking of' (<u>tingim</u>) each other, and hence in daily life material gifts can express what words cannot. When things go wrong because of disputes, people stop exchanging with each other, thereby marking the truth of their estrangement. Reconciliation is not effected by verbal apologies, but rather by a return to material exchange. Disputes end when those involved in them engage in highly ritualized exchanges in which they 'buy' (*dalamin*) each other's feelings of shame and anger through the exchange of matching objects to indicate with certainty that they are returning their relationship to good terms. To a North American observer, it often seems as if the Urapmin have recourse to the exchange of goods as often and as easily as we have recourse to the exchange of words, and that they have elaborated as great a range of formal and informal ways of exchanging things as we have of exchanging speech. This is because it is through the conversation of gifts that they establish the social truths of their lives.

Although this account of how the Urapmin establish social truth holds in broad outline today, much has changed since their conversion to Christianity. From the point of view of their Christian language ideology, the Urapmin believe that speech should always be sincere and thus should by itself be able to convey the truth of their relationships. As Keane (2002) argues, the demand for sincerity is in fact a cornerstone of Protestant thinking about language and about the person (see also Robbins 2001a; Schieffelin n.d., and chap. 7). Sanneh (2003: 101) provides a hint of the cultural logic behind this demand and the moral force that backs it when he writes "God does not dissemble or vacillate, nor should God's witnesses." In this language ideology, as it is understood in Urapmin and elsewhere, speech should make people's hearts and minds transparent to one another.

Despite the existence of this Christian model of language among the Urapmin, a life in which speech alone establishes the truth of relationships is still in many respects only an ideal for them: exchange remains crucially important in their lives. But it is nonetheless helpful in examining contemporary Urapmin cultural change to recognize that the Urapmin do very much desire to become sincere speakers, and that, as they see it, they have in important respects been working to move from a world in which the exchange of things is the foundation of sociality to one in which the exchange of speech plays that role (Robbins 2001a).

If we see the Urapmin as working to transform a materially mediated social past into a social present mediated by speech, we can note that the Spirit women have positioned themselves at the interface between these two epochs. Looking toward the present, they represent themselves and are represented by others as the epitome of modern truth speakers. When speaking on behalf of the Holy Spirit, or reporting what the Holy Spirit has shown or told them, they cannot lie. This is the import of the phrase I have already mentioned: "You cannot talk behind the Holy Spirit's back." The truthful status of their speech is rooted in the way the Holy Spirit communicates directly to their hearts, thus modeling the way that their own speech, conceived of as their reports on what the Holy Spirit has shown or told them, should be taken directly into the hearts of their listeners. The Holy Spirit's possession of the Spirit women, then, serves as a paradigm of what the spoken word taken as sincere can accomplish by way of establishing social truth if it can flow reliably from the hearts of speakers to those of hearers.[8]

At the same time, however, the Spirit women (and the Holy Spirit who informs them) also link themselves to the past. They do this by relating regularly and intensively to the nature spirits who represent that past. One can argue that all Urapmin keep the nature spirits present by becoming sick, and by the anxieties they feel about disregarding the taboos that formerly regulated their interaction with them. But it is Spirit women who make the world of the nature spirits a vivid reality for people. It is they who report on that world in detail and still live ritual lives deeply engaged with it—both through their healing sessions and through rites that are designed to clear spirits out of particular areas. It is true that most of their ritual work is aimed at ridding the Urapmin world of the influence of the nature spirits and the past they represent. They regularly ask God in prayer to remove particular spirits from the Urapmin world, and they plant wooden crosses in the ground around areas they have cleared to prevent spirits from coming back. But even as the Spirit women work to secure a future free of the spirits, they of all Urapmin most forcefully remind people that the spirits still remain powerful, a stubborn holdover from the past that continues to impinge on the present.

Crucially for the argument of this chapter, in their intercourse with the spirits, the Spirit women also remain engaged with the past in the sense that they promote the order of material exchange that formerly completely dominated the production of social truth in Urapmin life. This is true in the obvious but still important sense that the sacrifices they call for are material exchanges of pigs for people. But it is also true in a more momentous sense inasmuch as the nature spirits, as they are currently represented, epitomize the old order in which mediation was primarily material. This is so because one of the things that is distinctive about the nature spirits as compared with human beings, which they in some respects resemble, is that they engage in material exchanges but not in linguistic ones. In fact, they can be said to engage people in material terms precisely so as to make forceful their demands for freedom from linguistic contact. Put more concretely, the spirits give Urapmin the use of the natural resources they 'own', but in return they demand respectful treatment, which prototypically involves people either not speaking or speaking only quietly when around them. When people disregard the spirits' demands not to have to hear human speech, the spirits communicate their anger not by way of speech, but in the physical register of bodily harm. In response, victims and their families either draw on God's power to rout and bind the spirits physically (no one ever asks God to talk to the spirits) or, more important for our purposes, they give the spirits pigs in sacrifice.

Part of the sense in which the spirits belong to the past, then, inheres in their fully alinguistic approach to human beings. They show no interest in moving toward the modern regime of relationships based on truthful speech, preferring to remain at the level of material exchange. Because this is so, when Spirit women prescribe sacrifices to these spirits they use their newfound power of truthful speech to return people to a world in which such speech is relatively unimportant, a world in which its communicative functions are fulfilled by material exchange. Their insistence that people return to the pre-Christian regime of establishing social truth (here the truth of their social relations with the nature spirits), is one reason that the Spirit women's practice is so controversial and that people at least sometimes are willing to criticize them in spite of the risks of talking behind the Holy Spirit's back.

It is important to recall at this point, however, that outright criticism of the Spirit women is rare, and that people's relations with them are best characterized as mildly ambivalent rather then deeply hostile. Understood as such, peoples relations to the Spirit women—having regular recourse to them but also wondering about the moral status of the sacrifices they call for and sometimes going so far as to criticize them—quite accurately indicates Urapmin ambivalence about the shift from establishing social truth primarily by means of the material circuit to relying on the verbal one. In their ability to continue to trust sacrifice enough to sometimes carry it out and to believe at least some of the time that the Holy Spirit can call for it, the Urapmin demonstrate the hold the world of exchange still has on their own practices of establishing social truth. The day when any Urapmin can truthfully proclaim the end of material exchange in words given in the verbal circuit has not yet arrived. At the same time, the enduring quality of their discomfort with sacrificial exchange, their inability to shake their ambivalence over it, demonstrates the strength of their determination to move to a Christian regime in which social truth is conveyed by way of speech. The Spirit women inhabit the very place where the tensions between the new world of linguistic exchange the Urapmin want to achieve and the old material one in which they in important respects continue to live come to a head.

Spirit women and the analogy between linguistic and material exchange

I have just shown that in terms of the relationship of competition between linguistic and material exchange to produce social truth in contemporary Urapmin, the Spirit women occupy an awkward place: they both epitomize the power of a new kind of sincere speaker operating in the sphere of linguistic exchange and also on occasion, often on the most fraught occasions, use that power to promote a return to reliance on the material sphere. When we turn to considering how the Spirit women have made novel use of the analogy between speech and gift giving, we find them similarly enmeshed in a complex project of blending the old and the new in ways that defy the more general Urapmin project of creating a new world that is in debt as little as possible to the old. The analogic transfer they aim to effect draws on the important role the origins of material things play in traditional understandings of material exchange, a role they attempt to make origins play in Urapmin ideas about speech as well.

It is one of the hallmarks of systems that use exchange to establish social truth in places like Melanesia that people maintain a developed interest in where things come from. Urapmin people know in detail the exchange histories of most of the objects in their lives, even such mundane ones as foodstuffs that move rather quickly through their hands. As they think about their lives—both the major turning points that mark them and their more routine everyday flow—they are always thinking about who gave them what and where the donors originally acquired what they gave.

This concern with origins and routes of travel was traditionally and is still today far less marked in regard to speech. In traditional Urapmin language ideology, speech is not held to convey knowledge, so its origins are relatively unimportant. Speakers are very careful to mark the origin of the knowledge their own speech alludes to—whether they have only heard about or actually seen the things they talk about—because things seen have an epistemological value that far outstrips that of those only heard about (and the visibility of material exchange accounts in large measure for its importance in traditional Urapmin communicative ideology). This leads people to regularly convey reported speech explicitly as such to indicate the epistemological weakness of claims they are making about matters they have only heard about. But this commitment to reporting speech as speech does not ramify into a concern with the exchange circuits by which the knowledge conveyed by speech travels, because as soon as knowledge is conveyed in speech its origin becomes unimportant, or, put more precisely, the only aspect of its origin that remains important is that it originated in speech—its train of transmission becomes irrelevant, and only its status as something gained from the speech of others needs to be marked. Speech thus lacks the social history that is a crucial component of exchange goods.

Spirit women complicate this distinction between the role of origins in linguistic and exchange ideologies by demanding that people take their speech as true precisely on the basis of its origin in the speech and pictures that the Holy Spirit 'gives' them. People should trust what they say precisely because it is (in many cases) reported speech—speech whose original speaker (the Holy Spirit) has a special status. And even when they are reporting on what they have seen rather than heard, things they have been shown by the Holy Spirit, their own reports are only speech and as such should be taken as unreliable, since what they report on they cannot themselves show to others. In these cases, it is their own special status as an origin of speech that they highlight, asking that this status be taken as a warrant for the truth of what is heard.

In making such claims about the value of speech that originates with special kinds of speakers, the Spirit women draw on the widespread sense in Urapmin that Christianity is in important respects based on reported divine speech—the Bible as a document is full of such reported speech, which Urapmin themselves pass on when they preach. If, as the Urapmin say, "God is nothing but talk" (Robbins 2001a), they can be taken in some sense to mean he is nothing more than reported speech. To follow God's religion, then, is to learn to trust reported divine speech in a way the Urapmin traditionally could not trust human speech, reported or otherwise. Among the Urapmin, divine speech is the paradigm of speech that carries epistemological value and does not lose that value in the process of being heard and reported. It is this value the Spirit women ascribe to their own speech.[9]

Spirit women, I hope to have shown, understand the truthfulness of their own speech to be grounded in an exchange history that looks very much like the ones people track for the material goods they pass between themselves. It is the origin and transmission history of what they say that makes it worthy of trust. But once they back their speech with its origins, Spirit women open themselves to the charge that those origins may have been deceptive: it may be evil spirits posing as the Holy Spirit that gave them knowledge. In this way, it is their analogic reframing of the truth-value of speech in terms drawn from the ideology of exchange, an ideology that emphasizes where things come from, that leaves the Spirit women vulnerable to the kinds of criticisms they have faced from those made anxious by the way they bring linguistic and material orders into new kinds of relationships.[10]

Let me close with a contrast that though perhaps somewhat overdrawn is none-theless worth making at this point as a way to try to capture some of the direction of the complex kinds of negotiations and processes of change I have been sketching here. In traditional Urapmin thinking, it is probably fair to say that people evalu-ated speech on the basis of its effects and material goods on the basis of where they came from in chains of gift giving. The modern Protestant Christian world the Urapmin are reckoning with does roughly the opposite. Speech, especially speech metalinguistically marked as socially, relationally important, is evaluated on the basis of its origins: on the basis of whether it truthfully conveys the knowledge and intentions of its speakers. Christian moderns evaluate material goods, by contrast, by their effects, on the basis of what the recipient can do with them, rather than on the basis of their origins. The effort it takes to get people to care about the sweatshop labor that creates their sneakers, or the general lack of notions of bitter money in the West (Shipton 1989), are proof enough of this. Given this contrast, the truth-claiming practice of the Spirit women represents a step on the road to turning Urapmin language ideology in the modern Christian direction, for it links the value of speech to its origins. Yet the tensions that still inhabit the process of cultural change in Urapmin make it impossible for this innovation to be received without the kind of conflict the practices of the Spirit women sometimes, as we have seen, engender.

Conclusion

The rapid growth of the literature on language ideologies has opened up a host of new questions about how people's constructions of language relate to other aspects of their culture. In this chapter, I have joined Schieffelin, Keane, and others in argu-ing that a particularly rich area for exploration in this vein is that concerning how ideas about linguistic communication relate to those that shape the exchange of material goods. This is a particularly important topic of investigation in Melanesia, where ideologies of material exchange are of great traditional importance and where shifts in their relationship to ideas about language are a key aspect of contemporary cultural change.

In order to map such change among the Urapmin, I have suggested two models of the relationship between language and exchange ideologies. In one model, speech and material exchange serve as analogues of one another, and cultures elaborate both the similarities and differences between them in constructing broader ideologies of communication and relatedness. In the other, linguistic communication and material exchange are seen as potentially either competing or cooperating to accomplish the same tasks—tasks such as the construction of social truth. One of my claims is that these two models might be applicable in a wide variety of cases and can help us to accurately register the complexity of the relations that hold between the orders of linguistic and material exchange in different places.

In the Urapmin case, the two models bring out different aspects of current changes. The analogic model points to the Spirit women's appeal to the importance of the origins of speech as part of their efforts to modernize Urapmin language ideol-ogy. To the extent that those who criticized them also drew on arguments about the origins of speech—suggesting that in some cases Spirit women might be speaking for demons—they too are drawn into this part of the Spirit women's modernizing efforts. The model that sees linguistic and material exchange as potential competitors both brings out the general direction of change in Urapmin, which is toward giving the linguistic order a prominence in the establishment of social truth that it did not have in the past, and pinpoints one of the areas of greatest tension in people's efforts to promote speech over material exchange: the practice of Spirit women, and in particular the way in which they use their prominent position as modern truth speakers to foreground the importance of material exchange by prescribing sacrifices that demand that people reengage the nature spirits on material terms (the only ones the spirits will accept).

The intersection of ideologies of language and material exchange, and the way their changing relations to one another shape processes of cultural change, is an area of research with great promise for the future. I have only been able to hint at some directions it might take here. From the point of view of Melanesian ethnography in particular, it is clear that there is an opportunity to put the very sophisticated body of theory that has grown up around the topic of material exchange into dialogue with work in linguistic anthropology in ways that can produce new ways of looking both at social life and at processes of change (see Thomas 1991 and Sykes 2005 for discussions of the literature on material exchange). I have presented some aspects of the Urapmin case here in hopes that it might demonstrate the value of pushing this project forward.

Notes

The research upon which this chapter is based was funded by the National Science Foundation, the Wenner-Gren Foundation for Anthropological Research, and the University of Virginia. Bambi Schieffelin, Miki Makihara, and Rupert Stasch have all given me extensive commentary on various drafts. I thank them for all their help, and thank also the other contributors to this volume who have given me useful feedback as my argument has developed.

1. In making this generalization, I am leaving to one side the numerous studies that relate language and political economy—for in these studies, exchange appears, if it appears explicitly at all, primarily as only one part of wider economic processes.

2. In this chapter, terms in the Urap language are given in italics, and terms in Tok Pisin, the most widespread lingua franca in Papua New Guinea and a language that is very important to Urapmin Christianity, are underlined.

3. The time period addressed in this chapter is the early 1990s.

4. In domains other than the Christian one, I have some evidence that the Urapmin do routinely engage in calquing Tok Pisin words and phrases into Urap, as Schieffelin (this volume) reports for Bosavi, but it is precisely this kind of transformation they resist in regard to the vocabulary of Christianity.

5. Nature spirits are not capable of killing adults, but all childhood deaths are attributed to them—this is why cases in which nature spirits make children ill are subject to special treatment.

6. The Urapmin still kill pigs on ceremonial occasions when large numbers of people gather (such as during the Christmas season), but they refer to this as 'shooting' pigs (*kang sanin*) as opposed to sacrificing them to the nature spirits (kang anfukelang). In a sacrifice, the spirit causing an illness is understood to eat the 'smell' (*tang*) of the pig and is sometimes given the blood, while the meat is distributed to the group, usually quite small, that is gathered and to

key relatives of the family that owned the pig who are absent. Ceremonial pig kills are planned well in advance and involve wide distributions of meat. When forced to sacrifice, people in my experience inevitably choose the smallest pig they have as the victim (unless that is or is soon to be their only viable breeding female) so as to expend as little meat as possible in a context that is so little productive of human relationships.

7. Jebens 2005: 87 presents a case from the Southern Highlands of Papua New Guinea in which there did develop a full-fledged male critique of a predominantly female revival movement. In this case, the men succeeded in stopping the movement. Although Jebens does not present this case as turning on issues of language or exchange, it does bear comparison with the one I describe here. Certainly one reason the critique in Urapmin has not gone so far is that in Urapmin both men and women share the basic charismatic, revivalist understandings that underwrite the Spirit women's practice, a condition that did not hold in Jebens's case.

8. As I have discussed elsewhere, the one other context in which people most fully inhabit the role of the sincere modern speaker is when they pray (Robbins 2001a). During prayer, however, other humans occupy the role of legitimate overhearers of speech directed in the first instance to God. This lends the production of social truth in prayer an air of complexity that is lacking in the more straightforward way the Spirit women communicate with those to whom they speak. This gives the Spirit women pride of place when it comes to representing the ideal speaker posited by the new regime of verbal mediation.

9. Although the Urapmin do talk about God as nothing but talk, and such notions are key to their construction of the modern order as one built on linguistic exchange, it must be noted that their conviction that God exists follows more from things they can see—that is, the ecstatic effects of the Holy Spirit on their own bodies and the bodies of those around them, than it does on what the Bible says. It is only after one has become convinced of God's existence in this way that one turns to the Bible to gain understanding of the world God has made and comes to construe God as a sincere speaker of truth (see Robbins 2004a: 137–145).

10. It is interesting to consider in relation to this analysis another kind of charge that those men who were critical of the Spirit women's call for sacrifice sometimes leveled at them: on occasion they would suggest that perhaps they ordered sacrifice simply because they were hungry for meat. Unlike the charge that the Spirit women may be possessed by evil spirits when they order sacrifice, this criticism was never elaborated at all and in my experience was not taken up by the public. This is not surprising, for in speculating about the motives for the Spirit women's speech, it went against strong traditional language ideological norms against any such speculation. At the same time, however, such a deviant effort to publicly name other people's intentions can also be seen as a pointed response to the Spirit women's attempts to back their speech with its origins, for like the charge of evil spiritual inspiration, it invalidates their spoken demands for sacrifice by showing that the origins of those demands (in this case, the Spirit women's hunger) are illegitimate.

References

Jebens, Holger. 2005. *Pathways to Heaven: Contesting Mainline and Fundamentalist Christianity in Papua New Guinea*. New York: Berghahn.

Keane, Webb. 1997. *Signs of Recognition: Powers and Hazards of Representation in an Indonesian Society*. Berkeley: University of California Press.

———. 1998. Calvin in the Tropics: Objects and Subjects at the Religious Frontier. In *Border Fetishisms: Material Objects in Unstable Places*, ed. Patricia Spyer, pp. 13–34. New York: Routledge.

———. 2002. Sincerity, "Modernity," and the Protestants. *Cultural Anthropology* 17: 65–92.

Kulick, Don. 1992. *Language Shift and Cultural Reproduction: Socialization, Self, and Syncretism in a Papua New Guinean Village*. New York: Cambridge University Press.

Levi-Strauss, Claude. 1963. *Structural Anthropology*. New York: Basic Books.

Munn, Nancy M. 1986. *The Fame of Gawa: A Symbolic Study of Value Transformation in a Massim (Papua New Guinea) Society*. New York: Cambridge University Press.

Renck, Gunther. 1990. *Contextualization of Christianity and Christianization of Language: A Case Study from the Highlands of Papua New Guinea*. Erlangen, Germany: Verlag der Ev.Luth. Mission.

Robbins, Joel. 2001a. God Is Nothing but Talk: Modernity, Language and Prayer in a Papua New Guinea Society. *American Anthropologist* 103: 901–912.

———. 2001b. Ritual Communication and Linguistic Ideology: A Reading and Partial Reformulation of Rappaport's Theory of Ritual. *Current Anthropology* 42: 591–614.

———. 2004a. *Becoming Sinners: Christianity and Moral Torment in a Papua New Guinea Society*. Berkeley: University of California Press.

———. 2004b. The Globalization of Pentecostal and Charismatic Christianity. *Annual Review of Anthropology* 33: 117–143.

Sanneh, Lamin. 2003. *Whose Religion is Christianity? The Gospel Beyond the West*. Grand Rapids: Wm. B. Eerdmans.

Schieffelin, Bambi B. 1990. *The Give and Take of Everyday Life: Language Socialization of Kaluli Children*. New York: Cambridge University Press.

———. n.d. Reshaping Languages and Persons. Manuscript.

Shipton, Parker. 1989. *Bitter Money: Cultural Economy and Some African Meanings of Forbidden Commodities*. Washington, DC: American Anthropological Association.

Sykes, Karen. 2005. *Arguing with Anthropology: An Introduction to Critical Theories of the Gift*. London: Routledge.

Thomas, Nicholas. 1991. *Entangled Objects: Exchange, Material Culture, and Colonialism in the Pacific*. Cambridge, MA: Harvard University Press.

Weiner, Annette B. 1984. From Words to Objects to Magic: "Hard Words" and the Boundaries of Social Interaction. In *Dangerous Words: Language and Politics in the Pacific*, ed. Donald Lawrence Brenneis and Fred R. Myers, pp. 161–191. New York: New York University Press.

Woolard, Kathryn A. 1998. Introduction: Language Ideology as a Field of Inquiry. In *Language Ideologies: Practice and Theory*, ed. Bambi. B. Schieffelin, Kathryn A. Woolard, and Paul V. Kroskrity, pp. 3–47. New York: Oxford University Press.

7

BAMBI B. SCHIEFFELIN

Found in Translating

Reflexive Language across Time and Texts in Bosavi, Papua New Guinea

Language is not a neutral medium that passes freely and
easily into the private property of the speaker's intentions; it
is populated—overpopulated—with the intentions of others.
Expropriating it, forcing it to submit to one's own intentions
and accents, is a difficult and complicated process.

—Mikhail Bakhtin, "Discourse in the Novel"

Missionization in Papua New Guinea has transformed vernacular languages and
the social lives of their speakers in subtle and not-so-subtle ways. Even when there is
relatively brief contact between a mission using a proselytizing language and a monolingual society with an otherwise robust vernacular, intensive evangelizing can result
in hybridized, translocated, and dislocated language forms and practices. Local speakers themselves might not be aware that selective, significant changes have occurred in
their vernacular—or that they have been actively involved in producing those changes.
Thus, when speaking what they locally identify as their vernacular, they may be using
it in mission-introduced genres that have utterly foreign discursive structures. Even
when these new genres are indeed recognized as such and given names using another
language's metalinguistic labels, speakers still may not recognize more subtle semantic
or pragmatic shifts, or the social consequences connected with them.

For analysts, such changes are especially invisible in nonliterate societies if
there is neither written documentation of precontact language uses nor a language
ideology that explicitly valorizes purist varieties. Even when we recognize shifts in
a vernacular, we do not always have the methods or means to trace the linguistic and
cultural practices that have created new spoken vernacular forms. In missionizing
contexts, these new forms often emerge in Bible reading and translation practices.
Central to all domains of proselytizing, these should be seen as critical sites for

studying the linguistic and cultural processes involved in the creation of new speech varieties and genres. Activities of passing ideas from one language to another, as Bakhtin (1981) has pointed out, are never neutral. Not only are they imbued with language ideologies and culture-bound textual practices; in missionizing contexts, issues of power are never far from the surface.

Unraveling some of the dynamic processes of contact between texts and talk that occur over time requires both ethnographic and linguistic analyses of ideologies and practices. This essay analyzes language use in reading and translation practices that developed during Christian missionization and the introduction of literacy in Bosavi (1975–1995). In analyzing these practices, Bakhtin provides an entry point that is relevant from the perspective of language contact, change, and ideology. Though developed for literary genres, two of his notions are relevant. The first, heteroglossia, refers to the multiplicity of languages within a language, acknowledging the tension in that multiplicity. The second, dialogism, highlights the incorporation of a variety of voices, styles, and points of view, which may be independent and polyphonic. Both are relevant to situations of mission contact and translating where speakers from one society are engaged in making sense out of texts from another. Though some may think of translating as simply finding equivalencies between two language codes, interpretive struggles always occur in these contact zones where persons, languages, and texts encounter one another. In the case I consider, the contact zone is Bosavi, Papua New Guinea.The primary actors are fundamentalist Christian missionaries, Bosavi pastors, and me, a linguistic anthropologist. The languages are Tok Pisin, the major lingua franca in Papua New Guinea, and Bosavi, the vernacular. The texts are three successive versions of Mark 2:6–8 from the Tok Pisin Nupela Testamen, and my transcripts of oral translations of Mark into the Bosavi language, which I tape-recorded between 1975 and 1995 during church services. These components are all central to understanding transformations of the Bosavi language as a result of the introduction of Christianity.[1]

Translating Scripture, a context in which ideas are passed from one language to another, often presents significant cultural as well as linguistic challenges (Long 2005; Nida 1964; Renck 1990). Translating activities point out how certain epistemological frameworks, such as theories of mind, intersubjectivity, personhood, and ways of knowing, can be culturally and linguistically obscured or revealed in surprising places. Speakers' struggles to cross language boundaries can be telling when examined in relation to the texts and metapragmatic and cultural presuppositions upon which they are based. Moving across codes and searching for meaning while translating across texts and time causes boundaries between languages and their ideologies to shift, blur, and collide, more so in some domains of language than in others. Reflexive language, which includes language about language, is one of those domains. As I will show, it proved especially fraught for writing the Tok Pisin Bible and orally translating it into Bosavi, in ways that reflect broader metapragmatic issues found throughout Papua New Guinea.

Reflexive speech and translating across texts

Every language has a reflexive capacity, which includes ways to represent the everyday metalinguistic activities of reporting, characterizing, and commenting on speech.

These activities, like all speech practices, are culturally organized and variable, and their uses and meanings must be systematically investigated along with other forms of language use (Lucy 1993a). The most salient and explicit use of reflexive language is reported speech, "speech within speech, utterance within utterance, and, at the same time, speech about speech, and utterance about utterance" (Voloshinov [1929] 1986: 115). Reported speech may be direct, purportedly an exact quotation, or indirect, a restatement of another speech event that is not represented verbatim (Coulmas 1986). Speakers use various linguistic resources for reported speech, such as tense, to coordinate what they are describing—the 'narrated event'—with the ongoing action of speaking a 'speech event' (Jakobson 1957; Silverstein 1993).

Terms and distinctions for reported speech vary across languages and may make reference to a range of other reflexive practices, including reported thought and reported perception, which cross-linguistically and intrasystemically show many empirical and theoretical connections (Janssen and Wurff 1996: 4; Verschueren 1989). Verbs of speaking also indicate the nature and source of evidence, for example, another utterance (reported as direct or indirect speech). These metalinguistic verbs are often linked to more extensive evidential systems that mark epistemic stance, that is, speakers' attitudes toward knowledge expressed in the content of their talk. Chafe and Nichols view evidential systems as part of a "natural epistemology," how ordinary people naturally regard the source and reliability of their knowledge (1986: vii). Elsewhere, I have argued that these systems are part of a "cultural epistemology" (Schieffelin 1996: 443). In other words, the verbal resources of stance taking, and reflexive language more generally, are closely linked to cultural assumptions and epistemological frameworks for talking about how and what one knows and for communicating that knowledge to others (Besnier 1993). Speech act verbs also participate in this system, since a speaker's choice of a particular speech act verb communicates degrees of agency, responsibility, authority, truth, or certainty with which an assertion is made. Evidential systems are obligatory in some languages, that is, speakers must mark source of information as known from direct visual sources or inferred from indirect ones, and not present in others (Aikhenvald 2003; Whorf 1956).

Research has linked epistemological frameworks, as coded through reflexive language, to a set of other constructs, including notions of personhood and intersubjectivity, and to theory of mind—the human cognitive capacity both to recognize and attribute mental states (beliefs, desires, and intentions) to oneself and to recognize and understand that others have separate and different mental states.[2] In this sense, internal mental states, intentions and beliefs and how they are deployed in communicative activities provide a bridge between reflexive language and metalinguistic activities on the one hand, and the ethnographic literature on intentionality and theory of mind, on the other. For example, looking at how speakers verbally encode their intentions in culturally meaningful ways is especially revealing of prevailing epistemological frameworks (Du Bois 1993; Duranti 1993; Mitchell-Kernan 1972; Ochs 1988; Robbins 2001; Rosaldo 1982). Not all societies have an articulated or explicit theory of mind, so we must look to contexts of language use to make such ideas explicit. Analysts rarely address folk theories that distinguish the origin and expression of a speaker's intentions from those of another (but see Ochs 1984 and Schieffelin 1990). Furthermore, the extent to which speakers acknowledge that they can infer what others are thinking and make their inferences public through acts of speaking is central to folk epistemologies and ethnopsychological theories. The verbal practices and discursive structures that are linked to these folk epistemologies are part of cultural knowledge. Systematic attention to reflexive language can illuminate hard to get at theories of mind because it provides a context in which we can separate the cognitive and private (verbally unexpressed) dimensions of attributing specific mental states to others from practices that make such inferences social and public, through verbal expression. The similarities and differences between these two practices—thinking about others' internal states and/or talking about them—are often at the heart of culture.

There have been many approaches to analyzing metalinguistic activities (cf. Lucy 1993b), but most relevant here is Silverstein's formulation of reflexive practices (1976, 1985), which views much of metalinguistic activity as fundamentally metapragmatic—that is, as concerned with the appropriate use of language. From this perspective, reflexive speech, like other forms of talk, is a form of communicative action that requires specific social and linguistic knowledge to be culturally appropriate and meaningful.

Brief background to Bosavi people, mission, and anthropology

The Bosavi people live north of Mt. Bosavi on the Great Papuan Plateau in the Southern Highlands of Papua New Guinea.[3] In this rain-forest environment, two thousand or so Bosavi people inhabit scattered communities ranging from sixty to a hundred people. They practice swidden horticulture and hunt and fish for most of the animal protein in their diet. There are four dialects of the Bosavi language, one of which is called Kaluli, and all are mutually intelligible. Here I refer to the language as well as the people as Bosavi (Schieffelin 1986; Schieffelin and Feld 1998). The majority of Bosavi people are monolingual in their vernacular, and for the most part village life is carried out monolingually (this observation refers to the period from 1975 to 1995). Like most small-scale societies in Papua New Guinea, before contact with anthropologists, missionaries, and government representatives, Bosavi people lived in a nonliterate world (Schieffelin 2000).

Government contact in Bosavi has been intermittent,[4] as is often the case where populations are small, scattered, and hard to reach and where resources (e.g., timber) are not easily extractable. Such areas, however, are of interest to missionaries, and in 1964 two members of a small, nondenominational, fundamentalist Protestant mission (Unevangelized Fields Mission, later called the Asian Pacific Christian Mission) made brief contact with Bosavi people and began construction of a small airstrip. Missionization did not seriously begin, however, until the early 1970s with the arrival of two Australian missionaries, who over the years established a mission station with a clinic, hospital, school, and store. They interpreted the Bible literally and viewed original Scripture as the divinely inspired center of all preaching. Missionization was intensive as their goal was rapid conversion. They emphasized a doctrine of the "last things"—death, judgment, heaven and hell, elaborating the dire consequences of the Second Coming for nonbelievers. They told the Bosavis who wanted to become Christian to give up many important traditional practices; many did exactly that.[5]

The mission explicitly rejected the idea that knowledge about local cultural practices might assist proselytizing and viewed many local cultural practices as not only irrelevant to their project of conversion but an obstacle to its success. At the same time, its own long-standing language policy dictated working in vernacular languages, which they characterized as "the shrine of a people's soul" (Rule 1977: 1341). Like many other evangelical Protestant missions, Bible translation practices were based on Eugene Nida's (1964) notion of finding close functional equivalents to words. This mission held a Western reference-centered view of language, and treated the vernacular as a code that could be separated from local cultural practices and meanings and used independently of them. The vernacular could be expanded, contracted, and changed in myriad ways to express ideas that were foreign, and still remain the same vernacular. The missionaries who came to Bosavi knew little about the Bosavi language in terms of its genres, metalinguistic, pragmatic and ideological frameworks. As far as they were concerned, none of this mattered for the project at hand: everything one needed to know was already in the Bible; it just had to be translated and heard.

In practice, the Australian missionaries working in Bosavi lacked linguistic training and relied on Tok Pisin to communicate with local people. This limited the number of Bosavi people with whom they could interact initially to a small group of younger men who had learned Tok Pisin while working outside the area. Interested in what the missionaries promised (both spiritually and materially), and imagining possible benefits to themselves, they were willing converts. Though these converts lacked formal schooling, the missionaries taught them basic literacy in Tok Pisin, emphasizing reading but not writing skills, and within a few years they were working as village pastors and given the authority to preach to and baptize others. These recently missionized Bosavis then became active missionizers and played a major role in producing what Bosavi people understood Christianity to be about.

The setting for Bible translation

While not all Bosavis were interested in Christianity, Christian activities radically reorganized everyday village life from 1975 onward (Schieffelin 1996, 2000, 2002). Church services were held three to four times weekly, each lasting one to two hours. Local pastors followed the format of services used at the mission station. Thus services consisted of short routinized prayers, a few hymns, a reading from the New Testament in Tok Pisin, which was orally translated into the Bosavi language, and a lengthy sermon loosely based on the Bible reading. Except for the Tok Pisin reading and some of the hymns, services were in the vernacular.

Christianity introduced new forms of social hierarchy in Bosavi society, as reflected in the spatial and speaking arrangements of services. Pastors stood in the front of the church, while men and women, segregated, sat on the bark floor wearing whatever Western clothing they had—shirts or cloth wraps. As a congregation they were passive, never interrupting or questioning anything the pastor said. During the sermon, they remained silent when pastors posed questions about their sins or asked them to confess. Elsewhere, I have termed this "monologic domination" (Schieffelin 2003; cf. Knauft 2002) to capture the social and linguistic organization of church services. That characterization of the participant structure, however, stands in contrast to the unstable, heteroglossic nature of the processes and practices involved in Bible reading and translation, to which I now turn.

The performance of reading; the performance of translating

Central to church services was reading aloud from the <u>Nupela Testamen</u>, the Tok Pisin Bible. First published in 1969, it drew on Eugene Nida's (1964) dynamic or functional equivalency model of translation. It was modeled after the American Good News Bible published in 1966, which had as its target audience children and uneducated adults (see also de Waard and Nida 1986).

The <u>Nupela Testamen</u> was a work in progress until 1989. Following its 1969 publication, two successive editions were published (1978, 1989) in response to linguists' efforts to standardize Tok Pisin and input from local speakers (Mundhenk 1985).[6] These three editions showed significant revisions in Tok Pisin metalinguistics, verbs of speaking, feeling, and thinking, and other types of reflexive language that are culturally sensitive, linguistically variable, and central to Christian text and belief.

All three editions of the <u>Nupela Testamen</u> were used in Bosavi (1975–1995), and the linguistic differences for expressing reflexive language and speech act verbs across editions created problems for local pastors. Because many were not fluent readers to begin with, their reading in Tok Pisin was slow and labored, marked by false starts, repetition, paraphrases, and self-repair. In addition, their attempts to segment the Tok Pisin text into translatable phrases often resulted in mismatches between the read Tok Pisin text and the spoken Bosavi translation. Some of these difficulties were due to syntactic differences in the two languages, Tok Pisin being a verb-medial language, and Bosavi being a verb-final one. In part in response to these difficulties, many pastors ended up memorizing large portions of the 1969 edition of Mark, the most popular and often repeated of the Gospels. When reading aloud from later revised editions, pastors often inadvertently added memorized phrases that were by then obsolete. Some of these obsolete phrases in turn entered the Bosavi translations, resulting in variation between the Tok Pisin text and the Bosavi translation. These memorized wordings combined with difficulties in reading the printed text made both the Tok Pisin and its Bosavi translations sound uncertain and sometimes incoherent, unlike any other Bosavi speech event.

Pastors used two techniques when reading and translating from the <u>Nupela Testamen</u>. The most common, which I call *interlinear translation*, begins after announcing the title and verse numbers of the scriptural selection. Pastors read one verse at a time in Tok Pisin, sometimes breaking a single verse into two or more sections, followed by a translation of that verse into Bosavi. With interlinear translations, pastors often added cohesive devices and contextual information not in the read Tok Pisin to create textual and cultural meaning. A less commonly used translation technique, which I call *continuous translation*, refers to the practice of first reading the total verse selection (usually nine to twelve verses) in Tok Pisin, and then translating it into Bosavi as a continuous narrative. Verses or parts of verses were often omitted or abbreviated when this technique was used, as it required pastors to memorize or recall what was in the verses they had read.

Transcriptions from church services that used both translation styles reveal pastors' inconsistencies, extensive self-repairs, hesitations, and paraphrases; these flag culturally systematic and significant metalinguistic and metapragmatic differences.[7] These same domains of difference are not only found in pastors' translations from Tok Pisin into Bosavi, but parallel those found in linguists' and Bible translators' revisions of the Tok Pisin Bible. As we shall see, these difficulties are not random, but center on reflexive language and specific speech act verbs. These culturally sensitive issues surrounding reflexive language will be illustrated by close analysis and comparison of Mark 2:6–8 as read by Bosavi pastors in Tok Pisin and translated in Bosavi. These particular verses contain multiple examples of reflexive language, specifically reported speech and reported thought, and a culturally specific speech act verb, blaspheme.

Bosavi ideas about translation and translation practices

Like the missionaries, Bosavi people had their own ideas and metalinguistic expressions about translation, but it was not a topic they discussed among themselves. During trade exchanges with groups with whom they did not share a language, there were always speakers in bordering villages who could translate through a neighboring language. Government patrols and mission contact during the 1960s and 1970s introduced more formal translation events and, with them, official interpreters. In these situations, a designated <u>tanimtok</u> 'interpreter, translator' would <u>tanim</u> 'translate' (from English 'turn') <u>tok</u> 'talk' of a government officer (usually an Australian) from one of the lingua francas, Tok Pisin, or, less frequently, Police Motu, into Bosavi.[8] The Bosavi metalinguistic term for translation, *to nodoma* 'turn talk around to its opposite side', is semantically identical, but Bosavis claim it is a Bosavi word and not a calque or loan translation from Tok Pisin; my recorded evidence substantiates that. For Bosavi, then, translation involves two codes ("two sides"), and Bosavi people distinguish it metalinguistically from repeating and paraphrasing, both of which take place within the same code. Bosavi speakers use the expression *a:ma:la: nodolo:* 'turned completely around' for loan translations or calques referring to new expressions that entered Bosavi from Tok Pisin, reflecting the idea that the word is transformed back into the original code, or side.[9]

During Bible translation, pastors not only found many functional equivalents but also introduced new expressions in Bosavi. Tok Pisin was the main source of these new expressions. Through literally recoding or calquing Tok Pisin words and phrases word for word into the Bosavi language, they used calques to speak the vernacular. This successfully enacted the language ideology of the mission—to use the vernacular for proselytizing (or, to use Bakhtin's term, expropriate it) through word-for-word translations that were thought of as referentially straightforward. They believed this would assure that translations would stay very close to the literal meanings of "the original Bible text" (in Tok Pisin) (see Handman, chap. 8 of this volume).

Calques had an important influence on the Bosavi vernacular. In the domain of affective and cognitive states, some calqued forms expressed meanings that already existed in Bosavi words, some shifted the semantic and metapragmatic meanings from Bosavi to Christian ones, and others added new Christian concepts. One important shift was making explicit the source and location of private, affective, and cognitive states, whereas previously no such designation was made. The examples below illustrate how this shift resulted in the new verbal expressions for two internal states, worry and think. Examples 1 and 2 illustrate new Christian forms († = Christian usage) of prior Bosavi expressions, while example 3 introduces a new idea calqued from Tok Pisin.

1. *hida:yo:*   'I was worried; something is heavy in weight'

   †*kufo: hida:yo:*   'I regretted, was worried in my heart' < TP <u>bel hevi</u>
   stomach heavy

2. *asulo:*   'I thought'

   †*kufa: usa asulo:*   'I thought in my heart' < TP <u>tingting long bel</u>
   stomach center (loc)

3. †*asulo: nodolo:*   'I converted' < TP <u>tanim tingting</u>
   thought turned

Before mission contact, the only way to say (1) 'I was worried' was *hida:yo:*. The shift is from a monolexemic form (the adjectival use of a past participle) to a phrase that adds the source: *kufo: hida:yo:* 'I was troubled in my heart' (literally, stomach was heavy), a calque directly from the Tok Pisin expression <u>bel hevi</u> (literally, stomach/heart heavy). No pronouns or subject markers are needed as it is assumed that the speaker is self-reporting. A similar process pertains to (2) 'I thought' *asulo:*. The new Christian expression *kufa: usa asulo:* 'I thought in my heart' indicates the source (*kuf-a* 'stomach' + genitive) and a location, (*us-a* 'center' + locative). Bosavi word order as well as numerous syntactic relations differ from those of Tok Pisin. In both cases, however, a noun 'heart' (*kuf* 'stomach' from TP <u>bel</u>) makes explicit the interior source and location of the internal state, central to Christian ways of speaking, which required notions of sincerity and truth, related to belief. The final example (3), *asulo: nodolo:* 'convert' from the Tok Pisin expression <u>tanim tingting</u> (literally, turn thoughts), introduced a new concept.

Prior to missionization, "sincerity" was not a concept recognized or valued in the Bosavi speech community. People did not express concern that one's private feelings could be different from what one said. It was what one said in public that was taken seriously. If what one said was discussed, appropriate speech act verbs were used to directly report whether it was heard by the person who was repeating it or its source was second- or even thirdhand. People did not verbally speculate about whether someone had really meant something that he or she said. Christianity, in contrast, required sincerity, a match between the interior, private feeling and public talk—a direct correspondence between saying something and believing it or meaning it (Keane 2001; Robbins 2001, chap. 6 of this volume). Vernacular expressions had to be created to do that work, and Tok Pisin via the Nupela Testamen was the local source. Thus in learning Christian concepts, Bosavi people did not have to learn another code, or language, but instead incorporated new ideas and practices into their own lexicosemantic and pragmatic system. Created and adopted by Bosavi Christians, these verbal expressions were thought to give people access to the meanings contained in the Bible, but they also gave rise to a number of unintended outcomes. They restructured major portions of their lexicon in the domains of internal states, time (Schieffelin 2002) and place (Schieffelin 2003). Without anyone talking about it, they gave rise to a new speech register, which indirectly indexed a new Christian identity and new ways of knowing.[10] Whether these expressions gave Bosavi people insights into Scripture or changed the way they thought about their future are questions I cannot answer.

As a result of the mission's language policy and local translation practices, Tok Pisin has not only critically mediated the evangelical process, but it has caused significant changes throughout the Bosavi language. While language used in sermons and Christian settings still sounded like the vernacular and used a vernacular lexicon, it differed from the pre-mission-contact Bosavi language metalinguistically and metapragmatically. Two things make this situation unusual. First, it contrasts with the more common pattern of language change. Whereas vernacular languages are usually seen as influencing and changing the contact language (Tok Pisin) (Ross 1985), here that dynamic is reversed.[11] Second, though scholars usually expect orality to condition literacy, here the process is reversed, with written Tok Pisin read from the Nupela Testamen changing the spoken vernacular. We see in these new heteroglossic and dialogic expressions the traces of one language, Tok Pisin, encoded in another, Bosavi. These data point out that not all functions of language are equivalent in translation. Whereas some functional dimensions of language (e.g., referentiality) may lend themselves to calquing, others (e.g., metalinguistic and other reflexive dimensions) may not. I turn next to this domain of reflexive language drawing on translating Mark.

What is so difficult and interesting about Mark 2:6–8?

Like many Protestant missions, the Asian Pacific Christian Mission selected Mark as the first Gospel for translation because its narrative was seen as relatively simple for nonliterate indigenous people to understand. Mark 2:1–12, "Jesus heals a paralyzed man," was one of the Bosavi favorites, read and translated repeatedly over twenty years. Briefly, verses 1–5 describe Jesus' arrival in Capernaum to large crowds who had come to hear him preach. Four men approach carrying a paralyzed man, and, seeing their faith, Jesus tells the paralyzed man that his sins are forgiven. The man then stands up and walks. Such themes of sickness and healing were of particular interest in Bosavi because malaria and other diseases were common, and witchcraft was the only explanation of such maladies. Pastors challenged this thinking with a new explanation, telling Bosavi people that they were all sick and needed to be healed by Jesus. Using the Bosavi word *walaf* 'sickness' to translate sin, in sermons they elaborated particular instances of *walaf* 'sickness/sin' pointing to congregants' boils, coughs, and withered limbs as symptoms or evidence of their sin, which only further reinforced the truthfulness of their assertions.

Within this relatively straightforward miracle story about Jesus healing a paralyzed man, however, there is a subtle "controversy dialogue" (verses 6–10), significant in the larger trajectory of Christ's life (Camery-Hoggatt 1992) and which raises a number of important metalinguistic and metapragmatic issues (see Appendix for verses 6–8 from the English Good News Bible 1966 and the Tok Pisin Nupela Testamen 1969, 1978, and 1989 shown to represent their original print formats). This controversy dialogue recounts how several scribes observe Jesus and then, in their thoughts, challenge his authority to do two things: forgive sins and heal the sick.

Reported thoughts and interior views are rare in Mark and are used strategically in the parables. Verses 6–8 contain several examples of reported thought and verbs of speaking, signaling the importance and marked nature of what Jesus is doing and how the scribes view him. Verse 6 describes the scribes as "thinking to themselves." The nature of their thoughts is further revealed in verse 7 as a question challenging Jesus' right to speak in a particular way. They think Jesus is performing an infelicitous speech act, one that he does not have the right to perform (forgiving sins) and which they further categorize as "blasphemy," expressing contempt or disrespect for God. It is through their reported thoughts that the reader is informed that only God has the right to forgive sins and perform certain speech acts. Verse 8 shifts perspective and describes Jesus' special ability to know the private thoughts of others—"At once Jesus knew what they were thinking" (Good News Bible 1966)—which is followed by his verbal challenge of the scribes' thoughts and motives. Jesus not only knows what they were thinking; he lets them (and us) know by speaking about it.[12]

In my recordings, these dialogue verses stand out as especially challenging for Bosavi pastors to translate, as indicated by extensive hesitation, repetition, paraphrase, and other performance difficulties in finding appropriate "equivalencies" for their reflexive language and speech acts. Bosavi pastors, moreover, never referred to the content or meaning of these dialogue verses (including verses 9–10) in their sermons, focusing exclusively on the healing narrative. Why were these passages so difficult to translate and talk about?

Textual details of the Tok Pisin texts and situated practices of Bosavi pastors show us what gets obscured and what is revealed in translating as multiple factors contributed to difficulties in comprehension and translation. The first is historical coincidence. At the same time period that Bosavi pastors were starting to preach, Tok Pisin, the language of the source text, was undergoing revision as part of a broader standardization process. Reflexive language—for example, quotative formats for speech and thought as well as speech act verbs—was relatively unstable (see the appendix, bolded text). For example, to convey the idea of the scribes' reported thought as something that could be known, the 1969 Nupela Testamen used an expression composed of two verbs, think and speak *i tingting, i spik* (verse 6). The 1978 Nupela Testamen recognized the use of the complementizer *olsem* 'like, that' which was by then in widespread use in spoken Tok Pisin to introduce direct reported speech, i tok olsem, extending it to direct reported thought, i tingting olsem.[13] This shift is illustrated below, in the lines numbered 2 of each example.

Nupela Testamen 1969, Mark 2:6

1. Na sampela saveman bilong lo   ol   i sindaun i stap,
   and some   [wise men of law] they   [PM] sit [PM] CONT
   'and some legal scholars were [sitting] there'

2. na long bel bilong ol   ol   i tingting, i spik
   and in belly of them   they [PM] think   [PM] speak
   'and they were thinking in their hearts, saying, "…'

Nupela Testamen 1978/1989, Mark 2:6

1. Na sampela saveman bilong   lo   ol i sindaun i stap,
   and some [wise men of   law] they [PM] sit [PM] CONT
   'and some   legal scholars were [sitting] there'

2. na long bel bilong ol   ol i tingting olsem
   and in   belly of them they [PM] think that/thus
   'and in their hearts they were thinking "…'

A second factor concerns Bosavi speech resources. There were no equivalencies in the Bosavi metalinguistic and metapragmatic repertoire for reporting the private thoughts or internal states of others, except in traditional story genres that recounted Bosavi origins, or the bawdy adventures or social dilemmas of fictitious cultural heroes, schlemiels, and animals. These verbal forms for reporting thoughts of others (who were not real), however, were never used. There are several reasons for this. Bosavi Christians took literally the prohibitions against past cultural practices, including telling these stories, closely associated with traditional themes, because they included taboo topics, such as murder and lust. Marked forms of language, such as reporting others' thoughts, were associated with these genres of the past. Furthermore, Bosavi people called these stories *ba madali* 'not real' or 'for no purpose', though many contained moral lessons of broad relevance. Stories about Jesus, on the other hand, were represented as real, as were other Bible stories and the persons who spoke in them, and Bible translation as a new genre required new forms of language. Given the symbolic meanings associated with traditional genre-specific forms for reported thought, the expression of real third parties' reported thought did not translate smoothly for Bosavi pastors. Instead, pastors stayed close to the Tok Pisin lexicon and syntax, attempting to convey the language of the Tok Pisin Bible. The following examples I. A–D focus on verse 6 of Mark 2, specifically the phrase describing what the scribes were doing, "thinking to themselves," to illustrate some of the ways in which one Bosavi pastor worked on translating the quotation of others' reported thought.

Example I. A is from a 1975 church service, and the 1969 Nupela Testamen is the source text. Pastor Degelo: first reads verse 6 in Tok Pisin and then translates it into Bosavi, staying close to the Tok Pisin (see appendix, Text 2). The first part of the verse (line 1 in Tok Pisin and Bosavi) introduces the scribes (experts of law) who were sitting and observing Jesus.[14]

I. A.   1975   interlinear translation (NT 1969, Mark 2:6)

1. <u>na sampela saveman bilong ol -   ol i   - saveman bilong lo - ol i sindaun i stap</u>
   and some   wise men   of them   they [PM] wise men of law they [PM] sit [PM] stay
   'and some experts of theirs - they - experts of law, they were [sitting] there'

>2. <u>na long bel bilong - bel bilong ol   ol i tingting - tingting i   spik</u>
   and in belly of   - belly of   them   they   [PM] think - think   [PM] say
   'and in hearts of - their hearts,   they thought, saying, " ... '

1. *a:ta:ga:yo: kalu nolo: asulo: alan sa:la: a:no: aniba sen - a:no: aniba sen a:namiyo:*
   'so some men who really who really knew a lot sat close there - so sitting close there'

>2. *ili asulakiyo: a:la: asulo: - ili kufami asulakiyo: - iliyo: mada asulo: ko:li nowo:*
   miyo: sa:la: bo:bo:ge
   '(a) they were thinking their thoughts - (b) they were thinking in their hearts -
   (c) some different thoughts came really quickly'

My focus is on the second part of the verse (marked > 2), which contains a reflexive verb phrase, they were thinking. The hesitations, often self-repairs (indicated by single hyphens) show how Pastor Degelo: is trying to communicate this idea. Not finding word for word equivalencies, the first Bosavi phrase he uses, (a) *ili asulakiyo: a:la: asulo:* 'they were thinking their thoughts', is marked, redundant, almost a hypercorrection. Speakers would say either *ili asulakiyo:* or *a:la: asulo:* to translate "they were thinking" and not specify "thoughts," as it would be obvious. An initial self-repair (b) locates the scribes' thinking specifically inside, *ili kufami* 'in their hearts' (<u>long bel bilong ol</u>). A second self-repair (c) offers another formulation, that some different thoughts came really quickly, an idea that is not in the Tok Pisin verse.

Nine years later (1984), I recorded the same pastor in a Bosavi church service reading the same verses in Tok Pisin, but this time he used the 1978 edition of the <u>Nupela Testamen</u>. He read, then rendered the verses into Bosavi as a continuous translation. In example I. B below, his translation of the second line (>) contrasts what the scribes are not doing (talking with words) with what they were doing, thinking their private thoughts, making this distinction explicit. This shows that from a Bosavi perspective, it was still culturally problematic for anyone to know what was in the minds of the scribes.

I. B.   1984   continuous translation (NT 1978, Mark 2:6)

a:namiyo: kalu nolo: godeya: ene to man lo da:lab a:no: godeya: ene ele difa:
yo: asulo: ko:lo: sen –
'there some men, God's laws, God's rules those that knew the boundaries God
put down, sat'

> *i a:ma:yo: towa:yo: mo:sa:lai ko:sega asug ami a:la: asulo: –*
'they were not talking with words but they were thinking their thoughts'

In the following example recorded one month later, he used another periphrastic construction when translating what the scribes were doing, making clear that the scribes' thoughts were their own and *usa* 'inside'. The Tok Pisin expression locates the thinking in their hearts (<u>na long bel bilong ol</u>), and no reported speech verb indicates that they spoke.

I. C.   1984   interlinear translation (NT 1978, Mark 2:6)

1. <u>Na sampela saveman bilong lo   ol i sindaun i stap</u> –
    and   some wise men of   law they [PM] sit   [PM] stay
    'and   some experts of law,   they were [sitting] there'

>2. <u>na ol   i - na long bel bilong ol i tingting olsem</u>
    and they [PM] and in belly of them [PM] think that/thus...
    'and in their hearts they thought...'

1. *a:la:fo: ko:sega a:la: sa:lab godeya: to do:lefo:lo: asulo: – a:no:lo: a:na senka:*
    a:la: sa:lab
    'however, it says some who knew God's 10 commandments were sitting there,
    it says'

>2. *i a:namilo: sen a:ma: ini asulo: usa a:la: asulo:lo:boka: a:la: sa:lab*
    'they sat there with their own thoughts inside like that were just thinking it says'

Pastor Degelo:'s translation conveys that the scribes' thinking was of some duration, and that Jesus knew it by direct visual evidence, signaled by a visual evidential *-lo:b* as well as an emphatic marker *-ka:* suffixed on the verb 'think' *asulo:lo:boka:*. During this time period, pastors also added metapragmatic brackets to their translations, for example, 'it says' *a:la: sa:lab* to indicate that the source of their words was the text. In this way, they made verbally explicit that they were not the authors of the propositional content of the translated utterance and therefore not responsible for it (Goffman 1974: 512; 1979). This discursive feature is not in Tok Pisin, but central to Bosavi evidential marking. This is discussed in more detail below, as such metapragmatic brackets showed up in Bosavi translations in subsequent verses that were linked to the original proposition at hand.

A final example (I. D) of translating the quotation of others' reported thought is from a church service ten years later (1995). Translating Mark 2, Degelo: repeats verse 5 (having heard what Jesus said) to make the connection explicit between what the scribes heard and what they were thinking. Recapitulating information not in the current verse frequently occurred, for example in verse 7, discussed below. Unlike previous examples in which Degelo: reads verse 6 in its entirety before translating it, this time he breaks up the verse into two segments, translating each separately. Literally translating the Tok Pisin, he locates the reported thought in the scribes' hearts; what others were thinking became an explicitly interior act that could be reported.

I. D.   1995   interlinear translation (NT 1989, Mark 2:6)

1. <u>sampela saveman bilong lo i i sindaun   i   stap   long haus</u>
    some wise men of law   [PM] [PM] sit [PM] stay at house
    'some legal experts, they - they were sitting in the house'

1. *a:la:fo ko:lo: lolo: asulo: kalu a:no: iyo: a a:namiyo: sen*
    'so some men who knew the law they were sitting at the house'

2. <u>na long bel bilong   ol   ol i tingting olsem</u>
    and in belly of them they they [PM] think (that/thus)...
    'and in their hearts they thought...'

>2. *o: ya:suwa:lo: to siyo: a:no: da:da:sa:ga:yo: asulo:wo: - lolo: asulo:wo:*
    kaluwa: kufa:usamiyo: a:la: asulo:
    'having heard what Jesus said, they thought - the men who understood law
    thought in their hearts'

Pastors tried to align their translations with what was in each read verse, but they were usually not successful, especially when faced with translating others' reported thoughts. Translated material crossed verse boundaries, as information from one verse was repeated in the next in an effort to be explicit. Switching between verbs for speaking and thinking, they repeated and self-repaired their utterances as they attempted translations of reported thought. In addition, pastors added metapragmatic brackets to their translations to indicate the textual source of what they were saying. Two examples from Mark 2:7, recorded at different services in 1984, illustrate these difficulties encountered in passing the idea of others' reported thought from one language to another.

> II. A.   1984   continuous translation (NT 1978, Mark 2:7)
>
> *e Gode o:ga:igabo:lo:ka:* (a) *a:la: siyo:* - (b) *a:la: asulo:* – (c) *ene kufa: usa mo asulo:* –
>
> 'he (Jesus) is making fun of God like that (a) they said - (b) they thought – (c) in their hearts they only thought it – '

After asserting that Jesus is blaspheming God, this pastor adds two additional reflexive verbs to his translation. The first, (a) *a:la: siyo:* 'they said like that', is a quotative format referring to the scribes, which he then self-corrected (b) to another reflexive verb of thinking *a:la: asulo:* 'they thought like that', which is what they were doing, and further self-corrected (c) with the periphrastic phrase to explain that the scribes *only* thought it, but did not actually say it. Such self-repairs did not occur in everyday speech. This departure from the Tok Pisin verses indicates the active sense-making efforts on the part of the translators and the desire to provide evidence for the accusation of speaking about God in a particular way. A second example, recorded in 1984 one month later, shows that this was a persistent metalinguistic issue.

> II. B.   1984   interlinear translation (NT 1978, Mark 2:7)
>
> em i   tok bilas   long God - i   no   gat   man - i   no gat wanpela man
> he [PM] talk decoration to God [PM] [NEG] [EXIST] man [PM] [NEG] [EXIST]one   man
> 'He spoke boastfully to God - there's no man - there's not one person'
>
> em inap (long) tekewe sin. em i   wok bilong God wanpela tasol
> he able to   remove sin it [PM] work of   God one   alone/just
> 'who can forgive sin. It's the work of God alone.'
>
> >1. (a) *a:ta:ga: a:la: siyo:ka:* (b) *a:la: sa:lab* – (c) *ili sa:laiyo* – (d) *ili asulo:wamiyo:*
> (e) *a:la: asula:sa:ga:yo:*
>
> '(a) so they said like (b) that it says – (c) after they were saying – (d) after they were thinking (e) like that they kept thinking' [III. C provides the rest of this segment]

Like similar passages, this one is marked with hesitation between choosing the verb "say" or "think" to describe what the scribes are doing, as well as the addition of several metapragmatic brackets to signal the source. For example, the Bosavi text line 1 (a) *a:ta:ga: a:la: siyo:ka:* (b) *a:la: sa:lab*, the first use of the verb "say" (a) *a:la: siyo:ka:* 'they said like that' refers to the reported thought of the scribes, followed by a second verb phrase (b) *a:la: sa:lab* 'it says like that', which references the text as the source using the verb "say" as an evidential. This is followed by a self-repair (c) and a use of "say" (with a tense shift), which refers to the reported thought of the scribes which is self-repaired (d) *ili asulo:wamiyo:* 'after they were thinking' to mark it as reported thought, which is followed by an additional self-repair (e) to a nonfinite durative form using the verb think, 'like that they kept thinking'.

These enduring attempts, which eventually found a literal translation *kufa: usamiyo: a:la: asulo:* 'thought in their hearts' (example I. D), suggest that translating others' reported thought goes beyond finding lexical equivalencies. They signal important differences in metapragmatics and theories of mind that operate across specific cultural boundaries. If we were to restrict our attention to the Bosavi case, we might be led to conclude that this cultural incompatibility was an isolated or local phenomenon for a number of reasons. A focus on the Asia Pacific Christian Mission's language ideology could assign these difficulties to their translation practices and its literal scriptural interpretation and modes of teaching word-for-word translation, all of which were compounded by their lack of knowledge about or interest in Bosavi ethnopragmatics and metalinguistics. A focus on the pastors would attribute these difficulties to their undeveloped literacy and language comprehension, further complicated by the ways in which Tok Pisin and Bosavi syntax and semantics map on to each other. If we look at the Nupela Testamen, however, we see that these same verses underwent substantial revision in three successive Tok Pisin translations. This suggests that the difficulties Bosavi speakers had are not simply local or linguistic but are indicative of widespread metapragmatic issues in Papua New Guinea, where knowing others' thoughts is treated in culturally and linguistically specific ways that vary from Western and Judeo-Christian ideas encoded in Scripture (LiPuma 2000; Robbins 2001).

Culturally specific speech acts: gossip and blasphemy

As we have seen, finding the "right words" to express that the scribes were thinking to themselves but that Jesus could hear them as if they were speaking presented challenges both to the translators of the Nupela Testamen and to Bosavi pastors. What the scribes were thinking—that Jesus was committing the act of blasphemy—provides yet another critical piece of a larger epistemological puzzle. If we examine the same translating contexts, we will see how the ideology and practice of Bosavi reported speech and thought are deeply intertwined not only with other areas of reflexive language, but with wider cultural assumptions in Bosavi about personhood, privacy, and theory of mind. These broader cultural ideas help make sense of why the Bosavi concept of gossip (*sada:dan*) was selected as a possible gloss for the Christian concept of blasphemy, even though Westerners would not intuitively pair these speech acts.

To understand how blasphemy and gossip could be paired, it is necessary to understand local ideas about reported speech and thought. Reported thought is common in narratives and conversation in many parts of the world. Most Westerners do not hesitate to report their own internal states, beliefs, and desires, and they also attribute and verbally report others' thoughts, intentions, and emotions based on their own speculation. Most of us do this regularly without giving it a second thought. Bosavi people, however, did not share this orientation to the inner, private states of others. They claimed that only experiencers know their own internal states (affective and cognitive) and, furthermore, that only experiencers have a right or warrant to talk about those internal states. Thus, in Bosavi one should not say what another might think or feel. To do so is categorized as *sada:dan* 'gossip' and is among the most negatively sanctioned speech acts in Bosavi society and in other Pacific societies.[15]

The Bosavi notion of gossip differs from English usage in that it does not pertain to talk about the actions or speech of an absent third party. Indeed, such talk would present no problem for Bosavi speakers as they would invariably mark their speech with an appropriate evidential about their source of knowledge, be it direct or indirect perception (aural or visual) or habitual practice (Schieffelin 1996). *Sada:dan* 'gossip' specifically pertains to verbal speculation about the inner states of others, their unspoken desires and thoughts—a subject about which reliable evidence is never available.

This orientation as to what is and is not appropriate to verbally express is evident in the earliest language socialization of children. Caregivers never explicitly guess about what their children (or anyone else) might be feeling or thinking (Ochs and Schieffelin 1984), and children are taught not to talk about things about which they have no evidence. Evidential markers are learned early and used appropriately by very young children (Schieffelin 1986). Furthermore, missionary reports claiming difficulty in getting people elsewhere to talk about the unstated thoughts or feelings of others provide evidence that these cultural preferences are not limited to Bosavi. Joan Rule, a missionary linguist who worked in nearby Lake Kutubu, writing for a missionary newsletter reported the following in a short essay titled "Capturing words for Christ":

> None of us had found a word for "love" in this language (though of course there was one for "lust"). Every time we two [referring to herself and her husband, linguist Murray Rule] had demanded, "Why is that mother hugging her baby?", "Why are Omela's two little girls going arm in arm?" and similar questions, the same answers would always come back, "I don't know," or with a shrug of the shoulders, "Just because!" Then one day just recently a man was describing the steps a man takes here in acquiring a wife. It was the early part of it which arrested our attention: "He sees her. 'Ah,' he says, "I admire that girl. My heart goes to her.'" One's heart going to the loved one. (1954: 9)

Rule then goes on to describe how this expression, "one's heart going to the loved one," was adopted into the vocabulary for use in proselytizing. Tellingly, she does not appear to recognize that speakers' reluctance to talk about the internal states of others did not reflect a deficiency, but instead expressed a culturally preferred avoidance of speculating about others' internal states for which there is no evidence.

As a linguistic corollary, Bosavi, like many other non-Austronesian languages in Papua New Guinea, only uses direct quotation for speech, retaining the "verbatim" utterances of a speaker. Verbs of saying are central in the elaborate evidential system in the Bosavi language, which obligatorily marks how one knows something: the source of what is said and seen, among other dimensions of epistemic stance (Schieffelin

1996). Such evidential systems are not part of Tok Pisin; in fact, no creole language has obligatory evidentials. These issues of the cultural specifics of expressing epistemic stance are connected to other metalinguistic and metapragmatic domains, which also create related problems in translation. Indeed, it helps explain why the speech act of blasphemy does not find an easy equivalency in either Tok Pisin or Bosavi.

Blasphemy presupposes the concept of God or something sacred and, with it, associated forms of appropriate speech. We first examine examples of how "blasphemy" was translated in the first two editions (1969, 1978) of the <u>Nupela Testamen</u> and then shifted in the 1989 revision, evidence that its meaning was neither transparent nor easy to translate, from Mark 2:7:

1969/1978	<u>Em</u>	<u>i</u>	<u>tok</u>	<u>bilas</u>	<u>long</u>	<u>God</u>
	he	[PM]	talk	decoration of/from/to		God
	'he talked boastfully to God'					
1989	<u>Em i</u>	<u>laik</u>	<u>kisim</u>	<u>ples</u>	<u>bilong</u>	<u>God</u>
	he [PM]	want	take	place of		God
	'he wanted to take the place of God'					

Tok bilas is a metalinguistic term that means boasting. Composed of <u>tok</u> 'talk' and <u>bilas</u> 'decoration', when referring to God it means blasphemy. The later expression <u>kisim ples bilong God</u> uses a key Tok Pisin word, <u>ples</u>, which means one's home, village or place, and is used in expressions such as <u>tok ples</u> to refer to one's vernacular language. Neither expression really expresses the semantic dimensions of the English word blasphemy.

In Bosavi, the word for "blasphemy" resisted easy translation from the Tok Pisin phrases. Pastors tried to find equivalencies, and example III. A–D show their choices and shifts. Example III. A, recorded in 1975 exhibits several self-repairs as Pastor Degelo: reads this short phrase in Tok Pisin.

III. A.   1975   Degelo: interlinear translation (NT 1969, Mark 2:7)

1. em i -   em   i   tok - bilong - tok   bilas –
   he [PM]   he   [PM]   talk   of   talk   decoration
   'he - he talked - of - talked boastfully'

>2. mo:wo: sada:dan   aungu siyo: –
    'the reason is gossip they said like that'

Degelo: (and other pastors) translated <u>tok bilas</u> as *sada:dan* 'gossip', that is, saying something that one does not have a right to say about someone else, for example, verbally attributing intention, speculating about someone's desires or beliefs, usually out of hearing of that person, but not necessarily. *Sada:dan* 'gossip' does not carry the affective or semantic dimensions of maliciousness, ridicule, or disrespect conveyed by blasphemy. Accusations of gossip, however, are very serious in Bosavi, and anyone accused and proven to have gossiped is required to pay compensation to the aggrieved party or parties. In this Bosavi translation, the pastor has added a speech quotative marker not in the text, *aungu siyo:* 'they said like that', metapragmatically bracketing the reported thought of the scribes as something said, the only way it could be known. This example comes from early missionization (1975), when the idea of knowing what was in someone else's mind was especially foreign. This metapragmatic bracket was not in the Tok Pisin text, but indicates the importance of adding a Bosavi evidential marker to this textual translation.

The 1978 version of the <u>Nupela Testamen</u> continued to use <u>tok bilas</u>, providing additional evidence of Bosavi attempts at sense-making, as seen in example III. B, from a 1984 church service.

III. B.   1984   continuous translation (NT 1978, Mark 2:7)

e Gode o:ga:igabo:lo:ka: a:la: siyo: - a:la: asulo: – ene kufa: usa mo asulo: –
'he (Jesus) is really making fun of God doing like that they said - they thought
– in their hearts they only thought it –'

The pastor uses another Bosavi metalinguistic verb *o:ga:igab* 'make fun of' which in this context conveys the sense "mock or ridicule." Given the relatively egalitarian structure of Bosavi society,[16] however, it does not encode an asymmetrical power dimension or a sense of disrespect for the sacred, which might have been conveyed using the word for curse, but that word was not chosen. Using evidential suffixes on the verb, the pastor conveys that the scribes had direct visual evidence of Jesus making fun of God.

One month later, September 1984, Pastor Degelo: read verse 7 in Tok Pisin in its entirety (rather than breaking it into segments), struggling with the reading. In his translation of three lines, he uses the same verb *o:ga:igab* (line 2) for blasphemy, this time concatenated with the verb 'say' and suffixed with the evidential *-lo:b,* thus marking both direct visual and auditory evidence.

III. C.   1984   interlinear translation (NT 1978, Mark 2:7)

<u>em i tok bilas long God -</u>   <u>i   no   gat   man - i   no gat wanpela man</u>
he [PM] talk decoration to God [PM] [NEG] [EXIST] man [PM] [NEG] [EXIST] one man
'He spoke boastfully to God - there's no man - there's not one person

<u>em inap (long) tekewe sin. em i</u>   <u>wok bilong God wanpela tasol</u>
he able to   remove sin it [PM]   work of   God one   alone/just
who can forgive sin. It's the work of God alone.'

1. *a:ta:ga: a:la: siyo:ka: a:la: sa:lab – ili sa:laiyo - ili asulo:wamiyo: a:la: asula:*
    sa:ga:yo: –
    'so they said like that it says – after they were saying - after they were thinking
    like that they kept thinking –'

2. *kalu hoso Godeyo: ko:lo: o:ga:i sa:labo:lo:ka – mogago: kaluwa:lo: ko:lo:*
    hama:no: a:no:
    'that man (Jesus) is really making fun of God they say – the washing away of
    people's sins'

3. *Godeya: ina:li ene nanogo:ka:* (a) *a:la: siyo:ka:* (b) *a:la: sa:lab*
    'is only God's work   they really said it says'

Line 3 adds evidential and emphatic marking to the assertion made in the verse of reported speech (a), followed by the text source (b). The translation should have conveyed that the source was the scribes' reported thought, not reported speech.

The 1989 edition of the <u>Nupela Testamen</u> replaced <u>tok bilas long God</u> with <u>em i laik kisim ples bilong God</u> 'he wanted to take the place of God'. Reading from this edition in 1995, pastor Degelo: translates this Tok Pisin phrase literally as Jesus wants to take God's land.

III. D.   1995   interlinear translation (NT 1989, Mark 2:7)

em   i laik - i   kisim   ples   bilong   God
he [PM] wants - he take   place of   God
'he wanted to take the place of God'

o: we godeya: heno: e a:diabo:lo:ka:
'He (Jesus) really wants to take God's land'

In Bosavi, the word <u>ples</u> was translated by the word *hen* 'land', as one's place and one's land were the same. Suffixing the visual evidential *-lo:b* plus the emphatic *-ka:* to the verb *diab* 'take' expresses land theft, an idea that was culturally plausible. The scribes' negative meaning of Jesus' acts of speaking, forgiving, and healing were now obscured in translation, yet another possible explanation for why these verses were ignored in sermons. Bosavi pastors could not make sense of this controversy dialogue, so they put it aside.

Conclusions

My analyses raise a number of interrelated issues about reflexive language and metapragmatics in the context of Bible translating and suggest that detailed examinations of the translating process show that multiple factors are at play when turning one text into another. The domain of reflexive language is clearly problematic, and not just in Bosavi. Reported speech and thought, as speech acts *and* as evidential markers, contribute to the intertwined dimensions of metapragmatic use and meaning. There may be no such thing as simple translation, especially when one closely examines translating practices as socially and historically situated activities. Like other verbal practices, they are fundamentally cultural, and their cultural specificities make their travel across time, space, texts, and linguistic codes particularly difficult. While new verbal resources were created in Bosavi, for example, "Christian" expressions of internal states and neologisms (e.g., 'convert'), reporting others' thoughts resisted appropriation because of the salience and importance of local cultural meanings of personhood and mind.

As the Bosavi case shows, translating is a complex activity when both orality and literacy are involved. The ideologies of orality and literacy associated with each culture in contact are deeply implicated in the performance of border crossing, translating activities. Though literacy was limited in Bosavi, the practice of reading was never silent or solitary, but always an oral activity, a performance whether someone else was listening or not. The practice of reading made something visual into something oral. Sound and hearing were connected to ideas about saying and hearing as specific ways of knowing, remembering and reporting (Schieffelin 2000: 297).

Through the late 1990s, Bible reading and translation remained an oral activity in Bosavi. In church services, reading the Tok Pisin verses aloud gave voice to the pastor's authority, an authority that was often extended to settings outside of the church. Local pastors preferred their own performance of reading Tok Pisin and then turning it into Bosavi, keeping it oral and making it local, requiring that people listen to them to understand. Pastors developed genres for church services, and they were not willing to give up speaking the authoritative language, Tok Pisin, or reading the authoritative text, the Tok Pisin Bible.

Seeing what was found in translating was due to a particular methodology, one that seeks to capture the ephemeral nature of talk so as to make sense of changing discourse practices in context. Turning talk into text was a goal and result of my research, as I required an oral performance that could be transformed into a literate materiality through tape-recording and transcribing with local speakers to carry out ethnographic and linguistic analyses. No other methodology would allow me to begin to make sense of what was going on in these translating activities, which involved contact across multiple texts, practices, codes, and ideologies. These activities raise numerous questions, including What is "the vernacular," and how do we find the traces of where it has been, and with whom in situations of change? We usually see the results of such changes in our fieldwork situations, but may not recognize them, especially if people are still speaking what both they and we recognize as their vernacular.

Bible reading and translating practices vary across time and place, and as we see from these few examples, reflexive language is a domain that may be harder to translate than others and worth paying attention to more broadly. We see from the Bosavi example, in which both Christianity and literacy, and the textual practices that surround them, are emergent, that the distinction between communicative intent and overt utterance that shapes everyday social and verbal life does not disappear with the introduction of new texts and interpretative practices. If, as Protestants claim, the meaning of God's message is "in the text," we have to ask whose version of the text, what meanings are selected, and which meanings are ignored, and we have to look critically at language variety and linguistic ideologies. When speakers are trying to make sense of the words of others, both linguistic and social heteroglossia result (Bakhtin 1981: 263). Reflexive language provides a rich resource for examining both types of heteroglossia in contexts such as missionization where power, authority, identity and theories of mind are contested with words. What gets lost in translating can sometimes be found, if we keep listening.

Appendix (examples follow the print format of the original text)

1. Mark 2:6–10, Good News Bible (1966). Jesus heals a paralyzed man.

   [Jesus said to the paralyzed man, "My son, your sins are forgiven."]
   6 Some teachers of the Law who were sitting there **thought to themselves,**
   7 "How does he dare **talk like this**? **This is blasphemy!** God is the only one who can **forgive** sins!" **8 At once Jesus knew what they were thinking, so he said to them, "Why do you think such things? 9** Is it easier to say this to a paralyzed

man, 'Your sins are forgiven,' or to say, 'Get up, pick up your mat, and walk'?
10 I will prove to you, then, that the Son of Man has authority on earth to forgive
sins." So he said to the paralyzed man, "I tell you, get up, pick up your mat, and
go home!"

2. Mak 2:6–8, <u>Nupela Testamen</u> (1969). Jisas i mekim gut wanpela man han lek
   nogut.

		[Translation]
Na sampela saveman bilong lo ol i sindaun i stap,	6	
na long bel bilong ol ol i tingting, i spik, / "Bilong	7	
wanem dispela man em **i tok olsem**? **Em i tok bilas**		
long God. I no gat wanpela man em inap long tekewe		
sin. Em i wok bilong God wanpela tasol." / **Long**	8	/In His
spirit bilong en Jisas i save, ol i gat dispela tingting		spirit/mind Jesus knew, they had this thought
long bel bilong ol. Olsem na em i tokim ol, "Bilong		in their hearts. So then He said to them, "Why
wanem yupela i got dispela kain tingting long bel		do you have this kind of thought in your
bilong yupela? /		hearts?"

3. Mak 2:6–8, <u>Nupela Testamen</u> (1978). Jisas i mekim orait wanpela man han lek
   nogut.

   [6]Na sampela saveman bilong lo ol i
   sindaun i stap, **na long bel bilong ol ol i
   tingting olsem.** [7]"Bilong wanen dispela man em i tok olsem? **Em i tok bilas
   long God.** I no gat wanpela man em
   inap long tekewe sin. Em i wok bilong
   God wanpela tasol." [8]**Long bel bilong
   en Jisas i save, ol i gat dispela tingting
   long bel bilong ol.** Olsem na em i tokim
   ol, "Bilong wanem yupela i gat dispela
   kain tingting long bel bilong yupela?

4. Mak 2:6–8, <u>Nupela Testamen</u> (1989). Jisas i mekim orait wanpela man i gat han
   na lek nogut.

[6]Sampela saveman bilong lo i sindaun i stap long haus, **na long bel bilong ol ol i tingting olsem.** [7]"Olsem wanem na dispela man i mekim dispela kain tok? **Em i laik kisim ples bilong God.** I no gat wanpela man em inap long lusim sin. Em i wok bilong God wanpela tasol." [8]**Na wantu Jisas i save pinis long bel bilong en long dispela tingting bilong ol.** Na em i askim olsem, "Bilong wanem yupela i gat dispela kain tingting long bel bilong yupela?	(*bilong wanem* and *olsem wanem* both mean 'why') J. knew in His heart about this thought of theirs

Notes

Research support for fieldwork in Bosavi was generously provided by the National Science Foundation, the American Philosophical Society, and the Wenner-Gren Foundation for Anthropological Research and is gratefully acknowledged. I also thank the National Endowment for the Humanities, American Council of Learned Societies and the John Simon Guggenheim Memorial Fellowships, which supported time spent thinking and writing about this project. My *wantok* Gillian Sankoff provided generous assistance with Tok Pisin glosses, and Joel Robbins, Miki Makihara, Rupert Stasch, Steven Feld, and Graham Jones provided critical suggestions during various stages, including helping me translate my ideas from Bosavi into English. I alone am responsible for the translations presented here.

1. These engagements recall Pratt's 1991 notion of "contact zone": "social spaces where cultures meet, clash, and grapple with each other, often in contexts of highly asymmetrical relations of power, such as colonialism, slavery or their aftermaths" (34). In these spaces, such grapplings are often lost between literacy and orality.

2. The term "theory of mind" has been used differently in several literatures, especially philosophy and psychology, to describe the interpersonal understanding and use of mental states in talk and interaction. A conservative formulation has it referring to (1) a human cognitive ability to recognize and attribute mental states (beliefs, desires, and intentions) to oneself and to recognize and understand that others have separate and different mental states; and (2) the ability to form hypotheses about those states with some degree of accuracy and use one's theories to predict behavior. Throughout the literature, mental states include intentions, that of the self and the other, and thus imply intersubjectivity, a prerequisite for human communication.

3. In addition to the work on the Bosavi people cited in this chapter, see also E. L. Schieffelin 1976, 1981a, b; Feld [1982] 1990, 1988, 1996.

4. E. L. Schieffelin (1991: 262–268) provides an ethnohistorical account of first contact in Bosavi and a description of some of the subsequent changes in the area.

5. E. L. Schieffelin 1977 details Bosavi responses to Christianity in the early years of missionization. His example of spirit mediums who during séance performances comment on Christian ideas illustrates the tensions that existed between traditional beliefs and Christian beliefs, two versions of the world coexisting. In some ways, the translation practices discussed in this chapter also reflect an initial coexistence, but over time Christian practices overwhelmed traditional ones, including spirit mediums.

6. Franklin 1992 offers a taxonomy of English speech act verbs (drawn from the Gospel according to Mark), underscoring the importance of knowing their local meanings for translating. Other than this essay, there is no mention of translation difficulties in Tok Pisin specific to this domain of language.

7. Working with Swahili native texts, Fabian notes, "Their inconsistencies and linguistic deficiencies often contain precious information" (1986: viii). The Bosavi example has further parallels with Fabian's 1990 ethnographic inquiry into a grass-roots literacy document, the "Vocabulary of Elisabethville" written in Shaba Swahili. Without his interrogation, this document would have remained silent. Letting texts speak and listening to what they say raise profound methodological and theoretical implications for other found or constructed texts, such as transcripts that are produced between the boundaries of orality and literacy. The necessity for attention to details in such contact zones cannot be overemphasized.

8. Words in Tok Pisin are underlined; elements in the Bosavi language are italicized.

9. Feld 1990: 246–249 discusses the distinctions between the verbs for translate *to nodoma* 'turn around words' and interpret *to balema* 'turn over words'. They are part of an extensive

and sophisticated metalinguistic system in Bosavi that includes a range of conversational and poetic devices (138–144). As Feld so eloquently points out in discussing Bosavi ideas of interpretation and translation, the Bosavi view of meaning "is mindful of the subtle interplay of surface with intention, transparency with association, reference with resonance" (249), ideas that the missionaries willfully ignored.

10. Watson-Gegeo and Gegeo 1991 detail the development of Christian speech styles linked to nonverbal aspects of communication as markers of church affiliation (Anglicans and evangelicals) among the Kwara'ae (Solomon Islands).

11. Ross 1985 points out that scholars have paid little attention to the effects of Tok Pisin on the native vernaculars because the opposite processes have been more salient. However, in the few cases where some effects have been noted, Ross suggests that neologistic lexical transfers are based on speakers' perceptions that there is no equivalent in the vernacular for the objects and concepts for which lexical items are borrowed. This is often the case when they are new to the culture. In addition, transference occurs when speakers are bilingual (Ross, citing Laycock 1979) or are more "at home" in Tok Pisin than in their vernacular. This is not the case with most of the Bosavi examples.

12. Verses 8–10 are of course relevant to this sequence, but they are not included in this analysis. See appendix for the text.

13. Olsem, originally the preposition 'like', evolved into complementizer 'like/that', which Woolford 1979 claims is used for both direct ('thus') and indirect speech ('that'). Mühlhäusler 1985: 412–414 reports that olsem is only used with indirect speech and that direct speech is introduced by the verb phrase i tok or i tok i spik. This is not shown to be the case in the Nupela Testamen; there i tok olsem introduces direct speech.

14. Transcription conventions: examples I–III, which are transcribed from church services, use hyphens (-) to indicate hesitation in reading and speaking, which in many places are instances of self-repair. Double hyphens (–) indicate longer pauses. These are carried through in the glosses. Line numbers indicate a major pause or line break for both the read Tok Pisin as well as the translated Bosavi. For the Tok Pisin, [PM] is predicate marker.

15. This pattern of avoiding verbal speculation of the intentions of others, and its link to gossip as a negatively evaluated speech activity is reported in several Pacific societies. Besnier 1993 reports that in Tuvalu, "Nukulaelae islanders are remarkably wary of voicing conjectures, interpretations, and inferences from observable facts" (166). Only children, adolescents, and gossips engage in such asocial and irresponsible behavior. Thoughts are almost exclusively self-reported, and Nukulaelae avoid interpreting one another's linguistic and nonlinguistic behavior (166–167). McKellin, writing about Managalase (Papua New Guinea), describes their "avoidance of open displays or discussions of individuals' supposed intentions; they recognize that individuals' thoughts are often illusive, ambiguous, and imperfectly understood by others.... Although people privately gossip about others' activities, they hesitate to assign motives and control others' actions directly" (1990: 336). Weiner 1984: 166 discusses the Trobrianders' claim that no one has access to the minds of others, and Strathern 1979: 250 reports that Melpa of Mt. Hagen express an uncertainty of the source of intentions, whether in the mind or in the mouth. These ideas about intentionality have culturally specific verbal consequences, for example, the use of verbal disguise and indirection, but all signal a pervasive cultural preference.

16. I use the term "egalitarian" with some caution. There are no chiefs or established hierarchical structures, but there are inequalities in terms of gender, generation, and situation. Feld 1984 discusses these in terms of sound structure and expressive dimensions of Bosavi culture. In the context of missionization, hierarchy has been established through new social roles that have new forms of authority—for example, pastor and deacon.

References

Aikhenvald, Alexandra Y. 2003. Evidentiality in Typological Perspective. In *Studies in Evidentiality*, ed. Alexandra Y. Aikhenvald and Robert M. W. Dixon, pp. 1–31. Amsterdam: John Benjamins.

Bakhtin, Mikhail M. 1981. Discourse in the Novel. In *The Dialogic Imagination*, pp. 259–422. Austin: University of Texas Press.

Besnier, Niko. 1993 Reported Speech and Affect on Nukulaelae Atoll. In *Responsibility and Evidence in Oral Discourse*, ed. Jane Hill and Judith Irvine, pp. 161–181. New York: Cambridge University Press.

Camery-Hoggatt, Jerry. 1992. *Irony in Mark's Gospel*. Cambridge: Cambridge University Press.

Chafe, Wallace, and Johanna Nichols, eds. 1986. Evidentiality: The Coding of Epistemology in Language. Norwood, NJ: Ablex.

Coulmas, Florian. ed. 1986. *Direct and Indirect Speech*. Berlin: Mouton de Gruyter.

de Waard, Jan, and Eugene A. Nida. 1986. *One Language to Another: Functional Equivalence in Bible Translating*. Nashville, TN: Thomas Nelson.

Du Bois, John. 1993. Meaning without Intention: Lessons from Divination. In *Responsibility and Evidence in Oral Discourse*, ed. Jane Hill and Judith Irvine, pp. 48–71. New York: Cambridge University Press.

Duranti, Alessandro. 1993. Intentions, Self, and Responsibility: An Essay in Samoan Ethnopragmatics. In *Responsibility and Evidence in Oral Discourse*, ed. Jane Hill and Judith Irvine, pp. 24–47. New York: Cambridge University Press.

Fabian, Johannes. 1986. *Language and Colonial Power*. Cambridge: Cambridge University Press.

———. 1990. *History from Below: The Vocabulary of Elisabethville*. Philadelphia: John Benjamins.

Feld, Steven. 1984. Sound Structure as Social Structure. *Ethnomusicology* 28 (3): 383–409.

———. 1988. Aesthetics as Iconicity of Style, or, "Lift-Up-over-Sounding": Getting into the Kaluli Groove. *Yearbook for Traditional Music* 20: 74–113.

———. [1982] 1990. *Sound and Sentiment: Birds, Weeping, Poetics, and Song in Kaluli Expression*. 2nd ed. Philadelphia: University of Pennsylvania Press.

———. 1996. Waterfalls of Song: An Acoustemology of Place Resounding in Bosavi, Papua New Guinea. In *Senses of Place*, ed. Steven Feld and Keith Basso, pp. 91–135. Santa Fe, NM: School of American Research Press.

Franklin, Karl J. 1992. Speech Act Verbs and the Words of Jesus. In *Language in Context: Essays for Robert E. Longacre*, ed. Shin Ja J. Hwang and William R. Merrifield, pp. 241–261. Dallas, TX: Summer Institute of Linguistics.

Goffman, Erving. 1974. *Frame Analysis*. New York: Harper.

———. 1979. Footing. *Semiotica* 25: 1–29.

Good News Bible: Today's English Version. 1966. New York: American Bible Society.

Janssen, Theo, and Wim van der Wurff, eds. 1996. *Reported Speech*. Amsterdam: John Benjamins.

Jakobson, Roman. [1957] 1971. Shifters, Verbal Categories, and the Russian Verb. In *Selected Writings II. Word and Language*, pp. 130–147. The Hague, Netherlands: Mouton.

Keane, Webb. 2001. Sincerity, "Modernity," and the Protestants. *Cultural Anthropology* 17 (1): 1–28.

———. 2004. Language and Religion. In *A Companion to Linguistic Anthropology*, ed. Alessandro Duranti, pp. 431–448. Malden, MA: Blackwell.

Knauft, Bruce. 2002. *Exchanging the Past: A Rainforest World of Before and After*. Chicago: University of Chicago Press.

Laycock, Donald. 1979. Multilingualism: Linguistic Boundaries and Unsolved Problems in Papua New Guinea. In *New Guinea and Neighboring Areas: A Sociolinguistic Laboratory*, ed. S. Wurm, pp. 81–100. The Hague, Netherlands: Mouton.

LiPuma, Edward. 2000. *Encompassing Others: The Magic of Modernity in Melanesia*. Ann Arbor: University of Michigan Press.

Long, Lynne, ed. 2005. *Translation and Religion: Holy Untranslatable?* Clevedon, UK: Multilingual Matters.

Lucy, John A., ed. 1993a. Reflexive Language and the Human Disciplines. In *Reflexive Language: Reported Speech and Metapragmatics*, ed. John Lucy, pp. 9–32. Cambridge: Cambridge University Press.

————. 1993b. *Reflexive Language: Reported Speech and Metapragmatics*. Cambridge: Cambridge University Press.

McKellin, William. 1990. Allegory and Inference: Intentional Ambiguity in Managalase Negotiations. In *Disentangling: Conflict Discourse in Pacific Societies*, ed. Karen Watson-Gegeo and Geoffrey White, pp. 335–370. Stanford, CA: Stanford University Press.

Mitchell-Kernan, Claudia. 1972. Signifying and Marking: Two Afro-American Speech Acts. In *Directions in Sociolinguistics: The Ethnography of Speaking*, ed. John J. Gumperz and Dell Hymes, pp. 161–179. New York: Holt, Rinehart and Winston.

Mühlhäusler, Peter. 1985. Etymologizing and Tok Pisin. In *Handbook of Tok Pisin*, ed. Steven Wurm and Peter Mühlhäusler, Pacific Linguistics Series C–70, pp. 177–219. Canberra: Australian National University.

Mundhenk, Norm. 1985. Linguistic Decisions in the Tok Pisin Bible. In *Melanesian Pidgin and Tok Pisin*, ed. J. W. M. Verhaar, pp. 345–373. Amsterdam: John Benjamins.

Nida, Eugene A. 1964. *Toward a Science of Translating*. Leiden: E. J. Brill.

Nupela Testamen. 1969. Port Moresby: Bible Society of Papua New Guinea.

Nupela Testamen na ol Sam. 1978. Port Moresby: Bible Society of Papua New Guinea.

Nupela Testamen. 1989. In *Buk Baibel*. Port Moresby: Bible Society of Papua New Guinea.

Ochs, Elinor. 1984. Clarification and Culture. In *Meaning, Form and Use in Context, GURT '84*, ed. Deborah Schiffrin, pp. 325–341. Washington, D. C. Georgetown University Press.

————. 1988. *Culture and Language Development*. Cambridge: Cambridge University Press.

Ochs, Elinor, and Bambi B. Schieffelin. 1984. Language Acquisition and Socialization: Three Developmental Stories and their Implications. In *Culture Theory: Essays on Mind, Self, and Emotion*, ed. Richard Shweder and Robert Levine, pp. 276–320. New York: Cambridge University Press.

Pratt, Mary Louise. 1991. Arts of the Contact Zone. *Profession* 91: 33–40.

Renck, Gersink. 1990. *Contextualization of Christianity and Christianization of Language*. Erlangen: Verlag der Ev.-Luth. Mission.

Robbins, Joel. 2001. God Is Nothing but Talk: Modernity, Language, and Prayer in a Papua New Guinea Society. *American Anthropologist* 103 (4): 901–912.

Rosaldo, Michelle. 1982. The Things We Do with Words: Ilongot Speech Acts and Speech Act Theory in Philosophy. *Language in Society* 11: 203–237.

Ross, Malcolm. 1985. Current Use and Expansion of Tok Pisin: Effects of Tok Pisin on Some Vernacular Languages. In *Handbook of Tok Pisin*, ed. Steven A. Wurm and Peter Mühlhäusler, pp. 539–556. Pacific Linguistics C–70. Canberra: Australian National University.

Rule, Joan. 1954. Capturing Words for Christ. *Light & Life,* March 8–9. Melbourne: Australian Printing and Publishing Company.

Rule, Murray. 1977. Institutional Framework of Language Study: The Asia Pacific Christian Mission. In *Language, Culture, Society, and the Modern World, Fascicle 2, New Guinea Area Languages and Language Study*, Vol. 3, ed. Steven A. Wurm, pp. 1341–1344. Pacific Linguistics Series C–40. Canberra: Australian National University.

Schieffelin, Bambi B. 1986. The Acquisition of Kaluli. In *The Crosslinguistic Study of Language Acquisition*, ed. Dan I. Slobin, pp. 525–593. Hillsdale, N.J.: Lawrence Erlbaum Associates.

———. 1990. *The Give and Take of Everyday Life: Language Socialization of Kaluli Children.* New York: Cambridge University Press.

———. 1996. Creating Evidence: Making Sense of Written Words in Bosavi. In *Interaction and Grammar*, ed. Elinor Ochs, Emanuel A. Schegloff, and Sandra A. Thompson, pp. 435–460. New York: Cambridge University Press.

———. 2000. Introducing Kaluli Literacy. In *Regimes of Language*, ed. Paul Kroskrity, pp. 293–327. Santa Fe, NM: School for American Research Press.

———. 2002. Marking Time: The Dichotomizing Discourse of Multiple Temporalities. *Current Anthropology* 43 (S4): S5–S17.

———. 2003. The More It Changes …: Christianizing Language and the Displacement of Culture. Unpublished manuscript.

Schieffelin, Bambi B., and Steven Feld. 1998. *Bosavi-English-Tok Pisin Dictionary.* Pacific Linguistics Series C–153. Canberra: Australian National University.

Schieffelin, Edward L. 1976. *The Sorrow of the Lonely and the Burning of the Dancers.* New York: St. Martin's Press.

———. 1977. The Unseen Influence: Tranced Mediums as Historical Innovators. *Journal de la Société des Oceanistes* 33 (56–57): 169–178.

———. 1981a. The End of Traditional Music, Dance, and Body Decoration in Bosavi, Papua New Guinea. In *The Plight of Peripheral Peoples*, Vol. 1, Occasional Paper no 7. Peterborough, NH: Cultural Survival.

———. 1981b. Evangelical Rhetoric and the Transformation of Traditional Culture in Papua New Guinea. *Comparative Studies in Society and History* 23 (1): 150–156.

———. 1991. The Great Papuan Plateau. In *Like People You See in a Dream*, ed. Edward L. Schieffelin and Rob Crittenden, pp. 58–87. Stanford, CA: Stanford University Press.

Silverstein, Michael. 1976. Shifters, Linguistic Categories, and Cultural Description. In *Meaning in Anthropology*, ed. Keith Basso and Henry Selby, pp. 11–55. Albuquerque: University of New Mexico Press.

———. 1985. The Culture of Language in Chinookan Narrative Texts; or On Saying That… in Chinook. In *Grammar Inside and Outside the Clause*, ed. Johanna Nichols and Anthony Woodbury, pp. 132–171. Cambridge: Cambridge University Press.

———. 1993. Metapragmatic Discourse and Metapragmatic Function. In *Reflexive Language: Reported Speech and Metapragmatics*, ed. John Lucy, pp. 33–58. Cambridge: Cambridge University Press.

Strathern, Marilyn. 1979. The Self in Self-Decorating. *Oceania* 49: 241–257.

Verschueren, Jeff. 1989. Language on Language: Toward Metapragmatic Universals. *Papers in Pragmatics* 3 (2): 1–144.

Voloshinov, V. N. [1929] 1986. *Marxism and the Philosophy of Language.* Cambridge: Harvard University Press.

Watson-Gegeo, Karen, and David Gegeo. 1991. The Impact of Church Affiliation on Language Use in Kwara'ae (Solomon Islands). *Language in Society* 20: 533–555.

Weiner, Annette. 1984. From Words to Objects to Magic: "Hard Words" and the Boundaries of Social Interaction. In *Dangerous Words: Language and Politics in the Pacific*, ed. Donald Brenneis and Fred Myers, pp. 161–191. New York: New York University Press.

Whorf, Benjamin L. 1956. *Language, Thought, and Reality.* Cambridge: MIT Press.

Woolford, Ellen. 1980. The Developing Complementizer System in Tok Pisin. In *Generative Studies on Creole Languages*, ed. Pieter Muysken, pp. 125–139. Dordrecht, Netherlands: Foris.

8

COURTNEY HANDMAN

Speaking to the Soul

On Native Language and Authenticity in Papua New Guinea Bible Translation

When the Summer Institute of Linguistics (SIL) and its sister organization Wycliffe were incorporated in 1942 by William Cameron Townsend, SIL linguists and Wycliffe members thought that there were about a thousand languages in the world. Their organizing vision was that if SIL members worked hard enough, they could possibly see the translation of the Bible into every language in their own lifetimes. Imagine then their dismay when an SIL language surveyor sent to the Pacific, Robert J. Story, came to the biannual meeting in 1955 to announce that there were at least an additional thirteen hundred languages in the Pacific, possibly just on the island of New Guinea alone.

> For the first few hours of the conference while Story read page after page of evidence, including the names of the tribes and the number of souls involved, Wycliffe members in attendance were almost too stunned to react. They had not expected their job, already looming large, to double overnight. There were at least two thousand tongues to go. (Wallis and Bennett 1959: 297)

Devastated by their realization that they were probably not going to witness the completion of their goal, they nonetheless vowed to continue their work.

In the intervening fifty years, SIL members have grown accustomed to the enormity of their task—the total number of extant languages in the world is usually counted at around six thousand now—but their vision has not been clouded. The current SIL project is labeled Vision 2025, and the goal is to at least *start* a translation project in every language of the world that needs a translation by the year 2025. Some of the issues involved in deciding what counts as a language in need of translation are addressed below. In Papua New Guinea there are, by SIL's count, more than 800 languages, and as of April 2006, 159 of these had New Testaments. With 186 projects in progress, several translations already completed by other organizations, and several languages in the Sepik close to obsolescence which will probably not be translated, this still means that between 350 and 400 projects need to be started before 2025 in Papua New Guinea alone.[1] Moreover, though SIL Papua New Guinea has always had a large membership, several members feel that new recruits to SIL are now more interested in working in Asia as opposed to Oceania, and that recently it has been difficult to maintain the SIL Papua New Guinea membership size.

To achieve Vision 2025, SIL Papua New Guinea realizes that it cannot rely solely on existing or new membership, that it must forge partnerships with other organizations to see this project to completion. Currently, SIL Papua New Guinea is relying upon the steady growth of its sister organization the Bible Translation Association of Papua New Guinea (BTA), one of SIL International's many partner National Bible Translation Organizations, which are translation groups that use local people rather than expatriate missionaries. But in Papua New Guinea, BTA has had a slow growth. Started in 1977, two years after the independence of Papua New Guinea from Australia, BTA members have completed about ten translations.

Moreover, handing over responsibility to others is a tall order for SIL. Within mission circles, it is an organization known for its high academic standards and demanding requirements. Though its early orientations to and participations in the world of post-Bloomfieldian linguistics have changed as paradigms have shifted in academic linguistics, its translators continue to be trained in the latest theories and methods, with many translators receiving M.A.s and Ph.D.s in the field of linguistics. The organization has become not only the standard-bearer for Bible translation work around the world but also a major source of documentation of the world's smallest and most remote language communities. SIL Papua New Guinea is by far the largest national branch within the SIL family, and in a country where only a tiny fraction of the population receives a college education, many questions have emerged. Will Papua New Guineans be able to make a success of Vision 2025? How will SIL and BTA train all the needed personnel? Most important, what kind of training do they need? These are some of the questions that have been on the minds of SIL Papua New Guinea and BTA members recently, and they will be the starting point for this chapter.

As SIL and BTA reanalyze the training needs of various categories of members, we can examine the forms of knowledge necessary to Bible translation. At the same time, I would argue that this perspective allows us to get a handle on evangelical (conservative Christian) ideas about the structure of the self of the potential indigenous convert in the mission field, in particular the forms of knowledge that constitute selves open to the types of change envisioned by members of the evangelical community. What does SIL practice say about how members, especially translators, understand Christian cross-cultural communication? How do they speak to the soul of members of the communities with whom they work? The primary focus of the chapter will be a comparison of evangelical ideas of the location and form of linguistic knowledge as opposed to cultural knowledge, in part because SIL focuses so much attention on training its translators in linguistics and, to a lesser extent, anthropology.

Whereas other chapters discuss the effects of Christian conversion in local social formations (Schieffelin, chap. 7; Robbins, chap. 6), this chapter details the role of language in one organization that is dedicated to creating change. Neither SIL literature nor SIL members emphasize what kinds of change they hope for in the lives of the people they work with and try to help, although development, self-confidence, and Christian commitment are all common themes. However, by examining the role of linguistic and cultural knowledge as it is theorized for the translation process, we can begin to see how SIL and BTA techniques and training presupposes a certain kind of self and the conditions of change for that self. In particular, I examine various aspects of the SIL and BTA training regimes that pertain to issues of native speakerhood and the relationship between fluency and authenticity in Christian commitment. I demonstrate a linguistically oriented notion of group identity that establishes language as more central to authenticity than is culture within a process of Christian change.

On SIL

William Cameron Townsend (1896–1982) officially incorporated both the Summer Institute of Linguistics and Wycliffe Bible Translators in 1942, although summer linguistics schools had been held in Arkansas since 1934. SIL and Wycliffe form the main components of what members generally call "the Wycliffe family of organizations." The institutional, financial, and social links between these and other organizations in the SIL world are worthy of a paper in their own right,[2] but for the purposes of this chapter, I wish to highlight just a few characteristics.

It is important to first define the basic parameters of SIL. In particular, it is important to recognize the differences between SIL International, with headquarters in Dallas, Texas, and national branches of SIL—such as SIL Papua New Guinea—in target regions or nations. SIL International is primarily responsible for developing the training programs that members must complete; organizing and publishing *Ethnologue*, the UNESCO-sponsored database of languages and linguistic materials; and otherwise acting as the headquarters of an international nongovernmental organization. SIL International, in conjunction with SIL national branches, developed three main goals as part of a mission statement for the latter groups' work in local communities: access to and use of Scripture and other materials, language development for receptor communities, and advancement of academic knowledge and professional skills. SIL International established these goals, but each SIL national branch has had to ratify them, and in some cases national branches have amended or expanded on them. For example, SIL Papua New Guinea expanded upon each of these goals in ways that specifically addressed the unique sociolinguistic, political, and religious situation of Papua New Guinea. As this system of ratification and emendation suggests, the relationship between SIL International and its national branches is probably best described as one of guidance,[3] with SIL International ideally acting in an advisory capacity for the national branches. Because of this, it is important to point out that significant differences exist not only between the SIL national branches and SIL International but also between the various national branches of SIL themselves. Particularly relevant to this chapter is the very unique situation of SIL Papua New Guinea.

SIL Papua New Guinea (hereafter SIL PNG) dwarfs all other SIL national branches both in member size and in the complexity of its organization and infrastructure. SIL PNG is based near Kainantu town at Ukarumpa, Eastern Highlands Province, a sprawling compound known locally as "Little America." Built up over the last fifty years, Ukarumpa has grown from an isolated outpost into an excellent facsimile of a suburban subdivision, complete with its own post office, garbage pick-up, Internet service provider, meeting house/church, grocery store, school, and any number of other amenities that are routinely expected by the eight hundred-plus members coming from First World countries.[4] However, Ukarumpa acts as a hub for SIL PNG members, so that at no time would all eight hundred members be present on the compound.

There are, of course, positives and negatives to the size and development of Ukarumpa. On the one hand, SIL PNG is extremely productive in part because of these factors.[5] For example, members do not have to deal with the hassles of relocating themselves and their families to other countries while they typeset their publications because SIL PNG has typesetting facilities and staff on the Ukarumpa center. On the other hand, the size and development of Ukarumpa allows it to be a community unto itself, making it both expensive to maintain and inwardly focused. When living at Ukarumpa, members generally live, worship, work, and relax in a setting that is to a large extent divorced from the rest of Papua New Guinea. With the partial exception of SIL Philippines, which also has a large compound, no other SIL national branch has this kind of size, insularity, or convenience, according to SIL PNG members. In other countries, SIL might be little more than a storefront, with members' houses scattered around a capital city or around a country. Members in other national branches might share experiences and affiliations but do not form the kind of community that Ukarumpa provides.

Another way in which SIL PNG is unique is the extremely welcoming attitude that the Papua New Guinea government has toward the organization. Papua New Guinea's constitution states that it is a Christian nation, and as such it generally welcomes missionaries and Christian aid workers. SIL has occasionally had very tense relationships with host governments, but in Papua New Guinea, the organization is commemorated in postal stamps, honored with medals and awards, and has intimate access to government offices. Because of this, SIL PNG is able to put a primary focus on the first of the three SIL International goals mentioned above: giving to receptor communities access to Scripture—in other words, Bible translation. In contrast to members working in sensitive areas in which a New Testament translation would be unwelcome or even illegal and where members focus their efforts on linguistics and literacy to the exclusion of translation, SIL members in Papua New Guinea are encouraged by the government and indeed by many citizens to publish New Testaments in every one of the nation's languages. In fact, SIL members are so well liked by most Papua New Guineans that it was generally with disappointment that people discovered that my husband and I were not with SIL.[6]

Given the unique situation of SIL PNG, most of what I discuss in this chapter is with specific reference to it and to Ukarumpa, where I conducted several months of field and archival research during 2003 and 2006 as part of a larger project about the role of Bible translation in the missionization of the Guhu-Samane of the Waria

Valley, Morobe Province. However, a number of statements I make here are also based on an analysis of Wycliffe materials (either published in book form or on the Internet). Wycliffe is a specifically missions-oriented organization that provides support for many SIL members working in various host countries. Whereas SIL is a literacy and linguistics nongovernmental organization, Wycliffe is a Bible translation organization that works to recruit members, donors, and supporters for literacy- and translation-related work in SIL and other allied organizations. Most, but not all, SIL members are members of their home-country branch of Wycliffe, and many became interested in linguistics and Bible translation through Wycliffe advertising. For this latter reason, I have employed Wycliffe promotional materials in this analysis.

In some host countries, the separation between SIL as a literacy nongovernmental organization in the host nation and Wycliffe as a Bible translation organization in a member's home nation is quite obvious. But in Papua New Guinea, the lines between SIL and Wycliffe are fuzzy. Outside the Ukarumpa compound, SIL is synonymous with Bible translation work, and its members are referred to as missionaries, although Wycliffe as an organization is virtually unknown. Literacy, empowerment, Christian commitment, conversion, development, and any number of other topics that veer toward either SIL or Wycliffe regularly formed the basis of the interviews I conducted with SIL PNG members at Ukarumpa. Perhaps because of the two unique aspects of SIL PNG discussed above—the size and relative insularity of the Ukarumpa compound and the generally warm relationship with the government and people of Papua New Guinea—members of SIL PNG feel free to discuss the Christian and missions aspects of their work. This is not true of national branches in more sensitive areas, nor is it generally true of SIL International. My goal here is to present and analyze certain aspects of the translation work of SIL PNG in terms of those kinds of free-flowing conversations that occasionally blurred the boundaries of SIL and Wycliffe. For the most part, my discussion focuses on printed materials or conversations with SIL PNG members that are representative of how certain topics were discussed; this does not mean that those materials or discussions reflect official SIL International or SIL PNG policy.

The task of the Bible translator

To understand some of the difficulties of and issues related to having Papua New Guinean translators do the work that SIL has so far largely been responsible for, we need to look at how SIL translators theorize their task of New Testament translation.[7] SIL (and many current evangelical missions groups) see the world in terms of "people groups." SIL concerns itself not with the total population of the world or of a country that is in need of the message, but with the number of people groups that can still be considered either totally "unreached" or just without a New Testament translation in their own language. This contrasts sharply with the approach of the mainline missions in Papua New Guinea, such as the Lutherans and Catholics, which established gentlemen's agreements about provincially based spheres of influence. Even though individualism is stressed in analyses of Christianity (Dumont 1986), contemporary cross-cultural evangelism approaches the recipients of missionizing efforts in terms of groups. In Papua New Guinea, whether we are talking about the Melpa with 130,000 speakers or the Ama with 400 speakers (as they are listed on the SIL/BTA map of completed and ongoing projects), both are "people groups" and both had an equal need for the translators who worked there.

But why are the 400 Ama just as deserving as the 130,000 Melpa of the fifteen or more years that it takes to complete a New Testament? To understand this, we have to examine the concept of "heart language," which has been a cornerstone of SIL methodology. Heart language, in the most basic sense, refers to a speaker's first native language. But more important, heart language is the language through which God will be able to communicate to a group of people. In missions literature, it is the medium through which one speaks to the soul. Many contemporary evangelical missions groups use the concept of heart language in their missions strategy, requiring missionaries to learn the local language, but insofar as SIL's mission is to translate the New Testament for each group, it is particularly relevant to SIL's overall outlook. SIL members often discuss their local language translation work just in intellectual terms—they want to provide people with a translation of the New Testament in a language they understand. However, questions of intelligibility of the target text (i.e., translated New Testament) often slide into questions of the emotional and affective force of reading a potentially life-changing text in one's first, native language. Note that it is referred to as the *heart* language—not the brain language. As one of the most maximally presupposed terms of contemporary missions, it is rare to find much explicit discussion of heart language (also called simply "mother tongue") beyond the definition already given, although former Wycliffe President George Cowan's (1979: 62) remarks provide a standard elaboration: "When a person speaks in his mother tongue, it isn't just his intellect that is involved, but his whole self, including his emotions and will." That is to say, it is not just comprehension or competence ("intellect"), but a deep relationship between linguistic knowledge and the self that is involved when one speaks in one's heart language. Mother tongue, or heart language, presents the "whole self" to linguistic interactions, including reading the New Testament.[8]

Given contemporary evangelical Christianity's well-studied emphasis on talk as the foremost ritual medium (see Robbins 2001; Keane 1997; Harding 2000), a linguistic door on the soul, or the ability to speak to the soul, may in fact be the only one that many evangelical missionaries ascribe to. Luhrmann (2004) recently criticized Harding's exclusionary emphasis on talk in Christian conversion and practice; however, we should note that even in Luhrmann's materials, many of the metakinetic experiences are described as otherworldly linguistic communications (e.g., God spoke to me, I heard a voice, etc.). So whether or not analysts should focus entirely upon the linguistic aspects of Christianity, we should at least recognize that these are the primary ways in which evangelical Christians discuss their own religious experiences and, as I am arguing here, theorize the route to enabling those experiences for others (see also Ikeda 2002). As the "heart" in evangelical missionaries' concept of heart language is supposed to express, affective, possibly metakinetic conversion responses are the hoped-for results of evangelization. But methodologically speaking, they are results that are supposed to be possible because of this linguistic perspective. In the context of Papua New Guinea, those eight hundred heart languages are the necessary doors to the country's six million souls.

Note, also, that the question of speaking to the soul is not simply a problem of access to a readable Bible. For much of Papua New Guinea, people have a version of the Bible that they can understand, even if SIL or other organizations do not produce a vernacular language translation for them. Most Papua New Guineans speak the English-based creole lingua franca Tok Pisin and own a copy of the Tok Pisin Bible, Buk Baibel (1989). But a major aspect of a heart language is that it is not what SIL and many other missionaries and linguists call a "trade language." In these contexts, trade languages are lingua francas or vehicular languages and they are frequently pidgins or creoles. These types of languages have in common the fact that they are spoken by several ethnolinguistic communities rather than just one. They are often products of colonial interventions, and in many places, including Papua New Guinea, they have official or semiofficial status in the postcolonial governments. For SIL, Tok Pisin is exactly the kind of language that does not seem a promising route to the soul.

Heart language versus trade language

Pidgins and creoles that are based on European languages, such as the English-based Tok Pisin, or any of the French-based creoles of the Caribbean, have long been denounced as being less than languages because they are "simplified" from the lexifier language perspective—English or French, say. They have generally lost or changed the overt markings for common grammatical categories such as number, case, or tense. Additionally, they have significantly smaller lexicons than their standard European counterparts, usually leading speakers of the lexifier language to complain that one cannot express a full range of meanings in such a language. Even if objections to a pidgin or creole's ability to refer and predicate were overcome, critics would still maintain that the poverty of such languages do not allow for affective expression ("there aren't enough synonyms," or the like). Using the two functions of language recognized by many Euro-American speakers—(1) referring to a world "out there," and (2) expressing emotion—pidgins and creoles are almost always considered to be deficient. Since SIL is primarily concerned with the very affective processes ascribed to "natural language," this is essentially the death knell for the possibility of evangelizing in a pidgin or creole. In Papua New Guinea, most SIL members (and, for that matter, most evangelical missionaries and English-speaking expatriates) believe that Tok Pisin just doesn't have enough words to allow the Buk Baibel to accurately communicate the Christian message.[9]

Almost all trade languages are second languages (creoles are the exception) learned in addition to the language(s) of ethnolinguistic identity. Missions literature depicts a trade language, in general correctly, as the language of urban life and the majority culture. Jourdan (chap. 2 of this volume) discusses the nativized form of Solomon Islands Pijin that is now spoken among urban youth in Honiara (see also Smith 2002 for Tok Pisin). These are languages used away from hearth and home, in the hurly-burly of modern life,[10] and they are characterized in missions literature as lacking the relationship to self or soul that heart languages have.[11] And because missionaries assume that they lack the interiority and authenticity of first languages, trade languages, when used in evangelization, are seen as leading not to stable Christian commitment, but to the shifting grounds of syncretism or nominal Christianity. "The first key element in avoiding syncretism is communicating with people in their mother tongue—the language in which they learned their religion, values and cultural identity" according to the booklet "Making Disciples of Oral Listeners," which is posted on the Web site of the International Orality Network, a collaborative effort of several missions groups including Vernacular Media Services, an arm of Wycliffe.[12] You may be able to reach a larger audience evangelizing in the trade language, but you will most likely not reach potential converts' souls. Thus, the quality of converts is stressed in heart language evangelism, even if this means that the quantity of converts must suffer.[13] Note, then, that in focusing on translation for communities with non-obsolescent, non-trade languages, SIL has a de facto policy of seeking out those groups that are the classical Other, with a fully developed culture and language of their own.

Though most missionaries working in Papua New Guinea now accept that Tok Pisin is nativizing (i.e., becoming a first native language and, through that process, becoming grammatically and lexically more complex), few believe that Tok Pisin is able, on its own, to sustain Christian commitment. Many SIL members would want converts who speak Tok Pisin to supplement their study with local-language biblical resources.

The unity of heart language

Both the emphasis on people groups and the rejection of trade languages would seem to imply that a sense of cultural unity is what SIL is after in its methodological organization of the evangelistic process. One of the most interesting points about the concept of heart language is that it emphasizes the unifying force of native-ness of linguistic knowledge, with cultural unity being a common but not essential epiphenomenon. A heart language connects language not only to the "whole self" but to a whole community of selves—for SIL, it defines the boundaries of communities (Cowan 1979: 62–63). In this sense, it is close to the Saussurian concept of *langue*, in particular Saussure's image of language wherein each speaker has an individualized dictionary in his or her head.

> Language exists in the form of a sum of impressions deposited in the brain of each member of a community, almost like a dictionary of which identical copies have been distributed to each individual (see p. 13). Language exists in each individual, yet is common to all. Nor is it affected by the will of the depositaries. [The reference to p. 13 appears to be to the following: "If we could embrace the sum of word-images stored in the minds of all individuals, we could identify the social bond that constitutes language."] (Saussure 1959: 19, 13)

As later analysts have pointed out (e.g., Weinreich, Labov, and Herzog 1968), Saussure's famous dictionary metaphor constituted a foundational formulation of the relation between individual and group. Weinreich, Labov, and Herzog criticize this dictionary metaphor as one of the reasons that historical linguistic change had not been properly theorized in terms of its social (rather than simply structural linguistic) processes. However, I would suggest that part of the reason that heart language is such an attractive concept is precisely that it points the evangelist both to individual speakers and linguistic communities (people groups). That is, it defines groups through the knowledge that individuals have. If language constitutes a social bond, it is not so much because of a speaker's identification with or social interactions with the other members of the group but because each speaker has the same linguistic knowledge stored in her or his head. As such, heart language is both the site of epistemic ethnolinguistic group authenticity and the site of personal, interiorized truth. As a group definition, it delimits the breadth of access an SIL translator will have for a given translation program. As an individual definition, it identifies the self of the potential convert or reader. Heart language is a way to establish the people groups around which evangelical practice is structured as well as a way to engage individual speakers.

The dialectal problems that have plagued SIL work in Papua New Guinea, and perhaps in other areas of the world, can also shed light on the ways in which heart language is supposed to define groupness. Before beginning any translation project SIL conducts sociolinguistic surveys to determine social domains of language use and general dialectal variation. Often translations are supposed to cover several dialects of one language, and yet SIL orthographic choices represent the pronunciation of one dialect as opposed to another. Some SIL-produced New Testaments have hardly been used by the target community at all, and SIL translators generally feel that this is because people in certain cases refuse to read translations that are not in their local dialect. To combat this problem, SIL is developing a computer program called AdaptIt to allow translators to quickly adapt translations from one dialect into another or from one closely related language into another. However, it appears that a proliferation of dialects does not increase the total number of languages into which the New Testament must be translated. For example, the SIL/BTA Map of completed and ongoing projects lists the single language group Siane, but notes that two dialects have received translations. Similarly, Umbu-Ungu is listed as a single project, although it has three dialect translations. Dialects appear to be conceived as social groupings rather than as cognitive or affective ones. They are differentiated, but they establish a domain of political factionalization and not, it seems, a domain of the "heart."

Language and missionization in American evangelicalism

For many linguists who work in rural Third World areas, the main source of published linguistic data is often grammars and papers by SIL members. Though professional linguists might disparage the quality of SIL-produced grammars, it is important to point out that SIL's emphasis on scientific linguistics is unparalleled in evengelical circles. Even if SIL training seems less than adequate from the point of view of professional linguists, it is extremely rigorous from the perspective of the missions world. The emphasis on language and linguistics in evangelical missions is not an obvious one, and I hope to briefly sketch some of the influences at work in the history of American evangelicalism that led to this language-centric idea of missions practice.

In the late nineteenth and early twentieth centuries, modern American evangelicalism was coming into being in part as a response to the emerging liberal theology that would eventually take over such major U.S. seminaries as those at Princeton and the University of Chicago.[14] This liberal theology is itself traced back to the hermeneutic tradition of Higher Criticism coming primarily from Germany. One of the goals of Higher Criticism was to discover the historical relations between various books of the Bible, for example the idea that Mark was probably the source for Matthew and Luke. That is to say, it deconstructed the Bible into various sources, some hypothetical and not in the canon, and as such it turned the Bible into a historical text. To use Latour's (1991) terminology, Higher Criticism theorized that the historical authorizing "center" of the Bible might not be in the Bible itself.

In response to this perceived decomposition of the unity of the Bible, conservative theologians responded with a new evangelical, antiliberal movement that made belief in the divine authorship of the Bible a theological prerequisite. The tradition of dispensationalism was seen as the form of interpretation, or better, analysis, that adhered to this new requirement of divine authorship. Dispensationalism, unlike Higher Criticism, assumed the unity of the Bible and used this unity to read the text as a map of the history of the world—that is, as providing the key to the various "dispensations" of time. What is important here is not the difference between Higher Criticism and dispensationalism so much as the relatively heavy emphasis that dispensationalism puts on the unity of the Bible as, almost, a single linguistic utterance, interpretable within its own terms. That is to say, it projects the Bible as a unitary, given entity in need of objective analysis. Under dispensationalism, the Bible was its own center of authority.

As Latour (1991) has discussed regarding the emergence of experimental science, nature under Enlightenment assumptions is an autonomous object, and, in that sense, an object that authorizes itself. Scientific experimentation should simply make visible the secrets of that autonomous, natural world. In the same way, dispensationalism was, for its practitioners, a scientific analysis of the Bible, an object that was its own authorization and thus had an autonomy to reveal its secrets. According to its adherents, dispensationalism was a Baconian experimental and inductive science that took the facts at hand (i.e., the Bible) and was specifically contrasted to the deductive, theoretical, and hypothetical work of Higher Criticism (Marsden 1980: 55). Dispensationalism's goal was to "divide and classify" the ideas in the Bible, as opposed to the humanistic, philological work of Higher Criticism.

In that sense, liberal Christianity became associated with interpretive disciplines in the humanities, whereas conservative Christians oriented their biblical studies toward science, in particular natural science. Liberal Christianity became associated with hermeneutics, interpretation, or, for those most hostile to it, blasphemous speculation; conservative Christianity with the rigors of dispensationalist analysis. And though dispensationalism itself has come in and out of popularity, some of the basic tenets that underlie it—divine authorship, unity of the biblical text, the Bible as object of scientific analysis—have remained central to the continually shifting definition of what an evangelical is in the United States (see Marsden 1987).

As American scientific linguistics emerged in the early twentieth century, primarily through the work of Boas, Sapir, Bloomfield, and others who helped to form linguistics as a discipline, we see again the positing of a "natural" entity, language, that needed to be analyzed on its own terms. Linguistics, as opposed to the historical interpretive work of philology, was emerging as precisely the kind of science of language that could fit into the conservative side of the conservative/liberal divide that dominated American Christianity at the end of the nineteenth and beginning of the twentieth centuries. William Cameron Townsend, who corresponded with Edward Sapir, pushed his early students, notably Kenneth Pike and Eugene Nida, toward precisely this scientific version of language study as an essential precondition to successful and comparatively fluid Bible translation. Townsend thought that having the skills to scientifically analyze languages would make translation easier and more accurate. The science of biblical analysis then dominant in conservative Christian circles and the science of language would be the best way to ensure translations of good quality.

With this scientific background, SIL translators have a specific image of themselves as not being missionaries in the conventional sense of the term. By policy, SIL is not a church-planting organization, and members shy away from associating themselves too closely with any one church in areas where several churches are already established. SIL members are scientifically equipped to promote skills such as literacy and to disseminate information, which often is the "good news" as given in the New Testament.

SIL's rigorous training program for its translators is thus focused on linguistics and language learning, as these forms of knowledge are the most instrumental in attempts at the heart language evangelism that is at the center of the Bible translation organization. SIL schools take students through the same levels of linguistic analysis (phonetics/phonology, morphology, syntax, semantics, and pragmatics) that other graduate programs in linguistics do, although semantics is sometimes taught alongside translation principles.[15] Translators may take several anthropology courses and take courses on the Bible, meaning that they often spend about two years in training before going to their "allocations." SIL translators also have BA degrees, either from secular universities or from Bible colleges, where recent graduates often have studied Hebrew and Koiné Greek. Once they have settled into their allocations, SIL PNG translators will have to write three linguistics papers (referred to as the organized phonological data, grammar essentials, and grammar sketch papers), one sociolinguistics paper, and two major anthropology papers (referred to as the social organization and worldview papers), as well as take exams in the language into which they will be translating the New Testament and compile a dictionary of it. It is recommended that translators spend five years after allocating just learning the local language and studying the local social and cultural situation. So linguistics and language study is actually nestled into a wide range of requirements and disciplines that are part of the work one has to do before even attempting to translate the New Testament. Scholarly knowledge has to be put in the place of native knowledge for SIL translators. When one is not communicating to or about God in one's own heart language, education, rather than socialization, will be the key to opening the door. But we need to keep in mind that it is the Summer Institute of Linguistics, not the Summer Institute of Anthropology or Biblical Studies. In other words, it is this linguistic knowledge that has been considered most important to the task of Bible translation. Anthropology, and the study of culture more generally, is certainly a part of SIL training and procedure, but it does not hold the same pride of place that linguistics does. The point I want to make here is that the issue of language for SIL is not the same as the issue of culture. Which, finally, brings us back to the problem of training Papua New Guineans, or "mother-tongue" translators, to do the tasks that SIL has been doing up until now. If SIL's methodology and training are squarely focused on developing the knowledge needed to speak to the soul via "heart languages," then how does one train a person who is already fluent in this language? How do you teach a methodology of access—of speaking to the soul of receptor communities—to those who should already have it?

Fluency and familiarity

In 2000, BTA partnered with SIL, Pioneer Bible Translators, and the Bible Society of PNG to create a promotional video called, in Tok Pisin, *Kam, Yumi Pul!* ("Come On, Let's Row!"). The title and the opening shots of this thirty-three minute video imagine translation as a task of rowing a canoe—if only one person does it, you don't move very fast, but if we all row together then we can really get somewhere. It also has a more opaque reference to several books which use the metaphor of sailing or canoeing to discuss the history of Pacific Islanders' missionization to one another. Both *The Deep Sea Canoe* (Tippit 1977) and *Launch Out!* (Rowsome and Rowsome 1994) use this image of ocean travel to recuperate a history of Melanesians and Polynesians sailing the Pacific to missionize to one another in the nineteenth century as part of a contemporary push to get Pacific Islanders to engage in missions work of their own. Whereas the two books focus on encouraging Pacific Islanders to evangelize in other countries (see Handman 2003), the BTA video encourages Papua New Guineans to travel on the equally long and trying journey toward crafting a New Testament translation in their own communities.

In contrast to the daunting set of requirements and long pre-field training regimens of SIL, the promotional video for BTA tells its prospective Papua New Guinean recruits that BTA does not actually require much in the way of training or prerequisites. In the dialogue between an uncle who recently completed a translation and his nephew, who is desperate to improve his village situation, the uncle boasts that he has only finished grade 4 and yet was able to complete the translation task. The point here is supposed to be that anyone could make this happen—anyone could improve his village, his church, and his country by translating the New Testament. All over Papua New Guinea, the uncle tells his nephew, regular village Papua New Guineans are doing the work that only white missionaries used to do. Papua New Guinean native knowledge (of vernacular languages) is a sufficient substitute for academic knowledge, at least in the realm of Bible translation.

This implication that the field is open to all takers is not entirely true, since BTA of course screens its translators. Foremost among requirements is that the recruit be a "mature Christian," and a recruit needs a letter of support from his pastor to confirm this. Second, the recruit must have a good knowledge of both the source and receptor languages, in this case, English and the local vernacular. Third, he[16] must have "creative ability and editing skill in writing his own language" *(BTA Handbook* 1995: 13). In fact, the actual translator on whom the BTA video's "uncle" character was based was unusual in his lack of education—he was almost refused entry into BTA because of it. The average education level of recruits has gone up in the past few years, as more college-educated Papua New Guineans become interested in the task of translation. However, there is a general expectation that mother-tongue translators, who are translating *into* their mother tongue, will have training requirements different from those of expatriate translators, who are not necessarily translating into or from a language that they speak natively.

BTA mother-tongue translators (i.e., Papua New Guinean translators) are all trained in what is now called the Translator's Training Course, formerly called the National Translators' Course. The National Translator's Course was run in four segments, each six to eight weeks long, ideally with a year between the modules. National Translator's Course modules were held at Ukarumpa, the headquarters of SIL PNG, in the Eastern Highlands Province. Adjoined to SIL's land is the BTA field office and training headquarters. (BTA's main office is in Port Moresby, the capital.) The teachers are SIL and BTA members who have finished translations and have stayed on as mentors and consultants. In addition, each BTA student translator or translation team is mentored by an SIL or BTA member, whose long-term involvement in the translation project may range from leading it to simply helping the students during this particular module. Before proceeding to the next module, a BTA translator or translation team must complete a certain number of tasks (e.g., translating three chapters of New Testament connected narrative; doing a "village check" of one's translation) before he or they can return. Depending upon the level of involvement, the SIL adviser may also be required to complete assignments.

In the debate about how to implement Vision 2025 in Papua New Guinea, many SIL and BTA members asked if the National Translator's Course training was really the best way of getting Papua New Guineans into the role of translators. After several years of discussion, the National Translator's Course has been reworked so as to fit the new conditions of SIL's international goals (such as those detailed in Vision 2025) and renamed the training regimen the Translator's Training Course. Here I want to look at how the course was conducted in the past as well as how it has been restructured.

One of the things that the National Translator's Course used to focus on was the process of learning how to study one's own language and one's own culture. The *BTA Handbook*, which is based upon a Bible translation textbook developed for mother-tongue translators in Africa (Barnwell [1975] 1992), contains appendices about these subjects, which are striking in their asymmetry. As the titles to these appendices show, these two subjects are not the same endeavor. That is, "Discovering the Grammar of Your Language" is not the same as "How to Study Your Own Culture."

Language study

In an untitled introduction to the process of language discovery, the new BTA recruit reads:

> Every language has its own unique patterns. It is a fascinating study to discover the patterns of a language, and to become aware of the richness and variety of its grammar, and of the many neat ways of expressing subtle differences of meaning.
>
> Through studying his own language, a translator comes to appreciate its wealth and potential, and becomes more able to use all its richness in his own translation.
>
> He also becomes more alert to places where his language differs from English, or whatever source language he is translating from. Because of this he is better able to avoid the danger of keeping the traces of the form of the source language in his translation. (*BTA Handbook*, appendix I, p. 1)

Here we see a now commonplace musing on the "richness of diversity" that is well known to those familiar with the rhetoric of language preservation (see Hill 2002; Moore 2000). BTA student translators are introduced to an ideology of linguistic difference in which all differences can be put on the same plane. Grammatical structure becomes another way in which people are multiply comprehensible to others. We also begin to see the horizon that BTA focused on. Translators study their own language and study English so that they know how their languages differ from English.

The sections of the National Translator's Course devoted to "language discovery" attempted to get translators to understand how their languages differ from English, a central issue because BTA was then still emphasizing "dynamic equivalence translation." The dynamic translation approach was first developed by Eugene Nida (see Nida 1964), a former SIL translator and longtime leader in the United Bible Society. Although Nida's approach has fallen out of favor with SIL (see Gutt 2000 for a more contemporary approach), BTA training still used some of Nida's ideas. Dynamic equivalence translation is particularly concerned that translators do not follow the structure of the source language grammar (for BTA this is usually the English of the New International Version of the Bible), either seen as the problem of word-for-word translation or clause-by-clause translation. Part of the methodology of this translation approach is that all source text sentences can be decomposed from their grammatically formed structure in an English version of the Bible into a universal structure of semantic roles (see also Schieffelin, chap. 7 of this volume).

To give an example found in the *BTA Handbook* (1995: 38–41), the dynamic translator can take a verse such as Mark 1:4 (Revised Standard Version): "John the baptizer appeared in the wilderness, preaching a baptism of repentance for the forgiveness of sins" and decompose it into the following implied events and participants: "John PREACHED (a message), (John) BAPTIZED (the people), (the people) REPENT, (God) FORGIVES (the people), (the people) SIN." Putting this information into a sentence again, the dynamic translator arrives at a *revised source text sentence* on which he can base his translation: "John Preached: (people) (must) REPENT and (people) (must) be BAPTIZED so that (God) will FORGIVE (the people) who have SINNED." This process, a cornerstone of dynamic translation principles, depends upon a kind of universalization of semantic roles and assumes that these roles are, in one form or another, capable of being expressed in all languages. The method is vaguely based on transformational grammar's bifurcation of language into surface structures (the sentences we speak and hear) and deep structures (the universal grammar of all languages), wherein specific processes (transformations) turn the latter into the former (see Chomsky 1965 on transformational linguistics as practiced when Nida was developing his theories). In this case, the original source text sentence from Mark 1:4 would be the "surface structure," whereas the revised source text sentence would be the "deep structure" equivalent. A translator would then use this deep structure revised source text sentence to create a surface structure target language sentence that was in target language-appropriate style and construction. Whereas transformational grammar bases this ontology of language on cognitive universals of the human mind, SIL translators' universalizing can also be related to a more literal reading of the Bible, including the story of the tower of Babel and the division of languages from the Adamic original (cf. Comaroff and Comaroff 1991: chap. 6).

As such, the "language discovery" sections of the National Translator's Course were designed to show BTA translators the differences between English and their own vernacular languages in the hope that this would free them from trying to translate word-for-word from English. A grammar notebook, devised to guide a BTA translator through his language discovery and provide him with a place to document his findings, was the central text of this section of the course. Trying to explain linguistics without actually using much of its jargon, the notebook has roughly the same format for each section. It introduces the topic, either something that would be relevant to all languages of the world (e.g., word order) or something typologically probable for a Papua New Guinean language (e.g., switch reference, a feature of many Papuan languages). In some cases, the phenomena are exemplified with an English sentence; otherwise, they are simply described. Then the translator is asked to think of examples in his own language, come up with a rule of occurrence, find any exceptions, and finally relate this finding to his translation (quite a tall order!). The final task is usually asked in the form of a question, such as, "Are you following the rules of your grammar when you are translating?" or "Does your translation sound natural for your language?"

As it turns out, these mini-grammar courses and language discovery sessions sometimes created the very problem that they were devised to solve. After language discovery, some SIL and BTA advisors found that the BTA translators were becoming much more dependent upon the English source text grammar than they were before the course. Having been made aware of their grammar and its differences with English, translators were creating Anglicized translations of the Bible in their heart language by, say, following English clause order. When SIL and BTA realized that this was the case, the language discovery sections of the course were seriously reduced, and now grammatical issues are brought up on a need-to-know basis as the student translators tackle different problems with each new Bible verse. The Bible itself guides the grammar discussions as students practice their translation skills during the translator's training course modules. The instruction has in general switched to a more hands-on, less lecture-driven, approach.

SIL and BTA attempt to avoid the problem of Anglicization now by putting Hebrew or Greek in the place that English once had in the course. So rather than trying to translate from the English language translation of the New or Old Testaments, teachers point students to specific features of Hebrew exemplified in specific verses of the Bible and ask students if their languages have a similar feature as well. From Hebrew key terms introduced in the course, students learn tri-consonantal roots and are given example sentences from the Bible such as the following (illustrating *qadash*, 'to be holy, to make holy', etc.): "Gen 2:3 God blessed the seventh day and qadash-ed it." Now bypassing English in favor of Hebrew, the course tries to make the original biblical languages the standard for the class.[17]

Cultural study

When it comes to the opening paragraph of the *BTA Handbook* appendix on studying one's own culture (as opposed to language), we see a very different introduction. Titled "Why Study the Receptor Language Culture?" the introduction begins:

> Bible translators are generally well-educated people. You have learnt other languages, and been exposed to other cultures besides your own. Because of this education, you have become cut off in some ways from your own culture. You may have spent a number of years outside your own language area. For this reason, it is necessary to go back and sit with people in your home area in order to make a study of what they believe and do. You may need to rediscover the way in which they use words. You may need to rediscover the shades of meaning and implications that may be carried by particular words. You may need to rediscover too the assumptions and presuppositions that people have, that affect the way that they interpret and understand any message. (appendix J, p. 1)

Presumably the same translator who has spent time away from his home language area, who has learned other languages and been exposed to other cultures, is the same translator whose linguistic competence was unquestioned in the previous appendix. Though separation from culture is possible, even likely, for these translators, separation from language is not a question. Why is the same individual who has his cultural knowledge doubted because of "exposure" able to have his linguistic knowledge intact? This is another inflection of heart language: language, in particular native first language, is inalienable in a way that is not true for culture or cultural knowledge. All potential BTA translators are tested on their heart language ability before they can begin translation training, but that still suggests that language and culture are different entities—that one can pass a test for fluency in the first and yet perhaps only have a passing familiarity with the second.

In investigating culture and cultural knowledge, the student translator is told to gently query his own informants, with tape recorder at his side, about the meaning of various words and phrases. SIL translators seem to share the post-Bloomfieldian assumption that the lexicon is a messy collection of all of the unsystematic aspects of language. And this, it seems, is also where culture sits.[18] Compared with the systematicity, structure, and apparent inalienability of linguistic knowledge, cultural knowledge figures here more as an unstructured and thus alienable collection of phrases.

At the same time that the comparative (English to vernacular) linguistics of language discovery has been downgraded, a form of cultural discovery is quickly becoming one of the most popular aspects of the revised translator's training course format. Papua New Guineans are very excited to learn about the customs of the "ancient Jews," as they are talked about in Papua New Guinea, and SIL encourages this interest. Many SIL PNG translators have published booklets in the heart languages they are working on, called simply "Customs of the Ancient Jews" or "How the Jews Lived" as part of Bible background instruction. In interviews with SIL PNG translators, and in casual conversation with many non-SIL missionaries in Papua New Guinea, a common refrain is that the linguistic communities they work with are in certain aspects similar to the Jews of the Bible. This same comparison is evident in the training courses. In discussing how to do a "village check" of a translation, handouts suggest: "If you want to get a person's opinion on something that you found hard to translate, then go ahead and discuss this with them or ask their opinion. For example: If the Jewish customs are different from their own customs" ("Village Test" handout). This form of comparison has been a part of missionization since the discovery of the New World, and it is usually based on cultural traits such as kinship systems (especially anything that can be compared to the Levirate), sacrificial practices, and taboos (Eilberg-Schwartz 1990).

In Papua New Guinea, many missionaries from various organizations make comparisons between local people and the ancient Jews based in part on general livelihood; unlike people living in urban or suburban areas, the Papua New Guineans they cater to are subsistence farmers and in that sense are "closer" to the people who first responded to the message proclaimed by Jesus. Now BTA leaders are developing more in-depth sections on biblical background and ancient Jewish customs, hoping that this will foster more accurate and appropriate translations. In fact, the translator's training course as a whole is moving toward making biblical background a central emphasis of the program. Linguistics and language discovery are being pushed aside so that the "original context" of Jesus' good news can form the foundation of Papua New Guinean translators' knowledge base as they work toward Vision 2025.

Conclusion: the linguistic unconscious and ancient Jewish consciousness

With language discovery now relegated to a much lesser position than it had before, SIL is working on the assumption that the needs of expatriate translators are not the needs of Papua New Guinean translators. They are moving to a position that native speakers have a usable, if unconscious, relationship to their own linguistic knowledge. Now, minimal linguistic training is needed to create a successful translator. In some ways, this move is not a new one in SIL's history or in the history of linguistics.

The question of the role of the native speaker in analysis is a recurring one in the history of linguistics (e.g., Sapir 1933; Hale [1969] 1999; Coulmas 1981). During the 1940s and '50s, when the original SIL members were developing their methods and practices, several translators were either corresponding with or being taught by the Americanist linguist Edward Sapir (Wallis and Bennett 1959). In particular, SIL's academic guiding light, Kenneth Pike, was a Sapir student and lifelong devotee.

We can look to Sapir's seminal 1933 essay on the "Psychological Reality of the Phoneme" to see where SIL's vision of the usable linguistic unconscious likely came from.

In this essay, Sapir posits that sound inventories of languages are composed of mental or psychological entities, phonemes, with structured relations of alternation between what we now call underlying form and surface form. But the way in which he attempts to exemplify this psychologically defined level of grammar is very interesting. He relates five stories of trying to teach Native North Americans to write their own languages so that they can continue collecting texts for Sapir after he has left the area. In each case, what at first seemed to be errors or inconsistencies on the part of the informants in writing down their own languages turn out to be a kind of natural rising-to-the-top of the phonemes of the language. Though the intended purpose of the article was to prove the existence of phonemes in addition to phonetic segments, the other lesson that can be drawn from it is that, given a piece of paper, a native speaker will give voice to a coherent and accurate representation of his own language—that the kinds of psychological realities that distinguish native speakers from nonnative speakers will emerge the first time the informant touches pen to paper.[19]

It is this image of unconscious but usable native-speaker knowledge that SIL and BTA seem to be depending upon in their restructured training program for Papua New Guinean translators. Part of the reason that SIL and BTA gave up on the language discovery program was that it was making some student translators hyperaware of the differences between their languages and English. For whatever reason—perhaps as a way to hook themselves into a perceived linguistic center of Christianity, or perhaps because the course was set up with reference to English— these Papua New Guinean translators were trying to bring their languages into line with English. But this is the very opposite of SIL's philosophy of translation and of heart language. Heart languages are supposed to remain constant while a Christian transformation takes place.

In evangelical understanding, conversion should create a radical reformulation of ethics, behavior, and even parts of one's worldview. Amid all of this change, the intimacy of language seems to be the primary form of continuity that is stressed, as we also see in Schieffelin's analysis of missionization in Bosavi (chap. 7). To go back to George Cowan's discussion of heart language:

> It identifies the speaker as a member of one group in contrast to all others. This gives continuity to life, linking the present generation to past generations from whom the language was learned and with future generations now acquiring it. A translation of the Bible and native-authored writings in the mother tongue enter the stream of the group's cultural heritage. (1979: 63)

At the same time, conscious effort is put into establishing a comparative framework for understanding culture and cultural knowledge through the training course's new emphasis on biblical background. Viewing culture as a kind of Mosaic Law, it is the subject of explicit study. Indeed, in some ways it seems as though the comparisons to the ancient Jews allow one to imagine conversion as a replication of the New Testament dissolution of the Law for the sacrifice of Jesus. Mosaic Law, here understood as culture, is overcome by the cross. The ancient Jews, here understood as the original "cultured" people group, is an example for Papua New Guinean cultures. As such, any way to make the Papua New Guinean recipients of this version of the message more attuned to the "original" audience is a way of establishing the reiteration of this process. To return again to Cowan (1979: 145), SIL hopes to present Papua New Guinean groups with a choice: "By not imposing our cultural ways upon people but instead offering alternatives which they may choose, we recognize each culture's right to self-determination." The role of SIL is to access and organize the kinds of knowledge that will allow people to make this choice. If the lesson learned from the language discovery section was that a comparison to English leads to an Anglicization of translations, then perhaps it is acceptable if a comparison to the ancient Jews leads to a Hebraization of culture.

Though SIL training seems to connect language and culture, both for its own members and the BTA members, language and culture are theorized as having two very different relationships to the self. Linguistic knowledge is intimate and inalienable: the path to accessibility. Cultural knowledge is lawlike and partible, and one's relationship to it is necessarily altered if conversion is to take place. To return to the *BTA Handbook*, we can note that its definition of culture is primarily about words and concepts—the student must go back to his home language area to find out how his people use certain words. That is, the domains of language that might themselves need changing are relegated to the domain of culture. The intimacy and inalienability of language can be preserved while its cultural aspects can be altered through an introduced relationship to the cultural context of the ancient Jews. In that sense, heart language is language as unconscious grammar, whereas culture is the messy and unsystematic lexicon. It is the grammar of heart language that allows translation to be successful; it is the cultural lexicon that makes translation difficult. But as the founder of SIL/Wycliffe said, conversion happens from the inside out (Benge and Benge 2000: 153). With the grammar/language then on the "inside" and the lexicon/culture "out," we can see the organization of the self that is supposed to lead to Christian commitment.

Notes

This chapter is partially based on several months spent at SIL Papua New Guinea headquarters in Ukarumpa, Eastern Highlands Province, during 2003 and 2006. I would like to thank members of the SIL and BTA communities who warmly welcomed me and spoke with me during these times. I would also like to thank David Wakefield at SIL International for his encouragement of and careful engagement with the SIL portion of my research. During my 2005–2006 trip to Papua New Guinea which was spent in Morobe Province among the Guhu-Samane people and at Ukarumpa, my research was sponsored by an International Dissertation Research Fellowship from the Social Science Research Council and a Fulbright-Hays Doctoral Dissertation Research Abroad Fellowship. I thank the Council and Fulbright-Hays for this support. I would like to thank members of the Guhu-Samane community for graciously hosting my husband and I and for their perspective on SIL and BTA, to list only those topics addressed in this paper. I would like to thank the volume's editors and contributors for comments and help over the past several years. Members of the Interdisciplinary Christianities Workshop at the University of Chicago read and very helpfully responded to a version of the chapter. Finally, I would especially like to thank James Slotta and Robert Moore for their repeated efforts to improve this chapter.

1. See "Facts and Figures about Language Work in PNG," at www.wycliffe.org.au/PNG/png.htm, last accessed August 2006.

2. See Stoll 1982 for a discussion of the political aspects of SIL and Wycliffe's relationships to host governments in Latin America.

3. Some of the only situations in which SIL International has final and absolute say over the rules and conduct of national branches are legal ones. For example, there are SIL-wide policies on how to handle cases of child abuse.

4. A majority of SIL PNG members are from the United States. However, Australia, the United Kingdom, Finland, New Zealand, and South Korea each have a significant presence at Ukarumpa. This distribution generally follows international trends, with the United States sending by far the most missionaries, followed by South Korea and then other English-speaking nations (Johnstone and Mandryk 2001). In all, about twenty nationalities are represented among SIL PNG members. The label evangelical Christian is probably the best cover term for the members of SIL PNG, although it hides a good deal of variation within the Protestant tradition, from the more mainstream state-run Lutheran churches of German members to the newer Pentecostal churches (such as Assemblies of God) of some American members.

5. SIL PNG accounts for 12 percent of the total SIL membership across the globe, but it produces 25 percent of all SIL sponsored New Testaments. This reflects not only the capacity of SIL PNG but also the comparative freedom members of SIL PNG have to focus on the translation aspect of their work, discussed in more detail below.

6. As a young white couple living in remote Papua New Guinea and interested in linguistics and anthropology, my husband and I were initially assumed to be SIL members by almost all Papua New Guineans.

7. As mentioned above, it is very difficult to generalize about SIL and all of its national branches spread across the globe. Though SIL does foster a certain amount of uniformity across members through its training regimes, those regimes are continually being updated and changed, so that members who trained in the 1990s may have had a very different experience from members who trained in the 2000s. Moreover, each national branch, such as SIL PNG, has different policies and procedures, and different ways of relating to sister Bible translation organizations. This chapter examines practices that have been discussed by SIL International or Wycliffe USA on its Web sites or in its published literature, and practices either in place or under discussion at SIL PNG in recent years (2003 and 2006). Given the evolving nature of SIL International and its national branches, other concepts or procedures may have already supplanted those discussed here.

8. Interestingly, this is one of the few occasions when heart language is spoken of with respect to *speakerhood*. Usually, it is comprehension of a message, not production of one, that is stressed. This is not unexpected, since people who are talking about heart languages are usually missionaries learning a foreign language with the expectation of preaching in it. That is to say, they are missionaries who will be preaching in the heart language of their *hearers*.

9. See Hall 1955, Handman 2003, McDonald 1976, and McElhanon 1975 for a discussion of language policy in Papua New Guinea, in particular the intense controversies that have centered on whether Tok Pisin could or should have any kind of official or nationally recognized status within either the Territory of New Guinea or the independent state of Papua New Guinea. We can note that in contrast to colonial and government officials or missionaries, many anthropologists have conducted fieldwork in Tok Pisin. Although anthropologists often obscure the extent to which they depend upon Tok Pisin within their fieldwork, they do not seem to have the deep doubts that missionaries express about the language's communicative capacity.

10. See Kulick 1992 for an excellent example of Tok Pisin's use precisely in the intimate linguistic contexts that SIL associates with heart language.

11. See www.oralbible.com or www.chronologicalbiblestorying.com, for example. Both Web sites last accessed August 2006.

12. At www.oralbible.com/obc/Booklet_chap_4_page_1.php (last accessed August 2006).

13. The Wycliffe Web site (www.wycliffe.org/software/home.htm, last accessed August 2006) allows one to download or link to various video games, choose-your-own-adventures of Third and Fourth World Bible translation that specifically address this point. When you as missionary choose to work in the trade language, your number of converts goes up quickly, but the game specifically doubts the quality of these converts' commitment.

14. In this section, I am relying heavily on the arguments that Marsden 1980 makes (particularly chaps. 4–7).

15. SIL schools in the United States are programs run in association with and on the campuses of various universities, ranging from the University of Oregon to the Bible Institute of Los Angeles. Associated with the SIL International campus in Dallas is the Graduate Institute of Applied Linguistics. A full list of SIL schools around the world may be found at www.sil.org/training/show_programs.asp?by=all, last accessed August 2006.

16. A large majority of BTA translators are men, which probably has to do with the fact that men are more likely to have higher levels of education, are more likely to be leaders in their home churches, and are more likely to be supported in their translation work by their home communities.

17. Note that these "key terms" worksheets only partially provide the Hebrew form. *Va-qidesh*, with perfective aspectual prefix and appropriate number and gender marking, is the form found in this verse of Genesis. Unlike the comparisons with English, then, the move toward Hebrew seems to bypass grammar in favor of simple lexemes, although in other examples of the q-d-sh root, appropriate derivational morphology, as marked by the vowels, is included. (Many thanks to Alejandro Paz and Natalie Rothman for being my Hebrew informants.)

18. Many thanks to James Slotta for making this point to me.

19. The tradition in Americanist linguistics of using "native speakers" to collect data has been the subject of several recent works, among them Silverstein 1996 on Sapir's relationship with Pete McGuff, and Bauman and Briggs 2003 on George Hunt.

References

Barnwell, Katharine, comp. [1975] 1992. *Bible Translation: An Introductory Course in Translation Principles*. 3rd ed., revised. Dallas: Summer Institute of Linguistics.

Bauman, Richard, and Charles Briggs. 2003. The Foundation of All Future Researches: Franz Boas, George Hunt, Native American Texts and the Construction of Modernity. In *Voices of Modernity: Language Ideologies and the Politics of Inequality,* pp. 255–298. Cambridge: Cambridge University Press.

Benge, Janet, and Geoff. 2000. *Cameron Townsend: Good News in Every Language*. Seattle: WYAM Publishing.

BTA Handbook. 1995. Compiled and edited by Bill Martin. Ukarumpa: SIL PNG.

Buk Baibel. 1989. The Bible in Tok Pisin. Port Moresby: Bible Society of Papua New Guinea.

Chomsky, Noam. 1965. *Aspects of a Theory of Syntax*. Cambridge: MIT Press.

Comaroff, Jean, and John Comaroff. 1991. *Of Revelation and Revolution*. Chicago: University of Chicago Press.

Coulmas, Florian, ed. 1981. *A Festschrift for Native Speaker*. The Hague, Netherlands: Mouton.

Cowan, George M. 1979. *The Word That Kindles*. Chappaqua, NY: Christian Herald Books.

Dumont, Louis. 1986. *Essays on Individualism: Modern Ideology in Anthropological Perspective*. Chicago: University of Chicago Press.

Eilberg-Schwartz, Howard. 1990. *The Savage in Judaism: An Anthropology of Israelite Religion and Ancient Judaism*. Bloomington: Indiana University Press.

Gutt, Ernest-August. 2000. *Translation and Relevance: Cognition and Context*. Manchester, UK: St. Jerome Publishing.

Hale, Kenneth. [1969] 1999. Some Questions about Anthropological Linguistics: The Role of Native Knowledge. In *Reinventing Anthropology*, ed. Dell Hymes, pp. 382–400. Ann Arbor: University of Michigan Press.

Hall, Robert A., Jr. 1955. *Hands Off Pidgin English!* Sydney, Australia: Pacific Publications Pty.

Handman, Courtney. 2002. "Pidgin's Progress" Revisited: Tok Pisin and the Language Policy Debates in Papua New Guinea's Independence. M.A. thesis, University of Chicago.

———. 2003. "We Have a Very Big Debt": The Missionized as Missionaries in Papua New Guinea and Beyond. Paper presented to the Society for the Anthropology of Religion Annual Meeting, April, Providence, RI.

Harding, Susan Friend. 2000. *The Book of Jerry Falwell*. Princeton, NJ: Princeton University Press.

Hill, Jane. 2002. Expert Rhetorics' in Advocacy for Endangered Languages: Who Is Listening, and What Do They Hear? *Journal of Linguistic Anthropology* 12 (2): 119–133.

Ikeda, Elissa. 2002. Practice What You Preach: Constructing Language Ideologies in a Classroom for Future Missionaries. M.A. thesis, University of California at Los Angeles.

Johnstone, Patrick, and Jason Mandryk. 2001. *Operation World*. 21st Century ed. Carlisle, Cumbria, UK: Paternoster Lifestyle Publishing.

Keane, Webb. 1997. From Fetishism to Sincerity: On Agency, the Speaking Subject, and Their Historicity in the Context of Religious Conversion. *Comparative Studies in Society and History* 39 (4): 674–693.

Kulick, Don. 1992. *Language Shift and Cultural Reproduction: Socialization, Self, and Syncretism in a Papua New Guinean Village*. Cambridge: Cambridge University Press.

Latour, Bruno. 1991. *We Have Never Been Modern*. Cambridge, MA: Harvard University Press.

Luhrmann, Tanya. 2004. Metakinesis: How God Becomes Intimate in Contemporary U.S. Christianity. *American Anthropologist* 106 (3): 518–528.

Marsden, George. 1980. *Fundamentalism and American Culture: The Shaping of Twentieth-Century Evangelicalism 1870–1925*. Oxford: Oxford University Press.

———. 1987. *Reforming Fundamentalism: Fuller Seminary and the New Evangelicalism*. Grand Rapids, MI: Eerdmans Publishing.

McDonald, Bob, ed. 1976. *Language and National Development: The Public Debate, 1976*. Waigani: University of Papua New Guinea.

McElhanon, Ken A., ed. 1975. *Tok Pisin i Go We? Proceedings of a Conference Held at the University of Papua New Guinea, Port Moresby, P.N.G.* Ukarumpa: Linguistic Society of Papua New Guinea.

Moore, Robert E. 2000. "The People Are Here Now." The Contemporary Culture of an Ancestral Language: Studies in Obsolescent Kiksht (Wasco-Wishram Dialect of Upper Chinookan). Ph.D. diss., University of Chicago.

Nida, Eugene. 1964. *Toward a Science of Translating*. Leiden: E.J. Brill.

Robbins, Joel. 2001. God Is Nothing but Talk: Modernity, Language, and Prayer in a Papua New Guinea Society. *American Anthropologist* 103 (4): 901–912.

Rowsome, David, and Marilyn Rowsome. 1994. *Launch Out! A Call to the Local Churches of the South Pacific to Cross-Cultural Missions*. Mt. Hagen, Papua New Guinea: Christian Leaders' Training College.

Sapir, Edward. 1933. The Psychological Reality of the Phoneme. In *Selected Writings of Edward Sapir,* ed. D. Mandelbaum, pp. 46–60. Berkeley: University of California Press.

Saussure, Ferdinand de. 1959. *Course in General Linguistics*. Edited by C. Bally and A. Sechehaye. New York: McGraw-Hill.

SIL PNG. 2000. *Kam, Yumi Pul!* Video, joint production of the Bible Society of PNG, BTA PNG, Pioneer Bible Translators, and SIL PNG.

Silverstein, Michael. 1996. The Secret Life of Texts. In *Natural Histories of Discourse,* ed. M. Silverstein and G. Urban, pp. 81–105. Chicago: University of Chicago Press.

Smith, Geoff. 2002. *Growing Up with Tok Pisin: Contact, Creolization, and Change in Papua New Guinea's National Language*. London, UK: Battlebridge Publications.

Stoll, David. 1982. *Fishers of Men or Founders of Empire? The Wycliffe Bible Translators in Latin America*. London: Zed Press.

Tippit, Alan. 1977. *The Deep-Sea Canoe: Stories of the Spread of the Gospel by South Pacific Island Missionaries*. Pasadena, CA: William Carey Library.

Wallis, Ethel Emily, and Mary Angela Bennett. 1959. *Two Thousand Tongues to Go: The Story of the Wycliffe Bible Translators*. New York: Harper and Brothers.

Weinreich, Uriel, William Labov, and Marvin Herzog. 1968. Empirical Foundations for a Theory of Language Change. In *Directions in Historical Linguistics: A Symposium,* ed. W. Lehmann and Y. Malkiel, pp. 97–195. Austin: University of Texas Press.

9

SUSAN U. PHILIPS

Changing Scholarly Representations of the Tongan Honorific Lexicon

In Tonga over the last two hundred years, *lea faka'eiki*, or 'Tongan chiefly language', has undergone change. At the time of initial sustained Western contact with Tonga in the late eighteenth century, the documented targets of the two levels of lexical honorification constituting *lea faka'eiki* were human leaders who partook of the divine or sacred to varying degrees. Today, in contrast, the dominant language ideology in Tonga, reflected in the work of Tongan and non-Tongan scholars alike, associates the lexical honorifics with the constitutionally ratified secular governmental authority of the king and titled nobles. The purpose of this chapter is to describe and explain the process through which this transformation has taken place. Tonga is a Polynesian nation-state in the South Pacific. With a present-day population of approximately 110,000, Tonga is tiny as nation states go, but it is nevertheless one of the largest Polynesian populations in the Pacific.

I argue here that the move from sacred to secular is a result of collaboration between British Protestant missionaries and traditional and governmental Tongan leaders, who have mapped a British concept of constitutional monarchy onto the concept of a traditional Tongan polity to give the Tongan government the authority of both. I describe this transformation as the result of a Gramscian collaboration of church and state to produce a particular political hegemony. The ideological transformation of the honorifics is thus but one piece of a broader project, in much the same sense that Gal (2001) discusses for Hungary, of nineteenth- and twentieth-century Tongan nation-state formation.

The collaboration between missionaries and the Tongan chiefly class entailed an effort to downplay the sacred and supernatural quality of Tongan political leadership, consistent with a Protestant valuing of separation of church and state. However, the sacred persists today in the use of many of the same honorifics to address and refer to both king and God. But this continued connection between sacred and secular power through the use of the lexical honorifics does not appear in the contemporary scholarly literature. This is in part because such linking of king and God complicates the projection of the Kingdom of Tonga as a modern secular nation-state to the outside world. It is also the case that all Tongans do not agree today about who is or should be indexed through the use of the lexical honorifics, and they may never have agreed entirely, as will become apparent in this chapter.

There has been, then, a continual tension, ambivalence, and ambiguity in the meaning and use of the honorific terms in Tonga for at least two hundred years, centering on how the relation between the secular and the sacred should be conceived. Nevertheless, whereas some temporal frameworks for social change implicating language stress discontinuities and disjunctures, including many of the frameworks discussed in this volume, this particular tradition of language ideology stresses continuity.[1]

The historical ideological reconfiguration of indexical targets

Though the targets of Tongan lexical honorifics have changed in Tongan language ideology, as reflected in the scholarly literature on Tonga, other aspects of the honorification system have not changed. For example, some of the actual honorific lexical alternatives have stayed the same, as has their specific association with each of two distinct levels of honorification. I will refer here to the type of change that *has* occurred as entailing a historical reconfiguration of indexical targets. Most concretely, scholars write that the higher level of honorification used to be used to address or refer to the Tu'i Tonga, the sacred leader of Tonga in precontact times, whereas now it is reserved for the king, or Tu'i, the constitutional monarch of Tonga, although the picture is in fact more complex than that.

There is ample evidence of changes in the conceptualization of the indexical targets of honorification. Such shifts have often been represented in the broader literature on honorification as an aspect of overall changes through time in honorific systems. Most linguistic anthropological accounts of honorifics present them as in the process of change (Hill and Hill 1978; Errington 1985a, 1985b, 1988; Haviland 1979), though not all such accounts address the issue.

In general, scholarly accounts of linguistic honorifics include descriptions of who uses what linguistic forms to elevate or show respect to whom. It is difficult to know to what extent this is ascribable to the influence of conventions of descriptive linguistic writing and analysis, and to what extent it reflects informants' language ideology or descriptions of language practices. However, in spite of this difficulty, it is obvious that ideas about changes in speaker and addressee identities are pragmatically salient (to use Errington's 1985b term) in informants' accounts of their honorific systems.

Accounts of Asian honorific systems for Java (Errington 1985a, 1985b, 1988), Korea (Sohn 1981; Kim-Renaud 1990), and Japan (Wetzel 2004), which share broad areal influences with Pacific Island systems, offer a particularly coherent vision of changes in honorific systems. These systems consist of honorific lexical and morphological substitutes or alternatives for everyday linguistic forms that elevate the targets of the honorifics. The use of honorific forms is typically conceptualized as being determined by the nature of the relationship between the speaker and the addressee, yet at the same time this relationship is implicitly viewed from the speaker's point of view, since it is the speaker who is conceptualizing the relationship in order to be able to speak appropriately. The models then are typically dyadic or two-person models. In representations of these honorific systems, it is participant identities that are pragmatically salient, and other aspects of social context or social domain are secondary or unanalyzed.

Changes in concepts of participant identities are usually presented in a vision of a broader change in an honorific system as a whole, whereas changes in the entire honorific system are seen as caused by broader sociohistorical forces. For example, in his 1981 discussion of changes in the Korean honorific system, Sohn attributes those changes to a range of processes, including the eighteenth-century disintegration of the Yi dynasty, Japan's annexation of Korea, and the opening up of Korea after World War II to Western democratic values of democratization and modernization. Ultimately, out of this process Korea emerges as a nation-state with far more democratic ideology than before that affects the use of honorifics and who uses what forms to whom. Sohn proposes that some aspects of the shift in who uses what forms to whom involves a shift like that documented in Brown and Gilman's 1960 account of shifts in European languages in who uses honorific second-person address (e.g., <u>vous</u>) rather than nonhonorific everyday address (<u>tu</u>).[2] Brown and Gilman argued that the choice between the two alternatives used to reflect variation in the status differences between speaker and addressees, but now the choice reflects closeness versus distance. This is a shift from power to solidarity as the "function" of the honorific contrast. In suggesting that Korea has undergone such a shift, Sohn argues explicitly, as do other authors who see similar shifts (e.g., Errington 1985a; Hill and Hill 1978), that as wider social forces bring about a reconceptualization of the social identities of participants, this affects the choice of forms used from among the linguistic honorific alternates, and the actual function or meaning of the honorifics themselves undergoes a change.

This general model of changes in honorific systems is somewhat at odds with Tongan language ideology. Tongan language ideology suggests that the main change in Tongan use of honorifics has been in who is addressed by them; it has in other respects stayed the same, so that, as already noted, there is a powerful rhetoric of continuity, not change, in Tonga. Moreover, though characterizations of changes in Asian honorific systems of the sort I have just described convey a decidedly dyadic perspective that includes both speaker and person spoken to, Tongan language ideology focuses on the person spoken to.

However, even though much of the literature on linguistic honorifics is conceptualized dyadically from the speaker's point of view, as I have already noted, many language ideologies do focus more on either speaker identities or addressee identities to the neglect or lesser development of the other end of the interaction, or of the co-interlocutor (Silverstein 2003). For example, the women's liberation movement language ideologies initially focused primarily on contrasts between female and male speakers, a focus picked up by scholarly sociolinguistic work on gender and language. Inoue's (2002, 2003, 2004) work on historical changes in Japanese language ideology about women's language documents changing concepts of the Japanese women who use the language. This work is a good example of change in a language ideology that has focused on the identity of the speaker.

A good example of changes in addressee-focused honorific language ideology comes from the sociolinguistic history of changes in the English pronoun system. Basically, in both language ideology and in practice, the English second-person plural pronoun you underwent a change from being thought appropriate to address groups of persons to being thought appropriate to address individual persons as well.

In his observations on the growth of English, Jespersen (1938) summarized his version of the history of the shift from using you exclusively for plural address to its use in addressing individuals, a common honorific strategy across languages and cultures:

> The habit of addressing a single person by means of a plural pronoun was decidedly in its origin an outcome of an aristocratic tendency towards class-distinction. The habit originated with the Roman Emperors, who desired to be addressed as beings worth more than a single ordinary man; and French courtesy in the middle ages propagated it throughout Europe. In England as elsewhere this plural pronoun (*you, ye*) was long confined to respectful address. Superior persons or strangers were addressed as *you*; *thou* thus becoming the mark either of the inferiority of the person spoken to, or of familiarity or even intimacy or affection between the two interlocutors. English is the only language that has got rid of this useless distinction. The Quakers (the Society of Friends) objected to the habit as obscuring the equality of all human beings; they therefore *thou*'d (or rather *thee*'d) everybody. But the same democratic leveling that they wanted to effect in this way was achieved a century and a half later in society at large, though in a roundabout manner, when the pronoun *you* was gradually extended to lower classes and thus lost more and more of its previous character of deference. *Thou* then for some time was reserved for religious and literary use, as well as for foul abuse, until finally the latter use was discontinued also and *you* became the only form used in ordinary conversation. (223; italics as in original)[3]

By 1800, then, this shift in the target for you from plural to distant singular to all singular and plural had also resulted in the loss of use of singular thou, thee, thy, and thine in everyday use. However, these earlier singular forms for second person are still retained in some religious speech. Consider the Lord's Prayer and a Hail Mary, which have "hallowed be thy name" and "blessed art thou among women," respectively, where these second-person singular pronoun forms have a connotation of respected sacredness. The influence of the King James version of the Bible, which for centuries was admired as a model of English plain style, has been credited as a factor in the persistence of such language because it is perceived to be beautiful as well as sacred (Jespersen 1938: 225).

This distinction between everyday address and address directed to the religiously sanctified, with all its historically laden ideological baggage, had relevance for the Dissenting inheritors of the Calvinist Protestant tradition who brought Christianity to Tonga. Like the Quakers referred to by Bloomfield, for whom the religious and the political were deeply intertwined, the nineteenth-century Wesleyan missionaries to Tonga did not and apparently could not separate the religious from the political in their efforts to remake Tongans into Christians like themselves. And like the earlier Quakers, who manipulated English pronouns to accomplish both political and religious goals (Bauman 1983), the Wesleyans treated the language of address to both religious and political figures as of some relevance in their efforts to transform Tongan society.

Language ideology about Tongan lexical honorifics is, then, like language ideology about English second-person pronouns in that it is focused on the person addressed. And like the English language ideology about pronouns, Tongan language ideology intertwines the sacred and the secular. It is concerned with *who* those addressed and referred to by the honorifics are. It has little to say about who is doing the addressing, i.e. who the speakers are. The use of the lexical honorifics is thought to index addressees and not speakers. This chapter is concerned with how and why understandings about what addressees are being indexed by the use of honorifics has changed in scholarly representations of the honorific system.

Honorific language ideology versus honorific use in Tonga today

Today, the dominant Tongan language ideology, in both written sources (Free Wesleyan Church n.d.; Shumway 1971) and in what people say, is that the lower level of honorific lexicon is used to address and refer to chiefs, whereas the higher level of honorific lexicon is used to address and refer to the king. And so, for example, although the everyday term for 'stay' is *nofo,* the term used when speaking to or about a chief is *me'a,* and the term used when speaking to or about the king is *'afio.* Because of this variation among terms, I will have occasion to refer to the lower honorific level as 'chiefly' and the higher honorific level as 'kingly'. The same lexical items are used to both address and refer to the same persons. Words identified as honorific both by Tongans in their speech and in written sources for the two levels consist largely of greetings, nouns and verbs. Many nouns refer to the personal possessions of the target. Most verbs refer to the bodily actions and will of the persons they index.

Actual use of Tongan lexical honorifics is considerably more fluid and complex than the dominant language ideology suggests. Kingly terms are used for members of the royal family and for God, though not in identical ways, with contextual specificity in the nature and extent of the diversity of the forms used, and in their frequency. Kingly terms are also used for heads of state from other countries. Chiefly terms are used for members of the chief's family, for commoner members of parliament, and for people in positions of authority in other European derived institutional complexes, such as magistrates and judges.[4]

And even though who the speakers or users of honorifics are is not a focus of Tongan language ideology, the speakers who use the honorific lexicon in formal public contexts are usually of relatively high status themselves. For example, Wesleyan Methodist church ministers or preachers are prominent among those who address God,

and it is police prosecutors, not criminal defendants, who most often use chiefly honorifics in addressing court magistrates. What these uses have in common is the conveying
of respect, particularly in public interactions that are specifically associated with the
institutional complexes from which the authority of the persons for whom such terms
are used is derived. The remainder of this chapter explores not only how Tongan language ideology about lexical honorifics has changed over time, but also how and why
the language ideology has come to emphasize some aspects of use over others.

The reconfiguration of Tongan honorific language ideology over time

We turn now to consideration of how published scholarly characterizations of Tongan
lexical honorifics have changed over time. For each of three time periods, I briefly
describe the kind of writing about Tonga that was being published and then focus on
one key piece of writing in which discussion of Tongan honorifics can be found.

We will first look at what was written about Tongan lexical honorifics in the
period of initial sustained contact with Europeans. This begins with Captain James
Cook's second voyage to the Pacific, during which he twice visited Tonga, in 1773
and 1774, and ends in 1826 with the first sustained missionary effort there. Here
our key source is sailor William Mariner's two-volume account of his four years in
Tonga, from 1807 to 1811, first published in Great Britain in 1817.

Attention then shifts to the early twentieth century, specifically to the 1920s,
a decade that witnessed a flurry of publications by anthropologists and missionary anthropologists about Tonga, as well as the continued production of European
accounts of personal experiences in Tonga. Here I focus on the anthropological
accounts, most particularly the work of Edward Winslow Gifford, who provided the
chief published source on Tongan honorifics of this period.

Finally I consider the period from the mid-twentieth century to the present, by
which time multiple genres of writing about Tonga are in evidence. Here I give further
attention to the dominant Tongan language ideology described in the preceding section
of this chapter. Discussion is based on several published representations of Tongan
honorific language, particularly the written sources that are consistent with what Tongans nowadays say about *lea faka'eiki*. The key example here is drawn from a publication produced by the Free Wesleyan Church (n.d.), *Ko e Kalama 'i he Lea Faka-Tonga*.
This pamphlet was used as a text in government-sponsored schools and in Free Wesleyan Church schools throughout Tonga in the late 1980s and early '90s. Table 9.1
summarizes the historical shift in the targets of lexical honorifics discussed here.

The early contact literature (1773–1826)

As is true for many parts of the world, the earliest published accounts of Tonga come
first from the experiences of participants in European voyages of exploration of the
Pacific and then from the experiences of Protestant missionaries to the area. Tonga's
existence was first documented by Jacob Le Maire in 1616, then again by Abel
Tasman in 1643, but not again after that until 1773, when James Cook's exploratory

TABLE 9.1. Changing Representations of Tongan Honorific Targets

Scholar	Self-lowering speech	Everyday speech	Polite speech	Lower honorific level	Higher honorific level
1773–1826					
Mariner (1817)		tu'a 'commoner'		hau 'king or any chief'	Tu'i Tonga
1920s					
Gifford (1929)		Kakai 'people'		Lotoloto 'Middle Chiefs' Tu'i Kanokupolu	Muomua 'Leading Chiefs' Tu'i Tonga Tu'i Tonga Fefine Tamahā
1950–1990s					
Churchward (1953)	self	[everyday]	[polite]	chiefs and others	king and God
Shumway (1971)		Kakai		Hou'eiki	Tu'i
Free Wesleyan Church (n.d.)		Kakai 'Commoners'		Hou'eiki 'Nobles'	Tu'i 'King'
Taliai (1989)	Tu'a 'commoners'	Tatau 'equals'		Hou'eiki 'chiefs'	Tu'i 'king'

expedition established contact with people in Tonga. Written accounts of Cook's second voyage were first published in 1777 (Edwards 1999; Salmond 1991; Ferdon 1981, 1987), and were widely read. The wide dissemination of Cook's journals played a major role in arousing the interest of Protestant groups in Great Britain in saving the souls of islanders. Missionaries arrived as early as 1796, but a missionary effort was not sustained in an enduring way until 1826.

The account of Tonga from this period that is considered by scholars to be the most authoritative is that of William Mariner (1817). Mariner was a sailor on the British privateer *Port Au Prince* when it anchored off a Tongan island in 1807. The ship was taken over by the warrior Fīnau 'Ulukālala II and burned. Mariner was one of the few sailors not killed. 'Ulukālala II was a secular leader, or *hau*, who controlled the Ha'apai and Vava'u island groups, but not the main island of Tongatapu. Mariner lived under 'Ulukālala's protection and control in the northern Vava'u island group of Tonga from 1807 to 1811. He became fluent in the Tongan language and had extensive contact with chiefly people during his stay. Mariner was picked up by a ship in the area and returned to England, where his story was written down as a result of interviews with him by John Martin, M.D., and was published in 1818 through Martin's efforts.

In his discussion of Tongan social organization, Mariner[5] identifies the Tooitonga as the chief of highest rank, ruler of all of Tonga, with Veachi next in rank. Both are "acknowledged descendants of chief gods" (Mariner 1817: 84), but the Tooitonga is of far higher rank. According to Bott (1982), Veachi (pronounced Veasi'i) was the Tu'i Tonga's sister's son. In the Tongan cultural framework, the eldest sister of the Tu'i Tonga, and her children, particularly her eldest daughter, the Tamahā, were of higher rank than he, or *fahu* to him. But to the general population, he was the highest ranking person.

> The respect which is shown to Tooitonga, and the high rank which he holds in society, is wholly of a religious nature, and is far superior, when occasion demands it, to that which is shown even to the king himself; for the king...is by no means of the most noble descent, but yields in this respect to Tooitonga, Veachi, and several families related to them. (Mariner 1817: 84)

Mariner then lists a set of behaviors directed only to the Tu'i Tonga that show his highest rank, and it is here, among those behaviors, that his account of the Tongan honorific lexicon appears:

> 6. Peculiarities of speech, used in regard to Tooitonga. For instance, if the king or any chief but Tooitonga be sick, they say he is *tenga tangi*; but Tooitonga being sick, he is said to be *booloohi*. So with many other words that are used exclusively for him. (86).

At this time, the person that Mariner referred to as king, a term he used interchangeably with the term *hau*, was his sponsor, Fīnau II, the secular ruler. Mariner made clear that although the Tu'i Tonga had the greatest rank, Fīnau had the greatest power. He illustrates this with an example of a situation in which the Tu'i Tonga attempted to give the king some political advice and was basically told to mind his own business (125–126).

These same terms, identified in the quote above (*tengetange* and *pūluhi*), are listed in the most recent twentieth century sources as for the chiefs and king, respectively. The everyday term for 'sick' is *puke*. This one example suggests the stability of at least some of the terms over time, and the stability in their relative ranking, as well as a shift in who the terms are used for.

Mariner's characterization of Tongan language ideology, then, basically sets up pairs of contrasts in the hierarchy of Tongan leadership:

sacred	secular
Tu'i Tonga	*hau*/king
rank	power
higher honorific level	lower honorific level

Mariner argues that the Tu'i Tonga was highly respected because he was descended from gods. This raises questions about how the gods themselves were addressed. Mariner describes "priests" being possessed by gods and taking on their voices to offer predictions of the future. The people who were possessed by gods were treated with respect when in that state, but only when in that state. But there is no specific mention of honorific lexicon used to refer to priests or to address them. Mariner also describes chiefs addressing the gods and offering prayers, as well as sacrifices to them, but again there is no mention of any use of honorific lexicon. However, with regard to the word *egi* (today spelled *'eiki* and glossed as 'chief' when used as a noun or meaning 'respected' when used as an adjective), Mariner does say that this term is used both to address high chiefs and to refer to the gods (1817: 91). In the stories about the doings of gods and various Tu'i Tonga that have been published in this century (e.g., Gifford 1924; Collocott 1928; Fanua n.d.), kingly honorific words are used to refer to the doings of the Tu'i Tonga, but not to the doings of the gods.

There is, then, no clear evidence in written sources I have examined that the honorific lexicon had precontact Tongan gods as its target in language ideology or language use. And this is so in spite of the very clear Tongan idea during early contact with Europeans that the humans to whom the kingly terms were used received those words because they were descended from gods.

Early-twentieth-century scholarship (1920s)

Early-twentieth-century representations of Tongan lexical honorifics reveal a period in which the language ideology in the written scholarly literature was undergoing change, and different Tongans offered different views on who used what terms to whom (Gifford 1929). The diversity and change were in part a result of political and religious change in Tonga during the nineteenth century. For this reason, I will consider the nature of these changes and their influence on the honorific system before turning to the condition of diverse representations in the early twentieth century.

In the early 1800s, the Protestant missionary effort in Polynesia was similar across the several different groups working in the area—the London Missionary Society, the Wesleyan Missionary Society, and the ABC Missionary Society. All these groups came from an evangelical background and aspired to be interdenominational in their orientation, particularly the London Missionary Society. After several abortive attempts, the Wesleyan missionaries who set up a mission station in Tonga in 1826 were able to maintain a continuous presence and influence over the people.

These evangelical Christians, including Unitarians and Methodists/Wesleyans, were the inheritors of the British Calvinist tradition of the seventeenth century. In the late eighteenth century, the Church of England was the state church, and the king was considered the head of the church. The evangelical groups were known as Dissenters because of their opposition to the authority of the Church of England. Their religious denominations, under the influence of John Locke, emphasized the individual—rather than the Church of England—as the source of authority in the interpretation of the Bible (Hiney 2000; Clark 1994). This was the reason for their stress on education and literacy.

The Dissenters refused to take the sacrament in the Church of England. This barred them from holding government offices under laws that were not repealed until 1826. They were active in the antislavery movement and supported women's rights and so were advocates of both their own civil rights and those of others. Dissenters were strong supporters of the concept of constitutional monarchy, in which the ultimate authority was Parliament rather than a monarch, in an era that had rejected the concept of the divine right of kings.[6]

In Tonga, Tāufa'āhau, the powerful chief known for politically unifying the Tongan Islands in the 1830s and 1840s, aligned himself with the Wesleyan missionaries. He converted to Christianity and destroyed old gods to display their ineffectiveness. In so doing, he drew his followers to conversion to Christianity as well (Lātūkefu 1974). Although these conversions empowered the missionaries, they also empowered Tāufa'āhau. Futa Helu, who is a highly respected scholar of his own Tongan culture and the founder of 'Atenisi University in Tonga, argues that when Tongans gave their political loyalty to this chief and simultaneously converted to his religion, they were following a well-established Tongan pattern (personal communication). Different chiefs had different gods, and when Tongans moved into the territory of a given chief and under his authority, they typically converted to worship of his gods. And when a chief's political authority and good fortune waned, so did the belief that he was protected by his gods, and his followers would move to other chiefs. In this way, Tāufa'āhau's conversion to Christianity and the subsequent conversion of others fitted this pattern.

Thus, as Mariner explained, although there were powerful chiefs, *hau*, who were not descended from the gods, they were still viewed as protected by the gods. So under the "old order," the line between sacred and secular power was blurred, and secular leaders, however less sacred than the Tu'i Tonga, still had a sacred dimension to their authority. In other words, through his conversion, and that of his followers, Tāufa'āhau drew the sacred power of Christianity to himself, potentially threatening the power of the missionaries even as they benefited from these linkages.

Though the missionaries' goals were primarily religious, they also had political aims. Again throughout Polynesia, in the early 1800s, missionaries were pushing the idea to the local leaders, the chiefs, that it was in their interest to take actions to legitimate their political authority in the eyes of the British and the Americans in particular, but also the French and Germans. These powers were increasingly represented by the presence of government and military personnel (as opposed to traders and missionaries) in the Pacific who were interested in controlling trade and keeping sea lanes open for trade and under their control in the region. The idea here was that if local leaders could project a form of political authority to the Western powers that such powers could recognize as like their own—and hence would respect—then these island groups would be able to preserve their political independence (Daws 1974; Lātūkefu 1974; Powles 1979).

The missionaries also distrusted the completely unchecked power of any sovereign, especially a sovereign who claimed divinity. They saw the creation of laws as the way to contain chiefly autocracy (Koskinen 1953). In advocating laws to the Tongan chiefly class, they adapted the British model of government to the Tongan situation. Missionaries and European government representatives circulated drafts of laws and constitutions among themselves, which they offered as models to local chiefs (Powles 1979; Lātūkefu 1974; Daws 1974). Both the Hawaiian Constitution of 1840 and the Tongan Constitution of 1875 had in common a mapping of some basic features of the legal political form of a British constitutional monarchy onto indigenous forms of political authority. Paramount chiefs were to be called kings. In Tonga's case, this was Tāufa'āhau. Legislative bodies were conceived of as consisting of two "houses," even though they met together. The hereditary chiefs were represented by elected chiefs or "nobles" in one house, and the people, or "commoners," were represented by the elected non-chiefly members in the other house. So while Tāufa'āhau was busy "mapping" Christian notions of the sacred onto indigenous notions of the sacred, the missionaries were mapping European notions of political authority onto Tongan notions of political authority. This latter mapping preserved the relative hierarchy of Tongan rank groups, and Tongan commoner political power in the national legislature was largely illusory, in contrast with constitutional governments of the era in other parts of the world.

In some respects, it is puzzling that the missionaries imagined Tongans and other Polynesian groups as monarchies. They deplored the hereditary power the chiefs had over the people; after all, the missionaries themselves were from Protestant groups that had experienced religious persecutions under monarchical British rule quite recently. Other emerging constitutional governments rejected monarchy. However, Great Britain, the missionaries' primary model of government, was still a monarchy, and a monarchy was still a European governmental form. So priority may have been given to rendering Polynesian political authority in a European form over rendering it in a particular such form. There was also the model and practice of framing constitutions as selective schemas of some aspects of forms of authority already in place on the ground in the aforementioned circulating of drafts of laws and constitutions among missionaries and representatives of European governments. In addition, it was inconceivable to the missionaries that those in power in Polynesian political entities would surrender their powers. Finally, it was a huge conceptual break with the past for non-chiefs to have any power at all (Osorio 2002), so the missionaries may have felt they were achieving a great deal.

But while Polynesian monarchies were obviously acceptable to the missionaries on some level, the merger of secular and sacred power, as in the case of the Tu'i Tonga and potentially in the case of Tāufa'āhau, who became the first king, was clearly much less acceptable. The merger of church and state was part of the rejected past of Great Britain, anathema to these missionizing Protestants.

In the missionary effort to encourage governments that would be perceived as legitimate to Western nations, it was neither in their religious and political interests, nor in the Tongans' international (as opposed to internal) political interests to have a secular leader's political authority grounded in religious power. If the king's religious power came from precontact supernatural beliefs, then the Tongans were pagans and still savages. If the religious power was derived from Christianity, then the situation was more complicated. The missionaries wanted the Polynesian leaders to be Christians. This was a sign of civilization. But for the king to be perceived by his people as favored by God, or godlike, was not consistent with Dissenting Protestantism. It also threatened the power of the missionaries.

As noted earlier, however, Christianity was credited by Tongans for Tāufa'āhau's success as a warrior and political unifier of Tonga. His success was an indicator of the power of the Christian God. So there was a sense in which the missionaries' success in conversion depended on this link between the sacred and the secular. This created an ambivalence toward the linking of the sacred and the secular and an ambiguity regarding the source of the king's power and authority. In the case of Tāufa'āhau, this was theoretically less of a problem than it might have been because Tāufa'āhau's chiefly line was not that of the Tu'i Tonga, but rather that of the Tu'i Kanokupolu, the *hau* or secular leader.

It is not easy to learn how the missionary desire to render the Europeanized version of the Tongan nation-state as characterized by a separation of church and state affected language ideologies about the use of Tongan honorifics. However, what evidence there is indicates that there was a place for the lexical honorifics in the state building project and that the collaboration between Tongan leaders and missionaries during the reign of Tāufa'āhau led to kingly terms being reserved for God and not used for the king at all.

Futa Helu (personal communication) has suggested that the missionaries wanted to have the higher honorific terms reserved for God. Helu's examination of nineteenth-century Tongan government documents revealed no use of such terms for the king in earlier years of his reign but a gradual increase in their use over time. Some Tongans saw Tāufa'āhau, the first king, as also having assumed the Tu'i Tonga title in 1865 (Wood-Ellem 1999: 21; Gifford 1929: 59). Address to him using the higher level of honorifics was one of the sacred honors that went with the title, and according to Wood-Ellem he was addressed using the higher level of honorifics from that time on. However, many Tongans never accepted the king's right to assume that title (Wood-Ellem 1999: 21) and saw the title as having been extinguished after the death of the last Tu'i Tonga in 1865.

The clearest evidence for the missionary-led use of the higher honorific level for God that I personally have available comes from the present-day hymnal of the Free Wesleyan Church, *Ko e Tohi Himi 'a e Siasi Uesiliana Tau'ataina 'o Tonga* (Friendly Island Book Store n.d.). Free Wesleyan Tongans today say that this is the same hymnal produced by the missionary James Egan Moulton, during the period 1865–1888 when he was stationed in Tonga. Moulton was fluent in Tongan and composed many of the hymns himself (Moulton 1921). In this hymnal, the use of kingly honorifics to address God is widespread.

On the one hand, this use of terms for God that were formerly used only for the Tu'i Tonga, his sister, and her children, was consistent with the general missionary strategy of appropriation of all things sacred in the time prior to Tongan contact with Christianity. On the other hand, the use of honorifics to God in Tongan was also consistent with the use of "special" terms of address to God in English—thou, thee, thy, and thine—a consequence of the pronominal shift in English which had resulted in the loss of thou for second-person singular in everyday speech but its retention in religious speech.

By the early twentieth century, diversity and change in characterizations of Tongan lexical honorifics were evident in the writing of Edward Winslow Gifford (1887–1959). Gifford was an anthropologist, a curator at the University of California Museum of Anthropology in Berkeley at the time of his research in Tonga (Foster 1960). In 1920–1921, he led the Bayard Dominick Expedition to Tonga on behalf of the Bernice P. Bishop Museum in Hawai'i. As Patrick Kirch (n.d.) has described, Gifford's expedition was one of four separate Bayard Dominick Expeditions to the Pacific at that time sponsored by the museum. Research was carried out by teams representing all four fields of anthropology with the aim of taking a holistic approach to the problem of Polynesian origins. Gifford, the comparative ethnologist on the project, spent nine months in Tonga, producing three major publications from his work (1923, 1924, 1929).

This body of work as a whole, like that of Gifford's missionary friend E. E. V. Collocott, who gave Gifford large amounts of material he had collected in Tonga, was based largely on one-on-one work with Tongans rather than on participant observation. Much of it consists of texts of myths and other stories about the gods and the Tu'i Tongas of the past, as well as other pieces of verbal folklore. Although Gifford is not explicit about this, it was still thought by many anthropologists of this time that such stories could be studied for motifs that constituted "traits" which could be compared with the trait lists of other societies in the area as a way of determining historical connections among the groups. There was also the goal during this period, not entirely consistently, of doing 'salvage anthropology' to re-create the culture of a local people at a time in the past before there was contact with Europeans. Both approaches were ahistorical in that they did not see the societies being studied as having histories in the Western sense. In Gifford's final and culminating work on Tonga, *Tongan Society* (1929), there is no consistent attention to which of the cultural practices documented were still ongoing when he was in Tonga. Thus the work is characterized by a kind of flattening out of time.

Nevertheless, in part because of Gifford's interest in the origin and migration of the Tongans, and his belief that even geographical diversity within Tonga in cultural practices could provide clues to Tonga's relations to other Polynesian groups (Gifford 1923: 3), he does give considerable attention to who he got information from and to where within Tonga those persons came from. Accordingly, interwoven into his own accounts of Tongan culture, there are many texts from local Tongans, primarily of the chiefly class, some of which are rendered as translations into English only, but some of which include both Tongan and English versions of the accounts by Tongans, sometimes with even the identity of the translators of the texts, who were not always Tongans, included.

The aforementioned local Wesleyan missionary Collocott, who lived in Tonga from 1911 to 1923 (Wood-Ellem 1999: 309), was engaged in the same kind of anthropological research that Gifford came to Tonga to carry out (Collocott 1928; Collocott and Havea 1922). As Gifford himself acknowledges (1929: 3), Collocott generously gave ethnological materials to Gifford, including texts that he had collected, largely from the chiefly class, and perhaps more specifically the heavily missionized segments of that class. *Tongan Society* is, accordingly, a truly collaborative project of chiefly Tongans, missionaries, and anthropologists, and it is often possible to locate a number of individual voices in the text.

Gifford's section "Tongan Rank and Language" (1929: 119–122) consists of a general normative statement about the use of the honorifics, followed by three different accounts of actual words used and those to whom the words are used, thus perpetuating the ideological focus on the people addressed or, as I have called them, indexical targets. This multiplicity captures both diversity in Tongan views of the honorifics and ongoing change in how their use was conceptualized. Such multiplicity occurs in no other published account of the honorifics. Here is Gifford's normative statement: "One set of words was used in addressing or speaking of the Tamaha, the Female and the Male Tui Tonga, another for the Tui Haa Takalaua, the Tui Kanokupolu, and the chiefs, and still another for the people" (119).

Gifford's first list of honorific words is from "Elia Malupo, one of the Tui Tonga's ceremonial attendants, in a statement written November 27, 1905" (119). This list roughly matches Gifford's normative statement. Malupo's three categories are

"Muomua (leading chiefs), Lotoloto (middle chiefs) and Kakai (people)." Under each of these categories, ordered right to left from higher to lower, are columns of analogous words, such as "fakahifo, faele, fanau, To give birth" (120).[7]

In Gifford's second list, there is a simple contrast between the terms used for the Tu'i Tonga and the ordinary terms, again using a columnar format in which analogous words for the two levels are in parallel columns.

The third list, however, is the most interesting one for our purposes. This list was obtained "from Jioeli Pania, from other informants, and from Baker's Tongan Dictionary" (1929: 121). It is not laid out in columns, but as dictionary entries of Tongan terms ordered alphabetically with English glosses. This list, which deals almost exclusively with the higher honorific level, distinguishes among terms used for "the King"; terms used for "the Tu'i Tonga"; terms used for "the gods";[8] and terms used for "the Deity," as Gifford refers to God. Whereas the majority of the terms (23 of 37) are associated exclusively with the Tu'i Tonga (and his family), there were four terms for both the Tu'i Tonga and the king (e.g., *lakoifie*, 'well in health'), and two terms associated with the Tu'i Tonga, the king, and God (*folofola*, 'word, speech'; and *finangalo*, 'will').

This third list, then, shows the way in which words for the Tu'i Tonga were being extended to both king and God, bit by bit in a piecemeal fashion, and in ways that were contextually relevant. It includes targets of honorifics (God and king) that do not appear at all in the first two lists. Tongans, then, differed in their representations of the Tongan honorific system at this time.

When Gifford's account is compared with that of Mariner, some interesting issues emerge. Gifford's normative account, following Malupo, is very similar to Mariner's, although it deals with groups of people to whom a level of honorification is applied, rather than with specific individuals. The higher honorific level has the same sacred targets, the Tu'i Tonga and his sister's family. The lower honorific level has the same kind of secular targets, notably the *hau* or secular chiefs, the Tu'i Ha'a Takalāua and the Tu'i Kanokupolu. Gifford privileges this account over the others by foregrounding it and adopting it as his own. However, by this time, there was no longer a Tu'i Tonga, and no longer a Tu'i Ha'a Takalāua, both titles having been extinguished. And the king and the Tu'i Kanokupolu were the same person.[9] Logically, this would mean that the king was the only person to whom either level of honorification could be addressed, which clearly was not the case.

Gifford's privileging of the precontact model of honorification over one that reflected the practice of the time is consistent both with a 'salvage anthropology' mentality and with deference to the authority of Malupo, himself a figure of authority in chiefly circles. Gifford (and indirectly someone else from whom he obtained Malupo's 1905 text), can thus be understood to have been collaborating with the traditional chiefly class in his projected representation of rank in Tongan society.

The dominant view of the mid- to late twentieth century (1950s to 1990s)

By the mid- to late twentieth century, although there are more scholars publishing accounts of Tongan honorifics, there is more homogeneity in concepts of who is indexed when the two levels of honorification are used. There is still some variation in other respects that I will discuss further on. As noted in the beginning of this chapter, the dominant and widely shared view among Tongans is that the higher level of honorification is for the king, or *tu'i*; the lower level of honorification is for the chiefs, or *hou'eiki*; and the everyday lexical items are for the people, or *kakai*.

The third monarch of Tonga, Queen Sālote, who ruled from 1918 to 1965, contributed both directly and indirectly to the emergence of this view as dominant. When Gifford was in Tonga in 1920–1921, Queen Sālote had only recently taken over the throne. Her predecessor, Tupou II, who ruled from 1893 to 1918, had had a troubled reign by all accounts. There was disunity among Tongans under him, and during his reign Tonga became a protectorate under Great Britain. Queen Sālote not only brought unity to the country but also, with her husband, was a popular figure. She is best known today for her sponsorship of Tongan traditional arts, and she was herself a gifted and prolific poet whose love songs are still widely performed. Queen Sālote also played a major role in promulgating a coherent vision of the history of Tonga as a nation-state. She projected this vision to the outside world through the written accounts of Tongan and non-Tongan scholars alike with whom she worked closely, and who lived in Tonga for long periods of time during her reign (Bott 1982; Lātūkefu 1974; Wood-Ellem 1999).

This history is one of nation-state formation through cooperation between church and state. During her reign, the queen worked closely with the Free Wesleyan Church, *Siasi Uesiliana Tau'itania*. The Free Wesleyan Church has come close to being a state church in part as a result of her efforts.[10] This is the church to which the royal family belongs. The majority of Tongans belonged to this church during the latter part of the twentieth century, although this may no longer be true. Many believed that it was necessary to belong to this church to get key jobs in the government and support for economic projects or that it at least enhanced one's opportunities. This is also the one church among the three with Wesleyan missionary roots that has ties to international Methodist organizations.

In Queen Sālote's vision, the three traditional chiefly lines have been merged in her bloodline through the marriages of offspring of the royal family. Although in the late nineteenth century, not all Tongans accepted the idea that the first king, Tāufa'āhau, had been invested with the Tu'i Tonga title, they do seem to accept the idea that the queen's son, Tupou IV, the present king, embodies all three lines through the intermarriages among those lines of his ancestors. Thus he has some claim to the prestige of the Tu'i Tonga line and in this way to the higher level of honorific vocabulary, as well as having such a claim on the basis of the respect owed to him as king.

A key written source for promulgation of the view that the honorific vocabularies are used to show respect to the king and the chiefs comes from the Free Wesleyan Church itself. In the 1980s and earlier, the church published three pamphlets on traditional Tongan culture, written in Tongan: one on Tongan proverbs, one on Tongan kava circle etiquette, and one on Tongan grammar. The Free Wesleyan list of honorifics was part of this third booklet, *Ko e Kalama 'i he Lea Faka-Tonga,* 'The Grammar of the Tongan Language', distributed by the Free Wesleyan Church Office of Education to high school students. This pamphlet more briefly covers in Tongan many of the same topics as Churchward's 1953 *Tongan Grammar*, particularly parts of speech. The pamphlet was required reading for high school students in the state-run high schools and in the church-run Free Wesleyan high schools at the time of my field research in the late 1980s and early 1990s. The state-sponsored exam the students had to take on leaving high school, which included examination on the material in this pamphlet, determined whether the students could go on to college and whether they qualified for precious Tongan government jobs. Basically, then, the majority of Tongans who were going to school at that time were required to learn the church-promulgated and state-sponsored version of Tongan honorification.

The section on the honorifics is titled "Vocabulary for the Three Classes of People in the Tongan Society: Commoners, Nobles, and the Royalty." This title is in English, even though the pamphlet is a text written predominantly in the Tongan language. The format is the same as that introduced by Gifford: three columns of words, which are supposed to be the analogous words for people in the three different categories, headed by labels identifying the persons for whom the words are supposed to be used. (See Table 9.1 for comparison of labels for the indexical targets of the honorifics levels).

In this Free Wesleyan Church publication, the labels are in English (even though there is no translation into English of any of the lexical items), followed by their Tongan equivalents, ordered from left to right as: "Commoners (Kakai)," "Nobles (Hou'eiki)," and "King (Tu'i)" (Free Wesleyan Church n.d.: 32). The more usual translation of *kakai* would be 'people', and the more usual translation of *hou'eiki* would be 'chiefs', whereas the usual Tongan term for 'noble' would be the same word borrowed into Tongan, *nōpele*.

So the English glosses must be understood as an intentional mapping of state legal categories in English onto traditional Tongan categories of rank to represent the patterning of the use of honorific vocabulary. By 'state legal categories', I refer to the categories of king, noble, and commoner. These are the basic legal identity categories of Tongan persons that were defined in the Tongan Constitution of 1875, which still provides the legal foundation for the country. Each of these categories carries with it distinctive rights and duties that particularly affect landholding and governmental representation. The position of king is hereditary, as are the positions of nobles. The king and the nobles are the only people who "own" land (there is also the category government land). The king and the nobles give individual commoners use rights to individual pieces of their land. These use rights can themselves be inherited, but by law, as opposed to informal practice, they cannot be sold or alienated. By law, when a particular commoner line of inheritance is exhausted, the land reverts to the "owner," the king or a noble.

The king is the executive of the country. He appoints his ministers and his privy council. The national legislature consists of two elected groups, noble representatives and commoner representatives. The nobles elect their representatives and the commoners elect their representatives. The commoner representatives and the noble representatives are equal in number, even though there are only thirty-five nobles and over ninety thousand commoners. Because the king's ministers also vote in the legislature, the commoners have never been able to outvote a combination of noble representatives and cabinet ministers, although this situation is changing in Tonga today. Suffice it to say, these modern-day legal categories are profoundly determinative of the Tongan political process.

The Free Wesleyan booklet's treatment of the chiefly language then, in the context of instruction on Tongan grammar, projects a model of the Tongan state (in the English language) to schoolchildren that associates this model with traditional precontact Tongan social categories carried forward to the present (in the Tongan language).

This model is echoed in other characterizations of honorific use for the late twentieth century. The other major source for this period is Eric Shumway's *Intensive Course in Tongan* (1971). Shumway likewise schematizes his version of honorific usage into three columns, and he uses the same Tongan terms as the Free Wesleyan version—"Kakai," "Hou'eiki," and "Tu'i"—from left to right but with no translation of these terms into English (603).

Shumway prepared the *Intensive Course in Tongan* for the Peace Corps' use in training members assigned to Tonga. Shumway learned Tongan while on a Mormon mission to Tonga as a young man, and his book is still the only pedagogical textbook in print in English on how to learn Tongan. As was true for the Free Wesleyan Church publication, Shumway's language text links church and state through educational processes, albeit with a less direct link. For here there is, through the Peace Corps, a link between the Church of Jesus Christ of Latter-Day Saints, the United States government, and the government of Tonga. And in this case, the target audience is English-speaking learners of Tongan rather than Tongan-speaking learners of Tongan.

Here again, embedded in another widely disseminated prescriptive grammar, is a vision of the Tongan state as comprising three major secular social categories. Language learners from the United States are taught this three-way distinction and instructed that socially appropriate speech requires that this three-way distinction be maintained in discourse. In this way, people from the United States collaborate with Tongans in a transnational maintenance of a Tongan state vision of the Tongan nation.

The two other major sources on honorifics for the second half of the twentieth century are C. Maxwell Churchward's *Tongan Grammar* ([1953] 1985) and 'Opeti Manisela Taliai's master's thesis, *Social Differentiation of Language Levels in Tonga* (1989). Both begin with everyday speech and move to increasingly higher levels of respect in their accounts. Taliai uses the columnar format asserting lexical equivalences across levels that are used in the Shumway and Free Wesleyan accounts. Churchward does not use a columnar schema. He has a concept of "degrees of respect" (304) that are discrete and associated with different lexical items:

> In many cases Tongan courtesy requires the use, now of one word, now of another, and now of another, to express the same idea, according to the kind or degree of respect which is due to the person or persons addressed.

Churchward's account is quite brief, consisting of approximately a page in a section of his grammar titled "The Appropriate Word for the Appropriate Rank." But for this work, and for his dictionary (1959), he has been looked to as the most authoritative written source on the Tongan language by non-Tongan linguists until quite recently.

Both Taliai and Churchward preserve the three ranked identities of *kakai, hou'eiki, and tu'i* and their association with different lexicons that characterizes the Free Wesleyan Church account and Shumway's account. However, they both have more than three levels of respect in their frameworks. Churchward adds a level between everyday speech and chiefly speech, which he characterizes as "polite." Both Taliai and Churchward add a level below that of everyday speech in which the speaker engages in self-lowering by using derogatory words in reference to himself or herself. This then adds the element of ideology about <u>speakers</u>, though speakers remain otherwise undifferentiated in the models these two scholars use. This concept of vocabulary items that are associated with self-lowering is widespread among Tongans. However, it is not that often associated with the model of elevation in people's accounts of the use of lexical honorifics. In other words, this self-lowering can be either detached from or associated with the model of honorification. In any case, a four- or five-level model is not dominant in written and spoken accounts of honorific usage.[11]

Clearly, the number of levels can be said to have been contested during the second half of the twentieth century. However, this contestation does not seem to directly affect the robustness of the three categories of people, chiefs, and king across these four main written characterizations of the honorific system during this period.

One of the most important ideas that has been preserved across time in these accounts is that use to commoners, to chiefs, and to the king can be functionally equivalent: that one can say essentially the same thing to these different persons except for conveying different levels of respect. This idea is reinforced by Shumway's practice dialogue (1971: 602) illustrating contrasts in levels in use:

| PCV [commoner]: | *Mālō e **laumālie** 'a Nuku!* | 'Hello, Nuku!' |
| Nuku [a chief]: | *'Io, mālō e **lelei!*** | 'Yes, hello!' |

Thus both a chief and one of the people can be equivalently greeted, although with different degrees of respect conveyed by different lexical items in greetings. The columnar models reinforce this, with their rows of lexical equivalents.

God is not present at all in the Free Wesleyan, Shumway, and Taliai accounts. To introduce God into the picture causes a range of problems. First, it threatens the symmetry and coherence of the account of the honorifics. God is not a political category, and one cannot interact with God in the same ways one interacts with other people. One does not, for example, ask after and/or celebrate God's good health, as is true of talk to and about chiefs and the king.

Second, for Tongan state and church both, characterizations of the use of the Tongan honorific lexicon are part of a narrative of the Tongan nation-state—who the people were and who they are now, and how they became a modern nation (even when embedded in a grammar, as in the publications by the Free Wesleyan Church and by the missionary linguists Churchward and Shumway). To talk about how some of the same terms are used for both king and God can suggest to Tongans and to outsiders that the king and God are seen as being alike, including alike in their sacred quality. This idea is no more popular in the outside Protestant Christian and Western democratic traditions today than it was a hundred years ago, so there is pressure from both within and outside Tonga to obscure this possible interpretation.

A final reason for the omission of God as a target of honorifics is that although the honorific terms are used for God in the older Protestant groups (namely, the Wesleyan groups, who were still the great majority at the time of my research in the 1980s and 1990s), they are not used for God in the newer evangelical groups that have come into Tonga since the 1960s—Mormons, Seventh-Day Adventists, and others. This is a point to which I will return in the next section.

The transformation of the relation between the sacred and the secular is then key to the refiguring of the targets of Tongan honorification over the last two hundred years. This refiguring has been carried out by scholars who have essentially collaborated with Tongan rulers in the Tongan nation-state building ideological project. In Tonga at the time of contact, respect was split between the sacred Tu'i Tonga and the *hau,* or secular chiefs, so there was already a semi-split between the sacred and the secular. Missionaries wanted to eliminate the use of sacred terms for actual persons, and they succeeded in getting some of the terms used for the Tu'i Tonga shifted to God. However, over time, terms have also shifted from the Tu'i Tonga to the secular *hau* line of the king. So whereas once there was only one category of being that the higher honorific terms indexed, these terms now index two categories of beings—one of actual persons and one of God. But for all the reasons considered above, only part of that shift in use has been systematically incorporated into scholarly representations of Tongan honorific lexicons and their use, and that is the secular dimension of the shift of the sacred higher honorific level from the Tu'i Tonga to the secular leader, the king.

Continuing negotiation of the meaning of Tongan honorifics

There is diversity in Tonga today, just as there was in Gifford's time, with regard to what people say about the use and meaning of Tongan honorifics, in contrast to the homogeneity of the scholarly written accounts. The most salient systematic source of such diversity that I encountered was based on Christian religious denominational diversity.

In a Tongan village in western Tongtapu of approximately fifteen hundred individuals, I became aware of this diversity through my experience of a conceptual opposition between Mormons and Free Wesleyans. Here my closest research assistants were Tongan Mormons, but the Free Wesleyan Church dominated the village denominationally. Though these assistants readily recognized and labeled the honorifics by level in transcripts of tape-recorded data, as I have already noted, they professed to be unable to use the honorifics in actively addressing a noble. They attributed this inability to their having gone to a Mormon high school, where the honorifics were not taught as they are in Free Wesleyan and government schools, and where, moreover, they spoke English all day. They also said that the honorifics were not used in their church services. One of them recounted a situation in which she encountered a noble and, unable to use the proper honorifics, used English to him as a way of showing respect. I have heard several stories like this. This lack of ability to use the honorifics and its explanation were reported with a mix of embarrassment and pride. When I questioned a prominent non-native Mormon leader known for his fluency in Tongan about this at a later time, he said there was no policy to avoid use of honorifics in church. However, he did not use them in addressing God, but only in addressing the secular political leadership. He explained that he conceptualized his relationship with God as being very different from his relationship to the secular leadership. My understanding was that he saw his relationship with God as a personal, intimate relationship, whereas his relationship with the secular leadership was more distant.

Note clearly here, however, the separating of church and state, but with a reversal of the direction of the separation from that reported by Helu in his survey of nineteenth-century government documents, where the honorifics were reserved for God and excluded from the king. The Mormon strategy is to reserve the honorifics for the king and exclude them from God. What these strategies have in common is the separating of church and state. The Free Wesleyans from the same village as my research assistants saw this Mormon failure to use honorifics, of which they were well aware, as one of several key semiotically salient ways in which Mormons showed a lack of respect for traditional Tongan ways of doing things. Mormons also declined to drink *kava*, a traditional narcotic drink, and they often declined to wear the *ta'ovala*, the waist mat worn in public situations that conveyed respect to the social order in general (and, some would say, to the king).

Although my own experiences suggested a salient Mormon-Wesleyan opposition, anthropologist Ernest Olson's research (1993 and personal communication) in the same village and elsewhere in Tonga on variation among Protestant denominations in their social religious practices led him to conclude that whereas all three of the older Wesleyan denominations, and the Catholics, used the higher honorific level for God, none of the Protestant denominations that came into the country during the second half of twentieth century did so.

Olson had found that there was an emphasis in both ideology and practice on a more egalitarian relationship among leaders and members of congregations in the newer groups (Mormons, Pentecostals, Seventh-Day Adventists, and others). There was a conscious and deliberate turning away from or rejection of hierarchy in these churches that was part of the members' movement away from Wesleyan denominations, which were shrinking in membership as a result of the presence of these new groups. In a broader, indeed, national view, the non-use of honorifics in church in all these denominations was ideologically associated with the embracing of egalitarianism and a rhetoric of an equality-hierarchy opposition.

Recall that the nineteenth-century Wesleyan missionaries were generally hostile to Tongan hierarchy but simultaneously moved against it and embraced it in their engagement with Tongan leaders. Their domains were both political and religious. They saw themselves and are seen by Tongans today as having had a strong egalitarian ideology that transformed Tongan society. But in their religious work, they were more concerned about separating church and state than they were about getting rid of hierarchy altogether.

Today the denominational descendants of these same Wesleyans are being positioned by the newer Protestant groups as the hierarchical ones, and the newer groups are taking the "high ground" of egalitarian ideology and practice that once was the position of the earlier missionaries. Unlike their missionary predecessors, however, the new religious groups are essentially focused on religious matters. They leave the state and Tongan political processes out of at least their most overt efforts to convert Tongans. Instead, they give more emphasis to ideological differences among Protestant denominations. Undoubtedly this is partly for strategic reasons because the new groups don't want to be removed from the country by the king.

This same cyclical reproduction of a hierarchical-egalitarian opposition has occurred over time among Protestant denominations in Great Britain and its colonies. Repeatedly in these places also, newer groups criticize older groups for being too hierarchical.

There has thus been a continuous tension, ambivalence, and ambiguity in the meaning and use of honorific terms in Tonga now for at least two hundred years. The written characterizations of Tongan honorifics by late-twentieth-century scholars typically treat them as if there is only one view or vision of what they mean and how they should be used. But the above examples provide glimpses of multiple views of the honorifics in an evolving dynamic.

Conclusion

This chapter has documented changes in scholarly representations of Tongan chiefly language ideology. Over the last two hundred years, the degrees of respect and many of the words have remained constant, but the conceptualization of the indexical targets—those who are indexed by the use of the lexical honorifics—has changed. Such change appears to be a common feature of changes in language ideologies over time. The key shift in conceptualization of the targets of the higher honorific level has been from the sacred Tu'i Tonga of the traditional Tongan polity to the secular king of the Tongan nation-state, now a constitutional monarchy. This has entailed a submerging of the sacred, though not an entire erasure, from the dominant representation of the use of the honorifics. Discussion of the use to God interferes with the simplicity, coherence, and symmetry of the characterizations of the Tongan honorific system. It is also inconsistent with the larger ideological project of Tongan nation-state formation, a collaboration over time of church and state in Tonga facilitated by the scholarly representations of the honorifics. Finally, the use of the higher honorific level to index God is contested among Tongan Protestant religious denominations, and thus is not consistent with the projection of a single homogenous perspective on the honorifics within Tongan society.

Over the last century, since Gifford's iconic representation of the system, a format of three columns of lexically equivalent terms has become the norm for display of the honorifics. This inevitably static representation in itself obscures the extent to which the uses of the terms for different categories are nonanalogous and variable within each category.

Ultimately, the language ideology of *lea faka'eiki*, 'chiefly language', has consistently been an ideology of continuity between past and present political orders, of mapping European political concepts of legitimate political order onto precontact concepts of the Tongan political and religious hierarchy. This has been done by changing the labeling of the social categories identified as indexed by honorific lexical items, while presenting other aspects of the honorific system as remaining unchanged. In this way, the Tongan polity is projected to Tongans and non-Tongans alike as extending back into the depths of prehistory unchanged in its fundamental nature, even as it has undergone radical social change.

There are several aspects of this work that have broader implications for thinking about language ideologies, and Tongan language ideology can be better understood if compared with other language ideologies, especially honorific language ideologies such as those in Asia and the Pacific.

Clearly, participant identities are often salient in language ideologies. In the Tongan language ideology at issue, and in the particular kinds of discourse that constitute the language ideology, the social identities of the people addressed and the idea that these identities are linked to different levels of honorification are pragmatically salient. While it is more common for linguistic honorification ideologies to imagine an addressor-addressee dyad from the point of view of the speaker, here the focus on the person spoken to is very salient.

This focus on changing addressee identities can be attributed to broader social processes of change. Here, as in the work of Errington (1985a), Inoue (2002, 2003, and 2004) and Hill and Hill (1979), the changes in Tongan language ideologies are attributed to the influence of Western colonialism and nation-state formation. The addressee focus clearly reflects the appropriation of discourses about Tongan honorifics by the Tongan nation-state building project over the last two centuries. And presently the role of representations of lexical honorification in pedagogical materials is as much to instruct Tongan and American students about the national political structure of Tonga as it is to teach them how to use honorifics.

Tonga's experience of nineteenth-century Dissenting missionaries who had nation-state formation goals was not unlike that of other Polynesian societies, including Samoa, Tahiti, and Hawai'i. In these places, too, the separation of sacred and secular rule was a preoccupation. However, the historical transformations of these different Polynesian contexts have been very different.

Both Tonga and Samoa have honorification systems that were shaped by nation-state formation. Neither Tahiti nor Hawai'i had such ideologized lexical honorification systems, although they had the same semiotic framework for displays of respect that western Polynesia had. Both Tahiti and Hawai'i were early on engulfed by larger colonial processes that have nearly but not completely rendered nation-state formation moot. So the outcomes of these nation-state–forming activities have been quite variable, as have been their ideological effects, and they are ongoing.

Clearly, the idea that a modern state should have a secular leader was widely held, because Asian nation-states such as Indonesia, Korea, and Japan also have secular leaders, yet they encompass former states with sacred leadership strongly associated with the use of higher level honorifics. Sacred authority was superseded by secular authority in the process of nation-state formation in these countries. This process of nation-state formation has affected both the use of honorifics and the language ideologies about them, as demonstrated especially through Errington's documentation of Javanese honorifics. However, there are many aspects of the historical changes in honorific systems in these nations that are not extensively discussed in English accounts, and the shift from sacred authority to secular authority is one such aspect. Even so, it is apparent that in none of these situations would it be accurate to say—as it would be true to say of Tonga—that the present modern nation-state political structure is locally conceptualized as an outgrowth of the precontact political structure, embodied in the same family lines and in the same semiotic system for displaying respect through honorifics.

I have argued that the repression of the sacred in nation-state formation grew out of the theological epistemology of the Dissenting Calvinist missionaries in the Tongan case. The actual and potential effects of missionary epistemologies on the language ideologies and language use of local populations is a central theme in the chapters in this book by Handman, Schieffelin, and Robbins. In this chapter on Tonga, the aspect of missionary epistemology that is central to my argument is its vision of how the religious and political are and should be related. The Dissenters' religious positions entailed political positions. Political views about government were not separate from and merely correlated with religious views, but deeply part of their religious views, in a way that shaped historical changes in British as well as Tongan state formation.

The fact that so many chapters in this volume deal with the epistemological nature and consequences of missionary treatments of language is a testimony both to the continuing colonizing influence of Christian missionaries in the Pacific and to the continuing commitment of Pacific anthropologists to document this influence.

Ultimately, then, the changes in Tongan language ideology about lexical honorification are a consequence of processes of European colonialism and nation-state formation that have been widespread throughout the broader cultural regions in which Tonga participates, yet with far from uniform consequences as these processes interact with local circumstances.

Notes

I would like to acknowledge the Wenner-Gren Foundation and the National Science Foundation for their support of research leading to the analysis and writing of this chapter. My gratitude also goes to the government of the Kingdom of Tonga for permission to carry out this research, and to the many Tongans who have contributed over time both to the research and to my well-being. I thank Bambi Schieffelin, Miki Makihara, and the other contributors to this book for their comments on earlier drafts of my chapter, and Niko Besnier and Ernie Olson for discussions of issues in this chapter. Earlier versions of this chapter were presented at a Workshop on Honorifics in Action at the UCLA Conference on Language, Interaction, and Culture in May 2004, at a May 2006 University of Michigan Linguistic Anthropology Lab, and at an April 2006 University of Chicago Anthropology Department Colloquium. Comments from audiences at those presentations were most useful and are appreciated.

1. This does not mean that there are no temporally oriented accounts of social change among Tongans today that have a disjunctive quality. Thus Marcus 1980 documents a discourse of the missionaries freeing the people of Tonga from their enslavement by the chiefs that entails the idea of a sharp break from the past. There is also a discourse of a sharp break

between the chiefly rule of the past and the emergence of the present kingly line from lowly commoners that contests claims by the king's family to the rightful inheritance of the Tu'i Kanokupolu title.

2. Italics are used to identify Tongan language materials in this chapter, while underlining is used for European language materials discussed by the author.

3. Related enlightening discussions of this transformation include Brown and Gilman 1960; Bauman 1983; and Silverstein 1985, 2003.

4. This characterization is similar to that of Churchward 1985, Marcus 1980, and Philips 1991 for Tonga; and Milner 1961 and Duranti 1992 for Samoa.

5. Of course it is really John Martin and not William Mariner whose 'voice' is realized in this work, or rather one cannot separate the one from the other. In any case, the framing of what Mariner experienced is saturated with a British sensibility.

6. Late-twentieth-century scholarship on nation-state formation credits the Protestant Reformation of the sixteenth century and the denominations that emerged from it up through the eighteenth century with laying broad-based foundations for many of the ideals attributed to the supposedly nonreligious Enlightenment of the eighteenth century (e.g., Clark 1994; Herman 2001).

7. However, Malupo's Tongan version is different from Gifford's general statement and translation of Malupo. Whereas Gifford uses such phrases as "one of the leading chiefs," Malupo says, in giving examples of the different words one would use depending on whom one met or encountered, for all three categories, *kapau ko ha taha oe faahinga*, 'if it was one of a family/socio-political unit'. In other words, Malupo does not imagine meeting an individual who is a leading chief; rather, he imagines an individual who is of a leading chiefly family, such as a *fa'ahinga muomua*. I make this point because Helu 1992, in discussing Western scholars' analysis of the Tongan brother-sister relationship, argues that they consistently fail to recognize that Tongans are thinking in terms of categories of groups of people rather than in terms of individual role relationships. This contrast between Malupo's Tongan and Gifford's translation illustrates what Helu is criticizing.

8. This is the main context where there is evidence that the terms used for the sacred Tu'i Tonga were also associated with the precontact gods themselves. One term used for the Tu'i Tonga, the king, and the gods was *haele*, here glossed as 'to appear', but in other sources as *hā'ele*, kingly for 'to go'. The other term associated with the gods was *huafa*, here glossed as 'name, applied only to gods, king, chiefs'.

9. Elsewhere in Gifford, Malupo argues that the person who was king when he wrote his statement, Tupou II (1893–1918), was also the Tu'i Tonga, and deserved to be addressed using the terms reserved for the Tu'i Tonga (1929: 59) for that reason. However, as noted earlier, many Tongans did not accept the view that this title had passed to the king's hereditary line. This means that there had to be more than one kind of justification for extending the Tu'i Tonga terms to the king.

10. This is ironic, given the missionaries' concern to avoid such a situation—they seem to have played a role in reproducing that which they were resisting as Dissenting Protestants in Great Britain two centuries ago.

11. Unlike the other scholars considered here, Blixen has not actually worked in Tonga or with Tongans. His 1966 article, which presents a two-level model (chiefly and nonchiefly) with degrees of variation within the honorific or chiefly level, is based on the work of others. The purpose of his historical linguistic work is to discuss Samoan honorification and Tongan honorification together in a single framework because he is identifying them as part of a common honorific complex for western Polynesia. He seems to have been most influenced by

representations of the Samoan model, particularly that of Milner 1961, which is basically a two-level model. However, one of Gifford's informants, the second one, also had a two-level model of everyday speech versus speech to the Tu'i Tonga.

References

Bauman, Richard. 1983. *Let Your Words Be Few: Symbolism of Speaking and Silence among Seventeenth-century Quakers*. New York: Cambridge University Press.

Blixen, Olaf. 1966. Lenguaje honorifico y comportamiento reverente en Samoa y Tonga. *Comunicaciones Antropologicas del Museo de Historia Natural de Montevideo* 1 (6): 1–39.

Bott, Elizabeth. 1982. *Tongan Society at the Time of Captain Cook's Visits: Discussions with Her Majesty Queen Sālote Tupou* (with the assistance of Tavi). Wellington, New Zealand: Polynesian Society.

Brown, Roger, and Albert Gilman. 1960. The Pronouns of Power and Solidarity. In *Style in Language,* ed. Thomas Sebeok, pp. 253–276. Cambridge: MIT Press.

Churchward, C. Maxwell. [1953] 1985. *Tongan Grammar*. Nuku'alofa, Tonga: Vava'u Press.

———. 1959. *Tongan Dictionary*. Nuku'alofa: Government of Tonga.

Clark, J. C. D. 1994. *The Language of Liberty, 1660–1832: Political Discourse and Social Dynamics in the Anglo-American World*. New York: Cambridge University Press.

Collocott, E. E. V. 1928. *Tales and Poems of Tonga*. Bernice P. Bishop Museum Bulletin 46. Honolulu: Bernice P. Bishop Museum.

Collocott, E. E. V., and John Havea. 1922. *Proverbial Sayings of the Tongans*. Occasional Papers of the Bernice Pauahi Bishop Museum of Polynesian Ethnology and Natural History, Vol. 8, no. 3. Honolulu: Bishop Museum Press.

Daws, Gavan. 1974. *Shoal of Time: A History of the Hawaiian Islands*. Honolulu: University of Hawaii Press.

Duranti, Alessandro. 1992. Language in Context and Language as Context: The Samoan Respect Vocabulary. In *Rethinking Context: Language as an Interactive Phenomenon*, ed. Alessandro Duranti and Charles Goodwin, pp. 77–99. New York: Cambridge University Press.

Edwards, Philip, ed. 1999. *The Journals of Captain Cook*. Prepared from the original manuscripts by J.C. Beaglehole for the Hakluyt Society, 1955–1967. London: Penguin Books.

Errington, J. Joseph. 1985a. *Language and Social Change in Java: Linguistic Reflexes of Modernization in a Traditional Royal Polity*. Southeast Asia Series, no. 65. Athens: Ohio University Center for International Studies.

———. 1985b. On the Nature of the Sociolinguistic Sign: Describing the Javanese Speech Levels. In *Semiotic Mediation: Sociocultural and Psychological Perspectives*, ed. Elizabeth Mertz and Richard J. Parmentier, pp. 287–310. Orlando, Fla.: Academic Press.

———. 1988. *Structure and Style in Javanese: A Semiotic View of Linguistic Etiquette*. Philadelphia: University of Pennsylvania Press.

Fanua, Tupou Posesi. n.d. *Po Fananga: Folk Tales of Tonga*. Nuku'alofa, Tonga: Friendly Islands Bookshop.

Ferdon, Edwin N. 1981 *Early Tahiti as the Explorers Saw It, 1767–1797*. Tucson: University of Arizona Press.

———. 1987. *Early Tonga as the Explorers Saw It, 1616–1810*. Tucson: University of Arizona Press.

Foster, George M. 1960. Edward Winslow Gifford, 1887–1959. *American Anthropologist* 62 (2): 327–329.

Free Wesleyan Church. n.d. *Ko e Kalama 'i he Lea Faka-Tonga*. Nuku'alofa, Tonga: Free Wesleyan Church Office of Education. (In print and circulation 1987–1990.)

Friendly Island Book Shop. n.d. *Ko e Tohi Himi 'a e Siasi Uesiliani Tau'ataina 'o Tonga.* Christchurch: Sovereign Print.

Gal, Susan. 2001. Linguistic Theories and National Images in Nineteenth-century Hungary. In *Languages and Publics: The Making of Authority,* ed. Susan Gal and Kathryn Woolard, pp. 30–45. Manchester, UK: St. Jerome Publishing.

Gifford, Edward W. 1923. *Tongan Place Names.* Bernice P. Bishop Museum Bulletin 6. Honolulu: Bernice P. Bishop Museum.

———. 1924. *Tongan Myths and Tales.* Bernice P. Bishop Museum Bulletin 8. Honolulu: Bernice P. Bishop Museum.

———. 1929. *Tongan Society.* Bernice P. Bishop Museum Bulletin 16. Honolulu: Bernice P. Bishop Museum.

Haviland, John. 1979. Guugu Yimidhirr Brother-in-Law Language. *Language in Society* 8 (3): 365–393.

Helu, 'I. Futa. 1992. Brother/Sister and Gender Relations in Ancient and Modern Tonga. MS.

Herman, Arthur. 2001. *How the Scots Invented the Modern World.* New York: Three Rivers Press.

Hill, Jane, and Ken Hill. 1978. Honorific Usage in Modern Nahuatl: The Expression of Social Distance and Respect in the Nahuatl of the Malinche Volcano Area. *Language* 54 (1): 123–155.

Hiney, Tom. 2000 *On the Missionary Trail: A Journey through Polynesia, Asia, and Africa with the London Missionary Society.* New York: Atlantic Monthly Press.

Inoue, Miyako. 2002. Gender, Language, and Modernity. *American Ethnologist* 29 (2): 392–422.

———. 2003. Listening Subject of Japanese Modernity and His Auditory Double: Citing, Sighting, and Siting the Modern Japanese Woman. *Cultural Anthropology* 18 (2): 156–193.

———. 2004. What Does Language Remember? Indexical Inversion and the Naturalized History of Japanese Women. In: The History of Ideology and the Ideology of History, ed. Miyako Inoue. Special issue of *Journal of Linguistic Anthropology* 14 (1): 39–58.

Jespersen, Otto. 1938. *Growth and Structure of the English Language.* Chicago: University of Chicago Press.

Kim-Renaud, Young-Key. 1990. Parametric Change in the Korean Honorific System. Paper presented at the 42nd Annual Meeting of the Association for Asian Studies, Chicago, April 5–8.

Kirch, Patrick V. n.d. A Brief History of Polynesian Archaeology. Available at http://sscl. berkeley.edu/oal/background/polyhist.htm.

Koskinen, Aarne A. 1953. *Missionary Influence as a Political Factor in the Pacific Islands.* Helsinki: Suomalaisen Kirjallisuuden Seuran Kirjapainon Oy.

Lātūkefu, Sione. 1974. *Church and State in Tonga: The Wesleyan Methodist Missionaries and Political Development, 1822–1875.* Canberra: Australian National University Press.

Marcus, George E. 1980. *The Nobility and the Chiefly Tradition in the Modern Kingdom of Tonga.* Wellington: Polynesian Society.

Mariner, William. 1817. *An Account of the Natives of the Tonga Islands.* Compiled by John Martin. 2 vols. Edinburgh: Constable and Company.

Milner, George B. 1961. The Samoan Vocabulary of Respect. *Journal of the Royal Anthropological Institute* 91: 296–317.

Moulton, J. Egan. 1921. *Moulton of Tonga.* London: Epworth Press.

Olson, Ernest G. 1993. Conflict Management in Congregation and Community in Tonga. Ph.D. diss., Anthropology, University of Arizona.

Osorio, Jonathan Kay Kamakawiwoʻole. 2002. *Dismembering Lāhui: A History of the Hawaiian Nation to 1887*. Honolulu: University of Hawaiʻi Press.

Philips, Susan U. 1991. Tongan Speech Levels: Practice and Talk about Practice in the Cultural Construction of Social Hierarchy. In *Currents in Pacific Linguistics: Papers on Austronesian Languages and Ethnolinguistics in Honour of George W. Grace*, ed. Robert Blust, pp. 369–382. Pacific Linguistics Series C–117. Canberra: Australian National University.

Powles, C. Guy. 1979. The Persistence of Chiefly Power and Its Implications for Law and Political Organisation in Western Polynesia. Ph.D. diss., Australian National University.

Salmond, Ann. 1991. *Two Worlds: First Meetings between Maori and Europeans 1642–1772*. Honolulu: University of Hawaii Press.

Shumway, Eric. 1971. *Intensive Course in Tongan*. Honolulu: University of Hawaii Press.

Silverstein, Michael. 1985. Language and the Culture of Gender: At the Intersection of Structure, Usage, and Ideology. In *Semiotic Mediation: Sociocultural and Psychological Perspectives*, ed. Elizabeth Mertz and Richard J. Parmentier, pp. 219–259. Orlando, FL: Academic Press.

———. 2003. Indexical Order and the Dialectics of Sociolinguistic Life. *Language & Communication* 23 (3–4): 193–229.

Sohn, Ho-min. 1981. Power and Solidarity in the Korean Language. *Papers in Linguistics* 14 (3): 431–452.

Taliai, ʻOpeti Manisela. 1989. Social Differentiation of Language Levels in Tonga. Master's thesis, University of Auckland.

Wetzel, Patricia J. 2004. *Keigo in Modern Japan: Polite Language from Meiji to the Present*. Honolulu: University of Hawaiʻi Press.

Wood-Ellem, Elizabeth. 1999. *Queen Sālote of Tonga: The Story of an Era, 1900–1965*. Auckland: Auckland University Press.

10

J. JOSEPH ERRINGTON

Postscript

Making Contact between Consequences

$\mathbf{M}$uch of the rapidly growing anthropological literature on globalization has centered on what can be called, adapting a phrase from Mary Louise Pratt (1992), "zones of postcolonial contact." It may be a sign of the globalizing times that now, fifteen or so years after she borrowed the notion of "contact" from linguistics, work in that field is becoming populated with more socially descriptive labels: not just language "shift" and "death," but also language "collision," "competition," "conflict," and so on (see Joseph et al. 2003). Perhaps these mark growing awareness among linguists that the kinds of structural phenomena that concern them are intimately bound up with social dynamics like those described in the rich ethnographic accounts in this collection.

Recognizing language as constitutive of shared and shifting ways of life, these authors develop situated, fine-grained accounts of practices and ideologies that mediate broader engagements across lines of human difference. Each also speaks in different ways to suspicions or anxieties that might be behind such new labels for language contact, worries that linguistic diversity is part of a world which, Thomas Friedman tells us, is becoming flat. This collection sets out facts that are at odds with any such neoliberal version of world systems lite, and shows how oversimple it is to predict that such small-scale societies will inevitably be transformed into lesser likenesses and parts of societies at the vanguard of globalization. Marshall Sahlins rejects a weightier, theoretical version of this scenario to rebut the notion that "colonized and 'peripheral' peoples [are] the passive objects of their own history and not its authors." He asserts here very broadly what authors of chapters in this book demonstrate in nuanced detail: that language contact in such communities shows "their cultures" to be deeply engaged in situations of change, and as more than "adulterated goods" (Sahlins 1994: 412).

The chapters in this volume provide instructive, nuanced framings of such dynamics in different zones of contact. They relativize empirical dimensions of social and linguistic contact to the communicative practices and language ideologies that bind individual and collective life together, and so mediate dynamics of change affecting each. By moving beyond the more obvious, writable dimensions of human interaction, they open up broader engagements with outside forces that are engendering emergent forms, values, and situated meanings of language.

To foreground one common aspect of these authors' practice-centered orientations, I first contrast their ethnographic strategies with those centered on structural aspects of language contact. This helps to foreground limiting implications of commonsense notions of convention and use, and binary framings of language contact phenomena. With this narrow purview in mind, I next turn to the practice-centered, ethnographic strategies authors use to situate languages in the multiple temporalities of zones of contact. Rather than reframe any of these papers' ethnographic richness, then, I foreground some of the ways they make consequences of "local" contact more "globally" significant.

Locating "Contact"

Comparative approaches to language contact require strategies for establishing commensurability between two or more contact situations, so, between languages on one hand, and contexts of contact on the other. The grounds for establishing the first such commensurability are pregiven for linguists by their field's premises and goals, which key to structural properties of all language systems. Of interest here are two structure-centered strategies that linguists have devised to generalize across cases of languages in contact. Their comparative metrics have developed on one or the other side of a key heuristic binary: either language is a symbolic system internal to individuals, or a collective representation distributed across individuals. This is the binary Courtney Handman identifies, for instance, as crucial for the work of the Summer Institute of Linguistics (SIL) in New Guinea, where missionaries understand, as have linguists since Saussure, that languages are unitary at the same time they have multiple concrete representations, like a dictionary of which multiple copies are owned by different individuals.

This powerful heuristic for describing language structures offers no clear point of purchase on structural phenomena in emergent zones of contact between speakers who have different cultures, and not just different language systems. These situations require broader metrics of commensurability keying either to social biographies of individuals on one hand, or the histories of collectives of speakers on the other.

Foundational work by Uriel Weinreich (1953) locates contact phenomena within individuals, whose speech in one language bears traces of the shaping effects of another. Knowledge of the former language is prototypically internalized later in life than the latter: not "first" and "natively," but "second" and "nonnatively." Because it locates contact between language sytems within individuals, this scenario presupposes a biographical temporal trajectory that can be framed with minimal attention to forces (political economic, cultural, etc.) that shape contexts and modes of "second language" acquisition. It presupposes undifferentiated zones of interpersonal contact between (incipient) bilinguals and the native speakers who offer reference points needed to describe "interference phenomena" in their nonnative usage.

Even this minimally specified scenario lacks fit in important ways with several zones of contact discussed in this book. Certainly Marquesan French and Rapa Nui Spanish bear evidence of the shaping effects of their speakers' native languages, the "interference" phenomena whose social meanings I discuss below. But Tok Pisin, Pijin, and Indonesian usage in many communities of New Guinea, the Solomon Islands, and West Papua cannot be evaluated in this way: these languages are not acquired in situations of contact with native speakers, and so they lack pregiven reference points for gauging interference effects. As "un-native" languages, they do not fit this biographical scenario of language contact. It is no coincidence in this respect that SIL linguists, inheritors of a broadly European ideology of language and identity, discount Tok Pisin and Indonesian as being no one's heart languages. I discuss below other effects and meanings of this quality of un-nativeness in the zones of linguistic and cultural contact described by Robbins, Schieffelin, Stasch, and Jourdan.

The other comparative metric is used to frame contact between groups of speakers, and languages which count as their joint possessions or attributes. Beginning with the premise that the history of a language is the history of collectives of speakers, Sarah Thomason and Terrence Kaufman (1988) developed such a model of contact by focusing on dynamics of intergenerational continuity and discontinuity, rather than individual lives. When languages are thought of as being reproduced intergenerationally, their contours of change appear to reveal what Thomason and Kaufman call the cultural character of contact. Contact situations can be compared, they argue, on a continuum of "cultural pressure," strong to weak, which correlates sociohistorical dynamics with structural variation and change in language use. Stronger cultural pressure produces "deeper" structural change, extending into phonological and morphosyntactic systems. Relatively "shallow" lexical borrowing is a consequence of relatively weak cultural pressure exerted by speakers of one language on another.

This scenario also lacks fit with contours of change in communities in New Guinea and West Papua where, as described in this collection, "cultural pressure" does not correlate so easily with structural reflexes of contact between local languages and Tok Pisin or Indonesian. Although change in Urapmin, Korowai, and Bosavi communities involve restricted, shallow contact phenomena, speakers there engage Tok Pisin–ness or Indonesian-ness more profoundly because both languages are bound up with new communicative practices and language ideologies.

These two structure-centered approaches to language contact presuppose different temporal contours, and anonymize linguistic and cultural contact in different ways. When structure is abstracted from talk on either side of the individual/collective binary, issues of language contact are abstracted away from complex dynamics of interpersonal contact, variation, and change. Authors of chapters in this collection, on the other hand, work against the grain of both approaches by framing contact as having multiple temporalities, and showing how those temporalities mediate language together with broader dynamics of cultural change. By foregrounding consequences of contact that are marginal or invisible for structure-centered approaches, they demonstrate ethnographically how the interplay between uses and genres of language reflects both situated interests of speaking agents, and shared understandings of how speech is meaningful. Then contact does not name processes that "adulterate" cultures or languages, but that jointly transform speakers and communities.

At issue here, in one way or other, are situated immediacies of communicative experience: the "real time" of talk and intersubjective experience that is neither biographical nor historical, in the binary sense of those terms set out above. Rather, each author figures language in and as social conduct, and, through that conduct, as reproducing and transforming broader senses of communicative practice. By centering on interactional dynamics, the authors gauge differing, overlapping, and shifting senses of communicative practice, and significances they give to linguistic structures in broader institutional and ideological contexts.

Put differently, "contact" in this collection is a rubric for a range of event-centered perspectives, and for the work of tracing longer term consequences of occasion-bound, otherwise temporally distinct communicative acts in zones of contact. This requires strategies of interpretation centered not on individual and collective in an "either/or" binary, but on dynamic, dialogic "both/and" relations of simultaneity. From this angle, multiple modes of contact between languages, structural and generic, are interactionally situated on the shared and shifting grounds of communicative events. Because those grounds differ and vary—as do the interests they serve, capacities they presuppose, and projects they allow to be pursued—so too they mediate changing senses of self in and with others.

What Michael Silverstein (1998) calls event-centered perspectives allow communicative practices to be recognized as collectively grounded but also interested and strategic conduct, such that speakers of "weaker" languages in "weaker" cultures are capable of acting as more than what Sahlins calls "passive" subjects of history. Language contact then involves not just interference and borrowing, but assimilation of and resistance to broader senses of what different kinds of talk and writing presuppose and entail in different contexts. Foregrounding these points of juncture between sharedness and difference helps bring to the fore communicative practices' multiple temporalities as events, embodiments of structures, and instances of genres. Transient, real-time speech processes are meaningful in all these respects because they are (1) indexically situated in presupposed contexts in the present, (2) presuppose shared knowledge of prior communicative acts that they resemble, and (3) can entail shifts in contexts, including states of knowledge of participants. Real-time speech events reproduce and transform shared social experience because of their generic character, in Mikhail Bakhtin's sense of the term. Speech events in the present resemble and differ from those that are prior to them and that endow them with a "social accent." In this way, the shared dimensions of language use emerge as the "intentions of others" echo in a speaker's words, as Bakhtin observes in the passage cited by Bambi Schieffelin in the epigraph that opens chapter 7.

To read communicative events as reproducing and shaping shared senses of communicative practice, authors of these chapters deal with zones of cultural contact as matters of context: the types of social relations that genres of language can presuppose and entail, including multiple modes of international engagement and stances. They are especially interested in nuanced articulations of interactional engagements that refract biographical and collective incongruities arising from what Thomason and Kaufman call "cultural pressure." Riley, Jourdan, Makihara, and Philips extend these concerns to broader institutionally grounded, language-linked modes of difference and sharedness which make talk emblematic (iconic and indexical) of durable social identities.

To figure speech in these multiple temporalities involves some basic assumptions about the location and consequences of contact: because it is intrinsically eventual, talk's meanings and effects extend across events, with interrelations that need to be framed in discourse-centered ways. Bypassing anonymized, detemporalized framings allows features of language structure to be recognized as resources in ongoing, collective responses to shared senses of disequilibrium, and parts of efforts to devise new horizons of relevance for speech and social life.

Translating translation

The chapters about New Guinea in this volume trace consequences of "cultural pressure" on communicative practices that are "deeper" than their structural reflexes in local languages would lead one to suspect. In different ways, the authors of these chapters are concerned with consequences of contact with text-centered communicative practices, and far-reaching effects of the authority and meaning bound up with the work of translation. These chapters draw out what is presupposed about language and its users by Christian practices of translation, showing how it creates zones of contact involving not just new texts and beliefs, but radically new understandings of speech and speakers. The work of translation has entered and transformed the larger world of communicative practice because it presupposes what Schieffelin calls "cultural epistemologies" radically different from those of the Urapmin and Bosavi.

Handman's chapter articulates some of the conceptual and ideological grounds for this work of translation not just by SIL workers, or generations of missionaries before them, but also members of Western societies, religiously oriented or not, who use literacy in similar communicative practices. She helps in this way to trace the dislocating effects of work by the missionaries and pastors described by Schieffelin and Joel Robbins, even though their practical senses of literacy do not extend to an understanding of how the work of translating the Gospel presupposes a particular view of worlds of situated speech. Schieffelin and Robbins help to show how this failure of recognition makes missionaries and pastors unknowing but effective shock troops of modernity.

Practical assumptions about the dissociability of linguistic form and meaning, Handman shows, are imposed by SIL missionaries as part of their metric of commensurability between cultures and languages. Those assumptions license the work of Christianizing by allowing missionaries to do their work as if they did not need to expose "primitive" peoples to the dislocating effects of the outside, secular world. This is plausible only as long as they understand that there is a part-for-whole, "inner/outer" analogy between a unitary meaning and its translations in indefinitely many languages on one hand, and between persons' interior states and multiple modes of expression on the other. Projecting across these two conceptual spheres, missionaries can operate as if the inner/transcendent soul differs from the outer/secular world as does the "heart" language and foreign language. This trope grounds the SIL's text-centered agenda by helping to distinguish the "inner reality" of deep structures of a language, over and against the lexicon which, as the outer body of cultural (not sacred) knowledge counts as a "trash heap" to be freely manipulated and bent in the work of translation.

This text-centered conception of language is incongruent with communicative practice among Urapmin and Bosavi, and as a consequence dislocates talk from the broader sphere of exchange in which words and things are bound together. Schieffelin and Robbins describe different struggles to disentangle criteria for judging the "symbolic truth" of an exchange of speech from the "social truth" of an exchange of goods, which requires that they unravel two different modes of the accountability for speech over and against other types of conduct.

Robbins traces shifts in Urapmin senses of language and the world from multiple engagements with the idea of history ("the past is past, now is now"), with theology (unspeaking nature divided from the realm of God's Word), and with each other (in conversational and social practice). Central images in these shifting understandings of the world are gendered, ritualized words produced by bodies of women in possession, who figure as concrete targets for broader anxieties about talk's sources and authority, and understandings of "who is speaking" in any time and place.

Robbins draws on Schieffelin's insightful work on missionaries' influence on the Bosavi, which describes a different crisis in the work of translation. Schieffelin has documented conflicts arising from contact between practices of Bible translation and culturally grounded understandings of conditions of knowledge, or epistemologies. Institutionally framed translations have confronted the Bosavi not just with the content of a radically new body of faith, but the transformational uses of predicates of mental states and speech. Missionary practices of translation in this way both presuppose and entail new understandings of persons' internal states and external conduct, verbal and otherwise. Semantic shifts in these few verbs may appear structurally negligible, but they have enabled entirely new fashions of speaking with broader consequences for Bosavi conceptions of mental states as being open to referentially transparent objectification, like other things and states of affairs.

These new metapragmatic uses of predicates disconfirm local communicative practices which, like those among the Urapmin, split language off from broader practices of exchange and the modes of sociality they presupposed. So the Bosavi, like the Urapmin, find that Christianity is to be assumed as something more than an "adulterated" (as Sahlins might say) version of their old culture, because they are rearticulating local communicative practices in ways that enable new configurations of individual and collective life.

For the Urapmin and Bosavi, Tok Pisin is not a system of conventions, but a modality for engaging the larger world. To learn Tok Pisin is to recognize and adapt to larger ruptures between words and goods, nature and God, past and present. "Translation" in this respect names communicative practices that presuppose broader zones of cultural contact, not only because durable semantic content can be reproduced in multiple forms, but also because speakers are challenged to internalize new understandings of themselves as Christian, language-using creatures.

Rupert Stasch describes a different work of translation in which relatively "shallow" kinds of borrowing and loan translations from Indonesian into Korowai speech mediate profoundly disruptive forms of contact. Korowai find that discursive access to new senses of identity and place brings with it profound challenges of human difference. The structural business of replacing or adding parts to their vocabulary, finding new words for new things, belies the broader metasemiotic nature of their engagement with cultural Otherness, mediated by the borrowing of words. So a few words become fulcrum points for dealing with the "outside" world, standing in part-for-whole relations to languages, language users, and senses of the human condition.

By simultaneously assimilating and rejecting Indonesian, Korowai are negotiating conditions of dynamic simultaneity as alien words are made to figure against the ground of Korowai language and culture. An important element of this relation is Indonesian's lack of native speakers, which means that its zone of contact with Korowai life is detached from conditions of life the Korowai might recognize as comparable with their own. So too its un-nativeness makes it a kind of screen onto which Korowai translation practices project novel senses of difference between stasis and mobility, human and nonhuman, and, ultimately, anxieties about the ontological status of that which is not directly known or knowable. All these categories are in play as lexical similarity and difference becomes iconic of human similarity and difference.

The modes of linguistic commensurability presupposed by these practices of translation are both sources of and solutions for Korowai anxieties, as borrowing creates for them "endolingual" echoes of "exolingual" life. At the same time, Stasch portrays a situation in which structure and culture may coarticulate in a dynamic zone of contact. The Korowai word *laleo* already shows signs of shifting in structural function and semantic meaning, from a lexical item meaning "demon" to a semiproductive marker for lexical items that count, in one way or another, as falling into the category of the Other. Such a structural regularization in Korowai language may both presuppose and entail routinized modes of contact with "outside" things and forces. But beyond that shift are the existentially fraught occasions of talk which may be more intimately transformative of Korowai lives and communities.

Heteroglot communities

The chapters dealing with Rapa Nui, the Marquesas, Solomons, and Tongan Islands, describe contemporary communities that have been shaped by longer and more intense contact with (post)colonial powers and languages. In Honiara, and on Rapa Nui and the Marquesas, contact with formerly colonial institutions and languages— English, Spanish, and French—have firmly and durably grounded local communities in translocal economies, and imposed on them state structures whose oversight they accept. So, too, the missionary presence on Tonga, described by Philips, reflects long-standing dynamics of religion and politics in invented traditions of communicative practice.

The resulting situations are complex but familiar, in that the broad linguistic profiles described in these chapters can be aligned with hierarchies found in other parts of the postcolonial world, and can be modeled like sociolinguistic variation in other stratified, plural societies. Each structurally complex situation can be viewed as having emerged from zones of contact between languages of colonizers and colonized, as shaping effects of what Silverstein (1996) calls "cultures of standardization" have engaged with centripetal forces emanating from what Penelope Eckert (2000) calls "communities of practice."

The authors of these chapters situate this variation in larger historical dynamics to show how it figures ideologically and practically in multiple senses of identity. In this way, they trace links between different zones of contact, explicit norms of standard languages, and practical senses of interpersonal, appropriately used talk.

Christine Jourdan's chapter describes speech variation in long-term trajectories of social change that may lead, as she describes urbanizing Honiara, to language shift. The transition to distinctively urban Pijin from nonurban languages represents in this way a point of generational juncture between "urban adults" whose repertoires include languages "native" to earlier, rural generations, and the "younger crowd" whose repertoires do not. On this generationally stratified historical and geographical landscape, middle-class Honiarans are inventing urban identities by grounding images of traditional linguistic and cultural purity in modern cultures of standardization. Although these images can be projected onto a local, precolonial past with a discourse of nostalgia, they lack purchase in the lives of their children and grandchildren, and so their complaint tradition increasingly makes *kastom* a target, part-for-whole, for larger anxieties of failed social reproduction. *Kastom,* in turn, appears to be shifting in significance away from distinctively original attributes of lifeways and communities, and towards a category of discourse for understanding the past in the urban present.

Honiara differs from Rapa Nui, the Marquesas, and other heteroglot situations because these purist anxieties are emerging at the same time that Pijin emerges as socially and symbolically interstitial between the dominant language of power (English) and the originary languages and identities of *wantoks*. Pijin's historical and structural ties to English are obscured in these urban communities of practice as it changes from un-native lingua franca to a creole language (in the technical sense) of what Jourdan calls "cosmopolitanism and individualism." Pijin in this way mediates a zone of contact between two other languages, and is doubly mediating of Honiaran identity. Being nonstandard it stands in broad symbolic opposition to English (formal/informal, public/private, etc.). Being nonoriginal (unlike "native" languages) it can be jointly shared among speakers whose rural legacies differ but are now receding, if not yet invisible.

In the Marquesas, on the other hand, Kathleen Riley describes a different kind of interstitial speech. Like Pijin, it has emerged from contact between a dominant standard language (in this case, French) and local, rural dialects (of 'Enana). But whereas Jourdan applies the term "language" to Pijin, Riley identifies these interstitial Marquesan varieties as speech genres, because they have different roles in interactional contexts and different values in transforming identities.

Like Jourdan, Riley describes anxieties of identity that are leading "well-socialized products of the educational system" to project an ideal of linguistic and cultural purity onto a local, rural, precolonial past. But in Marquesan society, she shows, the hybrid *sarapia* speech genre mediates new identities in less obvious ways. From the normative perspective of the local cultural of standardization, *sarapia* is defined negatively: it is deviant structurally, inferior socially, and marginal interactionally. Within domestic, interactionally grounded spheres of life, though, it is a "tangling of languages," a label which better captures the genre's "social accent." Riley traces that accent to the communicative practices which presuppose *sarapia,* and the social dynamics *sarapia* can create. These are teasing (*keu*) and "say it" (*pe'au*) routines, which are practically if not officially "authentic" in that they figure in the fabric of (gendered) domestic life and the socialization of children into specifically Marquesan ways of acting and feeling.

As part of an alternative identity, then, *sarapia* endures because it is reproduced interactionally, and so in ways that seem covert and skewed relative to the norm- and structure-centered "classic French models of language maintenance." In the unofficial spheres of life, it can be emblematic of interactional identities opposed not just to those associated with dominant French institutions of literacy. This connection was made by Riley's inebriated friend who celebrated *sarapia*'s elusiveness for those who seek to reduce it to and capture it in writing.

Sarapia and Pijin can be considered as emergent contact phenomena in different historical trajectories, but both presuppose and entail modes of interactional sharedness which are tacitly oppositional to normative, codified languages. In this respect, Rapa Nui language differs as does the locale and zone of contact in which it is used. On Rapa Nui, a purist genre of usage of the local language is emerging not because literacy-centered norms are being imposed, but because new contexts for public speech require that new genres be devised. These new oratorical forms performatively presuppose and entail a space of institutional contact between Rapa Nui speakers as a corporate group and the Chilean state.

Miki Makihara has elsewhere described the parallel processes of massive social and language change on Rapa Nui resulting from exploitative colonial projects. The "pressures" that had the most leveling effects on the Rapa Nui language, more economic than cultural, extended beyond the leveling of its grammar and lexicon to extensive borrowing and calques from Spanish. The remarkable resurgence of Rapa Nui can be read similarly from shifting political and economic pressures, as renewed access to local resources has driven a renewed sense of collective identity. These identities are necessarily being invented along with new modes of linguistic and political contact between Rapa Nui and the state. Makihara shows how oratory performatively embodies these conditions of difference but, unlike the purist movements described by Riley and Jourdan, that Rapa Nui oratory is not "regimented." Because it is event-centered, rather than norm-centered, Rapa Nui oratorical genres are performed and evaluated (rather like *sarapia*) in effective performance, rather than as a category of rule-bound "language." That Rapa Nui oratory is quasi-improvisatory, rather than fully standardized, indirectly contributes to the oppositional stance presupposed by its use, reflecting (a bit like *sarapia*) a tacit refusal of the hegemonic purist categories of a culture of standardization. Rapa Nui language and society may have been more massively transformed by contact with the outside world than most, but with these newly and locally invented modes of public speech orators can represent those they address with a stance opposed to dominant outside forces and their cultures of standardization.

Susan Philips provides a historical review of another purist project, in which ideologies of power in the present have been recurrently projected onto speech genres in ideal Tongan pasts. Long-term, intimate negotiations of secular and religious authority between missionaries and elite segments of Tonga society have played out in prescriptive discourses for use of honorifics. She demonstrates how these theological and political negotiations key to honorific vocabularies, which map authority relations transparently onto objects of reference relative to agents of referential acts.

The shifting asymmetries of Tonga's referent-centered honorifics broadly parallel second person pronoun use in European languages described in a well-known article by Roger Brown and Albert Gilman (1960). Shifts in norms charted by Philips from the nineteenth century to the present, such that honorifics come to be used not for God but for the king, might be what they would call a shift from a theology of power to a theology of intimacy. Beyond this, though, she draws out what is hegemonic in this change and the controversy that drove it: partisans on both sides of the argument understood that honorific usage should presuppose the split between godly and human authority crucial to new regimes of power. Philips also observes, very suggestively, how the social meanings of these honorifics extend to the "profits of distinction" which accrue to their users because of unequal distribution of proper knowledge of their use in contemporary Tongan society. For this reason, use of honorifics presupposes not just a status relation between speaker and referent, but speakers' membership in the group of people capable of such actions of reference, membership associated diffusely but importantly with the literacy-related authority of ministers or other educated persons.

In this sense, Tongan purism, though restricted to a monolingual genre, broadly parallels purist ideologies described above for Honiara and the Marquesans. In all three cases, members of literate, Westernized classes are active participants in invented linguistic traditions: genres of speech that presuppose, part-for-whole, pure linguistic pasts which have their own meanings and uses in plural, unsettled contexts of ongoing contact in the present.

I noted at the outset of this postscript that globalization is creating anxieties and tensions not just outside but inside the academy, among linguists. I have tried to speak to those anxieties by reframing this book's eloquent arguments by example that a broader understanding of language contact can be a point of departure for broader efforts to frame globalization in local terms, and not just with easy, received images of a "flattening" world. In these chapters, "language" is taken as a rubric which extends beyond speech as social practice to speakers as social agents. Ongoing change in language ideologies and communicative practices are presented as more than consequences of a unilateral process, just as changing forms of talk are more than evidence of changing linguistic structures.

Bringing these chapters into contact with each other has helped to foreground the multiple mediating capacities of language in the fabric of individual biographies and collective histories. By taking "language" as a mode of entry into local lives, understood in local terms, these authors have drawn out some of the broader implications and complexities of "contact phenomena." By avoiding easy but limiting habits of thought about "language" and "the global," as global categories, they show what happens when "the local" is not just subordinated to but brought into genuinely dynamic contact with both.

References

Brown, Roger, and Gilman, Albert. 1960. The Pronouns of Power and Solidarity. In *Style in Language*, ed. Thomas A. Sebeok, pp. 253–276. Boston: MIT Press.

Eckert, Penelope. 2000. *Linguistic Variation as Social Practice: The Linguistic Construction of Identity in Belten High*. Malden, MA: Blackwell.

Joseph, Brian D., Johanna DeStefano, Niel G. Jacobs, and Ilse Lehiste. 2003. Language Conflict, Competition, and Coexistence: Some Preliminary Remarks. In *When Languages Collide*, ed. Brian Joseph, Johanna DeStefano, Niel Jacobs, and Ilse Lehiste, pp. vii–xii. Columbus: Ohio State University Press.

Pratt, Mary L. 1992. *Imperial Eyes: Travel Writing and Transculturation*. New York: Routledge

Sahlins, Marshall. 1994. Cosmologies of Capitalism: The Trans-Pacific Sector of the World System. In *Culture/Power/History: A Reader in Contemporary Social Theory*, ed. Nicholas B. Dirks, Geoff Eley, and Sherry B. Ortner, pp. 412–455. Princeton, NJ: Princeton University Press.

Silverstein, Michael. 1996. Monoglot "Standard" in America: Standardization and Metaphors of Linguistic Hegemony. In *The Matrix of Language: Contemporary Linguistic Anthropology*, ed. Don Brenneis and Ronald K. S. Macaulay, pp. 284–306. Boulder, CO: Westview Press.

———. 1998. Contemporary Transformations of Local Linguistic Communities. *Annual Review of Anthropology* 27: 401–426.

Thomason, Sarah G., and Terrence Kaufman. 1988. *Language Contact, Creolization, and Genetic Linguistics*. Berkeley: University of California Press.

Weinreich, Uriel. 1953. *Languages in Contact*. The Hague, Netherlands: Mouton.

AUTHOR INDEX

SUBJECT INDEX